Attracting Investment in Bangladesh—Sectoral Analyses

DIRECTIONS IN DEVELOPMENT
Trade

Attracting Investment in Bangladesh—Sectoral Analyses

A Diagnostic Trade Integration Study

Sanjay Kathuria and Mariem Mezghenni Malouche, Editors

WORLD BANK GROUP

1 2 3 4 19 18 17 16

ISBN (paper): 978-1-4648-0924-8
ISBN (electronic): 978-1-4648-0925-5
DOI: 10.1596/978-1-4648-0924-8

Cover photo: © Mariem Mezghenni Malouche/World Bank; further permission required for reuse.
Cover design: Debra Naylor, Naylor Design, Washington, DC.

Library of Congress Cataloging-in-Publication Data has been requested.

Contents

Boxes

Figures

Map

Photos

Tables

Foreword

Bangladesh can be justly proud of its track record in reducing poverty and achieving progress on key human development indicators, such as child mortality, school enrollment, and female empowerment, to name a few. In mid-2015, reflecting a decade of robust growth, the World Bank reclassified Bangladesh from "low income" to "lower-middle-income."

Over the next decade, the most important development challenge for Bangladesh will be to provide more and better jobs to its workers, as more than 20 million people join the labor force.

Achieving this goal will require Bangladesh to connect more deeply to the world market for garments and other labor-intensive products. Opportunities exist, particularly as wages continue to rise in China, gradually reducing China's dominance in labor-intensive manufacturing.

To benefit fully from international demand and emerging opportunities for export-based job creation, Bangladesh will need to craft a proactive strategy.

This comprehensive report lays out a path for doing so. It covers a lot of ground, including trade policy and institutions, logistics and infrastructure, and finance and foreign direct investment. It also anchors that thematic work in detailed studies of different sectors, such as shipbuilding, non-leather footwear, jute products, garments/polo shirts, bicycles, information technology, services, and pharmaceuticals.

We are confident that the depth and breadth of the report, combined with the high quality of its analysis, will contribute to the development debate in Bangladesh. In addition, policy makers and development partners will find a possible reform agenda, focused on areas critical to Bangladesh's development that they can support.

The World Bank Group is already supporting the government of Bangladesh in a broad range of areas related to private sector development, and, following the guidance of this report, expects to deepen this engagement, centering around job creation and trade and competitiveness.

We are grateful to the government of Bangladesh for entrusting the World Bank Group to carry out this important diagnostic work, and to the Enhanced Integrated Framework Secretariat at the World Trade Organization for funding and other substantive support.

Qimiao Fan
Country Director
for Bangladesh, Bhutan, and Nepal
The World Bank Group

Anabel Gonzalez
Senior Director
Trade and Competitiveness Global Practice
The World Bank Group

Acknowledgments

This Diagnostic Trade Integration Study (DTIS) has been prepared in response to a request from the government of Bangladesh under the Enhanced Integrated Framework (EIF) for Trade Related Technical Assistance to Least Developed Countries. The EIF is a multidonor program that supports the least developed countries in becoming more active players in the global trading system by helping them tackle supply-side constraints to trade. The ultimate objective of the study is to build the foundation for accelerated growth by enhancing the integration of the economy of Bangladesh into regional and global markets.

The World Bank thanks the government of Bangladesh for placing its confidence in the World Bank to conduct this study. The main counterpart for the DTIS is the World Trade Organization (WTO) Cell in the Ministry of Commerce of Bangladesh. The European Union is the donor facilitator, which means it is taking the lead in mobilizing resources to fund the identified actions. The government of Bangladesh has displayed strong ownership of the task, initiating its preparation and forming a National Steering Committee with concerned ministries, local think tanks, and the private sector to provide guidance to the work. The government's views and comments have been reflected at all stages of the report, from the concept note stage to the final action matrix. The team particularly thanks Mr. Amitava Chakraborty, Director General (Additional Secretary), WTO Cell, and the team in the WTO Cell, Ministry of Commerce, including Mr. Nesar Ahmed (Director), Dr. Md. Moniruzzaman (Director), Mr. Mohammad Zakir Hossain (Deputy Director), and Mr. Mohammad Mashooqur Rahman Sikder (Deputy Director).

Development partners, think tanks, the private sector, and other stakeholders have been consulted regularly at different stages in the preparation of the DTIS. Their views have been solicited through consultative workshops and one-on-one meetings. As an example, the team organized a consultative workshop with business leaders, development partners, government, academia, and researchers in June 2010. One-on-one meetings were also held with a number of individuals. The team organized two interim consultative workshops in December 2012. A two-day validation workshop was organized jointly by the WTO Cell, Ministry of Commerce, and the World Bank on October 22–23, 2013, in Dhaka. The prioritized recommendations of the action matrix were discussed in the validation workshop. The team has benefited from consultations with Dr. Mirza Azizul Islam

(Former Adviser to the government of Bangladesh, Ministry of Finance); Dr. Md. Mozibur Rahman (CEO, Bangladesh Foreign Trade Institute (BFTI)); Dr. Mostafa Abid Khan (Director, BFTI); Dr. M. K. Mujeri (Director General, Bangladesh Institute of Development Studies); and Dr. Zaidi Sattar, Dr. Sadiq Ahmed, and Dr. Ahsan Mansur (Policy Research Institute (PRI), Bangladesh).

The report has been prepared by a core World Bank team led by Sanjay Kathuria (Lead Economist) and Mariem Mezghenni Malouche (Senior Economist) and including Nadeem Rizwan (Research Analyst). The contributing team included several World Bank Group staff and consultants, including Charles Kunaka (Senior Trade Specialist, World Bank); Peter Kusek (Senior Investment Policy Officer, IFC); Michael Friss Jensen, Olivier Cadot, Nihal Pitigala, Hugh Baylis, Zaidi Sattar, and PRI Bangladesh; Dr. Selim Raihan (Dhaka University); Kay Dausendschoen (FutureShip); Glenn Surabian and Yasuo Konishi (Global Development Solutions); and Atdhe Veliu. Support was also received from Martha Denisse Pierola (Economist), Jose Daniel Reyes (Economist), Mohammad Anis (Energy Specialist), Iffath Sharif (Senior Economist), Ayesha Vawda (Senior Education Specialist), Tanya Primiani (Investment Policy Officer, IFC), and Sanjana Zaman (Research Analyst). The team thanks the development partners for their comments and cooperation. The team acknowledges comments received from World Bank Group colleagues, including peer reviewers Ndiame Diop (Lead Economist, MNSED), Philip Schuler (Senior Economist, AFTP1), Vincent Palmade (Lead Economist, SASFP), and Reynaldo Bench (Senior Port Specialist, TWITR); Salman Zaidi (Lead Economist); Zahid Hussain (Lead Economist); Vinaya Swaroop (Sector Manager, SASEP); Gladys Lopez-Acevedo (Lead Economist); Martin Maxwell Norman (Senior Private Sector Development Specialist); Manju Haththotuwa (Senior Private Sector Development Specialist); Arbind Modi (Principal Operations Officer, IFC); Sherif Muhtaseb (Senior Operations Officer, IFC); Hosna Ferdous Sumi (Associate Operations Officer, IFC); Raihana Rabbany (Consultant, IFC); Rodrigo Cubero and Seng Guan Toh (IMF); and Sadiq Ahmad and Zaidi Sattar (PRI). Mariem Mezghenni Malouche, Lalita Moorty, and Md. Abul Basher led the initial preparation of the concept note for the report. The team thanks Mehar Akhtar Khan and Kamrun Nahar Chowdhury for support with desktop publishing, logistics, and organizing the workshops in Dhaka. Rita Soni and Muhammad Shafiq helped with contracting and Sandra Gain and Michael Alwan edited the report. The team also thanks colleagues in the International Finance Corporation (in particular, Masrur Reaz and Paramita Dasgupta) for supporting a number of the sector studies, which greatly helped to increase the coverage of the DTIS, and Christine Kraus, Chief Coordinator for the Enhanced Integrated Framework at the World Trade Organization. Colleagues in the Trade and Competitiveness Global Practice (including Masrur Reaz, Nusrat Nahid Babi, and Victoria Dimple Penheiro) have been a key part of the team that is working on post-DTIS engagement with the government. Finally, the team acknowledges the support of the World Bank management team led by former Country Directors Johannes Zutt and Ellen Goldstein throughout the process of preparation.

About the Authors

Sanjay Kathuria is a lead economist and coordinator for regional integration in the World Bank's South Asia Trade and Competitiveness Global Practice, based in Washington, DC. Until August 2012, he was the World Bank's lead economist for Bangladesh, based in Dhaka. In 23 years at the World Bank, he has worked in the South Asia region, as well as in the Latin America and the Caribbean and Europe and Central Asia regions. Before joining the World Bank, he was a Fellow at the Indian Council for Research on International Economic Relations in New Delhi. He graduated from St. Stephen's College and received a master's from the Delhi School of Economics and a PhD from Oxford University. His research interests include economic growth, economic integration, international trade and trade policy, competitiveness, technology development, fiscal policy, and financial sector development. He has published several books and academic and popular articles on those topics. Recent books and report credits include coauthor of *Consolidating and Accelerating Exports in Bangladesh* (World Bank 2012); *lead author of Macedonia, FYR: Moving to Faster and More Inclusive Growth: A Country Economic Memorandum* (World Bank 2009); and editor of *Western Balkan Integration and the EU: An Agenda for Growth and Development* (World Bank 2008).

Mariem Mezghenni Malouche is a senior economist at the World Bank in Washington, DC. Her professional areas of interest include trade and competitiveness, economic integration, trade policy, nontariff measures, export diversification, trade finance, and diaspora. She joined the World Bank in 2004 as an economist in the Middle East and North Africa region in the World Bank International Trade Department. Before joining the Bank, Malouche earned a PhD in international economics from Université Paris-Dauphine, France, and a master's degree in business from the University of Tunis III with the highest honors. She is a coauthor of *Streamlining Non-Tariff Measures: A Toolkit for Policy Makers* (World Bank 2012); coeditor of *Non-Tariff Measures: A Fresh Look at Trade Policy's New Frontier* (World Bank 2012); and coeditor of *Trade Finance during the Great Trade Collapse* (World Bank 2011). She also participated in and contributed to a number of country-level policy dialogues, development policy loans, and reports in the Middle East and North Africa, South Asia, and Africa regions, notably in Bangladesh, Kazakhstan, Lao PDR, Libya, Mauritius, Morocco, and Tunisia.

Rupa Chanda is a professor of economics at the Indian Institute of Management Bangalore where she teaches Macroeconomics and International Trade. Before joining the Indian Institute of Management Bangalore, she worked as an economist at the International Monetary Fund in Washington, DC. She received a PhD in economics from Columbia University and a bachelor's from Harvard University. Her research interests concern the World Trade Organization, international trade in services, regional integration and migration. She has received several research grants and has undertaken research and consulting assignments for many international and Indian organizations. She has also been a member of several national and international committees. Dr. Chanda has published extensively, including professional books, journal articles, working papers, and book chapters in her areas of research interest.

Kay Dausendschoen is currently in charge of development of new businesses for DNV GL's Maritime Advisory division. For eight years, he was a management consultant for the maritime sector (shipping companies, yards, and financers), oil and gas companies, and the aircraft industry. His specialization is in investment advisory for high capital expenditure industries. He has degrees in mechanical engineering from the Hamburg University of Technology and the University of Minnesota and a degree in business administration from the University of Edinburgh.

Christine Elbert is a global strategy and marketing professional with 25 years of experience across public and private sectors and developed and transitioning markets. As the senior value chain and market development specialist at GDS, she leads competitiveness diagnostics of agriculture and agribusiness, manufacturing and tourism sectors, including analysis of value chains, supply chains, climate change and market linkages, for international financial institutions, government, and private sector clients. Before GDS, she worked for organizations including Citibank, General Motors Austria, the U.S. Treasury Department, Rochdale Investment Management (USA), and the MBA Enterprise Corps (Poland). She holds a BS from American University and an MBA from Kellogg School of Management at Northwestern University.

Nebiyeleul Gessese has more than 25 years of professional experience in promoting and implementing energy and environmental management systems in various industries in developing countries. He is recognized for his innovations and pioneering works in the fields of industrial energy, environmental issues, and global environmental affairs. His experience includes the development of policies and programs for sustaining environmentally friendly industrial products and optimal energy utilization. In conjunction with the United Nations Industrial Development Organization, Dr. Gessese has helped put into practice the theoretical knowledge of Life Cycle Assessment and has also had notable success in promoting energy and environmental management systems in Ethiopian manufacturing enterprises, providing both leadership and technical support for the implementation of United Nations Industrial Development Organization's Integrated Program for Ethiopia. He has a PhD from the Research Institute of Chemistry and Environment, Vienna, Austria. Since January 2006, Dr. Gessese has worked for GDS as a senior industrial and chemical engineer and environment and value chain specialist.

Yasuo Konishi is recognized for his innovations and pioneering work in the field of development, particularly in bringing together corporations with international organizations to tackle market and supply systems challenges in developing and emerging markets. With more than 36 years of professional experience, he has been successful in private business and think tanks, and has advised major international organizations such as the World Bank and the International Finance Corporation, the United Nations, the European Bank for Reconstruction and Development, and the Inter-American Development Bank, as well as developing country governments. His technical expertise in areas such as small-business development and foreign direct investment has proven beneficial to major corporations as well as local businesses in developing countries seeking market opportunities. Mr. Konishi has a master's in law and diplomacy from the Fletcher School of Law and Diplomacy through a joint program with the Harvard Business School and Harvard Law School. He is currently the managing director of GDS, a consulting firm in Reston, Virginia, specializing in value chain and supply chain analysis, and market development.

Selim Raihan is a professor in the Department of Economics at the University of Dhaka and the executive director of the South Asian Network on Economic Modeling. He holds a PhD from the University of Manchester in the United Kingdom. Dr. Raihan possesses vast expertise in research on international trade and trade policy issues related to the World Trade Organization, regional trading agreements, and domestic trade policies. He has worked extensively on applied economics, especially assessing the effects of trade and economic policies, using country-specific Computable General Equilibrium models, GTAP models, Social Accounting Matrix techniques, WITS/SMART partial equilibrium models, and dynamic stochastic general equilibrium models. He has the experience in research on poverty and labor market dynamics using household survey data and micro- and macroeconometric modeling and estimation techniques. His research interests also include analysis of economic growth and political economy analysis of growth and development. He has a long experience in teaching international trade, economic modeling, quantitative economics, econometrics, development economics and poverty dynamics at the Dhaka University. Dr. Raihan has worked for several national and international organizations including the Asian Development Bank, the World Bank, the United Nations Development Programme, United Nations Economic and Social Commission for Asia and the Pacific, the United Nations Conference on Trade and Development, the International Food Policy Research Institute, the Commonwealth Secretariat, the Food and Agriculture Organization of the United Nations, the European Commission, the International Labour Organization, the International Development Research Centre, and the U.K. Department for International Development.

Nadeem Rizwan is a development professional with more than eight years of experience. He worked in the World Bank Country Office in Dhaka, Bangladesh, as a research analyst in the Macroeconomics and Fiscal Management Unit for more than five years. He has contributed to numerous World Bank reports on Bangladesh (including the Diagnostic Trade Integration Study) on trade, remittances, and issues related to economic growth. Before joining the Bank, Nadeem worked as a senior business consultant in Katalyst where he developed expertise on agricultural value chains and agriculture market systems development. Nadeem has an MA in economics from the University of Alberta, Canada, and an MBA from the Institute of Business Administration, University of Dhaka, Bangladesh. He is currently pursuing a PhD in economics at North Carolina State University.

Glenn Surabian, lead consultant for the light manufacturing study in Bangladesh, is an engineering, marketing, and management strategy professional with 29 years of experience. For the past decade, he has been a core consultant for Global Development Solutions, LLC (GDS), focusing on competitiveness diagnostics through implementation of the integrated value chain analysis. His work at GDS also includes environmental impact, local content development, and global market linkages. Before employment with GDS, Glenn held long-term overseas assignments with various development agencies. Mr. Surabian began his professional career in high technology in the capacity of engineer (where his work resulted in two multinational patents) and subsequently as director of sales and marketing. He has received a BS in mechanical engineering from Columbia University, a BS in physics from Providence College, and an MBA from Kellogg School of Management at Northwestern University.

Atdhe Veliu is the the founder of Development Solutions, a management and economic development consulting firm that helps international financial institutions and companies identify, develop, and sustain business and industry-wide growth. With extensive experience in more than 30 countries and 20 sectors, Mr. Veliu specializes in industry competitiveness diagnostics, investment advisory, and supply chain development.

Abbreviations

6FYP	Sixth Five-Year Plan
AEO	Authorized Economic Operator
AGOA	African Growth and Opportunity Act
API	active pharmaceutical ingredient
ASEAN	Association of Southeast Asian Nations
ASYCUDA	Automated SYstem for CUstoms DAta
BASIS	Bangladesh Association of Software and Information Services
BEPZA	Bangladesh Export Processing Zones Authority
BFTI	Bangladesh Foreign Trade Institute
BGMEA	Bangladesh Garment Manufacturers and Exporters Association
BIDS	Bangladesh Institute of Development Studies
BIWTA	Bangladesh Inland Water Transport Authority
BKMEA	Bangladesh Knitwear Manufacturers and Exporters Association
BOI	Board of Investment
BPO	business process outsourcing
BSCIC	Bangladesh Small and Cottage Industries Corporation
BSTI	Bangladesh Standards and Testing Institution
BUILD	Business Initiative Leading Development
CPD	Centre for Policy Dialogue
CSIC	China Shipbuilding Industry Corporation
CSSC	China State Shipbuilding Corporation
DFID	Department for International Development (United Kingdom)
DGDA	Directorate General of Drug Administration
DTIS	Diagnostic Trade Integration Study
Dwt	dead weight tonnes
EEF	Equity Entrepreneurship Fund
EIF	Enhanced Integrated Framework
EPA	Economic Partnership Agreement
EPB	Export Promotion Bureau

EPZ	Export Processing Zone
ERP	effective rate of protection
EU	European Union
EVA	ethylene vinyl acetate
FDI	foreign direct investment
FOB	free on board
FTA	free trade agreement
FY	fiscal year
GDP	gross domestic product
GSP	Generalized System of Preferences
GT	gross tonnes
HHI	Hyundai Heavy Industries
HS	Harmonized System
ICD	inland container depot
ICT	information and communications technology
IFC	International Finance Corporation
IMF	International Monetary Fund
IPS	Internet Protocol Suite
ISIC	International Standard Industrial Classification
IT	information technology
ITES	information technology–enabled services
IWT	inland waterways transport
JDPC	Jute Diversification Promotion Center
kWh	kilowatt hour
L/C	letter of credit
LDC	least developed country
LFMEAB	Leather Goods and Footwear Manufacturers and Exporters Association of Bangladesh
LPI	Logistics Performance Index
MOC	Ministry of Commerce
MPV	multipurpose vessels
MRA	Mutual Recognition Agreement
MW	megawatts
NBR	National Board of Revenue
NTB	nontariff barrier
NTM	nontariff measure
ODM	original design manufacturing
OECD	Organisation for Economic Co-operation and Development
OEM	original equipment manufacturer

PRI	Policy Research Institute
R&D	research and development
RCA	revealed comparative advantage
RMG	ready-made garment
SAFE	Safety Advancement for Employees
SBSRB	Ship Building and Ship Recycling Board
SBW	Special Bonded Warehouses
SME	small and medium enterprises
SPS	Sanitary and Phytosanitary Standards
TEU	20-foot equivalent container unit
TIR	Transports Internationaux Routiers (International Road Transport)
Tk	taka
TRIPS	Trade Related Aspects of Intellectual Property Rights
UNIDO	United Nations Industrial Development Organization
UNWFP	United Nations World Food Programme
UPS	uninterruptable power supply
U.S.	United States
US$	U.S. dollar
USITC	U.S. International Trade Commission
USTR	United States Trade Representative
VAT	value-added tax
VCA	value chain analysis
WTO	World Trade Organization

GOVERNMENT FISCAL YEAR
July 1 – June 30

CURRENT EQUIVALENTS
Currency unit = Bangladeshi taka (Tk)
US$1 = Tk 78.4 (June 2016)

CHAPTER 1

Assessment of the Shipbuilding Sector in Bangladesh: Capabilities and Future Potential

Kay Dausendschoen

Introduction

The shipbuilding sector in Bangladesh has recently shown increased activity and potential as a future growth area. The objective of this chapter is to assess the current situation of the industry and Bangladesh's possibilities for development, keeping in view competition from other shipbuilding nations. In particular, the chapter assesses how the country can increase exports and employment by enhancing its current production capabilities from small-scale vessels mainly for the domestic market toward higher-value and more sophisticated ships for export. This assessment was based on existing reports as a starting point, complemented by in-depth analysis through further desk research, consultation with experts from the Germanischer Lloyd network, and interviews with ship owners and European shipping and shipbuilding experts with experience in Bangladesh shipbuilding. These sources have been complemented by consultation with local shipyards and banks and the government of Bangladesh. The chapter compares the development of Bangladesh's shipbuilding sector with that of China, the Republic of Korea, and Vietnam.

The analysis presented in this chapter highlights that as international demand has dried up and will most likely not recover right away, Bangladesh has to rely on domestic demand over the next few years, with demand for additional tonnage evolving from domestic and coastal trade. This represents an opportunity for yards to deepen experience with classed vessels and broaden their capability base. However, for the benefits of this demand to be fully realized, it will need to more closely resemble international demand, for which the enforcement of vessel standards and safety procedures is critical. Higher technical requirements on domestic vessels, more closely resembling "class" standards, will help bridge the standards between the domestic and international markets and improve the safety and overall performance of domestic vessels. Another area of opportunity lies in expansion of maintenance and repair services, which are more stable and labor-intensive businesses than building new ships. Since larger and smaller vessels ply Bangladeshi waters, there is a general opportunity to benefit from this traffic and expand maintenance and repair facilities for larger vessels as well, which would require establishing further appropriate sites or dry docks beyond the existing dry dock in Chittagong with its maximum capacity of 20,000 deadweight tonnage (dwt).

Sector Profile

The story of building seagoing vessels for export in Bangladesh began with Ananda Shipyards and Slipways Ltd. in Dhaka, which is currently the second largest shipyard in the country. In 2005, after participating in an international tender, the yard was awarded an order for two multipurpose vessels (MPVs), with 2,900 dwt each, from Danish Stella Shipping. The yard already had some experience with building tugs, pontoons, and ferries "under class"—that is, vessels adhering to the design, building, and quality requirements of a shipbuilding classification society. After Ananda, Bangladesh's Western Marine Shipyard in Chittagong followed, building on its experience in ship repair and maintenance of classed vessels. Western Marine entered the new building market in 2008 after having attended the Shipbuilding, Machinery and Marine Technology International Trade Fair in Hamburg. The first orders from Stella Shipping were followed by orders for larger MPVs from European owners such as Komrowski, Wessels Reederei, and Grona Shipping. Although several of these orders were cancelled, more than 20 vessels have been delivered by these two shipyards to date, with an export value well above US$100 million. Although Bangladesh has demonstrated capabilities to build different types of vessels (see figure 1.1), only MPVs and ferries have been exported up to now.

In 2008, international ship owners were facing a steep upturn of the shipping cycle with increasing freight demand and subsequently increasing order activity at shipyards across the world. With limited capacity, China and Korea—the largest players in the international market—were going for orders of larger vessels to utilize their yards in the most economical way. An opportunity existed for other countries to enter the stage, especially in the segment of small, less sophisticated vessels such as MPVs. Bangladesh already had a basic yard industry and availability of skilled workers. The experience of building bigger ships existed but was not formalized. The yards were not able to show a track record, facilities were not fully ready, import of steel and components posed a major problem, and export incentives were nonexistent. Nevertheless, international ship owners started ordering ships from Bangladesh. It helped that the increased demand was driving up prices for new buildings, making owners willing to go for a venture at a new yard with moderate pricing. At that time, even many yards in China that had never built a ship before received new build orders.

This development was a stretch for Bangladeshi yards not only on the commercial side, but also on the technical side. Production of classed ships for export

Figure 1.1 Ship Types and Sizes Built at Yards in Bangladesh, as of 2008

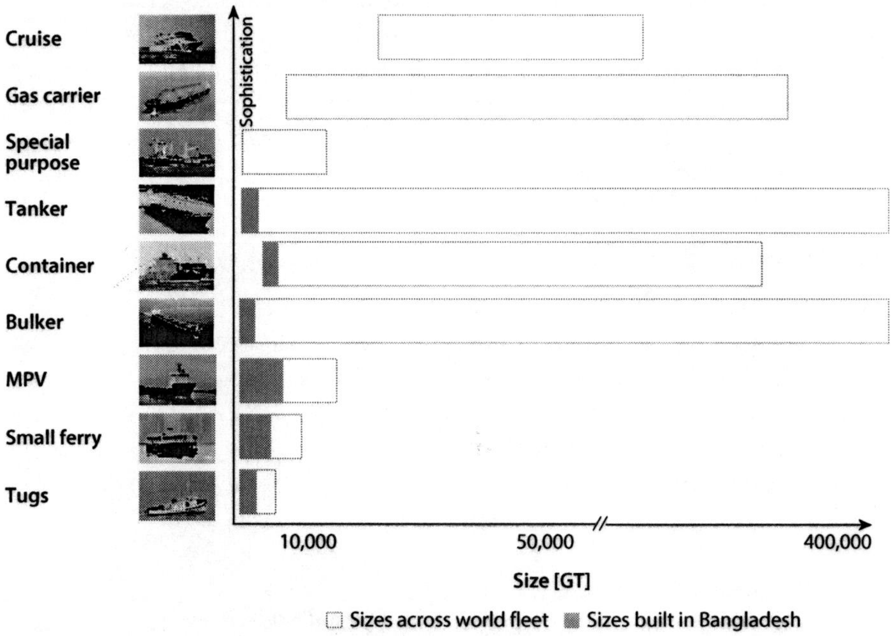

Sources: Fairplay, expert interviews.
Note: GT = gross tonnes; MPV = multipurpose vessels.

follows different standards from domestic shipbuilding. This skills gap was closed with engineers and other technical staff with international experience, especially Bangladeshis who had worked in Singapore and Dubai and were able to transfer knowledge. Technical assistance for the building process was largely supported by the owners. It included training programs conducted by the Danish International Development Agency at the yard, extensive hands-on teaching by classification societies, and advice from overseas experts who were hired on a project basis. However, previous experience with classed vessels through repair and maintenance jobs was the basic enabler, as yards were already familiar with certain regulations and quality standards. Shipbuilding is a complex process, but a big advantage is that technology can be "unpackaged." Sophisticated components may be bought and assembled without the support of industries in the component supply chain.

However, shipping and shipbuilding markets are in a poor condition at the moment. This will not change significantly over the next few years. Against this background, the question is how Bangladesh can further build up its capabilities, broaden the shipbuilding value chain, and establish its shipbuilding sector as an important part of the economy. Stable and growing domestic demand will help the sector improve its quality and productivity. In a more positive market situation and with improved competitiveness, Bangladesh could increase the volume and quality of its exports in the long term. This chapter aims to find out which vessel segments may provide opportunities for Bangladesh based on the current strengths, supply situation, and impediments such as bottlenecks. By learning from competing countries that have developed a shipbuilding sector over the past decades, key success factors are derived for the industry. Finally, by mapping capabilities with key success factors and bottlenecks, the chapter prioritizes improvement areas that need to be worked on in the future and develops future scenarios and a policy roadmap.

Market Perspective

Because of the size and infrastructure restrictions of the yards, Bangladesh's market focus is on smaller and relatively simple vessel types, such as MPVs, bulkers, and tankers. In the following discussion, long-term contracting demand forecasts will be presented (Clarkson Research 2012). These forecasts are based on assumptions on tonnage increase requirements and capacity replacement requirements, which are in turn derived from assumptions about scrapping age.

International Demand

In line with global economic development and global trade, demand for shipping and shipbuilding grew significantly during the past decade. The financial crisis of 2009 brought growth to an abrupt halt. However, the order books of the yards were still full and deliveries of new vessels continued into the crisis, thus adding even more transport capacity. Ordering activities in the main ship segments, including container, bulker, and tanker, almost dried up, leaving shipyards with significant overcapacities. It will most likely take several years for markets to regain a healthy balance between supply and demand. Contracting was expected to stay low for several years, and yearly deliveries were projected to decline 43 percent between mid-2012 and 2015 (see figure 1.2). In the medium to long term, contracting will slowly increase again, but likely not to pre-crisis levels. The most significant catalyst for this moderate growth will be bulk carrier and container ship contracting, of which the strongest development is projected for larger container vessels.

For the "very small vessel" segment—the types and sizes that could potentially be served by Bangladesh now or in the future—global demand is expected to stay low (figure 1.3). It is a rather fragmented segment that includes tugs, MPVs, bulkers, tankers, dredgers, drill vessels, and passenger ferries. Of these, tugs represent by far the largest portion of the fleet, with close to 35 percent. Smaller vessels tend to stay in service longer than larger vessels, with an average age of 26 years (compared with 10–24 years for larger vessels, depending on type). Old vessels are often replaced with larger vessels. But there continues to be a positive outlook for small MPVs and passenger vessels because of an increase in intra-continental service in Southeast Asia, where only a few trading arrangements justify large vessels.

The size cluster 2,000–10,000 dwt consists mainly of small tankers, general cargo vessels, MPVs, and small feeders. Consolidation in the market, especially in

Figure 1.2 Global New Shipbuilding Deliveries, 2001–11, and Expected Deliveries, 2012–20

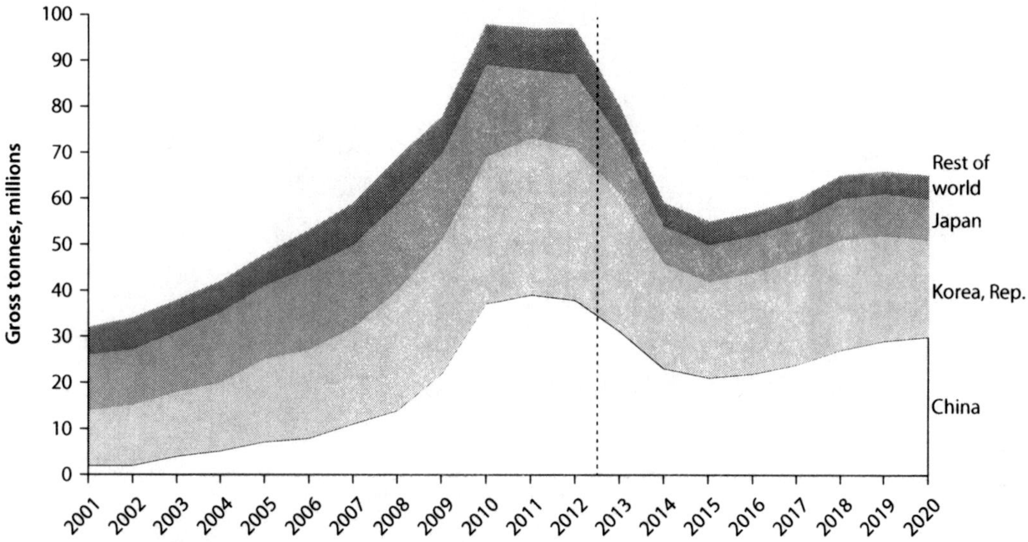

Source: Clarksons, Shipbuilding Forecast Club.

Figure 1.3 Global Demand Forecast for Very Small Vessels, Less Than 2,000 Deadweight Tonnage, 2012–21

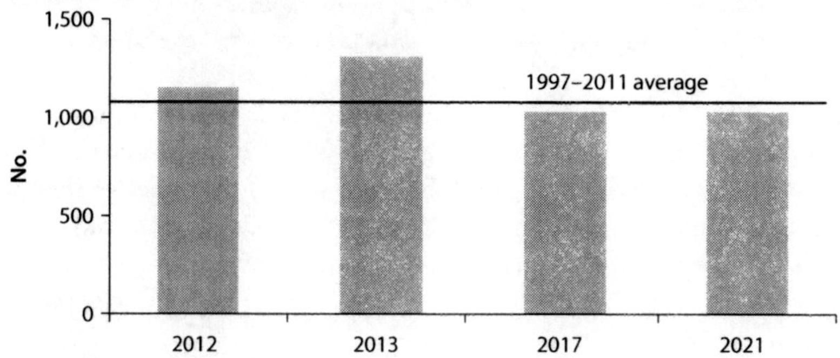

Source: Clarksons, Shipbuilding Forecast Club.

Europe, will keep orders low for MPVs (figure 1.4). Some replacement demand is likely to continue to be apparent. However, the demand is expected to fall by 3 percent per year in this segment until 2021. The feeder container fleet will come under significant pressure, reflecting the trend by operators to upsize small, aged vessels and gain greater economies of scale, especially on the intra-regional routes. The outlook for the general cargo and mini-bulker sector is bleak, with declining demand caused by the shift to other ship types (MPV and container) and general upsizing.

Figure 1.4 Global Demand Forecast for Small Vessels, 2,000–10,000 Deadweight Tonnage, 2012–21

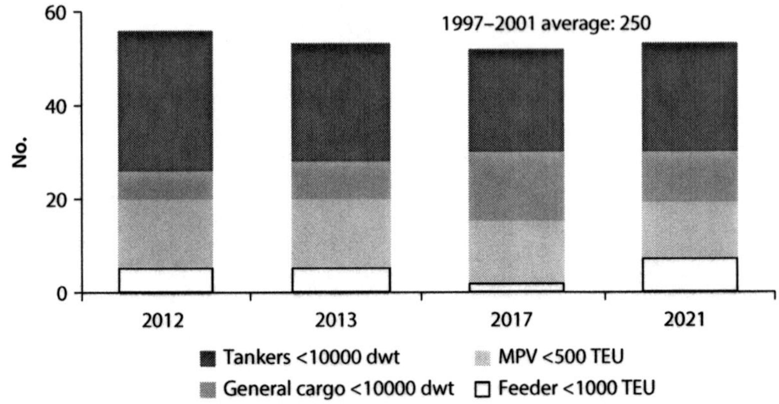

Source: Clarksons, Shipbuilding Forecast Club.
Note: dwt = deadweight tonnage; MPV = multipurpose vessels; TEU = 20-foot equivalent units.

Contracting for larger MPVs is expected to remain at very low levels in the short term, as oversupply in the bulk and containership market absorbs the transport demand. However, in the mid to long term, significant scrapping activity should produce considerable replacement demand. The handysize bulk fleet (10,000–40,000 dwt) is projected to decline as elderly tonnage is increasingly not replaced. Growth in transport of minor bulks is likely to be served by more economical handymaxes (40,000–50,000 dwt) because of upsizing pressure (figure 1.5).

Midsize container vessels are showing robust growth as box volume increases on intra-regional trades. However, this growth will be in the segment of 2,000–3,000 20-foot-equivalent unit (TEU) (25,000–40,000 dwt), rather than in the segment that would benefit Bangladesh more, 1,000 TEU (12,500 dwt). Demand is expected to be stagnant in the latter segment. Demand for small-to-midsize tankers will stay relatively stable in the future, supported by developing Asian demand on intra-regional trades.

In summary, demand for very small vessels (less than 2,000 dwt) will be stagnant but comparably good, especially for MPVs and passenger vessels. The size segment just above this (12,500 dwt) is hit hardest across vessel types and thus will provide limited growth opportunity. In the midsize segment, prospects are a bit better, particularly for the larger vessels closer to 50,000 dwt.

Domestic Demand

Sources are limited for forecasting the demand for domestic shipping in Bangladesh. Therefore, assumptions have been based on past developments as well as influencing factors, such as Bangladesh's economic outlook and trends in regulatory policies and infrastructure projects.

Figure 1.5 Global Forecast for Midsize Vessels, 10,000–50,000 Deadweight Tonnage, 2012–21

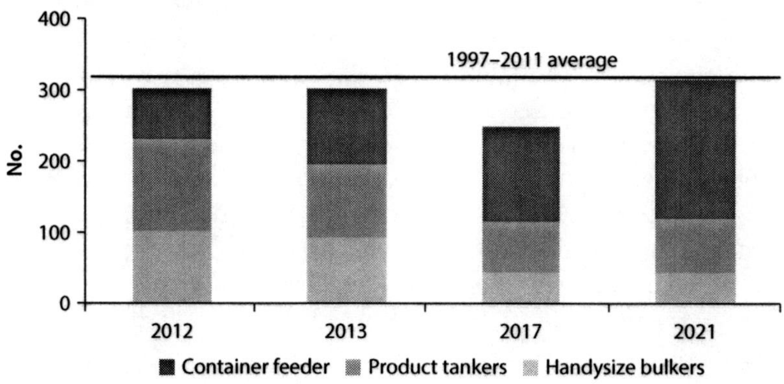

Source: Clarksons, Shipbuilding Forecast Club.

Figure 1.6 Number of Inland and Coastal Vessels Produced in Bangladesh, 2001–11

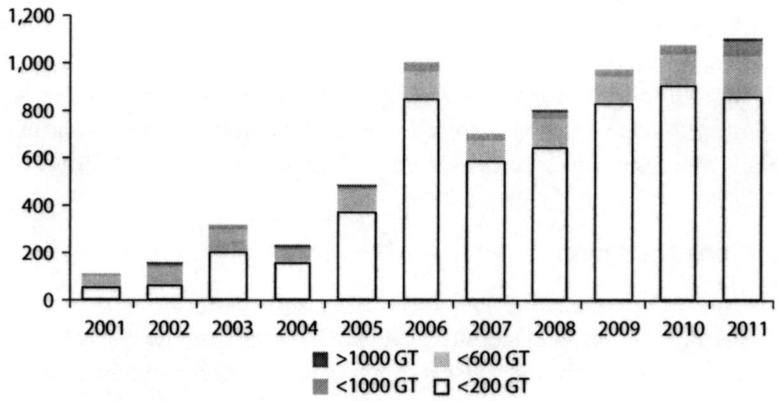

Source: Department of Shipping 2012.
Note: GT = gross tonnes.

Domestic demand has been growing constantly over the past decade, with average growth rates of 25 percent by number of vessels (figure 1.6).[1] Larger vessels are usually more complex and require more capabilities. In addition to the general economic growth forecasted at around 5–7 percent (IMF 2011), the Bangladeshi government and private investors have initiated infrastructure projects that create an additional demand for domestic water transport. Several fuel power stations are being built across the country. To transport the oil to these plants, 60 tankers of approximately 2,000 dwt have been planned and are under construction. Furthermore, two inland container terminals are already built to handle container traffic on inland waterways, which is currently transported by land. The government has assigned 32 licenses for container vessels of 140 TEU (2,000 dwt) to various parties to operate on container lines in the country. It is expected that another 32 licenses will be granted soon. Both vessel types, tankers and container vessels, need to be built under class, which makes them export quality. However, as the Bangladeshi shipbuilding industry is not able to deliver sophisticated vessels in sufficient quantities, it is expected that half these vessels need to be built in China.

Overall, domestic demand in Bangladesh will likely be detached from international shipping markets. Solid domestic growth rates will provide good opportunities to develop the sector further. In addition to oil tankers and container vessels, demand for inland passenger vessels could increase. Because of high accident rates, safety regulations for these vessels could change. Experts predict there will be demand for 300–400 smaller ships over the next 10 years.

Key Buying Factors

When selecting a yard for building a vessel, owners consider various factors along three major dimensions: price, quality, and delivery date. These factors change with the market. In buyers' markets, where building spots are readily available, price and quality dominate, whereas in sellers' markets, timely delivery becomes more important and buyers are willing to compromise on price and quality. There are differences among vessel types, as shown in table 1.1. In relative terms, price is more important for simpler vessel types, whereas quality becomes more important with sophisticated vessels. Thus, in the current market situation, it is important that Bangladesh compete in terms of both price and quality.

Capabilities and Competitiveness of the Shipbuilding Industry in Bangladesh

Export shipbuilding in Bangladesh is considered a success story and has significantly improved over the past decade. Nevertheless, the industry is still in its infancy. The production of the vast majority of Bangladeshi shipyards is still directed toward the domestic market. Total output is estimated to be around

Table 1.1 Perceived Importance of Key Buying Factors for Different Ship Types

Level of sophistication	*Price*	*Quality*	*Timely delivery*
MPV	5	3	2
Bulker	5	3	2
Tanker	4	4	2
Container	4	3	3
Chemical tanker	3	5	2
LNG/LPG	2	5	3
Passenger	3	4	3

Source: FutureShip Expert Survey 2011.
Note: Importance is indicated by a total of 10 points distributed among factors by industry experts.
LNG = liquefied natural gas; LPG = liquefied petroleum gas; MPV = multipurpose vessels.

Box 1.1 Khan Brothers Shipyard

Khan Brothers Shipyard is an example of a shipyard that was basically built from scratch. In 2008, the founders diverted funds from their bagwear business to acquire land and set up a shipyard. In the same year, they attended the Shipbuilding, Machinery and Marine Technology International Trade Fair in Hamburg with just a banner and a layout plan. This led to several serious negotiations with international ship owners, although no contracts were realized afterward. Nevertheless, the yard was built and became operational in 2011. Now the Khan Brothers have several vessels under construction, including oil tankers, tourist vessels, and ferries—all for domestic use.

Source: Khan Brothers.

250,000 gross tonnes (GT) per year, of which 185,000 GT are for the domestic market (registered production). To date, of around 200 shipyards in total (of which 124 are registered) in Bangladesh, only two yards have produced export-quality vessels of up to 7,000 dwt—Western Marine Shipyards and Ananda Shipyards and Slipways. Production conditions have improved significantly since the mid-2000s. In particular, Western Marine Shipyard has achieved the reputation of a quality player that delivers good ships on time. In addition, some yards have export shipbuilding capabilities but no demand, including Highspeed Shipbuilding & Engineering, Khan Brothers Shipbuilding, Khulna Shipyards, Meghna Shipyard, and Narayanganj Shipbuilders (box 1.1). Many of the remaining yards in Bangladesh lack the infrastructure, reputation, and experience to move quickly into the export segment, but the entry barrier is not insuperably high if enough capital is invested upfront.

Status and Capabilities of the Industry

Shipyards

Major vessel types produced at Bangladeshi shipyards nowadays include MPVs, small container vessels, bulkers, and tankers, as well as passenger ferries and tugs. Only MPVs and ferries have been exported so far.

Technology

Exporting shipyards have equipment and shops for computer numerical control machining, bending, welding, and shot blasting, as well as heavy lifting. These are prerequisites to operate steelworks and assemble the components for larger vessels at the level of quality required by international owners. However, these basic facilities are present at only a few yards in Bangladesh.

Sites

With the current spatial limitations of the sites and the low river draft across the country, it is only possible to build ships of up to 15,000 dwt. This is comparatively small by international standards. Realistically, Western Marine Shipyards could currently build 5 to 10 vessels of such sizes per year on its current sites. Ananda Shipyards, employing fewer staff, has a capacity of fewer than five vessels. With other yards estimated at a maximum of five vessels, currently Bangladesh's annual capacity is estimated at 20 or fewer export-standard vessels.

People and Employment

The actual number of people employed in the shipbuilding industry in Bangladesh could be fewer than 100,000. The number of semiskilled and skilled employees of Bangladeshi shipyards often quoted in publications is 150,000 to 200,000. However, this results in a high average figure of 750 staff at each of the 200 yards with a total production volume of 250,000 GT. The largest yards—Western Marine Shipyards and Ananda Shipyards—employ around 3,000 and 2,000 people, respectively, whereas smaller yards employ fewer than 100 people. As a comparison, in 2008 China employed 400,000 people in 2,000 shipyards and related industries, with a production volume of 14 million GT; in 2010, Vietnam employed 110,000 workers for a production volume of 600,000 GT.

Although the availability of labor has often been rated as good, industry stakeholders report a scarcity of good welders and engineers. Especially for higher quality and more sophisticated vessels, the industry faces a shortage of high-caliber staff. These shortages have negatively influenced the delivery time of vessels and productivity in the past.

The successful track record of building vessels for export has strongly relied on support from foreign experts and Bangladeshi staff with international experience. Going forward, it is crucial for shipyards to acquire and retain such employees, especially as they can transfer knowledge to other staff. Furthermore, proper management is one of the success factors missing at most yards.

Training and Education

Training is conducted mostly by informal, hands-on teaching directly at the shipyards. Western Marine Shipyards and Khulna Shipyards are the only yards that operate proper training institutes or training programs to educate skilled workers. There is a Naval Architecture and Marine Engineering Department at the Bangladesh University of Engineering and Technology, currently educating 30 engineers per year. In addition, the Marine Academy offers a curriculum in Marine Engineering. The quality of these curricula is perceived as sufficient. However, this number of graduates is too low to develop the sector, especially as graduates often leave the country for better job opportunities abroad.

Forward and Backward Industry Linkages

In Bangladesh, the ship design industry is developing slowly. It currently focuses on domestic vessels such as small oil tankers designed for the home market. Often, the work consists of refining existing designs within a frame of limited capabilities. Ship design is a task requiring solid to sophisticated engineering capabilities. Foreign ship owners mostly bring their own designs, which gives Bangladeshi designers limited opportunities to add improvements. A viable way of enhancing design capabilities to develop proprietary designs over the long term is time-limited employment of Bangladeshi staff in higher-income countries.

Because of the lower quality requirements, domestic demand for ships is higher than for exports. Local materials and equipment may include steel plates, angles, winches for mooring, anchor windlasses, chain cables of 10–15 millimeters diameter, furniture, upholstery, kitchen utensils, electric cables, switch boards, and power transformers. Against international standards, Bangladesh is currently able to produce steelworks and minor items, such as electrical cables, furniture, and welding electrodes. However, engines installed in Bangladesh-built vessels originate exclusively from foreign suppliers. Capabilities in the maintenance sector are sound, but expansion of activities is limited by the lack of dry dock facilities for vessels larger than 20,000 dwt.

Therefore, the value chain has much potential for broadening. The share of value creation besides actual building—if produced for the domestic market—is up to 25 percent; but it is only 1 percent for export ships.[2] The main reasons why no linkage industry has grown around shipbuilding are the comparably small size of the market and, especially, the unavailability of skills and technology. The technological threshold of building high-quality and certifiable components is high. However, there are potential areas where the linkage industry could be developed, especially with help of foreign producers. Over the short to medium term (up to five years), steel, pipes, flanges, and paint could be developed. Over the medium to long term (up to 10 years), generators, purifiers, compressors, and valves seem possible.

Investment Climate

A general shortage of suitable land in Bangladesh makes it difficult for shipyards to expand. Infrastructure around shipyards has been rated rather problematic by many stakeholders. Reliable road and rail connections do not exist for many shipyards, making transportation of supply goods difficult. Furthermore, the supply of power, gas, and water is not reliable. Existing sites are sufficient to maintain levels of production for small vessels, but growth and scaling up is hardly possible. The Ministry of Industry estimates that about 2,000 acres of land needs to be declared as shipbuilding zones to attain significant growth of the sector. Furthermore, the depth of waterways and clearance of bridges put a natural cap on ship size.

Foreign direct investment (FDI) in the shipbuilding sector is close to zero at present. Reasons often mentioned are the poor infrastructure, absence of proper management structures, no critical mass for shipbuilding products in the domestic market, lack of a skilled workforce, and widespread corruption (Transparency International 2011). Bureaucratic and nontransparent decision making, including allegations of corruption at the top, has also turned away foreign investors. In past years, Bangladesh has conducted efforts to attract more FDI with the help of the International Finance Corporation and in partnership with the U.K. Department for International Development and the European Union.

Competitiveness

Cost Position

To assess the competitiveness of Bangladesh's shipbuilding industry, a comparison of the cost position against reference countries was conducted. China and Vietnam were chosen as references for three reasons. First, both Asian nations share with Bangladesh comparable cost structures and limitations to their share of domestic value creation. Second, both have shown a fast development trajectory from similar starting points. Third, both have experienced strong governmental and institutional steering in strategic planning and tactical plan implementation of their respective shipbuilding industry segments.

For merchant shipbuilding, materials represent the largest cost position (57 percent, including components), followed by overheads (27 percent, including financing, indirect labor, and other costs), and direct labor (17 percent) (Stopford 2009). In low-income countries, which often have a labor cost advantage, the cost structure will lean further toward materials and less toward labor. To understand the overall relative cost positioning of Bangladesh against China and Vietnam, each of the cost groups' materials, labor, and finance costs are reviewed.

Bangladesh has little local supply and is largely dependent on importing raw materials and components. This also holds true for Vietnam, but to a lesser extent. China, by contrast, now has significant own capacities for steel and marine components, with substantial competition among national and international suppliers. Basic commodities such as iron ore and coal are traded on the world market and are similar for all buyers, but China enjoys abundant availability through its sheer size. Therefore, it will remain difficult for Bangladesh to create a beneficial position for the most important single cost position, materials.

Compared with China, Bangladesh has significantly lower nominal labor cost, but also lower productivity, which levels out some of the labor cost benefit.[3] Vietnam has better productivity levels than Bangladesh and comparable nominal labor cost. Bangladesh presently has an effective labor cost advantage over China and a disadvantage compared with Vietnam; but total effects range in the lower single-digit percentage, as shipbuilding is a material and component–intensive rather than a labor-intensive business. Nevertheless, a positive outlook can be sketched. Bangladesh's modern shipbuilding industry is still in its infancy and is making fast progress on the learning curve. Therefore, productivity is likely to increase faster than nominal labor cost, resulting in a more favorable position in the future.

Bangladesh has a disadvantage in the cost of financing, as commercial banks currently lend at interest rates of 15 percent on average. In addition, for imported raw materials and components, it is necessary to open import letters of credit (L/Cs), with fees of up to 8 percent. Furthermore, bank guarantees are a topic of concern, as they add additional cost to ship owners. These guarantees are issued on advance payments made by the owner, as confidence in capabilities and commitment to strict delivery schedules is lacking. Because guarantees from

Bangladeshi banks are not accepted, counter-guarantees from foreign banks are needed. Shipbuilders in China and Vietnam can finance their working capital at significantly lower rates, often supported by governmental guarantees and state funding. Of total ship costs, financing conditions in Bangladesh cause a cost disadvantage of approximately 2 percent.

Export shipbuilding is exempt from all tariffs and has been granted full green channel customs support, but domestic shipbuilding is subject to import duties for almost all sorts of materials and components. These duties range from 3 percent for sophisticated components and steel to more than 100 percent for components that are easy to manufacture. However, this has to be seen in relation to the import duty for complete vessels, which is at a rate of 12 percent for most vessel types. Although there are no tariffs on material and components for export vessels, customs clearance of shipbuilding components requires improvements, as it reportedly represents a bottleneck to the industry.

Quality Position

Although there is a broad quality range of ships manufactured, classification ensures elevated quality levels and low variation. The spectrum ranges from classed, reasonable quality vessels for export markets and an increasing number of "partly classed"[4] domestic oil tankers, down to nonclassed, low-quality vessels built from recycled scrap without any standards for domestic markets. Classed vessels follow the technical rules and guidelines of an independent body—that is, a classification society (class). Classified vessels are both designed and produced under the supervision and rule application of the class society. Moreover, personnel have to be qualified and trained and components have to meet class-established criteria. Most owners that have bought ships in Bangladesh attest to good vessel quality, as do class surveyors. However, as only short-term experience exists, long-term quality cannot be judged properly.

Smaller domestic vessels are often built without application of international (class) or national standards (such as Bangladesh's Domestic Vessel Code)[5], for several reasons. International classification is expensive and legally not required for inland waterway and coastal vessels. Furthermore, most yards do not have the skill to produce under class standards. These vessels must adhere to local standards, which are enacted and enforced by the government. However, local rules and standards are low quality and in many cases they are not even enforced. According to government officials, only three surveyors have been taking care of design approvals and supervision tasks for the entire domestic fleet in Bangladesh. As a result, domestic nonclassed vessels generally have quality levels that are low and that vary greatly depending on the executing yard.

Buyer's View and Implications

The main strengths of Bangladesh's shipbuilding are steelworks, overall cost position, and business environment. In spite of this, perceived excellence is scarce and benchmark nations surpass Bangladesh in most criteria (figure 1.7). Ship design has recently started in Bangladesh for smaller domestic vessels, but it is difficult

Figure 1.7 Qualitative Rating of Shipbuilding Capabilities by Industry Experts, Bangladesh and Comparators

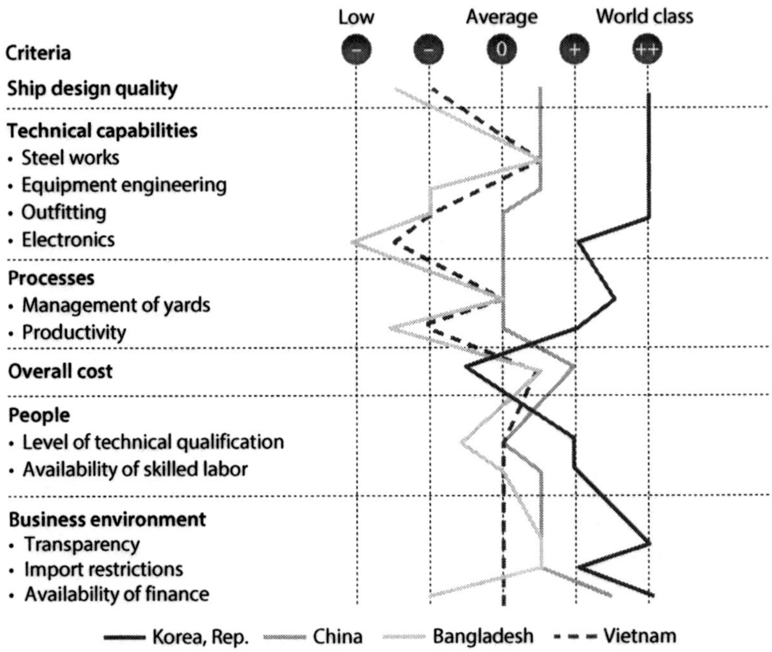

Source: FutureShip Expert Survey 2012.

to progress quickly to export designs as the field builds up mainly on experience. This is also the reason why design is still done mainly in high-income European countries, Japan, and Korea. However, China is investing heavily in this field by buying competency from abroad. In technical capabilities, Bangladesh is competitive in steel works, at least in the export-oriented yards. Most of a ship's equipment, outfitting, and electronics are still produced by manufacturers in high-income countries or by licensees in China. To close the gap with other competitors, it is essential to broaden the value chain with help from abroad—for example, through joint ventures (see box 1.2). Processes at Bangladesh's export-oriented yards are rated competitive. However, in productivity, Bangladesh is surpassed by its competitors. Here, work organization improves strongly with the industry experience of foremen and engineers. With respect to qualification and availability of people, Bangladesh is still behind its competitors. Graduates from universities and skilled workers often leave the country and training is not available on a broader scale for most workers. Bangladesh's business environment is perceived as good within the peer group. Only the financing problem is a major issue, which may be mitigated by more FDI (see box 1.3).

Summing up, Bangladesh's capabilities are adequate to serve the international market with small vessels on a limited scale. Domestic demand for higher-quality vessels is present but cannot be satisfied unless progress is made in several areas. Developing capabilities for building domestic vessels is a key

Box 1.2 China's Shipbuilding Industry: Technology Transfer through Joint Ventures

Since 2010, China's shipbuilding industry has been the largest in the world, with 37 million gross tonnes (GT) of deliveries in 2010 and 39 million GT of deliveries in 2011. China defended its position at the top in 2012.[a] The Chinese shipbuilding industry is dominated by the two state-controlled companies, the China State Shipbuilding Corporation (CSSC) and the China Shipbuilding Industry Corporation (CSIC), both founded in 1999. CSSC has more than 60 and CSIC 46 industrial subsidiaries and 28 research institutes. Both hold strong positions in shipbuilding and ship repairing and operate as engine and equipment manufacturers.[b] In addition to CSSC and CSIC, there are up to 2,000 shipbuilding yards that hold small shares of the market. The total workforce amounts to 400,000 employees (OECD 2008).

The expansion of the Chinese shipbuilding industry was initially aimed at securing domestic economic development and meeting the demand of growing international trade. With its comparatively low labor costs, China's shipbuilding industry has also gained an important position on the world markets. In 2007, 81 percent of Chinese new shipbuilding was directed toward the export market (Ecorys Research and Consulting 2009). With the launch of the 11th Five-Year Economic Plan in 2006, the Chinese government established several measures to strengthen its shipbuilding position and broaden the local value chain of the maritime sector in China. These measures include opening the sector for foreign investment and joint ventures, exempting imported components from tariffs (whereas there are tariffs on imports of entire vessels), and direct and indirect financial aid (for example, refund guarantees) (KPMG 2008; OECD 2008). Cooperations with Japanese, Korean, and Singaporean yards have helped bridge the technology gap China used to have compared with developed shipbuilding nations. One condition for joint ventures is that foreign companies establish technology centers to foster knowledge transfer. Foreign shipbuilding companies are allowed to hold up to 49 percent of ownership in Chinese enterprises. Moreover, several Chinese companies are licensed to produce propulsion equipment and engines for foreign suppliers. Some of these agreements date back to the 1980s, but complex equipment continues to be imported (Collins and Grubb 2008; OECD 2008). Government support is limited to shipyards in three regions: Bohai Bay, the Yangtze Delta, and the Pearl River Mouth (Ludwig and Tholen 2006).

For a long time, the main strength of Chinese shipbuilding has been building competitively priced, simple vessels. Bulkers are still the backbone of the industry and comprised 29–67 percent of all delivered vessels between 2007 and 2011 (Clarksons Database 2012), but diversification into more complex vessel types has also taken place during the past five years. At the same time, the volume of locally produced equipment and components has risen and will continue to grow to 80 percent in 2015 (Collins and Grubb 2008). This development shows that Chinese shipbuilders are not only relying on their (diminishing) cost advantage, but are also transferring knowledge into adjacent markets requiring more sophistication.

Source: FutureShip.
a. Clarksons Database 2012.
b. CSIC 2012, http://www.csic.com.cn/en/default.htm; CSSC 2012, http://www.cssc.net.cn/en/.

Box 1.3 Vietnam's Shipbuilding Industry: FDI for Quality Improvement

The Vietnamese shipbuilding industry is the fifth largest in the world, with 603,000 and 659,000 gross tonnes (GT) of deliveries in 2010 and 2011, respectively (Clarksons Database 2012) and a workforce of around 110,000 (Norad 2010). The industry is dominated by the state-owned Vietnam Shipbuilding Industry Group (Vinashin), which has a market share of 70–80 percent. Vinashin is a conglomerate that mainly specializes in the shipping industry; it is composed of more than 160 subsidiaries and over 30 shipyards.[a] Vietnam's shipbuilding industry began to soar in 2004 and has been backed by the industry's shift from the West to Asia. It has also been supported by dedicated government measures, including direct investments and additional loans at preferential conditions for shipyards, exemption from export and import taxes for equipment, and financing of working capital. These measures are aimed at increasing local content to 60 percent, improving the quality of building, and making the industry more competitive on the world market (Norad 2010). Some foreign-owned shipyards and several equipment producers act on the Vietnamese market as well as joint ventures. Both are said to produce more efficiently than local companies. In 2008, Vinashin's order book showed that export contracts comprised 60 percent of production. Strengths and competitive advantages of the Vietnamese maritime sector include a qualified workforce, low labor costs, new building and repair facilities, and government backing. Weaknesses are low productivity, poor management capabilities, and a weak supply industry that requires imports of 70 percent of total value.

Vietnam specializes in simple vessels. From 2007 to 2011, multipurpose vessels less than 8,000 GT and bulkers less than 35,000 GT represented between 79 and 92 percent of deliveries (Clarksons Database 2012). Different forms of foreign direct investment (FDI) have played an important role in the fast development of the shipbuilding industry. Several joint ventures and cooperations between Vinashin and foreign manufacturers have been established. These partnerships produce knowledge transfers that support quality and productivity enhancements, as well as the ability to produce more complex ships. Moreover, there are 100 percent foreign-owned companies that produce mainly for the export market. Vietnam has created economic and industrial zones with good infrastructure and easy and fast site planning to attract foreign investors. FDI amounted to US$67.4 billion over two decades as of June 2007 (Norad 2010; OECD 2008).[b] Although these have contributed to the success of the maritime sector over the past 10 years, further advances are being constrained by the current economic downturn and the resulting, ongoing financial problems of Vinashin. According to the press, Vinashin was "on the verge of bankruptcy" caused by insufficient management of public funds, lack of supervision and transparency, and lack of expertise in senior management, nepotism, and corruption (Philip 2011). These factors led to the imprisoning of nine former managers and contributed to the downgrading of Vietnam's credit rating.

Source: FutureShip.
a. Vietnam Shipbuilding Industry Group (Vinashin), 2012, http://vinashin.com.vn/.
b. Investment volume is calculated from figures in OECD 2008, 17.

to increased export competitiveness on a broader base. With appropriate capacity building, more yards can enter export shipbuilding in the future when markets pick up.

Key Success Factors

The analysis suggests that relying on stable domestic demand while improving quality and productivity is the most viable strategy for Bangladesh's shipbuilding industry. The background analysis and interviews with industry stakeholders highlight obstacles and some opportunities that can be leveraged. In a more positive market situation and with higher competitiveness, Bangladesh may increase the volume and quality of its exports in the long term. To assess this development potential, the key success factors identified in the previous section are analyzed and mapped against Bangladesh's boundary conditions and the market situation. Possible future scenarios are laid out for Bangladesh's shipbuilding industry, including a specific roadmap.

Five key success factors apply to shipbuilding in Bangladesh based on the experiences of China and Vietnam, as well as of other countries.

Key Success Factor 1: Grow the Industry during Periods of Increasing Demand

In almost all cases, new entrants to the shipbuilding sector emerged during phases of increasing demand. Shipbuilding is much more cyclical in term of its amplitudes of supply and demand than other sectors. Thus, the entry barrier is lower in phases of strong demand. International shipbuilding entered a severe crisis, with demand for tonnage forecasted to shrink by over 40 percent by 2015, leading to overcapacities and falling prices. Yard overcapacities exist in most countries, including nations with comparable cost positions, such as China and Vietnam, and in shipbuilding segments relevant for Bangladesh, such as bulkers, tankers, MPVs, and container feeders. However, demand for additional tonnage evolving from domestic and coastal trade represents an opportunity for yards to deepen their experience with classed vessels and broaden their capability base. Therefore, demand for small vessels for domestic and coastal trade needs to be fostered.

Key Success Factor 2: Ensure Government Support

The government has given growing attention to shipbuilding, including declaring it a thrust sector, easing import procedures, granting green channel support, and creating shipbuilding zones. However, no comprehensive master plan for the sector exists. Future establishment of the Ship Building and Ship Recycling Board (SBSRB) by the Ministry of Industry will demonstrate full support and guidance. SBSRB is intended to be a business incubator for the maritime industry. Implementation through concrete measures is vaguely formulated, if at all, and specification of detailed tasks and actions is pending. However, some milestones have been defined, as outlined in the following list. These measures can lead to improved infrastructure and quality, but they need to be implemented.

- Regulate the number and quality of new shipyards through issuance of "No Objection Certificates."
- Report to the government about the implementation of shipbuilding policies.
- Evaluate shipyards every five years.
- Look after the interests of workers; supervise on safety, work environment, and health issues.
- Take action to prevent environmental pollution.
- Facilitate connections for electricity, water, and gas.
- Register all shipyards. Registration or refusal has to be issued three months after application.
- Assist in establishment of ship design firms and backward and forward linkages.
- Develop a long-term plan for the shipbuilding industry.

Probably the greatest challenge to the industry at the moment is intermediate financing. It is a key enabler and is related to other factors such as cost, quality, and growth. Shipyards finance themselves at high interest rates of 15 percent on average. In addition, they bear the cost for import L/Cs and bank guarantees. The administrative effort for L/Cs is significant for suppliers and yards, which affects export and domestic shipbuilding. For export vessels, it drives up cost significantly and diminishes the competitive advantage that can be generated from low labor costs. For domestic vessels, it has another important implication. Local materials and components are more extensively used in domestic vessels, since regulations for building these are less strict than for export vessels and local materials are cheaper and do not bear the cost and administrative burdens associated with L/Cs. However, this lack of regulation has a negative effect on quality and does not allow firms to build experience in the production of quality components.

Moreover, industry stakeholders have reported the scarcity and cost of suitable sites as major obstacles for developing larger shipbuilding yards. Connection to roads, rail, and electrical power is a major problem for existing and new sites. However, for the future, the government intends to establish shipbuilding zones with space for yard building and reliable infrastructure. Appropriate areas for medium to large vessels are in the southeastern part of the country on the coast of the Bay of Bengal and Anwara and Kutubdia at Chittagong. Sites for smaller vessels are on the bank of Meghna River and at Narayanganj Dhaka, on the bank of the Pashur River and Mongla. Furthermore, the government intends to help scrapyards move into shipbuilding. In addition, the construction of a deep-sea port south of Chittagong is being considered, but even if this occurs, full operations can be expected no earlier than 2022.

On the tax front, the National Board of Revenue of Bangladesh has approved a 12-year tax rebate facility that cuts corporate taxes to 10 percent from 18.75 percent for shipyards. Imports of foreign marine components are subject to duties of 3–126 percent, with the highest tariffs applicable to components that could be manufactured domestically. The purpose of this system is to foster local content. However, it tends to drive up shipbuilding costs and leads owners of technically more complex vessels to award construction to non-Bangladeshi yards.

Another area where the government can play an important role is quality upgrade. Whereas quality is rated "good" for export vessels, only a small number of export vessels have been built by only two yards in Bangladesh. The majority of yards are building vessels under lower quality standards as classification is not legally required and would mean higher cost. Quality for local sales is not enforced, although measures such as the domestic vessel code exist in theory. The code is not applied for several reasons, mainly lack of resources. The supervisory body (the government) does not have enough qualified staff and employees at the yards do not have sufficient training to put the rules into practice. To build up quality, the following actions are considered essential: (a) enforce the current rules by appropriately educated surveyors employed by the government, (b) update and improve the domestic vessel code with stricter technical rules and standards, and (c) increase the share of classified vessels among domestic vessels. Most countries delegate the quality control and enforcement of their local standards to so-called recognized organizations for cost reasons.

Key Success Factor 3: Attract FDI and Foster Joint Ventures

FDI and joint ventures help bridge the capability gap with more advanced shipbuilding nations and increase reputation (box 1.4). FDI in the shipbuilding industry is currently close to zero in Bangladesh. Reasons often mentioned are the poor infrastructure, absence of proper management structures, lack of a critical mass for shipbuilding products in the domestic market, and widespread corruption. FDI could bring shipbuilding in Bangladesh forward, especially in linked industries, as it fosters technological advancement, improves processes, and enhances the capabilities of people in the industry. It is difficult to build up the industry to provide more complex marine components without technological

---

Box 1.4 Spotlight on the Republic of Korea: Hyundai Heavy Industries

Hyundai Heavy Industries (HHI) of Korea made the best of a downturn in world shipbuilding production by partnering with more experienced firms. In interviews with Amsden (1989), HHI explained the four specific ways that they obtained advanced shipbuilding technologies: "obtaining dockyard designs from a Scottish naval architecture firm, A&P Appledore; ship designs and operating instructions from a Scottish shipbuilding firm, Scottlithgow; experienced European shipbuilders who worked as employees of HHI for the first three years of operations; and production know-how from the Kawasaki shipbuilding company of Japan."

Source: Amsden 1989, 276–77.

---

know-how from foreign manufacturers. Improvement of the local market and the infrastructure situation would help attract more FDI, especially for those product families that have applicability in other sectors, such as generators.

FDI could also provide an important source of financing, as shipbuilding is a capital-intensive industry and investment in large yard facilities is associated with significant risk. An investment of approximately US$50 million is needed for setting up a shipyard with an annual capacity of ten 40,000 dwt vessels. It is questionable whether private investors are willing to take such risk, given the current market climate and against the background of Bangladesh's infrastructure problems and missing competitive advantages.

Key Success Factor 4: Broaden the Domestic Supply Industry

Up to now, the supply industry for export ships has not been developed in Bangladesh. This affects shipbuilding negatively in two dimensions. First, since all components have to be imported and yards order only small volumes, components may not be available on time; often ship owners have to help with procurement. In addition, communication and building relationships with suppliers are difficult, leading to higher administrative effort, production delays, and higher cost of procurement. Second, the value added in the country is low, affecting buildup of skills and negating a possible virtuous circle of higher employment. However, the value chain provides much opportunity for broadening. According to the 2011 Indian Steel Report, with production of steel, steel items, paints, generators, compressors, and other items, the value added in Bangladesh could be pushed beyond 50 percent (International Metalworkers' Federation 2011). This would have a positive effect on employment of up to 2,500 additional employees in the steel industry (based on production of 500,000 tonnes of steel and 200 tonnes per worker per year) and 20,000 to 30,000 additional employees in other industries.[6]

Key Success Factor 5: Provide a Low-Cost, Skilled Workforce and Proper Yard Management

In Bangladesh, lack of adequate management and technical staff for yards is another constraint to the growth of the shipbuilding sector. Limited capabilities in work organization and planning by senior staff are a problem often mentioned by industry stakeholders. This affects the productivity and the time taken to produce a vessel. For senior staff, high-quality shipbuilding has relied to a significant extent on foreigners or Bangladeshi staff educated and trained abroad. Universities and marine academies have recognized the demand for qualified graduates and have increased enrollment and made the curricula more relevant, which will influence the situation positively in the long term. In the workforce, shortages of good welders have been reported. Proper training is the most urgent need, as formal training for workers is rare. The training at Western Marine Shipyards is a good model to follow. In summary, the situation at the management and engineering levels is more challenging than at the shop floor level, where productivity gains are leveraged more easily.

Future Development Potential and Challenges

Three key areas could be leveraged in the near future to influence the sector positively. First, there is the growing use of small vessels in domestic and coastal trade. Demand for additional tonnage evolving from domestic and coastal trade represents an opportunity for yards to deepen experience with classed vessels and broaden their capability base.

Second, benefits will accrue from rule enforcement. Vessel safety is a major concern and a high number of accidents with many fatalities have occurred in the past. This is partly because of the poor quality standards of domestic vessels. But it is also an opportunity for the industry to improve. Bangladesh's shipbuilding industry will benefit from stronger rules and standards through an expected increase in workload and improved capabilities fostered by higher technical requirements.

Third, expansion of maintenance and repair services will create new opportunities. Maintenance and repair services for fleets in service are more stable and labor-intensive businesses than building new ships. Since larger and smaller vessels ply Bangladeshi waters, there is a general opportunity to benefit from this traffic and expand maintenance and repair facilities for larger vessels as well. This would require establishing further appropriate sites and dry docks beyond the existing Chittagong dry dock with its maximum capacity of 20,000 dwt.

Future Development Scenarios

This section uses the key success factors and opportunities to create scenarios over the next 5 to 10 years for shipbuilding in Bangladesh. Factors can be separated into those that are fairly predictable, the so-called trends (box 1.5), and factors with unclear outcomes, so-called uncertainties (table 1.2). The trends and uncertainties are discussed in the following subsections. For the uncertainties, a variety of assumptions leads to three scenarios: realistic, positive, and negative. The analysis assumes that government support and incentive programs are broadly the same across competing countries.

Realistic Scenario: Moderate Growth

As international demand has dried up and will most likely not recover until 2015, Bangladesh has to rely on domestic demand over the next few years. In the most

Box 1.5 Trends in Bangladeshi Shipbuilding

- Moving toward larger vessels
- Increasing complexity of vessels
- Increasing energy efficiency of vessels
- Increasing demand for inland container and oil transport vessels
- Creating mid-term shipyard overcapacities

Table 1.2 Uncertainties in Bangladesh's Shipbuilding Industry and Possible Reponses

	Scenario		
Uncertainty	*Realistic*	*Positive*	*Negative*
International market demand	Weak short-term growth, moderate growth after 2015	Strong rebound after 2015	Constantly weak
Cost competitiveness in comparison with China and others	Competitive	Highly competitive	Not competitive
Availability of adequate financing for yards	No direct support, slight decrease of interest rates	Direct governmental support, decrease in interest rates	No change to current situation
Level of investment in backward linkage industries and yard infrastructure	Moderate investment	High investment	No or low investment
Investment in education	Moderate	High	Low

likely scenario, Bangladesh's shipbuilding sector—currently a half-billion-dollar industry, according to industry experts—will grow moderately at an average of 10–15 percent over the next 10 years, taking the produced tonnage to 800,000 GT. Direct employment will not rise as much because of productivity gains, but it will still double. Domestic demand is mainly driven by increased demand for river transport and by the replacement needs of the old fleet in service. High fuel prices and safety concerns are the favorable factors. International orders only complement the order book. The average quality of vessels built in Bangladesh will rise, enhancing international competitiveness. This will happen for two main reasons: First, around one-third of all newly built vessels greater than 600 dwt will be classed according to the new, internationally competitive standards. Second, concentration of yards will lead to knowledge accumulation and accelerated learning for individuals.

Compared with 2012, the value chain will broaden to include a significant share of locally produced goods, leading to moderate employment growth in linked industries. The domestic steel industry will be able to produce marine grade steel and pipes. FDI will help to build up local production of paint, smaller generators, purifiers, compressors, and valves; this will increase the value added of classed ships to above 50 percent. In addition to shipbuilding, maintenance activities will develop as a stable business. Toward the end of the decade, Bangladesh will start producing more export vessels, primarily in the smaller vessel segments. In addition to good quality, Bangladesh will be known for excellent business relations with foreign ship buyers. Nevertheless, Bangladesh's international orders will not boom because financing of yards and shipbuilding—despite slight decreases in interest rates—will remain a major impediment to Bangladesh's competitiveness.

Positive Scenario: Strong Growth

Within 10 years, Bangladesh will be recognized as a mature player for vessels up to 20,000 dwt, fulfilling local and international standards. Production will increase by 20 percent per year on average and direct employment will triple. In 2022, output will reach 1.5 million GT per year.

Two main assumptions shape a positive scenario for Bangladesh's shipbuilding sector in the next decade. First, international demand will pick up much faster than expected by industry experts. Although there is a lot of capacity available worldwide, Bangladesh will succeed in increasing its net tonnage built, thus strongly increasing market share. Reasons for growth will include a good reputation for quality, internationally competitive classification standards, and increased labor cost competitiveness through productivity growth that exceeds the impact of wage increases. Moreover, increased coastal trade among Bangladesh, India, and Myanmar will lead to increased demand for tonnage. Second, the government will launch a major shipbuilding growth program consisting of tax incentives for FDI, duty exemptions, guarantees for investments, and an own-investment program in the Chittagong deep-water area. In addition, direct support will be given with low-interest financing. These measures taken together will multiply local and foreign investments in yards as well as in supply and maintenance and repair industries.

Negative Scenario: Stagnation

First, domestic demand will be stable, requiring no investments in new yards and leading to small productivity growth. Wage pressure from other industries will drive up wages in the shipbuilding industry and thus international competitiveness will decrease. Moreover, international demand for tonnage will almost exclusively be absorbed by yard overcapacities in China, Korea, and a few other countries. Second, without orders for international vessels, the government will keep classification standards at a low level, just sufficient for domestic registration. With little trust in the potential for improvement, the government will lose focus on the shipbuilding sector and will not create incentives for expansion. As a result, Bangladesh's shipbuilding industry will face zero growth.

Suggested Roadmap for Development

Future development may be influenced positively by government policies. Seven areas have been identified that could be targeted by government policy makers. These are summarized in table 1.3.

Conclusions

Bangladesh's history in building ships for international markets is short, with just above 20 vessels delivered to international ship owners. In the past, ships for export have been awarded to Bangladeshi shipyards because of lack of yard capacity in traditional suppliers. Given Bangladesh's basic to average capability,

Table 1.3 Seven Areas for Shipbuilding Development: Policy Action for the Government of Bangladesh

Policy goal	*Time frame*	*Measures or policies*
1. Funnel domestic demand to domestic shipyards	Short term	Enable more yards to produce quality vessels: prioritize attention and support on yards with potential by evaluation and short listing. Attach licensing for operation of new builds to domestic building (for example, licenses for inland container lines).
2. Make shipbuilding more attractive for the domestic market	Short term	Review the duty regime for critical materials and components to make shipbuilding for the domestic market cheaper.
3. Bundle competencies for shipbuilding in government	Short term	Make the Ship Building and Ship Recycling Board operational. Define responsibilities and decision rights (vs. government). Establish key tasks, work agenda (for example, fostering infrastructure), and timetable. Staff board with experts.
4. Bundle and enable quality shipbuilding	Medium term	Establish shipbuilding zones. Designate and prepare appropriate land for the shipyards and supply industry. Create local clusters with access to water and workforce. Provide central infrastructure for shipbuilding zones: water supply, power supply, river and sea access, and road connections into the hinterland. Initiate repatriation program for Bangladeshi shipbuilding talent with foreign work experience (for example, through tax exemptions).Foster foreign direct investment through global communication.
5. Foster local supply industry	Medium term	Identify focus areas (business case development and selection). Provide industrial zones (in combination with shipbuilding zones). Provide legal support for foreign investors.
6. Ensure vessel safety and build up local standards	Medium term	Establish dedicated governmental authority to take full ownership and responsibility of vessel safety in national waters: define tasks, responsibilities, organization, processes, and staff authority (administration and surveyor organization). Update content of rules and standards: develop toward international standards in breadth and strictness. Ensure execution of rules and standards through skilled surveyors.
7. Incentivize water transport, foster shift of transport mode	Long term	Direct funds toward projects favoring water transport. Review taxation of different means of transportation based on carbon emissions.

Note: Short term = 1–3 years; medium term = 3–5 years; long term = 5–10 years.

quality and cost positioning have been supporting but not decisive factors. An average 25 percent annual growth in tonnage built since 2001 has largely been fueled by construction of smaller vessels for domestic markets. This pattern is unlikely to change, because international shipbuilding has just entered its most severe crisis in years. A modest recovery was not expected before 2015. Therefore, export contracts could be considered as supporting rather than driving shipbuilding growth.

The main challenges to shipbuilding, in addition to depressed international demand, are intermediate yard financing, infrastructure development, and quality. Key opportunities for growth include leveraging domestic demand, benefiting from increased national safety regulation, and expanding maintenance and repair services. To overcome the present challenges and leverage the identified opportunities, the roadmap requires action and focused implementation. In this case, moderate growth of Bangladesh's shipbuilding industry with a significant effect on employment but moderate export revenue growth is realistic. Extreme growth rates greater than 30 percent over the long term, as seen in China and Vietnam in the past decade, seem unachievable, given the lack of international demand. Overall, there is a positive outlook if the right measures are taken.

Notes

1. Although this is the officially reported number and shipbuilding at unregistered yards (of the approximately 200 shipyards in Bangladesh only 124 are registered) might have a significant share, it can be expected that the number for large vessels above 200 gross tonnes is fairly exact.
2. Western Marine Shipyards, procurement department.
3. The labor cost position has two components: nominal labor cost (US$/hour) and productivity (capital gains tax/hour).
4. Domestic oil tankers currently under construction have "hull class" only.
5. Published in 2001 in accordance with Inland Shipping Ordinance, 1976.
6. Expert estimates.

References

Amsden, A.1989. *Asia's Next Giant: South Korea and Late Industrialization*. Oxford: Oxford University Press.

Clarksons Database. 2012. "Shipping Intelligence Network." London.

Clarksons Research. 2012. "Base Case Assumptions." Forecast Report, The Shipbuilding Forecast Club. http://www.crsl.com/.

Collins, G., and M. Grubb. 2008. "A Comprehensive Survey of China's Dynamic Shipbuilding Industry." China Maritime Studies 1, U.S. Naval War College, Newport, RI. http://www.usnwc.edu/Research---Gaming/China-Maritime-Studies-Institute/Publications/documents/CMS1_Collins-Grubb.aspx.

Ecorys Research and Consulting. 2009. *Study on Competitiveness of the European Shipbuilding Industry*. Report to the Directorate-General, Enterprise & Industry, European Commission, Rotterdam. http://ec.europa.eu/enterprise/sectors/maritime/files/fn97616_ecorys_final_report_on_shipbuilding_competitiveness_en.pdf.

IMF (International Monetary Fund). 2011. *World Economic Outlook Database*. IMF, Washington, DC. http://www.imf.org/external/ns/cs.aspx?id=28.

International Metalworkers' Federation. 2011. *Indian Steel Report*. International Metalworker's Federation, Geneva. http://www.imfmetal.org/files/08040111112266/IMF_Indian_ steel_report.pdf.

KPMG. 2008. "Indian Shipbuilding Industry: Poised for Take-Off?" https://www.kpmg.de/Themen/10354.htm.

Ludwig, T., and J. Tholen. 2006. "Shipbuilding in China and its Impacts on European Shipbuilding Industry." Institute of Labour and Economy, University of Bremen. http://www.iaw.uni-bremen.de/downloads/ShipbuildingChina2006.pdf.

Norad (Norwegian Agency for Development Cooperation). 2010. *Study of the Vietnamese Shipbuilding/Maritime Sector*. Norad Report 10/2010 Discussion, Oslo. http://www.norad.no/en/tools-and-publications/publications/publication/_attachment/196523?_ download=true&_ts=12a37fd2177.

OECD (Organisation for Economic Co-operation and Development). 2008. "The Shipbuilding Industry in Vietnam." Council Working Party on Shipbuilding, OECD, Paris. http://www.oecd.org/dataoecd/34/20/42033324.pdf.

Philip, B. 2011. "Massively Indebted Vietnamese Shipbuilder Misses Payment." *Guardian Weekly*, January 4. http://www.guardian.co.uk/world/2011/jan/04/vietnam-financial-crisis.

Stopford, M. 2009. *Maritime Economics*. 3rd ed. New York: Routledge.

Transparency International. 2011. "CPI Index." http://cpi.transparency.org/cpi2011/.

CHAPTER 2

Light Engineering: Bicycles

Atdhe Veliu and Glenn Surabian

Introduction

This chapter assesses the performance of the bicycle value chain in Bangladesh in the context of global competition. The objectives of the value chain analysis are: (a) to review the detailed breakdown of costs and productivity for bicycles and identify the main reasons for the productivity and cost gaps; (b) to identify the most important and common constraints across the value chains; (c) to generate insights into the possible practical solutions to address a critical mass of the identified constraints; and (d) to benchmark the competitiveness (productivity and costs) of the selected products against competitors (China and Vietnam).

The chapter provides a basic description of the bicycle sector's value added, domestic market, imports and exports, and employment; it then provides a detailed breakdown of the value added for each critical step along the value chain. In addition, each critical step along the value chain will be provided with an additional breakdown and analysis to show the underlying issues for each of these steps and provide the breakdown among input, labor, capital, and other costs. This section will also discuss the quality drivers, such as the quality of key inputs and services at each step of the value chain, the quality of processing, as well as the quality of delivery and marketing (time to market).

Bicycle exports are the single largest product export of Bangladesh's engineering sector, contributing about 7.5 percent of engineering exports. Bicycle exports began around 1995 and have been growing gradually since then. It is a large cluster in the Bangladeshi context, with a few large firms, along with many more small enterprises. Potential links with the rest of the economy are substantial, given the nature of the product as an assembly of a large number of parts. Production is not very energy intensive. As such, it was felt that a case study of bicycles could help provide insights on the potential of not only bicycles, but also the engineering industry.

The detailed value chain analysis in this chapter suggests that continued growth of Bangladeshi bicycle exports is not obvious. Exports currently enjoy a price preference because of EU antidumping duties against China's bicycle exports. In a more open regime, the price edge may be wiped out.

Critical issues that affect the international competitiveness of bicycles are not unique to the sector. Most of the more sophisticated parts are imported, which means that domestic economic links with the exporting sector are lower than is potentially possible and brings up the question of lead times between order receipt and delivery. Lack of a domestic supply base raises the question of scale economies in production, along with a skill base that leads to low-productivity production. These issues will be explored in greater detail.

Sector Profile: Bicycles and Bicycle Parts

Global production of bicycles is highly concentrated, with the top 10 countries commanding about 92 percent of global production value. The top three countries account for three-quarters of the production value. Leading producers of bicycles by value include China, with US$27.5 billion or 51.6 percent of the market; Indonesia, with US$7.1 billion or 13.2 percent; and India, with US$6.6 billion or 12.4 percent. Global bicycle production reached US$53.3 billion in 2011 and grew 30.8 percent in the five-year period from 2007 to 2011 (table 2.1). Production of bicycles is growing fast. In 1965, world production of cars and bicycles was nearly 20 million each, but as of 2003, annual bike production had climbed to over 100 million per year compared with 42 million cars produced worldwide (figure 2.1).

It is estimated that more than a billion bicycles were present in the world as of the mid-1990s, with approximately 450 million in China, 100 million in the United States, and 72.5 million in Japan.[1] Consumption statistics are difficult to pinpoint at the country level. Demand for bicycles in high-income markets is growing because of a trend toward environmentally friendly transportation and in developing markets because of the desire for affordable transportation as

Table 2.1 Leading Producers of Bicycles by Value, 2007–11
US$, thousands

Rank	*Country*	*2007*	*2008*	*2009*	*2010*	*2011*
1	China	18,712,700	22,589,900	22,923,700	24,374,300	27,516,600
2	Indonesia	4,757,600	5,610,400	5,983,300	6,696,100	7,059,900
3	India	4,044,200	4,500,200	5,112,600	5,830,800	6,590,100
4	Japan	3,043,400	2,684,200	2,153,000	2,071,900	2,185,400
5	Germany	1,338,300	1,328,300	1,134,300	1,413,200	1,432,200
6	United States	1,476,600	1,355,100	1,174,400	1,157,600	1,269,600
7	Netherlands	1,452,300	1,471,600	998,300	1,064,500	1,100,200
8	Italy	1,019,000	975,300	930,700	826,100	730,100
9	Canada	788,900	843,400	799,500	692,600	718,100
10	France	540,000	596,300	545,800	542,300	636,200
	Other	3,573,200	3,774,100	3,600,000	3,862,500	4,053,100
	World	40,746,200	45,728,800	45,355,600	48,531,900	53,291,500

Source: Euromonitor International, www.euromonitor.com.
Note: Data shown are International Standard Industrial Classification (ISIC) 3592: Manufacture of bicycles and invalid carriages, which correspond to Harmonized System (HS) 8712: Bicycles and other cycles (including delivery tricycles), not motorized.

Figure 2.1 World Bicycle and Passenger Car Production, 1950–2007

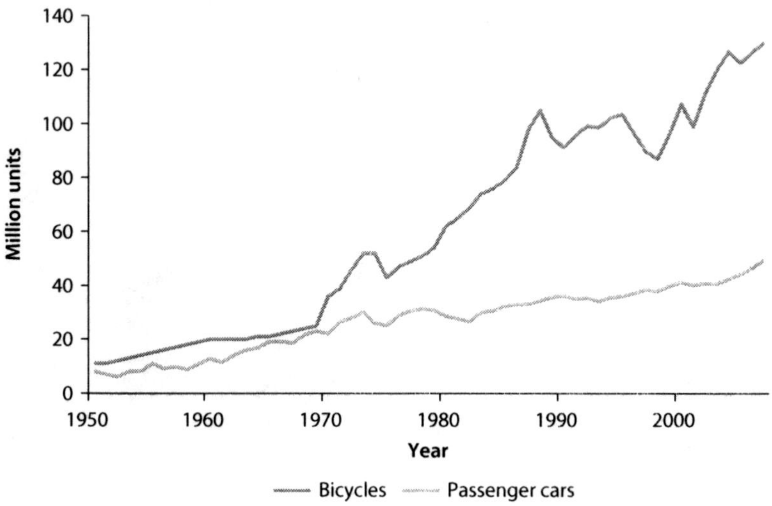

Sources: Compiled by Earth Policy Institute with bicycle data from Gardner 2009, 53–54; car production for 1950–70 from Worldwatch Institute 2004; car production for 1971–2007 from Ward's Automotive Group 2008, 239–42.
Note: Bicycle data include electric bicycles; car data do not include commercial vehicles.

household income improves. In addition, higher-end, more technically advanced bicycles appeal to sports enthusiasts. Particularly in Europe, urban design facilitates riding and bicycles are a popular form of transport. In the Netherlands, for example, 25 percent of all trips occur via bicycle. The figure is only 1 percent for the United States, where on the whole bicycles are favored more for recreation than transport (figure 2.2).

Exports of bicycles totaled US$6.6 billion and more than 71 million units in 2011.[2] The top 10 exporting countries comprised 82 percent of total value and 85 percent of total units. Leading exporters included China (44 percent of value and 79 percent of quantity), the Netherlands (12 percent of value and 1.5 percent of quantity), and Germany (7.6 percent of value, quantity unknown) (table 2.2). The average value for an exported bicycle worldwide is US$92. Of the top 10 exporters, China commands the low-priced value space, with an average unit value per export of US$51.98, while the Netherlands and the United States are targeting more up-market consumers via an average price per unit export of US$730 and US$550, respectively.

Bangladesh's bicycle exports are highly concentrated in three key markets that together capture about 87 percent of export market share. In 2011/12, Bangladesh bicycle exports were US$106 million (table 2.3). Total exports rose 27 percent from the levels in 2008/09, although they were US$5.3 million below the 2009/10 peak of US$111 million. Leading destinations in 2011/12 were the United Kingdom (US$67 million or 64 percent), Germany ($15 million or 14 percent), and Belgium (US$9.2 million or 8.7 percent). Figures by unit

Figure 2.2 Bicycle Trips as Share of Total Trips in Selected Countries, 2008–09
percent

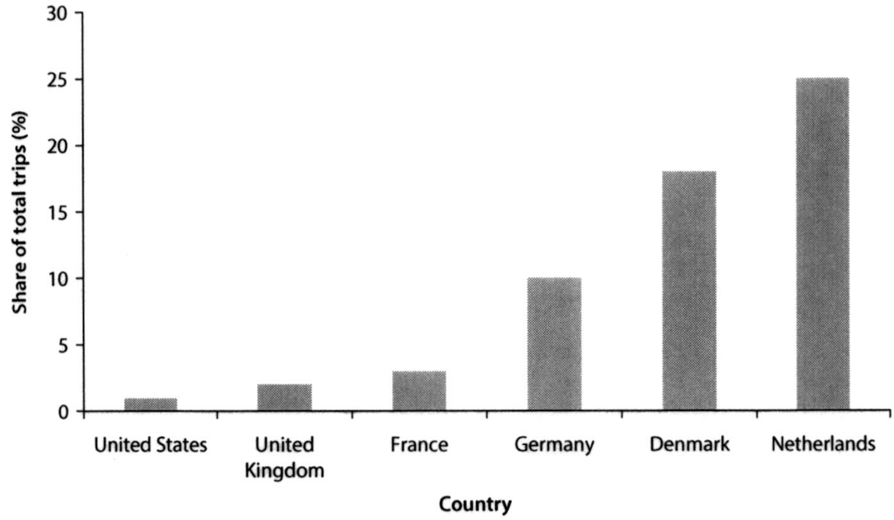

Table 2.2 Top 10 Exporters of Bicycles by Value and Quantity, 2011

				Share of global exports (%)	
Rank	*Country*	*Value (US$)*	*Quantity*	*Value*	*Volume*
1	China	2,919,683,604	56,164,600	44.4	78.6
2	Netherlands	798,857,918	1,094,183	12.1	1.5
3	Germany	499,281,309	—	7.6	n.a.
4	Belgium	268,635,240	1,163,888	4.1	1.6
5	Italy	214,968,058	1,585,835	3.3	2.2
6	Portugal	193,351,968	—	2.9	n.a.
7	France	146,864,763	697,369	2.2	1.0
8	Thailand	116,408,877	—	1.8	n.a.
9	United States	111,498,021	202,567	1.7	0.3
10	Cambodia	109,261,969	—	1.7	n.a.
	Other	1,200,682,242	10,568,145	18.2	14.8
	World	6,579,493,969	71,476,587	100.0	100.0

Source: United Nations Statistical Division, UN Comtrade, http://comtrade.un.org/db/.
Note: — = not available.

quantity were not available. Based on data from the Export Promotion Bureau, export value in 2011/12 would place Bangladesh near the top 10 exporters, not far behind Cambodia's $109.3 (table 2.2).[3]

Global imports of bicycles totaled US$7.5 billion and nearly 63 million units in 2011. The top 10 importing countries comprised 71.6 percent of total value and 60 percent of total units. The import market is much more fragmented than the export market. Leading importers included the United States (19 percent of value and 25 percent of quantity), Japan (12.5 percent of value and 15.0 percent of quantity), and Germany (9.8 percent of value, quantity unknown) (table 2.4). The average value for an imported bicycle worldwide is US$119. Of the top 10 importers, the United States and Japan are making a value play, with an average unit value per import of US$90 and US$99, respectively, while Switzerland demands much higher-value bicycles, with an average value per unit of US$483.

Table 2.3 Leading Export Markets for Bicycles from Bangladesh by Value, 2008/09–2011/12
US dollars

Rank	*Country*	*2008/09*	*2009/10*	*2010/11*	*2011/12*
1	United Kingdom	52,353,829	72,124,123	66,179,318	67,386,507
2	Germany	6,819,491	11,859,977	11,289,987	14,825,992
3	Belgium	12,969,410	11,688,875	8,999,693	9,205,061
4	Ireland	4,597,616	7,121,688	3,354,404	4,479,141
5	Denmark	110,533	1,080,324	1,346,265	2,264,866
6	Italy	976,302	3,260,548	721,432	1,251,901
7	Portugal	34,478	—	244,473	1,128,182
8	Netherlands	688,097	546,034	1,103,062	1,003,583
9	Spain	303	—	65,653	831,248
10	Austria	35,664	289,906	633,809	824,235
	Other	4,365,509	2,891,974	5,894,196	2,389,983
	World	82,951,232	110,863,448	99,832,293	105,590,700

Source: Export Promotions Bureau, Bangladesh.
Note: — = not available.

Table 2.4 Top 10 Importers of Bicycles by Value and Quantity, 2011

				Share of global imports (%)	
Rank	*Country*	*Value (US$)*	*Quantity*	*Value*	*Volume*
1	United States	1,419,601,493	15,793,254	19.0	25.1
2	Japan	936,137,141	9,450,592	12.5	15.0
3	Germany	732,033,662	—	9.8	n.a.
4	Netherlands	500,059,174	1,772,882	6.7	2.8
5	United Kingdom	470,750,959	3,435,904	6.3	5.5
6	France	374,054,159	2,631,313	5.0	4.2
7	Belgium	302,885,493	1,537,953	4.1	2.4
8	Canada	212,809,157	1,320,719	2.8	2.1
9	Australia	211,470,458	1,238,667	2.8	2.0
10	Switzerland	197,491,117	409,179	2.6	0.7
	Other	2,120,978,436	25,297,776	28.4	40.2
	World	7,478,271,249	62,888,239	100.0	100.0

Source: United Nations Statistical Division.
Note: — = not available.

The Bicycle Industry in Bangladesh

Industry Emergence

The bicycle and bicycle parts export industry has emerged relatively recently in the industrial landscape of Bangladesh. As international trade liberalization was growing in the mid-1990s, the use of various trade protection instruments was frequent. In 1993, after continuous lobbying from the European Bicycle Manufacturers Association, the European Union imposed antidumping duties of 30.8 percent on bicycles made in China.[4] This duty provided an opportunity for existing producers and new investors in other countries to enter the lucrative bicycle market of the European Union (estimated at US$7 billion in 2011). At the time, Bangladesh did not have a domestic bicycle exporting base, but investment opportunities for capturing EU market opportunities were greatly improved with the imposition of antidumping duties on Chinese exporters.

Foreign direct investment was critical to the emergence of the bicycle export sector. Malaysian investors were the first to seize the EU market opportunity by establishing the first bicycle exporting firm in Bangladesh in 1995. They invested US$2 million in a new plant named Alita in Chittagong. A domestic trading group, Meghna, was the next firm to enter the bicycle export manufacturing industry after Alita. Meghna's founders had been involved in bicycle and parts trading in the 1960s, manufacturing bicycle spokes in the 1970s, and doing bicycle assembly for the local market in the 1980s. After diversifying and becoming a highly successful trading conglomerate, the Meghna Group grew to become the largest bicycle and bicycle parts manufacturer in the country. It now has two factories dedicated to the export market, two factories dedicated to bicycle manufacturing for the local market, and five bicycle components factories. The third and last market entrant in the bicycle exporting industry is German Bangla Bicycles, established in 2009 as a joint venture between a German bicycle manufacturing firm (Panther) and a Bangladeshi company (Powertrade Engineering) whose major business interests are in heavy manufacturing (telecom towers, electrical grid infrastructure, and so forth). Like the other two firms, German Bangla is an original equipment manufacturer (OEM), but by and large only for European brands, as is the case for Meghna and Alita. Table 2.5 provides an overview of the industry at present. These figures are broad estimates based on interviews with participants in the industry.[5]

Bangladeshi bicycle exporters continue to rely almost exclusively on preferential market access in the European market arising from the antidumping duty on Chinese exports.[6] However, because of a severe slowdown in the European market, the industry's export levels, capacity utilization (and employment), and other performance indicators have been impacted negatively.

Alongside the export-oriented bicycle industry, Bangladesh has a cottage industry of small-scale bicycle assemblers, parts manufacturers, and retailers, with beginnings dating to the 1970s. This cottage industry remains understudied and

Table 2.5 OEM Bicycle and Bicycle Parts Sector Profile, Bangladesh, 2012

Details	*Units*			
Number of firms	3			
Number of bicycle manufacturing/assembly factories, of which:	7 4 by Meghna (1 idle, M&U) 2 by Alita (1 for steel, 1 for alloy frames) 1 by German Bangla (low capacity utilization, idle for parts of the year)			
Number of bicycle components factories	5 (all owned by Meghna); other OEMs produce some components for own use only			
Estimated bicycle production (units/year)	1,100,000			
For export market	900,000			
For local market	200,000 (Meghna only)			
Estimated size of the local market (bicycles/year)	1,000,000			
Industry capacity utilization, bicycle assembly	40–70%			
Estimated number of people employed in the industry	2,000			
Estimated male-to-female ratio, employees[a]	50:50			
Reported export value, 2008–12 (US$/fiscal year)[b]				
	2008/2009	*2009/2010*	*2010/2011*	*2011/2012*
Bicycles[c]	82,951,232	110,863,448	99,832,293	105,590,700
Bicycle parts	4,655,496	5,541,322	6,953,527	7,905,120
Total bicycles and parts	**87,606,728**	**116,404,770**	**106,785,819**	**113,495,820**

Source: Global Development Solutions, LLC.
Note: OEM = original equipment manufacturer.
a. http://www.thefinancialexpress-bd.com/2008/08/10/42241.html.
b. Export Promotion Bureau; the fiscal year is July to June.
c. As reported under category HS87120000 (bicycles and other cycles, not motorized), which includes tricycles and similar nonmotorized cycles that are not exported by Bangladesh (the entire value can be attributed to bicycles).

statistical information is extremely limited. Nevertheless, based on interviews with the Business Owners Association of the Bongshal Market in Dhaka—the hub of the cottage bicycle industry in Bangladesh—general features of the market can be discerned. An estimated 1,500–2,000 people work in the Bongshal market in businesses directly related to bicycle assembly, component manufacturing, and retailing. Firms are small (typically, up to 10 employees), have extremely old machinery (in many cases over 30 years old), and are limited in their ability to graduate from the low-quality segment of the market. Typically, many small firms combine parts manufacturing with bicycle assembly and retailing of "complete knockdown" or "semi-knockdown" kits imported from China and India. Table 2.6 illustrates the general characteristics of this cottage industry for the Bongshal market, based on interviews with members of the Bongshal Bicycle Assembly and Importers Association.

Low tariffs on inputs and high tariffs on outputs (56 percent) create effective protection rates that average 219 percent for the domestic market. Thus, there is a strong incentive for firms to focus on the domestic market (see Kathuria and Malouche 2016, chapter 2).

Table 2.6 Cottage Bicycle and Bicycle Parts Industry, Bongshal Market, Dhaka, 2012

Details	*Units*
Finished bicycle selling shops	105
Bicycle parts sellers	120
Importers of cycles and having trading shop	35
Importers of parts and having trading shop	25
Importers from China	20
Importers from India	16
Bicycles sourced from importers of CKD and SKD kits with own retail shop(s)	70
Bicycle parts sourced from importers with own retail shop(s)	95
Shops selling bicycle frames exclusively	8
Shops selling bicycle wheels/rims exclusively	12
Shops selling bicycle tires and tubes exclusively	7
Manufacturing/service unit in Bongshal Market	
Fork producers	8–10
Frame producers	15–20
Nickeling units	6
Bicycle parking stand producers	5
Mudguard producers	3
Seat posts, steering posts, and similar parts producers	2
Employment in the market	
Estimated number of people employed in the cottage industry, of which:	1,500–2,000
Salespeople in the market	350
Experienced bicycle assembling specialists (employed in assembly shops)	150
Freelance bicycle assembling specialists (not employed in assembly shops)	50
Bicycle market size	
Average monthly imports of bicycles as CKD and SKD (units)	4,000 (low season) to 45,000 (high season)
Country of origin	China, India
Average daily sales of bicycles in the market (units)	500–600

Source: Compiled by Global Development Solutions, LLC, based on data from Bangladesh Bicycle Merchants Assembling & Importers Association.
Note: CKD = complete knockdown; SKD = semi-knockdown.

Supply Chain

The bicycle manufacturing sector in Bangladesh is split into two distinct supply chains: (a) modern export-oriented OEM manufacturers and (b) the small-scale cottage bicycle and bicycle parts industry catering exclusively to the local market. These two supply chains operate independently with extremely limited interactions and linkages between the two (figure 2.3), owing to a differences in market demands.[7] There are no suppliers in Bangladesh that occupy the middle

Figure 2.3 Bicycle Manufacturing Sector Supply Chain, Bangladesh

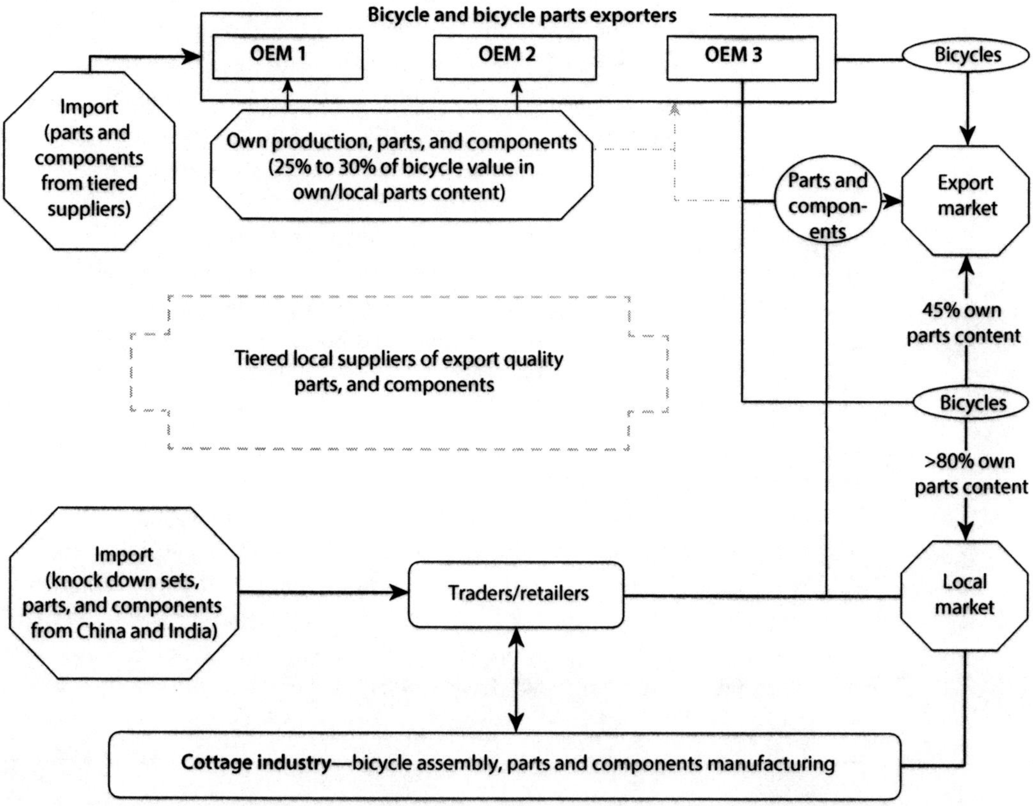

Global Development Solutions, LLC *- - - Dashed lines indicate missing linkages in the supply chain*

part of the supply chain consisting of specialized parts and component manufacturers; local suppliers cannot produce parts and components of the quality required for export-oriented OEMs. Suppliers of bicycle parts and components in Bangladesh historically have been exclusively oriented toward the local market, where quality requirements and standards have been low. Local producers of parts and components have few incentives to make significant quality improvements in their products geared solely to export market demands.

Moreover, opportunities for links to local suppliers to access the supply chain of exporting OEMs are probably decreasing because OEMs have increased the level of vertical integration of their production. Meghna, for example, has five parts and components factories and Alita and German Bangla can produce a number of parts themselves for their own needs, including wheels and spokes, frames and forks, handlebars, chain covers, seat posts, pedals, saddles, and many other parts.

The lack of a local base of suppliers of quality parts and components has significant implications. First, OEMs that do not have deep enough pockets for investing in additional parts and components manufacturing must source parts in foreign markets. Currently, two of the three Bangladeshi OEMs import parts worth 60–75 percent of their ex-works bicycles' export value. Interviews suggest that these producers will likely increase the foreign content of parts and components in the future to the maximum allowed by EU rules of origin.[8] Second, OEMs that are strong financially, like Meghna, have made significant investments in parts and components manufacturing. For bicycles sold locally, Meghna's share of own parts and components is estimated at 80 percent and for exported bicycles, up to 45 percent. This, combined with the lack of scale economies in the manufacture of parts, probably limits opportunities for independent suppliers of export-quality parts and components suppliers to emerge.

The third implication stemming from foreign sourcing of export-quality parts is a negative impact on lead times (box 2.1). For example, Bangladeshi exporters' lead times to the U.K. market are estimated to be 30–50 percent longer compared with Chinese exporters (see table 2.7). It is estimated that the bulk of the lead-time gap arises from the Bangladeshi firms' need to source a large part of parts and components from abroad, which can take up to a month after all the required paperwork and shipping. Chinese exporters can rely on a vast local supplier base that enables them to source parts and components within a few days.

Furthermore, shipping transit times to and from Chittagong are uncompetitive.[9] For example, it takes approximately the same number of days (27) to ship a container from Chittagong to the United Kingdom and to ship a container from much farther east in Shanghai to the United Kingdom; it takes half as many days to ship a container from Sri Lanka (two weeks).

Box 2.1 The Importance of Lead Times in the Bicycle Industry

Compared with other goods, such as garments, footwear, and similar consumer goods, bicycles are bulky items to store, cost relatively more to buy and stock on a per unit basis, and have significantly longer supply chains with more composite parts (up to more than 100 in certain bicycles). Thus, although bicycles have one seasonal cycle (late spring and summer season in the largest markets in Europe and North America), lead times are extremely important in bicycle supply chains. The following quotes from participants in the industry may help shed light on lead time and other supply chain developments in the bicycle industry that have a long and complex history.

"Lead times are mostly a problem in late spring when the selling season is ramping up and both retailers and suppliers have to gamble on quantities without knowing when the weather will turn favorable or if any economic setbacks will affect buying … by the time the season actually kicks off, it is often too late to react to spikes in demand since the factories have already begun the transition to the next model year." General Manager, Giant Bicycle, June 2011, http://www.bicycleretailer.com.

"The lead-times for alloy frames produced in China are on the rise. Volume bike makers in Europe are now planning to start a joint frame facility in the Ukraine to become more flexible. For years the regular lead-time in China for produced alloy frames was 15 weeks. Currently that

box continues next page

Box 2.1 The Importance of Lead Times in the Bicycle Industry *(continued)*

lead-time stands at about 25 weeks. The situation could even deteriorate further...." Rising Lead-Times for Alloy Frames: Bike Makers Turning to Eastern Europe, June 2010, www.bike-eu.com.

"What it all boils down to is the fact that lead-times are on the rise. That is a fact we at Accell Group cannot deal with. It is frustrating our business as there's no time left to react on actual bike sales. When the selling season starts in Europe—beginning of April—we get accurate sales info on which models are popular and which not. We want to be able to order frames in April for bike production in July." Chief Operating Officer, Accell Group NV (leading bicycle producer in Europe), April 2010, www.bike-eu.com.

"Industry's ordering cycle is changing. More suppliers move forward placing their orders in September and start production for the upcoming season in April/May. They clash with those suppliers relying on the traditional product cycle.... In October 2011 we received an extremely high number of orders. Since then our production is running at full capacity. The ordering level in Europe is notably higher compared to the number of bikes being sold in Europe. We can't explain why this is happening and I can only say that this situation makes it very, very difficult to plan our production." Managing Director, Shimano Europe, February 2012, www.bike-eu.com.

Source: Compiled by Global Development Solutions, LLC.

Table 2.7 Comparative Lead Times, Bicycle Exports, Bangladesh versus China, 2011

Lead time (days)	*Bangladesh*	*China*
Preprocessing (parts ordering), lead time A (L/C and other paperwork)	8–15	1
Preprocessing (parts ordering and delivery), lead time B (shipping and transportation)	15–20	2–7
Processing lead time (bicycle manufacturing/assembly)[a]	25	25
Post-processing lead time (shipping to United Kingdom)	27–30	27
Total lead time (days)	75–90	55–60
Lead time difference (Bangladesh/China)	+35% to +50%	

Source: Global Development Solutions, LLC.
Note: L/C = letter of credit.
a. For illustration, assumes identical order size, processing time, and destination market for both countries. This comparison is for illustration purposes only; lead times vary significantly depending on bicycle complexity.

Supporting Institutions and Policies

Two private sector associations are directly involved in the bicycle industry in Bangladesh. The Bangladesh Bicycle and Parts Manufacturers and Exporters Association is the official association of bicycle exporters or OEMs. However, its role seems quite limited and OEMs do not share with or receive industry information from the association. The one OEM outside Dhaka (Alita) was even surprised that there is a formally registered association of bicycle exporters in the country. The cottage industry of small and medium enterprises (SMEs) engaged in frame assembly, parts manufacturing, and import has its own association in the Bongshal market named the Bangladesh Bicycle Merchants Assembling and Importers Association. Although the association is formally registered, the functioning of the cottage industry itself is highly informal. The information shared by the association during interviews was limited. Precise membership figures are not published, but interviews with the association suggest that it has more than 100 active members in any given year. The main benefit of participating in the association is that it tends to bring some level of order to this highly informal market. In addition, the Bangladesh Small and Cottage Industries Corporation (BSCIC), which is under the Ministry of Industry, has a mandate to support industrialization of small and cottage industries, but a review of BSCIC's ongoing projects does not reveal any support activities related to the cottage bicycle assembly and parts industry.

The sector benefited from the export stimulus provided by the government in the form of export incentives until 2012/13. Until the end of 2011/12, the bicycle-exporting industry was on the list of 19 export sectors that were eligible to receive cash incentives. For bicycle exporters, the eligible rate was 15 percent of the assessed free on board value of exported goods. In 2012/13, however, the list of export-oriented sectors eligible for incentives was reduced to 15 sectors and bicycle exports are not on the list.[10] According to public pronouncements of the Ministry of Finance, one of the primary reasons for leaving the bicycle export sector off the export cash incentive scheme is that the sector already enjoys duty-free access to its main market in the European Union.

Value Chain Analyses: Bicycles and Bicycle Parts

Product Profile: Bicycles

In the age of computerized designs and sophisticated materials, consumers can choose from a wide variety of bicycles available in the market depending on desired features: means of propulsion (motorized or nonmotorized), type of construction or function (ranging from basic steel frame city bicycles to carbon fiber racing bicycles), or other features. The most common bicycle categories or types are: utility, hybrid, mountain, motocross (BMX), touring, and racing bicycles (table 2.8).[11]

Bangladeshi OEMs produce a range of bicycles for the export market (table 2.9). The number of models produced is extremely large; typically, OEMs may produce anywhere from 100 models for a single client to more than 200 different models in total for various clients. As a result, Bangladeshi OEMs typically define their product ranges by price categories in which they compete rather than by functional categories of bicycles. According to Meghna's chief executive officer, for example, "[the company] is shipping bicycles in the price bracket of US$120 and we have been working on the

Table 2.8 Common Bicycle Types and Categories

Bicycle type/category	*Features*
Utility	Designed for basic transportation (commuting, shopping, and leisure) rather than recreation or competition. The European city bike and the English roadster are commonly referred to as category representatives: typically weighs 16–23 kilograms; typically steel frame; components and frame designed for strength, safety, and durability rather than performance; generally fewer technological improvements compared with performance or sports bicycles, although lightweight aluminum and derailleur (instead of hub gearing) models are available and marketed as "sports" variants of city bikes. Common in Asia and Africa. Less common in North America and most parts of Europe. Produced by Bangladeshi OEMs for export mainly to the U.K. market.
Hybrid	Designed for general commuting on a variety of surfaces with a combination of features from racing and mountain bicycles. Includes variations such as city, cross, and commuter bicycle. Typically weighs 10–15 kilograms (with medium- to light-weight composite frames), is designed with wide derailleur gear ranges for various terrains, and has a limited number of accessories. Common in high-income countries and one of the key export categories of Bangladeshi OEMs.
Mountain	Designed for off-road, unpaved environments for activities typically called mountain biking. Typically weighs 10–13 kilograms, with multiple gears (up to 30), with shock absorbers for off-road stresses. Includes many variations such as cross country, endure all, mountain, trail bikes, downhill bikes, and many others. Produced by Bangladeshi OEMs.
Bicycle motocross (BMX)	Designed mainly for dirt and motocross cycling but used in casual and sport activities on paved streets and dirt. Frames typically made of steel (cheaper, low-end products), aluminum (for racing), or high-performance chrome alloys for high-end models. Some variants: freestyle, dirt jump, street, park, race. Produced by Bangladeshi OEMs.
Touring	Designed for bicycle touring with features to provide ride comfort and capabilities to carry heavy loads: long wheelbases, heavy-duty wheels and tires, and multiple load-carrying and mounting points.
Racing	Designed for competitive road cycling. Generally sophisticated technologically. Higher-end bicycles extremely sophisticated, with high-tech carbon fiber frames used instead of steel and aluminum frames. The low weight and high tensile strength of the frame is paramount; a typical carbon frame weighs less than one kilogram and the bicycle can weigh as little as 0.6 kilogram. High-end range of products generally not produced by Bangladeshi OEMs.

Source: Global Development Solutions, LLC.

higher price bracket for some time now and the time has come when we will soon start getting into the over US$150 price range" (BIKEEurope 2012).

As is the case with other OEMs, a bicycle from a given price bracket usually will include features from various categories: a basic or low-price bicycle may have a combination of features from the hybrid or utility category; a mid- to high-priced model typically would have features of a mountain bicycle, but also a mix of city or commuting bicycle characteristics. In this context, value chain

Table 2.9 Bicycle Categories Produced by Bangladeshi OEMs

Type of bicycle	*Estimated production cost range, Bangladesh (US$)*	*Estimated retail price, Europe (US$)*	*Produced in Bangladesh*
Basic utility or hybrid	50–60	100+	Yes
Mid-end city or hybrid	75–120	200+	Yes
Higher-end city, hybrid, mountain, or BMX	100–150	350+	Yes
Racing	n.a.	700+	Limited

Source: Global Development Solutions, LLC.
Note: n.a. = not applicable.

analysis was undertaken for a typical bicycle exported by Bangladeshi OEMs: a hybrid bicycle in the production cost range of US$75–US$90 per bicycle and with an estimated retail price in end-markets in Europe starting from US$200 per bicycle or higher depending on distribution channel (see photo 2.1 for a sample hybrid or city bicycle from a typical client of Bangladeshi OEMs).

Value Chain Analysis for Bicycles, Export-Oriented Industry

Bicycles are made of hundreds of parts and components. Photo 2.2 illustrates the key building blocks of a typical bicycle and their technical nomenclature. In the manufacturing process, the process of making a bicycle is typically as follows:

- Assembling of frame, which consists of two processes: (a) cutting tubes for the frame, fork, and seat and chain stays and (b) welding tubes, with or without lugs (metal sleeves that join two or more tubes)
- Washing the welded frame from impurities and painting it
- Assembling the wheel, including attaching the tire and tube (rims, spokes, tires, tubes, and other parts needed at this stage may or may not be produced by the bicycle assembler)
- Assembling the bicycle by attaching to the frame the wheels and all other parts and components, including, among others, handlebar, stem and headset, brakes, saddle and seat post, derailleur(s), crankset or chainset, and all other components
- Testing, quality control, and inspection of the finished product (usually performed at each stage as well as at the final stage), after which products are packed, warehoused, and ready to be shipped to clients.

Imported parts and components dominate the exportable bicycle value chain in Bangladesh. The final assembly stage dominates the cost structure of bicycle manufacturing, with a little over 51 percent share (figure 2.4), consisting essentially (98 percent) of costs of parts and components. Bangladeshi OEMs import the bulk of bicycle parts and components from China; Singapore; Taiwan, China; Hong Kong SAR, China; Malaysia; and Thailand. The cost of assembly is followed by frame assembly (21 percent) and wheel and tire assembly (10 percent).

Photo 2.1 Hybrid or City Bike

Photo 2.2 Technical Parts of a Bicycle

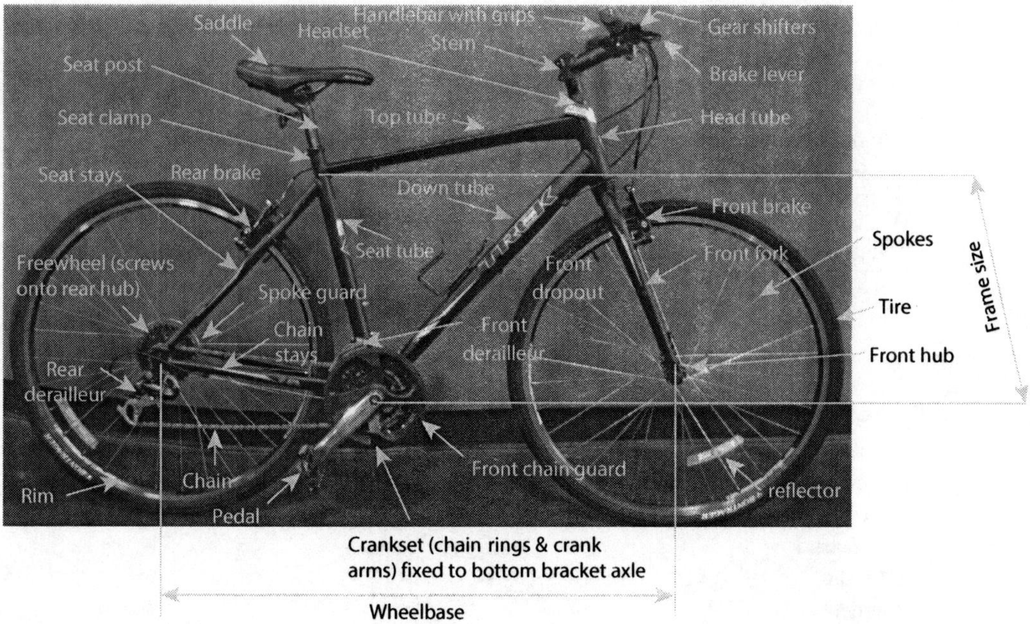

Source: Global Development Solutions, LLC.

The availability of export-quality parts and components in the local market is extremely limited (table 2.10).[12] Some components can be produced by OEMs, but generally the make-versus-buy decision is driven by price and quality considerations. OEMs report that many parts can be sourced cheaper from abroad than it would cost to make them in-house.[13] For most high-value components,

Figure 2.4 Bicycle Value Chain Analysis, Bangladeshi OEMs

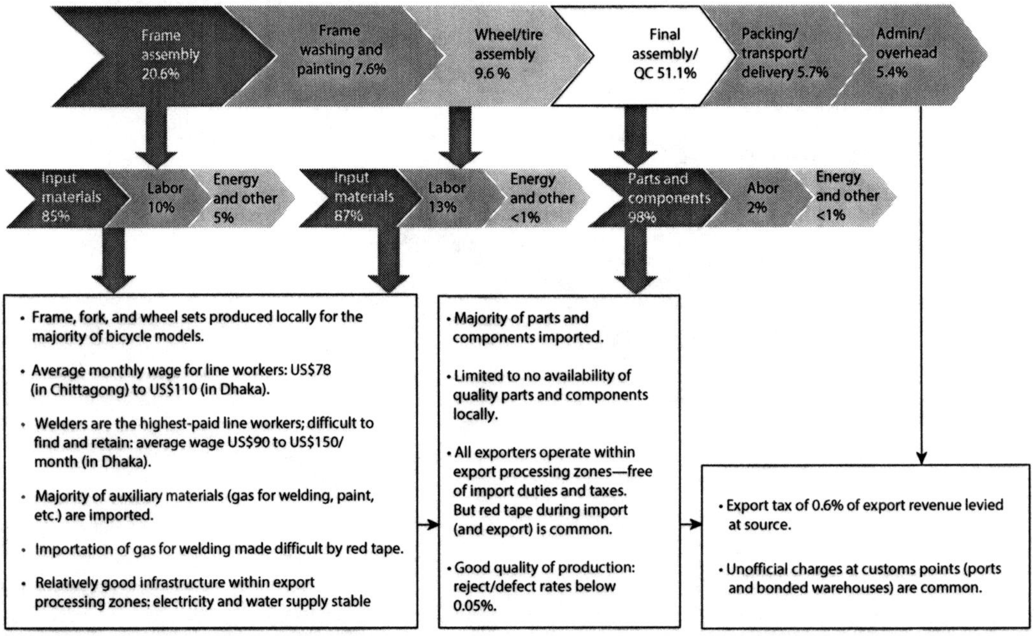

Source: Global Development Solutions, LLC.

Table 2.10 Availability of Bicycle Parts and Components in the Local Market, Bangladesh, 2012

Parts and components group	*Local sourcing possible (sufficient quality/price)*[a]	*Own production possible*[a] *OEM 1*	*OEM 2*	*OEM 3*
Derailleur(s)	No	No	No	No
Chain set	No	No	No	No
Freewheel and hub(s)	No	No	No	No
Brake set(s)	No	No	No	No
Bearing(s)	No	No	No	Yes
Saddle	No	No	Yes	Yes
Rack (carrier)	No	No	No	Yes
Steering column	No	No	Yes	Yes
Mudguard	No	Yes	No	Yes
Pedal(s)	No	Yes	Yes	Yes
Handlebar	No	Yes	Yes	Yes
Grip(s)	Yes	Yes	No	Yes
Seat post	Yes	Yes	Yes	Yes
Chain cover	Yes	Yes	Yes	Yes
Frame assembly set (tube and fork)	No	Yes	Yes	Yes
Wheel assembly set (rims and spokes)	No	Yes	Yes	Yes
Tire and tube	No	No	No	Yes

Sources: Global Development Solutions, LLC. Meghna data from www.meghnagroup.com.bd/cycle/parts.html.
Note: OEM = original equipment manufacturer.
a. "Yes" does not necessarily mean the specific parts or components are sourced locally or produced by OEMs themselves.

however, OEMs' make-versus-buy choice does not exist: derailleurs, chain sets (crank, chain, etc.), brake sets, freewheel or hubs, and many other high-value parts cannot be made by Bangladeshi OEMs. Meghna Group is the only OEM that has the capability to produce a wider variety of components such as bearings, pedals, and racks; nevertheless, it also has to rely on imports for many parts and components. The bicycle industry in competing countries (most notably China) has a large base of OEMs and parts and components manufacturers that enables it to source parts and manufacture bicycles with much shorter lead times. OEMs typically build their own frames and forks and then, depending on manufacturers' level of vertical integration, build some parts on their own and source other parts and components from specialized suppliers or from their clients.[14]

Frame and wheel manufacturing and assembly are also dominated by input material or parts costs. Typical for the industry, Bangladeshi OEMs manufacture and assemble the frame and wheel sets in their own facilities. Depending on client requirements, Bangladeshi OEMs can produce a variety of frame and wheel sets in terms of the design and materials used (steel and alloys). The value chain analysis suggests that the frame and wheel assembly stages constitute approximately 28 percent of total bicycle manufacturing costs. These stages generate the bulk of local value added in bicycle manufacturing in Bangladesh.[15]

Thus, Bangladeshi OEMs have an estimated 35–50 percent lead time gap compared with Chinese suppliers, primarily because of heavy reliance on time-consuming import of parts and components.

The value chain analysis reveals that the share of labor costs in the production of a bicycle is quite low across all manufacturing stages in Bangladesh. The share of labor costs is about 10 percent at the frame assembly stage, 13 percent at wheel assembly stage, and 2 percent at final bicycle assembly stage. When all stages of production are included, the direct labor costs associated with producing a bicycle in Bangladesh range from US$3 to US$5 per bicycle, depending on capacity utilization at any given time and on production location.[16] Labor costs, although important, have a relatively lower importance in determining the competitiveness of the product compared with other labor-intensive industries such as garments and similar industries. This is evidence that bicycle manufacturing across all stages, including frame and wheel manufacturing and assembly, is relatively capital intensive.

As a consequence, bicycle manufacturing can be and is successful in countries with relatively higher labor costs than Bangladesh. In China, for example, the average monthly payroll per employee in the transport equipment industry (including bicycles) is US$500 (table 2.11).[17] In Taiwan, China the average monthly payroll in the industry is US$1,300.[18] Notwithstanding these comparatively high labor costs, producers in these countries are market leaders in the bicycle industry: China is the world leader in bicycle exports in general and Taiwan, China is among the leaders in medium- to high-end bicycles.

The competitiveness of Bangladeshi OEMs across all stages of bicycle production suffers from unnecessary bureaucratic practices.[19] For example, OEMs need to obtain two permits to import welding gases (argon-based and

Table 2.11 Comparative Labor Costs, Bicycle Industry, Bangladesh and China, 2012
US dollars

Cost	*Bangladesh*	*China*
Average monthly wage, direct labor	US$95	US$520–US$550
Cost of direct labor per bicycle	US$3–US$5	US$10–US$12
Bicycles/worker/day—reported estimate at current production levels	1.0–1.3	2.0–2.2
Bicycles/worker/day—reported estimate at full capacity production	2–3	3

Source: Global Development Solutions, LLC.

other specialized welding gases) that are not available locally: a "prior permission" to import and then a "final permission" to import. Both permits are issued by the Explosives Department of the Ministry of Energy, which regulates the trade in these generally dangerous materials. According to OEMs, this two-stage process is a typical example of an approval process designed for rent-seeking. The so-called prior permission is almost identical to the final permission: most information sought in the prior permission (gas content and cylinder specifications) is also provided to the authorities at the final permission stages (via packing lists, invoices, and specifications). The current regulations (the Explosives Act or the Gas Cylinder Rules amendments) are not sufficiently clear about the necessity of a prior permission as a procedure.[20]

According to the Explosives Department, the prior permission is indeed an informal procedure. It is designed to facilitate trade because it assists various importers during the import process when commercial banks require this permission to open letters of credit. This may be the case in certain situations, but as far as OEMs are concerned, they have long-standing relationships with their banks and they do not report prior permission as being a requirement from their banks for processing import transactions. An OEM in Bangladesh typically would import at least 500 gas cylinders (two containers) per month from established suppliers that are well known to OEMs' banks in terms of supplier origin, gas or cylinder specifications, and all other pertinent details.

The cost of obtaining prior permission is significant in time and money (table 2.12). At US$550 per shipment of imported gas, the total transaction costs associated with import permits can add approximately 5 percent to the cost of imported welding gas inputs. To put these transaction costs in perspective, assuming an estimated 30 containers of welding gas are imported each year in separate shipments, the total cost for obtaining welding gas permits alone, depending on the amount of unofficial payments, can amount to an estimated US$16,500 per year. This amount corresponds roughly to the total monthly bill for 200 workers. Combined with other reported official and unofficial payments, these costs strain OEMs' cash flows considerably and represent a costly burden on their competitiveness.

Unofficial costs have a large impact on overhead cash outlays. The unofficial payments in table 2.13 consider the lowest amounts reported in firm interviews, which are 18 percent of overhead cash outlays. These levels of payments can

Table 2.12 Transaction Costs and Procedures in Bangladesh, Input Importation per Shipment, 2012

Fees and costs (US$) and time (days)	*Prior permission*	*Final permission*	*Notes*
Official fees paid	US$12	0	US$6 per 100 cylinders.
Unofficial fees paid	$60	US$60–US$120	"The more you pay the sooner they issue the papers to you," says one OEM owner.
Other transaction costs	0	US$180–US$360	For the final permission, companies have to involve own employees or intermediaries to handle the file personally for each shipment. The company pays for cost of transportation, lodging, and other related costs.
Total fees paid	US$72	US$240–US$480	At US$550 per shipment, total transaction costs are roughly 5 percent of the value of the shipment. At current prices, a container of imported argon welding gas with 260 cylinders costs US$11,000 delivered to the factory gate in Bangladesh.
Time to obtain permit (as reported by officials)	3 days	3 days	According to the head of the Explosives Department, "If all of applicants' papers are in order, we issue the permits in three days at most. But most applicants have errors in their applications so it generally takes up to a week to issue the permits."
Time to obtain permit (as reported by companies)	7–14 days	7–14 days	"We apply for prior permission well ahead of time so it has no major impact on delaying inputs. But then the vessels cannot unload our shipment unless the final permission is sent to Customs. And here is where most glitches occur. Shippers increasingly are reluctant to transport welding gas to Bangladesh due to many glitches with final permissions," says one OEM owner.

Source: Global Development Solutions, LLC.

have a major impact on firm competitiveness. The advance income tax (levied at 0.6 percent of export revenues) constitutes 28 percent of overhead cash outlays, but this is merely early payment and would have been collected anyway in the form of taxes on profits.

OEMs report difficulties in finding qualified workers in several areas. Finding the qualified welders needed for the frame assembly stages of production is reported to be particularly difficult. Welders are among the highest-paid members of the workforce in assembly plants, earning up to US$150 per month in Dhaka.

Table 2.13 Overhead Costs, Bicycle Assembly, Bangladesh, 2012

Overhead cost	*Share of total overhead costs (%)*
Administrative labor	16
Rent	21
Marketing	5
Financing[a]	3
Advance income tax	28
Unofficial payments	18
Other	8
Total[b]	100

Source: Global Development Solutions, LLC.
a. For operating activities.
b. Excludes depreciation.

This is a relatively high manufacturing wage in Bangladesh. Yet despite the significant premium over standard assembly line wages (up to 50 percent), finding and attracting a sufficient number of qualified welders is a challenge. Finding and attracting qualified middle managers is also reported to be difficult as management and business graduates are reported to prefer working in the telecom and other service sectors. Migration, particularly to Gulf countries, is reported to be particularly challenging to the industry. A 2010 survey on the international demand for semiskilled and skilled Bangladeshi workers confirms that welders are in high demand:

> "The survey revealed that a typical semiskilled or low-skilled migrant does not have a general or technical education or training, and is employed in a lowly job with wages up to a meager Tk 13,000 a month [US$190].... Welders are the largest of the better-paid groups with wage levels of Tk 26,000+ per month [US$380+]. Workers in certain skill categories have fairly high demand. They are steel frame fixers/fabricators, welders, tiles fixers, plaster technicians, and masons." (Maxwell Stamp Limited 2010)

The export competitiveness of the industry may be challenged if the European Union lifts antidumping duties against Chinese bicycles. Bangladeshi bicycle exporters readily admit that the heavy antidumping duties on Chinese bicycle exports to Europe helps keep them afloat. They estimate that without antidumping duties, Chinese bicycles could reach European markets with a price tag at least 10–20 percent lower than Bangladeshi bicycles. And Chinese exporters can ship bicycles to the EU market with 35–50 percent shorter times. In March 2012, the EU Commission initiated a review of antidumping measures on Chinese bicycles. According to official review documents, "[T]he continued imposition of [antidumping] measures at the existing level may no longer be appropriate to offset the effects of injurious dumping."[21] Without antidumping duties, Bangladesh's bicycle exports to the United States would likely suffer dramatically. In other markets that do not impose antidumping duties, most notably the

United States, Bangladeshi bicycle exporters have found it difficult to compete (table 2.14).

Vietnam is an emerging competitor for Bangladeshi bicycle exporters. It is recovering from EU antidumping duties imposed between 2005 and 2010. The case illustrates the importance of industry linkages in the bicycle industry. Although industry insiders in Vietnam report that the industry is not yet competitive, the bicycle industry in Vietnam is reportedly developing into a "near self-supporting network of factories." The emergence of a local base of producers of export quality parts and components in Bangladesh appears to be vital to the country's bicycle export competitiveness.

Value Chain Analyses for Bicycle Parts and Components: Local Market SMEs[22]

The SME value chain of a bicycle steering column consists of cutting long aluminum pipes into smaller slugs ready for extrusion and machining. Precut slugs then are greased and sent through impact extrusion: slugs are placed inside a die cavity and struck through a punch. Extruded pipes then are machined (lathed), washed, and ready to be packed and delivered. Figure 2.5 illustrates the value chain for bicycle steering columns produced by SMEs in Bongshal, Dhaka.[23]

The value chain analysis suggests that SME bicycle parts manufacturers face multiple challenges, including high levels of reported informal imports from China and India (box 2.2). Imported parts from China and India often come through informal channels that make it difficult to compete because SMEs source raw materials through local traders with all duties and taxes included in the price. This is particularly difficult when the cost of raw materials generally constitutes the bulk of the value chain and where all interviewed SMEs report the price of raw materials to be rapidly increasing (see table 2.15).

Importers of parts from China and India effectively set the ceiling price for parts and components sold in the local market. As is the case with many

Table 2.14 Bicycle Exports to the United States, 2007–11
US$, thousands

Exporter	*2007*	*2008*	*2009*	*2010*	*2011*
World	1,138,719	1,386,818	1,104,679	1,447,336	1,419,601
China	865,060	1,031,464	776,256	1,059,264	964,818
Chinese Taipei	248,560	333,371	310,040	354,643	420,373
Cambodia	—	—	1,458	5,663	8,164
Germany	1,163	1,649	1,609	5,056	7,996
Canada	7,454	7,346	6,153	9,632	5,276
Indonesia	2,184	2,737	2,678	1,672	2,519
Vietnam	178	688	261	426	428
Bangladesh	—	—	—	—	—

Source: Global Development Solutions, LLC, from ITC/UN Comtrade.
Note: — = not available.

Figure 2.5 Bicycle Steering Column Value Chain Analysis, Bangladeshi SMEs

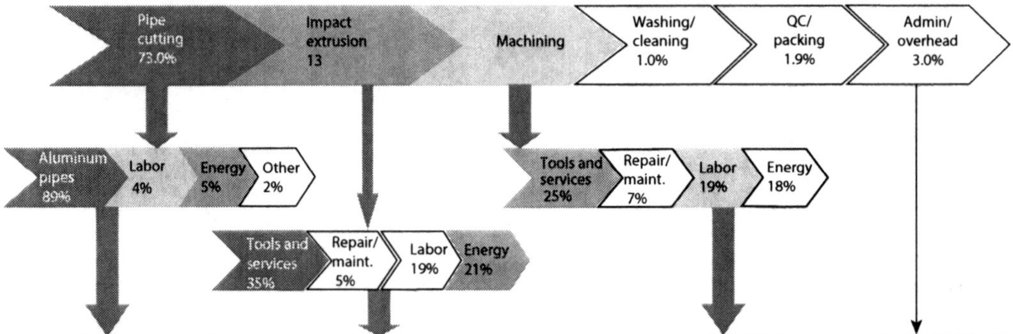

- "We buy aluminum pipes from a local trader at full price with all duties and taxes. Importers flood the market with imported goods from India and China and pay no duties and taxes."
- "I [the manager] am the most educated person in the workshop. I finished secondary school."
- "We have three pipe cutting machines, two lathing machines, and four impact extrusion machines. Age of machinery is 25 to 40 years."
- "Workers earn US$18 per week. We work from 8:30 am to 6:00 pm. Sometimes we work until 10:00 pm depending on how many hours we lost waiting for electricity to come back on."
- "We can buy lathing and some die tools in the local market but they are of poor quality. They break constantly. The punch has to be of high-grade steel. I buy it from shipbreaking scrap dealers. I cannot find it anywhere else. Then I temper and level the tools in local workshops. Quality of service is very poor. The punch may bend and/or break at any time. Then the electricity stops every day, sometimes for 3–4 hours. So in the end I lose so much of my production that I have to sell as scrap metal. In a batch of 3,600 pieces, we scrap 300."
- "We applied for a loan with a local bank three years ago. They never bothered to reply. We don't bother to apply again."
- "Rent has increased by 20 percent from last year and the landlord announced another rent increase of 20 percent starting next month.

Source: Global Development Solutions, LLC.
Note: SMEs = small and medium enterprises.

Box 2.2 SME Bicycle Parts Manufacturer Suffering from Imports from China and India

"We are two brothers who run this workshop. Our father started the business 40 years ago producing bicycle frames and forks, steering columns, seat posts, and some other parts. We worked in the workshop and learned all about it from him. He passed on the business to us in 2003. Twenty years ago, we employed 55 people. Now we employ seven to eight people. At the time, we had an established brand name in the local market but then imports from India and China started flooding the market. A big Indian firm, Hero Cycles, sent us to court claiming that we infringed on its brand name. We won the court case, but this cost us a lot of money."

Today, this small firm in Bongshal produces only aluminum bicycle steering columns (called fork pipes) and seat posts. The firm can also cut frame and fork pipes, but according to the manager, the market is flooded with imported and local frame pipe sets (from OEM Meghna), which makes it impossible to compete. The interview suggests that the firm is barely competing in its existing product line as well.

Table 2.15 Survey of SME Parts Manufacturers, Bongshal, Dhaka: Share of Raw Materials and Profit Margins by Part, 2012
percent

Bicycle part(s) manufactured by SME	*Reported share of raw materials in value chain (%)*[a]	*Reported profit margin (%)*
Steering column	66	9
Frame and lugs	62	11
Frame	56	11
Parking stand	85	8
Fork	65	4
Mudguard	65	7

Source: Global Development Solutions, LLC.
a. Auxiliary input materials such as welding and painting materials, components (springs, nuts and bolts, and others), grease, oil, packaging, and other materials are not included. When auxiliary material costs are included, the share of all materials in the value chain is over 80 percent for most parts or components.

SMEs that do not have brand recognition and pricing power, the steering column producer sells its products in the price range of Tk 460–Tk 560 (US$5.55–US$6.75) per dozen, well below the price for steering columns imported from India (Tk 600 [US$7.15] per dozen units). Steering columns sold by Meghna sell at par with or slightly higher prices than Indian imports, but Meghna has established a brand and quality recognition that smaller local firms cannot match. As a result, SMEs operate under intense competition from imported parts with thin profit margins (see table 2.15), although the parts they produce may not necessarily be of lower quality than imported parts. Table 2.16 lists market prices of some other parts and components sold in Bongshal market depending on their origin.

The quality of electricity is extremely poor and creates major problems for SMEs that cannot afford generators. Although SMEs consider the price of electricity to be high (US$0.09 per kilowatt-hour), it is generally the quality of electricity in relation to price that generates this perception.[24] Daily brownouts are a frequent occurrence in Dhaka. The duration of brownouts is reported to range from fractions of an hour to three to four hours at least once a week. Frequent brownouts create major production problems. In the example of the steering column producer highlighted in the value chain analysis, all the processes come to a halt and all the cutting, extrusion, and lathing machines have to be retooled. This generates losses in time, materials, and quality of product. Poor electricity combined with other production bottlenecks leads to major losses in this particular SME that amount to as much as 8.3 percent of production.

The impact of the poor quality of electricity is felt across the board by SME producers and service providers alike. Providers of tempering, nickel plating, and other services also depend heavily on consistent supply of electricity. Tempering, for example, involves maintaining specific high temperatures constant during the

Table 2.16 Survey of SME Parts Manufacturers, Bongshal, Dhaka: Price Ranges

	Origin (price range in Tk/unit)		
Part name	*Bangladesh*	*China*	*India*
Frame	580; 700; 800; 1,050	1,800	n.a.
Frog	160; 350 (Meghna)	250	220
Rim	500	n.a.	n.a.
Tire	150;180; 250; 350	400	n.a.
Mudguard set	180; 350 (Meghna)	200	n.a.
Stand	140; 180; 250 (Meghna)	220; 230	200
Spokes set	190; 250	n.a.	n.a.
Free wheel	60	80	60; 70
Tubes	100; 120; 160	100	n.a.
Seat nut	4	6	10
Cake light	4; 10	10	n.a.
Chain	100	90	110
Handle	n.a.	350; 390	320
Chain cover	n.a.	80	60
Break	n.a.	130; 135	n.a.
Hub set	n.a.	135; 160	140
Seat	n.a.	145; 150	130; 180
Pedals	n.a.	90; 100	110
Bell	n.a.	80; 90	50; 60
Chain key	n.a.	10	n.a.
Lock	n.a.	120	80
Ball	n.a.	25; 30	n.a.
Ball bearing set	n.a.	100	80

Source: Global Development Solutions, LLC.
Note: n.a. = not applicable.

heat treatment process. During nickel plating, chemical mixtures have a narrow timeframe of utility in the production process; any work stoppage caused by sudden electricity brownouts renders premixed chemicals useless and causes financial losses.

SME competitiveness is critically weakened by the poor availability and reliability of tools and dies and service suppliers. In the case of the bicycle steering column producer, impact extrusion and lathing processes require various tools and dies as well as services. While tools like high-grade steel punches (used for pushing slugs though dies) are not produced locally, SMEs cannot afford to import them; they use scrap iron rods from ship breaking yards instead. They then send the rods to tempering and leveling shops in Dhaka. On paper, impact extrusion and lathing tools and services cost the firm US$570 per month, but as table 2.17 illustrates, the real cost is much higher because tools break or bend frequently, thus contributing to high amounts of production waste. In combination with other bottlenecks, the poor quality of tools and related services leads to extremely high waste levels of 8.3 percent. Although the firm recovers some production costs by selling rejected steering columns as scrap, the damage from poor tools is significant (see table 2.17).

Old machinery contributes to production inefficiencies and losses among SMEs, in large part owing to lack of access to finance. The value chain of the steering column producer suggests that the SME has three pipe-cutting machines, two lathing machines, and four impact extrusion machines, all of which are at least 25 years old and some of which are 40 years old. The owner would like to replace some of the machines, but was not able to obtain a loan from a local bank three years ago. In fact, none of the SMEs interviewed had received any loans from local banks. The few producers that had purchased relatively new machinery (see table 2.18 for more details) recently did so with own funds.

Table 2.17 Cost of Waste, Steering Tube Manufacturing, SMEs in Dhaka, 2012

	US$ per month of marketable production	
Cost	*With rejects/current*	*Without rejects*
Production cost	(6,504)	(6,504)
Sales	7,333	8,000
Gross profit/margin	829	1,496
	11%	19%
Sale of rejects as scrap	98	0
Agent commission	(261.90)	(285.71)
Net profit/margin	665.81	1,210.45
	9%	15%

Source: Global Development Solutions, LLC.

Table 2.18 Survey of SME Parts Manufacturers, Bongshal, Dhaka: Machinery and Workforce, 2012

Bicycle part(s) manufactured by SME	*Reported age of machinery (years)*	*Education level of workforce*	*Workforce experience level (monthly wages)*
Steering column	25–40	90% without any education	50% with > 5 years of experience (US$72) 50% with 2–5 years of experience (US$58)
Frame and lugs	25+	"Most are primary school dropouts."	20% with > 5 years of experience (US$72) 80% with < 5 years of experience (US$48)
Frame	n.a.	"Most have no education."	20% with > 5 years of experience (US$78) 80% with 2 years or less experience (US$45)
Parking stand	7–14	"Most have no education."	40% with > 5 years of experience (US$108) 60% with 2 years or less experience (US$53)
Fork	15–20	"Most have no education."	40% with > 4 years of experience (US$67) 60% with < 4 years of experience (US$48)
Mudguard	5–12	"Most have no education."	30% with > 5 years of experience (US$58) 70% with 2 years or less experience (US$40)

Source: Global Development Solutions, LLC.
Note: n.a. = not applicable.

Technological upgrades of SMEs are highly dependent on access to finance that is currently not forthcoming.

The level of education of the workforce is very poor. Most of the workers producing parts and components in the interviewed SMEs typically are young and have little to no education (table 2.19). Typically, SMEs have at least one experienced technician, equally uneducated, to pass on process and other knowledge to less experienced workers; "learning by doing" is the mode of operation in all SMEs. Some SME business owners see the uneducated workforce to be an advantage, since it is not complicated to make the product and allows for lower wages. Most owners, however, recognize that any future technological and process upgrade in their operations is extremely difficult to accomplish with the current level of know-how and education of its workforce. The case study in box 2.3 illustrates in more detail the typical working environment and profile of employees in the parts and components cottage industry of Bangladesh.

Table 2.19 Profiles of Three Typical Workers in Parts and Components SMEs, Bongshal Market, Dhaka

Worker characteristic	*Bilal*	*Jashin*	*Mamun*
Age	"28 or 30, I am not sure."	"19 or 20, I am not sure."	"I don't know my age, probably 24."
Job duties	Welding and assembly	Assembly	Welding
Education	Primary school dropout	None	None
Originally from	Narayangang	Shariatpur	Meghna
Years of experience	12 (third job)	2.5 (first job)	5 (second job)
Weekly wage, Tk (US$)	1,500 (US$18)	850 (US$10)	1,100 (US$13)
Daily food allowance, Tk (US$)	20 (US$0.25)	20 (US$0.25)	20 (US$0.25)
Working hours	8:30 am to 6:00 pm, with a 30 minute lunch break		
Working days	Six days a week		

Source: Global Development Solutions, LLC.

Box 2.3 SME Frame Assembler

"My father started this business 30 years ago. He passed on the business to me eight years ago. We assemble frames and produce frame lugs for the local market. The way the business is going, I may have to close the lugs business as Indian lugs come here at half the price. We are lucky to own our workshop as rent is very high. Otherwise the business environment would be tougher."

This small firm in Bongshal market employs eight people. The typical profile of its employees does not differ from other firms: they are young and uneducated men from villages and peri-urban settlements near Dhaka. Table 2.19 illustrates in more detail the profile of typical employees working in Bongshal market.

Key Market Drivers and Options for Growth

Currently, Bangladesh's bicycle industry relies heavily on EU policies to support the export market, most notably through EU antidumping penalties on Chinese bicycle imports. However, these penalties are due to expire in 2016. When this happens, Bangladeshi OEMs will be hard-pressed to compete with Chinese manufacturers, given their advantages in cost, delivery lead time, and other factors. Therefore, Bangladesh must look to expand its market beyond the European Union while working to remove impediments to sector efficiency and productivity.

Global Macroeconomic Trends

The world's population is estimated to have surpassed seven billion in 2011 and is expected to reach 9.3 billion by 2050, with nearly all the growth taking place in low- and middle-income countries, predominately among the poorest populations in urban areas.[25] As the bicycle is the most efficient method of transport, it is the most easily affordable one in lower-income countries. Thus, population growth in low- and middle-income nations can fuel global bicycle consumption.

As noted in the section on imports, annual world imports of bicycles in 2011 exceeded US$7.4 billion, and price points for bicycles are wide-ranging, with the average value for an imported bicycle worldwide at US$118.91 (cost, insurance, and freight). Within the top 10 importers, the United States imports bicycles at an average unit value of US$89.9 versus US$482.7 for Switzerland. The United States and Japan are the top two importers by value and both have an average unit price below US$100. In developing markets, the unit price is even lower. For example, the charitable organization Women for Women International provides US$72 bicycles to women-led households in Rwanda and the Sudan to facilitate organic farming and economic development.[26] According to Women for Women International, "the women we serve often use bicycles as their means of transportation from the farm to the market and back. A bicycle helps a woman quickly transport more goods to market."[27]

The value chain analysis suggests that a hybrid bicycle manufactured in Bangladesh costs US$75–US$90 to produce, placing Bangladesh within the lower end of the price range. However, to diversify its market to include the United States and Japan, Bangladesh will need to reduce production costs further, as it currently is uncompetitive relative to other countries, most notably relative to China.

Urban Planning Trends

Although demand for bicycles is fueled in developing markets by a desire for affordable transportation as household income improves, in high-income markets demand increasingly is driven by trends toward environmentally friendly transportation and green growth. Concerned about traffic congestion, noise, air pollution (such as diesel particulates), and the environment (including carbon dioxide emissions), urban planning increasingly is looking to bicycles as a solution. Throughout the world, countries and cities have made strides in implementing and expanding on- and off-street bicycle networks, improving cycling safety, enhancing bicycle access on bridges and mass transit, and institutionalizing cycling in public and private organizations. Some of these initiatives are detailed in table 2.20.

In addition to being one of the most environmentally efficient modes of transportation, the bicycle is economically efficient. According to estimates by Transportation Alternatives, bicycle riding costs the frequent cyclist only one-quarter as much as driving, assuming cyclists must replace their bicycles every three years because of bicycle theft and bad pavements. Transportation Alternatives estimates that the annual savings would average $1,100 per motorist.[28] A survey by the U.K. Department of Transportation noted that a typical journey within Central London took on average 38 minutes by bus, 33 minutes by car, 31 minutes

Table 2.20 Selected Bicycle Promotion Initiatives around the World

Country	*Initiative*
Australia	Planned to double bicycle use by developing a network of trails, end-of-trip facilities, and improved bicycle safety.
Chile	In Santiago, a 30–40 km bike path pilot project funded by the Global Environment Facility could grow to 1,000 km over 10 years.
Colombia	In Bogotá, 300 km of bicycle paths have been completed, cars are banned from 120 km of city streets on Sundays and holidays, and a referendum was passed to prohibit car circulation during rush hours by 2015.
France	The French Environment Ministry, together with the Transportation Ministry, created a national bicycle plan in 1994, granting nearly US$2 million for 10 bicycle promotion projects based on the Dutch model.
Germany	More than 31,000 km of paths and lanes are exclusively for bicycles.
Japan	In Tokyo, anti-car policies promote alternative transportation: fuel taxes are double those of the United States and account for almost half the price of gas and automobile tax levies, and vehicle inspection fees amount to an average of almost US$2,000 annually. In Nagoya, employer contributions for commuting by bicycle doubled in 2000, while allowances for automobile commuters were halved.
Netherlands	The first country to establish an official national bicycle policy; currently almost 19,000 km of paths and lanes are exclusively for bicycles.
Peru	In Lima, low-interest loans available to low-income families for the purchase of a bicycle are helping the city to meet its goal of increasing the percentage of trips by bicycle from 2 to 10 percent. Over 60 km of bike paths have been built along major traffic corridors.
United States	From 2008 to 2012, the Federal-Aid Highway Program committed to funding 12,845 bicycle and pedestrian projects totaling US$4.4 billion. In New York City, commuter cycling more than doubled from 2007 to 2011. The Bicycle Network Development (BND) program funds an annual "NYC Bike Month" and the BND Bicycle Master Plan has identified and planned for a 900-mile (1,148 km) bicycle network of on-street bicycle lanes and off-street paths. In Los Angeles, nearly 55 miles (88 km) of bike lanes have been installed since 2005. In 2012, NBC Universal committed US$3 million to fund bike path improvements in the 391-acre NBC Universal Studios park.In San Francisco, there are 215 miles (326 km) of bicycle paths, routes, and lanes.Chicago plans to create 100 miles (160.9 km) of separated bike lanes by 2015.

Sources: International Bicycle Fund; U.S. Department of Transportation (Federal Highway Administration); New York City Department of City Planning; New York City Department of Transportation; Los Angeles Department of Transportation; San Francisco Municipal Transportation Agency; *San Francisco Bay Guardian.*
Note: km = kilometers.

by rail, 20 minutes by taxi, and only 18 minutes by bicycle, thus emphasizing the role of bicycles in reducing congestion and enhancing economic productivity.[29] In addition, the bicycle is space saving, an important feature in densely populated urban areas. It has been estimated that one single-occupant car requires 75 times the amount of urban space as a pedestrian, 20 times that of a cyclist, and 13–40 times that of rail transit per unit of personal movement achieved.[30]

The Local/Regional Market

With the looming expiration of EU policies that favor Bangladeshi bicycles over Chinese ones, Bangladesh should consider other markets, domestic and international. Areas of high population and high population density are ideal target markets for bicycle transportation given space, economic, and environmental concerns. As shown in figure 2.6, among the urban areas with population more than 2.0 million, Bangladesh has an extremely high population density, with Dhaka taking first place as the most densely populated urban area in the world (44,400 people per square kilometer) and Chittagong in fifth place with 26,800 people per square kilometer. Moreover, Dhaka ranks as the 16th largest urban area in the world by population, with 15.4 million, and its population density is estimated to be up to one million per square kilometer in slums and informal dwelling areas.[31] Nine of the 10 densest urban areas with more than two million in population are in Asia, with the majority in Bangladesh, India, and Pakistan. These are target markets, provided Bangladesh develops the capability to produce simple, durable bicycles in sufficient scale to be cost-effective.

Figure 2.6 Top 10 Most Dense Urban Areas Worldwide, 2012

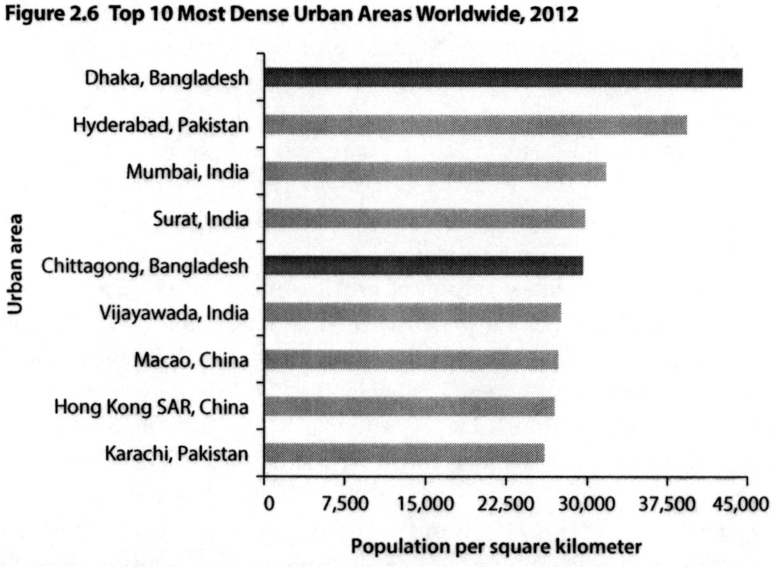

Source: Demographia World Urban Areas, 9th Annual Edition, Demographia, March 2013 (http://www.demographia.com/db-worldua.pdf); compiled by Global Development Solutions, LLC.
Note: The top 10 densest urban areas have population over 500,000.

Bicycles as a Means of Poverty Reduction

Just as innovations like clean cookstoves balance household and environmental needs, bicycles can contribute to household economic development and green growth. Recent studies have noted that bicycles can contribute significantly to poverty reduction in rural areas by helping households save money and time while expanding their economic reach. Compared with walking, bicycles improve access to education, health care, and economic opportunity by increasing carrying capacity and accessible travel distance while decreasing the time it takes to commute to and from schools, clinics, and markets. For every 10 miles traveled, a bicycle saves three hours of time versus travel by foot. Riding a bicycle increases an individual's carrying capacity by five times. And, over equal units of time, an individual can ride a bicycle four times the distance as someone walking.[32] Time saved can be used to expand agricultural production or diversify into nonagricultural income-generating activities.

A field study by World Bicycle Relief (United States), which distributed 24,000 free bicycles in Sri Lanka following the tsunami, surveyed 221 bicycle owners for the impact made and the contribution to livelihood security.[33] Among survey findings, savings from bicycle use over other transportation alternatives contributed 10–30 percent (18 percent on average) of a household's annual income. Bicycle distribution effectively mobilized and empowered women, with 82 percent of women recipients reporting that they use the bicycle for income-generating activities. Daily income was enhanced 17 percent (US$0.52 per day) if the time saved from bicycle use was spent on productive endeavors.

A study by the International Forum for Rural Transport and Development (United Kingdom) of 248 households in eight villages in Makete District, Tanzania, examined the benefits of nonmotorized transport interventions in rural areas and found that households can benefit greatly in time savings when bicycles are introduced (Sieber 1998). In rural areas in low-income countries, foot transport to procure water and energy requires more than 1,000 hours annually. Further, the largest share of the transport burden is carried by women, thus limiting the productivity and economic contributions of half the population. The physical and time requirement for foot transport drains the household's labor resources and significantly hampers the growth of labor-intensive agricultural production. The study noted significant time savings in households that use bicycles, with an average savings of 200 hours per household per year when a bicycle is used to reduce the transport burden. Monetary benefits also were noted, as bicycle use enabled farmers to cultivate bigger fields, use more fertilizers, and sell on average 40 percent more in quantity of agricultural products. Bicycles reduced isolation, enabling trips outside the village and improving access to public facilities and markets. The main restriction noted on the purchase of nonmotorized transit was the relatively high procurement cost, which amounted to 80–90 percent of annual income. At the same time, the average monetary benefit from a bicycle was US$45 per household per year, meaning that the bicycle essentially could pay for itself within two years if financing were available.

A study by the Institute for Transportation and Development Policy examined the cost-benefit of rural household bicycle ownership.[34] Three hundred poor households from different regions of Uganda were given subsidized bicycles and a one-time guidance on how to apply the time saved from bicycle use. The study found that all bicycle households either enlarged the area of land used for agricultural purposes or intensified the level of cultivation. Roughly half the households began or intensified nonagricultural activities during the survey period, thus diversifying the composition of household income. Transport time saved was almost two hours per day per household. Households made substantially more frequent visits to markets and medical facilities and realized 35 percent higher income.

Bicycles already are beginning to make an impact in rural Bangladesh via the Info Ladies Project. Created in 2008 by local development group D.Net, the program recruits and trains women for three months in how to use computers, the Internet, printers, and cameras; arranges bank loans for the women to buy bicycles and equipment; and sends the women into remote Bangladeshi villages to provide Internet connections, laptop access, and social services (Hossain 2012). Apart from technology access, the Info Ladies lead community discussions about a range of relevant issues, including best agrarian practices and public health matters such as contraception and HIV/AIDS prevention. They perform a vital service in a country where only five million people have Internet access. In 2012, nearly 60 Info Ladies were working in 19 of Bangladesh's 64 districts. The program hopes to train 15,000 women by 2016, which means there is an immediate local market for affordable, rurally compatible bicycles.

As agriculture comprises 18.3 percent of gross domestic product and 45 percent of employment in Bangladesh,[35] bicycles could be an important contribution to the productivity of the agriculture and manufacturing sectors and help bring poverty in Bangladesh below the current level of 31.5 percent of the population below the national poverty line.[36] Two of the primary challenges in increasing bicycle density per capita in rural areas are the affordability and the quality of bicycles. Often the bicycle is a significant investment for poorer households and they cannot envision the immediate return on investment versus something like a buffalo. In addition, the bicycle must be compatible with the intended use in rural areas, which necessitates carrying heavier loads over uneven and challenging terrain. Bicycles manufactured for rural markets should be appropriately rugged and engineered for the terrain and load requirements. A rural program also would need to establish maintenance infrastructure by training local field mechanics, stocking spare parts and tools, and providing means to ownership or access, such as bike share, work-to-own, or microfinance programs.

Improving Competitiveness: Policy Options

The bicycle export story is different from other sectors, in that there is a high degree of dependency of bicycle exports on antidumping duties levied on Chinese bicycles in the European Union. Without such duties, exports could decline sharply. How can Bangladesh reduce the costs of its bicycles to become more competitive in a more contested market setting? How can it diversify its markets and break into markets like the United States and Japan and regional urban clusters in South Asia?

Fortunately, most of the answers to these questions involve support at a broader policy level, rather than support that is specific to bicycles.

In modern bicycle production, scale economies and precision engineering are clearly important and this has allowed China and even higher-wage countries to remain competitive in different segments of the bicycle market. In Bangladesh, modern export firms have vertically integrated to partially overcome the lack of a modern parts supply industry, but rely on imports for the bulk of their needs for parts. This approach has meant that their export prices are 10–20 percent higher than China's export prices.

A modern parts and components industry that progressively produces more and more in-country would help the overall competitiveness of bicycle exports. For this, the parts industry will need to invest in modern tools and equipment, such as semi-automated and, where necessary, automated precision equipment. This kind of programmable equipment will allow different kinds of parts to be produced on the same assembly line with low downtimes and high precision. Additional scale economies can be reaped by focusing on standardized parts that are common to different types and makes of bicycles.

Better access to finance will help those producers whose desire to invest in equipment has been hampered by financial access. One way is for the large OEMs to support such investment by guaranteeing bank borrowings of the suppliers on the basis of their (OEM) orders. This can be complemented by improved financial access for the SME sector as a whole.

Bicycle production for the domestic market is highly protected, as seen in high nominal and very high effective rates of protection. This helps to perpetuate keeping the domestic and export markets separate. Reducing output tariffs and thereby domestic effective rates of protection, and increasing competition in the domestic market could help provide consumers with a choice of high-quality bicycles and in time potentially narrow the gap between the two markets. As in other industrial sectors, a growing domestic base of export quality products could help existing and potential manufacturers to export. Of course, lower domestic effective rates of protection also help reduce the anti-export bias.

Bangladesh could court foreign direct investment and seek to become part of international and regional supply chains in bicycles and parts. Development and exports of particular components would help achieve scale economies and create positive externalities for the sector as a whole. Large firms in India and China could potentially invest in Bangladesh or be encouraged to make its firms part of their supply chain.

The issue of skill inadequacy is a recurring theme in the sector studies done for this Diagnostic Trade Integration Study. This is a key reason for low productivity in Bangladeshi plants. These issues have been raised elsewhere in the study and in recent World Bank reports on education and skills and exports.

Last, but by no means least, is the constraint imposed by long lead times. Long lead times make products more expensive and less competitive. To the extent that lead times are reduced, the handicap imposed by lack of local input industries is reduced, but imported inputs can never provide the flexibility and range of options to the exporting sector that a strong local parts industry can. The set of trade facilitation issues is been addressed in Kathuria and Malouche (2016, chapter 6).

Notes

1. Country quantities are as of 1992, 1995, and 1996, respectively. Estimates are compiled from a variety of sources and no single source provided data for all countries for a single year.
2. Bicycles are classified under HS8712 or HS871200, while the parts used for production or repair may be listed in several other HS categories (HS401150, HS401320, HS851210, HS871495, and HS871499).
3. Bangladesh has not reported statistics to UN Comtrade after 2007. Later trade data may be inferred through Comtrade via mirror data from corresponding trade partners, but there are wide discrepancies between these data and data from the Export Promotion Bureau. More current export data by volume are available directly from the Bangladesh Export Promotion Bureau.
4. Regulation Number 2474/1993 was initially extended by regulation number 71/97 and subsequently maintained and gradually increased. The current antidumping duty is 48.5 percent, up to October 2016.
5. Since the industry effectively is composed of only three competing firms, precise data such as installed capacity, current capacity utilization, sales figures, and other indicators typically are confidential and were shared on an estimation basis.
6. Zero-rated General System of Preferences duties for Bangladesh, Most Favored Nation duties of 14 percent, and an additional 48.5 percent antidumping duty for Chinese exporters until 2016.
7. The only exception is Meghna's supply of some components to the local market (mostly steel frame tubes, frame joints, wheels and spokes, and tires and inner tubes).
8. In January 2011, EU rules of origin were relaxed significantly. First, an exporter from a least-developed country, including Bangladesh, could import up to 70 percent of the ex-works price of a bicycle in components from the European Union. Second, regional cumulation allowed component sourcing between different groups of countries, including between East Asia (Brunei, Cambodia, Indonesia, the Lao People's Democratic Republic, Malaysia, the Philippines, Singapore, Thailand, and Vietnam) and South Asia (Bangladesh, Bhutan, India, the Maldives, Nepal, Pakistan, and Sri Lanka).

9. Most mother vessels do not call at Chittagong Port because of poor navigability. As a result, transshipment through major regional ports increases transit times.
10. Light engineering products other than bicycles, however, will continue to be eligible to receive cash incentives.
11. Categorization of bicycles varies significantly depending on various markets, distribution channels, and consumer and other classifications or nomenclature. Bicycle characteristics often cut across some categories, because for many bicycle manufacturers the differences in type or nomenclature may have more to do with marketing focus than with differences in specifications and design.
12. Parts and components are grouped into functional sets. The total list of each separate part and component is much longer.
13. Data on production cost versus import prices of specific parts and components are closely guarded information by OEMs.
14. Typically, clients of OEMs are original brand manufacturers (OBMs) or original design manufacturers (ODMs). OEMs may have exclusive arrangements with clients whereby OBMs or ODMs supply them with parts and components from their designated plants or tiered suppliers. This is the case with all OEMs in Bangladesh, albeit to different degrees.
15. Meghna is an exception, with a higher local content (up to 45 percent in total for exportable bicycles).
16. Wages in Dhaka are reported to be at least 20 percent higher than in Chittagong.
17. Bicycle industry wages in China's key bicycle manufacturing province, Guangdong, are US$520–US$550 per month (Global Development Solutions, LLC, from industry sources).
18. Global Development Solutions, LLC, from industry sources.
19. For example, interviews with OEMs suggest that "speed money" is prevalent as a means to expedite customs procedures. Reported aggregate amounts of unofficial payments, at different stages of interaction with customs officials, range from 0.30 percent to 0.75 percent of the value of a finished product (bicycle).
20. The Explosives Act dates from 1884. The Gas Cylinder Rules amendments to the Act were first introduced in 1991 and were amended in 2003. The Explosives Department refers to Rule 43(1) of the Gas Cylinder Rules of 1991 as the legal basis for its Form B (prior permission).
21. Official Journal of the European Union (9.3.2012, C71/11), available at: http://eur-lex.europa.eu/LexUriServ/LexUriServ.do?uri=OJ:C:2012:071:0010:0022:EN:PDF.
22. Interviews with several bicycle assemblers, parts and components manufacturers, and traders were undertaken in the Bonghsal market in Dhaka, the hub of the cottage bicycle industry of Bangladesh.
23. Reported production waste levels (8.3 percent) include raw material costs (aluminum pipes) and factor in added costs associated with subsequent production stages (impact extrusion and machining) where losses or waste occur.
24. Electricity prices below US$0.10 per kilowatt-hour are generally considered competitive at the international level.
25. United Nations Population Fund.
26. The implied value of the US$72 bicycle is based on a Women for Women International solicited donation of US$100 and a charity program expense ratio of 72.2 percent, according to Charity Navigator.

27. http://pinterest.com/source/give.womenforwomen.org/.
28. New York City Department of City Planning, http://www.transalt.org/files/resources/blueprint/chapter1/chapter1g.html.
29. UKDOT Journey Times Survey 1996, published by the Stationery Office and featured in DOT Press Release 106 of 28.5.96, as reported by International Bicycle Fund.
30. Professor John Whitelegg (1993), as quoted by International Bicycle Fund, http://www.ibike.org/library/statistics-data.htm).
31. Demographia World Urban Areas, 8th Annual Edition: Version 2, Demographia, July 2012 (http://www.demographia.com/).
32. World Bicycle Relief (http://www.worldbicyclerelief.org/).
33. World Bicycle Relief (http://www.worldbicyclerelief.org/).
34. BicyclePotential.org. (http://www.bicyclepotential.org/search?q=Institute+for+Transportation+and+Development+Policy).
35. CIA World Factbook.
36. Estimate from World Bank (2010).

References

BIKEEurope. 2012. "Bangladesh 2011: Meghna Marches On." *BIKEEurope*, March 28. http://www.bike-eu.com/Sales-Trends/Market-Report/2012/3/bBangladesh-2011b-Meghna-Marches-On-BIK005683W/.

Gardner, Gary. 2009. "Bicycle Production Reaches 30 Million Units." In *Vital Signs 2009*. Washington, DC: Worldwatch Institute.

Hossain, Farid. 2012. "Internet Rolls into Bangladesh Villages on a Bike." Associated Press, November 1. http://bigstory.ap.org/article/internet-rolls-bangladesh-villages-bike.

Kathuria, Sanjay, and Mariem Mezghenni Malouche. 2015. *Toward New Sources of Competitiveness in Bangladesh*. Washington, DC: World Bank.

———, eds. 2016. *Strategies to Strengthen Bangladeshi Competitiveness: Thematic Assessments*. Washington, DC: World Bank.

Maxwell Stamp Limited. 2010. *Study on the International Demand for Semi-skilled and Skilled Bangladeshi Workers*. Final Report for TVET Reform Project, Bangladesh.

Sieber, Niklas. 1998. "Appropriate Transport and Rural Development in Makete District, Tanzania." *Journal of Transport Geography* 6 (1): 69–73. http://www.niklas-sieber.de/Publications/TransGeo98.pdf.

Ward's Automotive Group. 2008. *World Motor Vehicle Data 2008*. Southfield, MI: Ward's Automotive Group.

World Bank. 2010. *World Development Indicators 2010*. Washington, DC: World Bank.

Worldwatch Institute. 2004. *Signposts 2002*. CD-ROM. Washington, DC: Worldwatch Institute.

CHAPTER 3

Light Manufacturing: Diversified Jute Products

Glenn Surabian and Yasuo Konishi

Introduction

This chapter assesses the performance of the diversified jute products value chain in Bangladesh against the backdrop of global competition. The objectives of the value chain analysis are: (a) to review the detailed breakdown of costs and productivity for jute products and identify the main reasons for the productivity and cost gaps; (b) to identify the most important and common constraints across the value chains; (c) to understand possible practical solutions to address a critical mass of the identified constraints; and (d) to benchmark the competitiveness (productivity and costs) of the selected products against competitors (China and India).

The chapter provides a basic description of the sector's value added, domestic market, imports and exports, and employment, followed by a detailed breakdown of the value added for each critical step along the value chain. There is an additional breakdown and analysis of each critical step along the value chain to show the underlying issues for each of these steps, in the breakdown between input, labor, capital, and other costs. The chapter also discusses quality drivers, such as the quality of key inputs and services at each step of the value chain, the quality of processing, and the quality of delivery and marketing (time to market).

Sector Profile: Production, Consumption, and Exports

Bangladesh is the second-largest producer of jute in the world, after India, and the leading exporter of jute and jute products (box 3.1).[1] Total world production of jute was estimated at 3.1 million metric tons in 2010.[2] More than 96 percent of world jute production is concentrated in India and Bangladesh, which produced 1,743,000 tons or 57.0 percent and 1,200,600 tons or 39.3 percent of world production, respectively, in 2010 (table 3.1).[3]

Box 3.1 Jute Sector Definition

Jute is natural fiber extracted from the jute plant, a principal agricultural product of Bangladesh. Nicknamed the "golden fiber" of Bangladesh (more for its money-generating ability than for its color), jute's inherent characteristics include tensile strength, low extensibility, long durability, heat resistance, silkiness, luster, and long staple length.[a] Many products can be produced from the jute plant and stalks, including fashion apparel, fabric, yarn, rope, industrial products, handicrafts, agricultural products, and others (figure 3.1).

In addition to jute's commercial uses, jute leaves are edible. According to wisegeek.com, "People who cook with jute leaves use them in soups, stews, curries, vegetable dishes, and sometimes tisanes or teas. The jute tends to get rather gluey and mucilaginous, like okra, another common vegetable thickener. It is also said to have its very own distinct flavor, which some people find quite enjoyable. Jute leaves are also a good source of nutrition, particularly beta carotene."[b] One hundred grams of jute leaves provide two grams of fiber, 104 percent of the U.S. Department of Agriculture daily recommended dose of vitamin A, 21 percent of calcium, and 17 percent of iron.

The current systems for tracking international trade do not lend themselves well to tracking the diversified jute goods market. For example, the Harmonized Commodity Description and Coding System (HS) classifications noted in annex 3A are potential categories for trade in jute products. However, none of these is easily matched with the nomenclature for finished goods. In addition, even at the six-digit level, the category includes jute and non-jute products, making it challenging to track the success of jute. For several of the categories, the International Jute Study Group has proposed a new code to capture jute sector trade data. The Jute Diversification Promotion Center (JDPC) of Bangladesh has also suggested alternative codes for diversified jute products (annex 3B). However, manufacturers and exporters do not always use these codes in classifying their own products. For example, it was observed that Bangladeshi shopping bags are exported under codes including, but not limited to, HS42022200: Handbags, including those without handle, with outer surface of plastic sheeting or of textile materials, HS56090090: Articles of yarn, strip or the like of heading 54.04 or 54.05, twine, cordage, rope or cables, n.e.s.; and HS63051000: Sacks and bags, used for packing goods. Absent from the JDPC list but included in diversified jute products is footwear from jute, such as espadrilles, and shoe components, such as jute soles. Analysis of whole jute footwear (complete shoes) is discussed in chapter 4 on non-leather footwear.

a. Bluebell Enterprise, www.jutebangladesh.com.
b. http://www.wisegeek.com/what-are-jute-leaves.htm.

During the same year, the jute area under harvest in Bangladesh was 466,800 hectares, compared with 790,000 hectares in India.[4] (Bangladesh is considered to produce higher-quality jute than India.)[5] Production capacity for all jute, raw and processed, is higher than demand, indicating an opportunity to add value and manufacture products in demand in domestic and international markets. Bangladesh is a bigger player than India in the export market. While Bangladesh exports over 60 percent of its jute products, India exports only

Table 3.1 Top 10 Producers of Raw Jute by Quantity, 2010

		Production volume	
Rank	*Country*	*Million MT*	*Share of total (%)*
1	India	1,743,000	57.0
2	Bangladesh	1,200,600	39.3
3	China	40,000	1.3
4	Uzbekistan	21,700	0.7
5	Nepal	20,965	0.7
6	Vietnam	12,447	0.4
7	Myanmar	3,800	0.1
8	Zimbabwe	3,700	0.1
9	Sudan (former)	3,200	0.1
10	Thailand	2,300	0.1
	Other	4,144	0.1
	Total	3,055,856	100.0

Source: FAOSTAT.
Note: MT = metric tons.

Figure 3.1 From Jute to Diversified Products

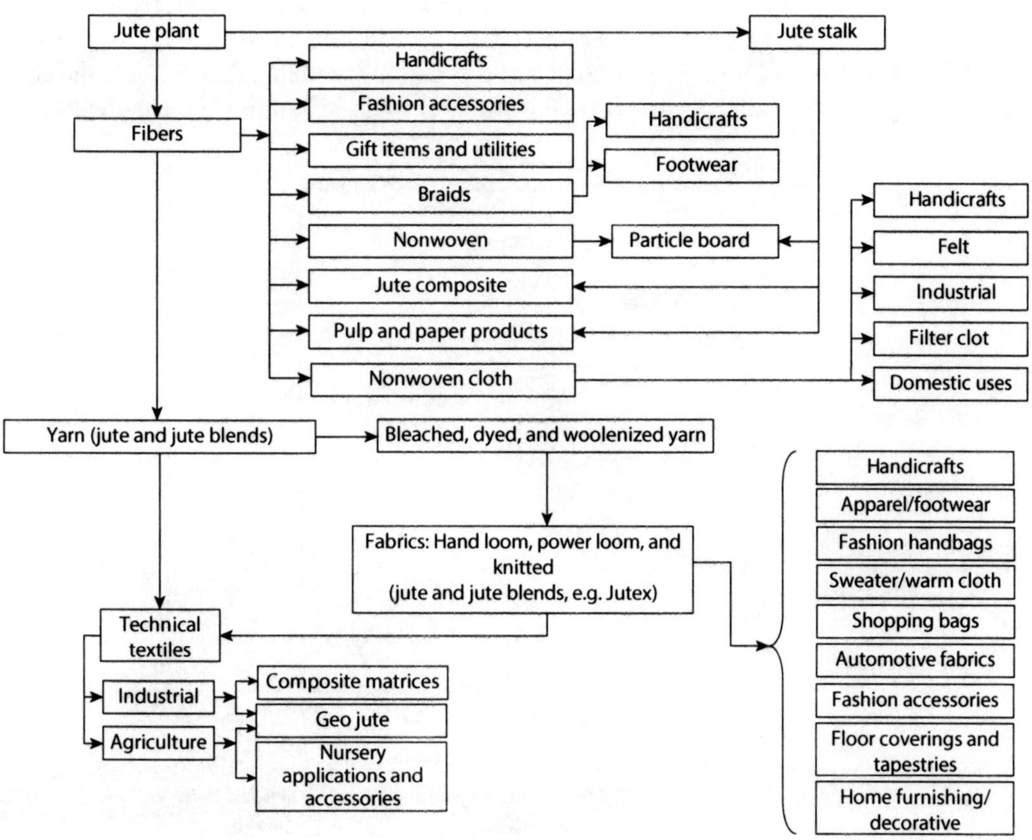

10–12 percent (Dash 2012). Jute and jute products constituted 39 percent of Bangladesh's agricultural exports[6] and in FY2014 they accounted for 2.7 percent of all exports.[7] Within the overall jute sector, low value-added and traditional products account for more than 99 percent of exports; thus, diversified jute products currently represent less than 1 percent of jute sector exports. The private sector accounted for 79.74 percent of total exports of jute goods during 2011/12. Combined earnings of the public and private sectors totaled Tk 50 billion (US$609.8 million) from the export of jute goods.

Bangladesh has the potential to broaden its scope within the jute sector and realize higher value added from its rich jute resources. Despite the small share of diversified jute products relative to the jute sector as a whole, there is a wide range of products within the subsector. Manufacturers and exporters of jute products often are involved in traditional and diversified products. For example, one firm that was interviewed exported hessian cloth, hessian bags and sacks, mesh soil savers, twine, yarn, carpet backing cloth, webbing, shopping bags, wine bottle bags, women's handbags, gift bags, children's bags, and food bags (for tea, coffee, flour, rice, and so forth), all made of jute. Looking at the jute goods product mix on a metric ton basis, Bangladesh's predominant categories are other goods, specifically yarn and twine (55.4 percent), followed by jute sacks (30.5 percent), whereas India's jute products consist primarily of jute sacks (64.9 percent) and hessian cloth (19.0 percent) (figure 3.2). For producing high volumes of yarn, Bangladesh is better positioned than India in the area of nontraditional jute goods. However, as India makes much of its diversified

Figure 3.2 Jute Goods Production, Bangladesh and India, 2007–10

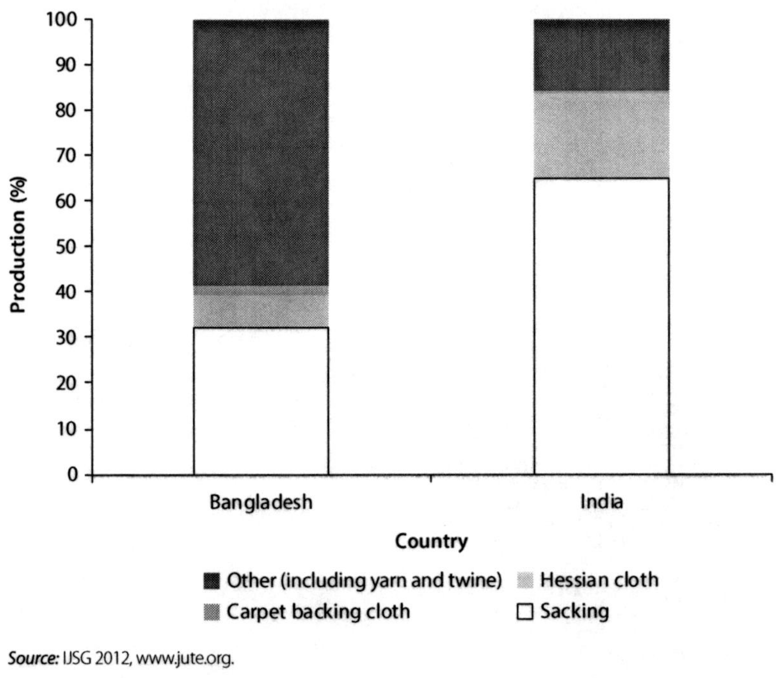

Source: IJSG 2012, www.jute.org.

jute goods output from Bangladeshi fibers and cloth, Bangladesh is not fully realizing its value-added potential in the subsector. Further, India has first-mover advantage in diversified jute fashion goods and is perceived globally as more fashion-oriented compared with Bangladesh.

Nearly all the sacks produced by India are consumed internally, largely because of India's 1987 mandatory jute packaging law.[8] Using its indigenous jute, Bangladesh produces approximately 0.5 million tons of gunnysacks each year versus 1.1–1.2 million tons in India. Nepal produces 15,000 tons of gunnysacks (Dash 2012). Indian packaging regulation contributes to an annual demand of 1.2 million tons of sacks (1 million tons for food grains and 0.2 million tons for sugar). According to the Indian Jute Mills Association, the Indian jute industry has the capacity to produce 1.5 million tons of sacks and sacking capacity is almost 0.55 million tons higher than peak government demand (Dash 2012). Thus India rejected recent proposals from Bangladesh and Nepal for India to import their sacks. India is introducing new labeling requirements for Bangladeshi jute sacks that will add to production time and cost. By contrast, Bangladesh's internal consumption is only 7 percent of that of India, as Bangladesh is a major exporter of raw jute and jute goods. A comparison of the top two jute-producing countries, Bangladesh and India (annex 3C), indicates that Bangladesh has 19 percent higher yield rates than India. Bangladesh is able to produce 66 percent of the amount of jute India produces on only 56 percent of the land as in India.

The spot market price for raw jute is set in Bangladesh. The price of raw jute has risen dramatically in the past 10 years, more than doubling (107 percent) between 2001 and 2011, from US$331.47 to US$687.78 per ton (figure 3.3). The majority of the price rise has occurred in 2006–11, when prices rose 79 percent, because of increased demand for jute as a substitute for other fibers as well as mandatory packaging laws that required (in the case of India, sacks)

Figure 3.3 Historical Spot Market Prices for Jute, 2001–11

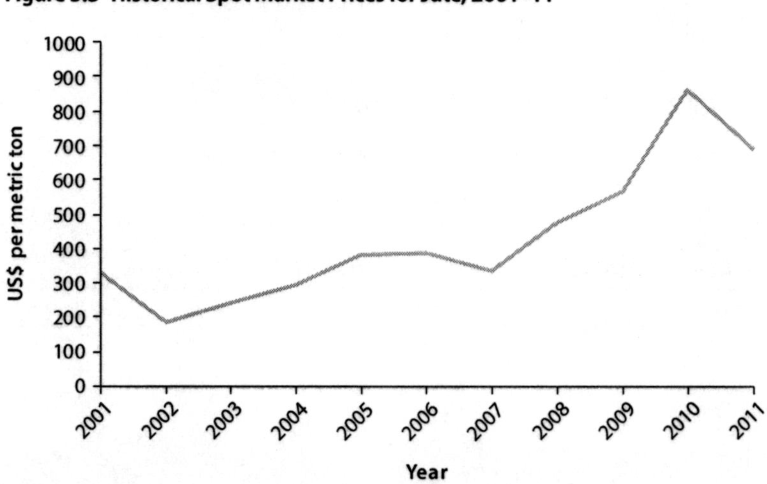

Source: Bangladesh Jute Mills Corporation–The Public Ledger, as quoted on FAOSTAT.
Note: Prices are annual averages, Jute-BWD (FOB Mongla, at sight, Friday closing price).

or encouraged (in the case of plastic shopping bag bans) use of jute. Rising prices in 2010 led to expanded jute cropping in 2011, which resulted in oversupply and depressed prices. However, the overall trend is still positive, given the many and expanding uses of jute in various products and applications. Among major jute-producing countries, while Bangladesh enjoyed the lowest producer prices in 2005, by 2009 that advantage had eroded and Bangladesh, China, and India had similar producer prices. Thailand now has a cost advantage and Nepal is expensive relative to other major jute producers (figure 3.4).

The top consumers of jute and related fibers are India, China, Turkey, Bangladesh, and Pakistan (table 3.2). Information on the current consumption of diversified jute products in detail is not available given the diversity of the sector. Estimates provided by the United Nations Common Fund for Commodities in 2006 noted that among all jute products, sacking, hessian cloth, and jute yarn represented the largest consumption of jute (table 3.3). Diversified jute products with the greatest projected growth potential as measured by increase in jute tons include decorative and household furnishings (+3,900 percent), webbing (+233 percent), market garden products (+233 percent), felt (+200 percent), jute carpets (+200 percent), and geotextiles (+100 percent).

Figure 3.4 Producer Price of Jute in Major Producing Countries, 2005–09

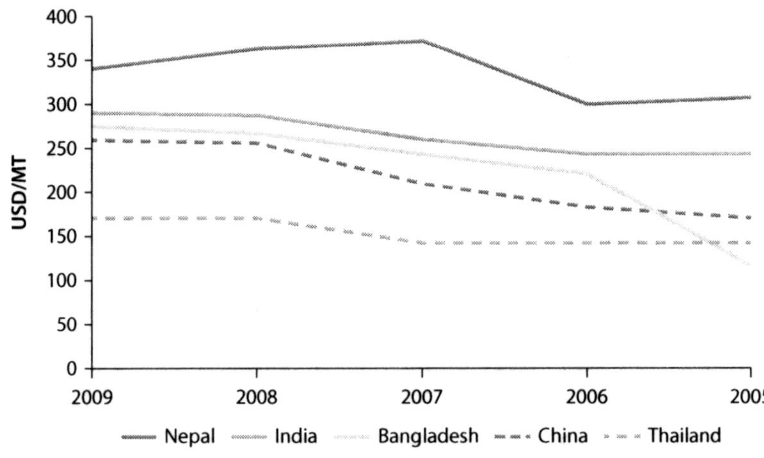

Source: IJSG 2012.

Table 3.2 Top Five Consumers of Jute, Kenaf, and Allied Fibers, 2010

Rank	*Country*	*Volume (MT, thousands)*
1	India	1,628
2	China	180
3	Turkey	166
4	Bangladesh	140
5	Pakistan	111

Source: International Jute Study Group.
Note: MT = metric tons.

Bangladesh's diversified jute products enjoy Generalized System of Preferences privileges in most major markets, given Bangladesh's status as a least-developed country. Import duties by country depend on the classification of the product and corresponding duty. Although duties are frequently based on the majority product component (for example, cotton versus leather), this is not always the case and jute itself does not have any inherent duty attached. Thus, across the diversified jute product spectrum, a range of duties applies.

Bangladesh would appear at the top of the exporters in 2011 if it was included in UN Comtrade after 2007 and assuming export trends continued. Bangladesh export data do not appear after 2007, when exports of raw or retted jute of 563,809 tons valued at US$190,166,866 were reported (table 3.4). According to 2011 UN Comtrade data, globally the top exporters by value of raw jute (HS530310: Jute and other textile bast fibers, raw or retted) were India, Tanzania,

Table 3.3 Global Consumption of Jute Goods, 2006 and Projected

Item	*Consumption in 2006 (MT/year)*	*Potential consumption, 5–10 years (MT/year)*
Sacking	1,400,000	1,400,000
Hessian cloth	483,000	473,000
Jute yarn	322,000	450,000
Twine	100,000	120,000
Canvas	50,000	48,000
Tarpaulin	38,000	40,000
Carpet backing cloth	25,000	60,000
Jute carpets	10,000	30,000
Geotextiles	10,000	20,000
Market garden products	3,000	10,000
Felt	2,000	6,000
Webbing	600	2,000
Decorative and household furnishings	500	20,000
Other textiles	10	30,000
Shopping bags	—	60,000
Plastic reinforcement	—	60,000

Source: International Jute Study Group; estimated by UN Common Fund for Commodities.
Note: MT = metric tons.

Table 3.4 Bangladesh Exports of Raw Jute, Jute Yarn, and Jute Fabric, 2007

HS Code	*Commodity*	*Trade (US$)*	*Quantity (MT)*
530310	Jute and other textile bast fibers, raw or retted	190,166,866	563,809
530390	Jute and other bast fibers, not spun, nes, tow, waste	6,625,736	17,656
530710	Yarn of jute or textile bast fibers nes, single	184,967,637	281,035
530720	Yarn of jute, textile bast fiber nes, multiple, cable	30,575,258	36,696
531010	Woven fabric of jute/bast fibers, unbleached/bleached	49,727,438	70,290
531090	Woven fabric of jute/bast fibers, not unbleached/bleached	10,918,677	14,334

Source: UN Comtrade.
Note: MT = metric tons; nes = not elsewhere specified.

and Belgium, while the top exporters by quantity were India, Pakistan, and Tanzania (table 3.5). The UN Comtrade 2011 list is conspicuously missing Bangladesh. In addition, from the data, it is apparent that countries such as Pakistan either are exporting very low-grade jute or have data errors, while countries such as Tanzania either are exporting high-value jute or have data errors.

According to the Bangladesh Jute Association, Bangladesh's exports of raw jute totaled 411,281 tons valued at Tk 1.541 billion (US$198.4 million) in 2011/12 (table 3.6). Over the past 10 years, average annual exports were 389,457 tons valued at US$152,662 per year or US$407 per ton. While quantity exported fluctuates annually, on a U.S. dollar value basis, exports increased 151 percent from 2003/04 to 2011/12, reflecting to a large extent price

Table 3.5 Top Exporters of Raw Jute by Value and Quantity, 2011

		Export value		*Export quantity*	
Rank	*Country or area*	*US$*	*% Total*	*MT*	*% Total*
1	Bangladesh	297,990,000	91.1		
2	India	16,087,622	4.9	25,292	53.6
3	Tanzania	10,571,072	3.2	8,057	17.1
4	Belgium	689,208	0.21	1,703	3.6
5	United States	666,073	0.20	416	0.9
6	EU-27	335,560	0.10	296	0.6
7	Germany	262,432	0.08	296	0.6
8	France	243,478	0.07	517	1.1
10	Italy	201,600	0.06	55	0.1
11	Pakistan	115,690	0.04	9,880	20.9
12	Ethiopia	102,247	0.03	30	0.1

Source: UN Comtrade.
Note: UN Comtrade does not report data for Bangladesh after 2007. Bangladeshi data are from the Export Promotion Bureau. MT = metric tons.

Table 3.6 Bangladesh's Raw Jute Exports, 2002/03–2011/12

Fiscal year	*Quantity (bales)*	*Quantity (MT)*	*Value (Tk, thousands)*	*Value (US$, thousands)*
2003	2,518,831	453,435	517,660	n.a.
2004	1,905,917	342,970	454,910	78,911
2005	1,703,812	306,717	563,100	93,257
2006	2,447,077	440,518	977,270	144,860
2007	2,442,945	439,774	914,150	131,294
2008	2,870,985	516,829	1,033,400	151,510
2009	1,749,514	314,944	921,000	134,649
2010	1,598,912	287,833	1,130,840	165,327
2011	2,112,400	380,270	1,906,760	275,768
2012	2,284,666	411,281	1,540,660	198,384
Total	21,635,060	3,894,571	9,959,750	1,373,960

Source: Bangladesh Jute Association.
Note: Conversion factor for tons to bales: 5.555. MT = metric tons. n.a. = not applicable.

increases over the period. Bangladesh exports raw jute, which leaves importing countries to add value to the raw jute and produce traditional and diversified jute products. The largest segment by volume and value was traditional jute products, followed by raw jute. Diversified jute products represent less than 1 percent of jute exports on a volume and value basis. In addition, when looking at the value per unit, traditional jute products were valued at a rate 7 percent higher than that of diversified jute products (US$0.00123 per ton versus US$0.00115 per ton, respectively). This indicates that the diversified jute goods sector has not yet realized its value potential, which should be higher than that of traditional goods since there are more value-added processes involved in diversified jute product manufacturing.[9]

Export values for 2011/12 were down because of unstable markets in the Middle East and UN trade sanctions against the Islamic Republic of Iran.[10] The Middle East has experienced business and economic interruption because of ongoing political unrest and Iranian international banking activities have been curtailed by UN trade sanctions, causing nonpayment and cancellation of orders by Iranian importers (who prefer jute carpet backing cloth for Persian rugs, among other uses of jute). The Bangladesh Jute Exporters Association estimated a loss in millions of U.S. dollars caused by the Iran sanctions and noted that, although Bangladesh is looking for new markets, India's jute sector was less affected by the sanctions, since it creatively bartered jute and food for oil (*Al Jazeera English* 2012). Bangladeshi exports of raw jute to the Islamic Republic of Iran were US$6.05 million in 2010/11, but only US$4.52 million in 2011/12.

The top export markets for Bangladesh's raw jute were India, China, and Pakistan in 2011/12, purchasing 71 percent of all raw jute exports by value (table 3.7).[11] Bangladeshi jute products reach around the globe, except for South America and with limited presence in Africa. Export destinations for Bangladesh's jute products vary by product (table 3.8). For diversified jute products, the top export markets include the United States, the United Kingdom, and

Table 3.7 Top 10 Export Markets for Bangladeshi Raw Jute, 2010/11–2011/12

		Export value	
Rank	*Country*	*US$*	*Total (%)*
1	India	63,421,893	25.2
2	China	61,039,216	24.2
3	Pakistan	54,407,851	21.6
4	Nepal	13,914,934	5.5
5	Côte d'Ivoire	9,146,176	3.6
6	Sudan	8,389,648	3.3
7	Vietnam	4,737,604	1.9
8	Thailand	4,734,306	1.9
9	Iran, Islamic Rep.	4,515,515	1.8
10	Russian Federation	4,150,637	1.6

Source: Export Promotion Bureau, Bangladesh.

Table 3.8 Primary Export Destinations of Bangladeshi Jute Products

Category	*Product(s)*	*Destination*
Traditional jute products	Hessian	Europe; Iran, Islamic Rep.; United States
	Sacking	India, Sudan, Thailand
	Carpet backing cloth	Europe, Japan, United States
	Yarn/twine	Belgium; Egypt, Arab Rep.; India; Russian Federation; Syria; Turkey; United Kingdom; United States
	Other traditional jute goods	Turkey, Middle East, India
Diversified jute products	Braided rugs, carpet, mats, table mats, table runners, cushion covers, curtains	Denmark, Germany, Greece, Hungary, Italy, Japan, Netherlands, Norway, Russian Federation, Saudi Arabia, Sweden, Switzerland, United Kingdom, United States
	Jute toys, show pieces, handicraft items, carry bags, shopping bags, handbags, wine/bottle bags, ladies' bags, school bags, laundry bags	Australia, China, Europe, Japan, Thailand, United States, other Asia
	Soft furnishings, home furniture, crocheted products	Australia, Canada, Germany, Italy, United Kingdom, United States
	Jute cotton apparel	Canada, Italy, Japan, Malaysia, Nepal, Turkey, United Kingdom, United States

Source: International Jute Study Group.

Germany, for rugs, mats, and cushions; Europe, Australia, and the United States for toys, handicraft items, and bags; the United States, Canada, and Italy for home furnishings; and Canada, the United Kingdom, and Turkey for apparel. Top importing countries, depending on the products made with the imported jute, potentially represent the leading competitors for Bangladesh's diversified jute products. Since India purports to be self-sufficient in its gunnysack needs, many of its jute imports may be going toward the manufacture of diversified jute products. This concurs with the fact that Bangladesh's jute is of higher quality than Indian jute, since higher-quality jute is required for higher value–added diversified jute products (home furnishings, garments and accessories, flat weave and braided rugs, and so forth).

New Market Drivers and Opportunities for Growth and Diversification

The encouragement to "bring your own bag" has provided a boon to the diversified jute products sector, in particular to jute shopping bags. Although there was a collapse in the jute sector two decades ago, in large part because of the rise of synthetic replacements for jute products, such as packing bags, shopping bags, and twine, environmental concerns have led consumers and the public sector to shun plastic bags in recent years.[12] Regulations have been enacted in various countries worldwide that outlaw plastic shopping bags (including Australia, Italy, Uganda, the United Arab Emirates, and many cities throughout North America[13]), in an attempt to reduce plastic bag use and deter it from entering the waste stream. In addition to the regulations, many stores, in an effort to encourage "green," charge for shopping bags or give a rebate to customers who bring their own bags. For example, some Walmart stores in the United States charge for plastic bags.[14] Whole Foods, a U.S. grocer, gives a discount to customers who bring their own bags. Globally, stores such as IKEA do not provide any bags and thus customers are encouraged to purchase (albeit recycled poly) bags from IKEA or bring their own.

Demand for jute shopping bags has increased, as has demand for other alternatives to plastic bags. As a consequence, orders for Bangladeshi shopping bags reportedly have increased from 300,000 units in 2010/11 to nearly 2,000,000 units in 2011/12. Among the buyers are prominent international corporations such as Walmart, The Body Shop, Home Depot, and Tesco. Jute bags are favored because they are perceived to be less harmful to the environment while still retaining the durability and convenience of plastic. Despite the recent success, jute shopping bags represent a negligible portion of the total annual world demand for shopping bags of approximately 500 billion pieces. In selecting reusable shopping bags, shoppers seek bags that are affordable, durable, washable, and sometimes fashionable. Those who are more environmentally conscious may want to buy a more "natural" bag, that is, one made from natural textiles, biodegradable, or recyclable. In this respect, while the "bring your own bag" movement represents an opportunity for jute shopping bags, there are many materials of which such bags can be made, including cotton, canvas, linen, or recycled polyester. Many bags are marketed as eco-friendly simply because they are durable enough to be reused, even if the underlying material is not of natural fiber. Thus the jute sector needs to make a strong case for its product, perhaps in cooperation with India and the Jute Study Group.

Continuing the shift away from plastic, food producers are also returning to jute bags for their products. According to the International Cocoa Organization, the cocoa industry desires 32 million food grade jute bags, but Bangladesh and India together are supplying only 12 million bags. Similarly, coffee bean producers desire food grade jute bags, but their needs presently are unmet.[15] Currently there are three mills in Bangladesh producing food grade jute bags; their production totaled 14,529 million tons in 2011/12.

Geotextiles are starting to be made of jute too. Geotextiles used for civil engineering, coastal engineering, and soil erosion control are traditionally made of synthetic materials. Nowadays, jute geotextiles are favored over synthetic since the raw materials are plentiful and renewable, the jute enhances soil nutrition when it biodegrades, and jute geotextiles are less expensive. Two jute mills in Bangladesh export 2,000–2,500 tons of jute geotextiles annually to the European Union, Australia, and Canada. India uses domestically produced jute geotextiles in national road construction. In 2010, the United Nations Common Fund for Commodities awarded US$2 million to a five-year project to help develop and expand production capacity of jute geotextiles in India and Bangladesh (*Specialty Fabrics Review* 2010). Ten field trials of geotextiles have been approved in Bangladesh and two of these are already completed, including one to prevent riverbank erosion and another for renovation of rural roads (*Daily Sun* 2012). Potential global demand for geotextiles to prevent soil erosion is estimated at more than five million square meters for the United States, up to one million square meters for Europe, and around 10 million square meters in Japan and Australia.[16]

Demands for green fashion and green products in general are rising globally along with increased environmental and social awareness (see box 3.2). Although undefined officially, green fashion broadly can include the following:

- Eco-friendly materials, such as organic, recycled, nonpetroleum-based, and non-PVC vegetable dyes
- Vegan or nonanimal materials, such as non-leather, animal-free adhesives
- Earth-friendly manufacturing, such as use of hydro or solar power or overall minimized use of electrical or fuel powered machinery, as with handmade products
- Socially responsible manufacturing or marketing, such as fair trade, non-sweatshop, no child labor, ethical treatment of workers, living wage, and buy-one-give-one.

Bangladesh has yet to realize the opportunity to replace wood or bamboo paper products with jute-made paper products. World demand for paper and paperboard was 359 million tons in 2004 and is estimated to grow 2.1 percent annually to reach 490 million tons by 2020. Although traditionally paper and paperboard are made with wood pulp, jute paper production requires less chlorine and other chemicals, usually consumes less energy, and, because of the low lignin composition in jute, creates cleaner wastewater that can be used for direct irrigation. A mill in Myanmar that used dried jute plant raw materials has been producing 5,000 million tons of paper a year (IJSG 2012).

Several industrial applications for jute exist and are only recently beginning to be explored. Jutin, for example, is an innovative building material based on jute fiber and is lightweight, heat-insulating, and rustproof. By mixing it with resin, it can be transformed into a sustainable and affordable building substance to construct shelters in poor countries and disaster-stricken areas. Greenovation Technologies, the Bangladeshi firm creating jutin, took the top award at the 2012 Global Innovation through Science and Technology "I Dare" business plan competition. The firm is exploring the most cost-effective machinery and method for mass production prior to global launch (Yusuf 2012). Bio-composite is another industrial application of diversified jute products. Jute is blended with other materials and incorporated into bio-composite for automotive interiors (fabric and body parts) by manufacturers, including Mercedes Benz, Daimler Chrysler, Ford Motors, Toyota, Hyundai, and Suzuki. Estimated demand for bio-composites is up to 10 million tons of jute annually (IJSG 2012).

Box 3.2 The Green Fashion Industry

Photo B3.2.1 FEED Fashion Tote Bag

Source: FEED Projects LLC.

Photo B3.2.2 Promotional Shopping Bag

Source: Quality Logo Products.

In addition to traditional fashion items such as jute handbags, green fashion has evolved into branded items that express the environmental and social consciousness of the wearer or the provider. At the high end are jute bags by FEED Projects (United States), a charitable foundation launched in 2006 whose bags are sold in higher-end retail establishments such as Nordstrom and Saks Fifth Avenue. The basic bag retails for US$80, but designs can run up to US$200 or more. The bag design is inspired by traditional gunnysack bags used to distribute large quantities of food rations to countries in need. The bag shown in photo B3.2.1 is made of natural hessian/burlap (exterior) and organic cotton (interior), with a utilitarian design that is reversible and has side and interior pockets. Each product is tied to a specific social benefit and works through beneficiaries such as the United Nations World Food Programme (UNWFP), the United Nations Children's Fund, and others. For example, purchase of the bag pictured is stated to provide for school meals for one child for one year through the UNWFP School Feeding program. To date, FEED product sales have raised enough through the sale of the basic bag to provide more than 60 million school meals. The bags and other FEED fashion products are made with fair labor production in countries including Guatemala, Haiti, India, Kenya, and the United States. Given its status as a jute producer (thus sourcing closer to the point of origin and reducing carbon footprint) and a least-developed country, Bangladesh can make a case for involvement in the manufacture of FEED or other charitable fashion products. At the low end of green fashion bags are those that can be sold or given away for promotional purposes, such as that shown in photo B3.2.2. Given the lining and flat bottom, such bags are specifically designed for shopping. Depending on the quantity purchased, the bag pictured wholesales from a U.S. firm for around US$2.40 per bag plain or US$5.00 per bag with logo imprint.

Institutional and Regulatory Environment, Market Structure, and Supply Chain

Bangladesh has public and private sector jute mills, all operating below capacity.[17] Bangladesh Jute Mills Corporation (BJMC) is the largest public enterprise and operates 27 mills. There are also private jute mills (represented by the Bangladesh Jute Mills Association, BJMA) and spinning facilities (represented by the Bangladesh Jute Spinners Association) in the country (table 3.9). In addition, in Bangladesh, there are 177,315 installed spindles in jute spinning mills, of which 150,025 (85 percent) are operating. All firms operate below capacity. For example, for mills under BJMC (public sector), utilization of looms is 63 percent of installed capacity, while at BJMA (private sector), utilization is only 38 percent of installed capacity (table 3.10). In addition to commercial producers, diversified products open the door for handicraft artisans and cottage industries. Three large fair trade companies exist and each has a network of artisans. One of the companies, with 4,020 member artisans and 6,000 associate member artisans, specializes in diversified jute products.

Much of the milling machinery in Bangladesh is 50–60 years old. China, India, Japan, Turkey, and other countries purchase raw jute from Bangladesh and process it on modern, more cost-effective equipment than is available in Bangladesh. Part of this challenge comes from the lack of information and awareness regarding available technology and equipment in the market. New entrants to jute milling are purchasing new machines, but these mills (private sector) are typically small enterprises.

Table 3.9 Selected Public and Private Sector Jute Milling Operations in Bangladesh, 2012

					Average internal consumption of jute goods		*Average export of jute goods*		
Organization	*Status*	*Number of mills*	*Number of employees (estimated)*	*Average production of jute goods (MT)*	*MT*	*Type*	*MT*	*Tk million*	*US$ million*
BJSA	Private	81	62,000	422,000	27,000	Yarn/twine	387,362	2,972	36.2
BJMA	Private	106	45,000	160,000	35,000	Sacking/hessian	97,891	713	8.7
BJMC	Public	27	64,000	207,000	31,500	Sacking/hessian	123,025	932	11.4
Total		221	171,000	789,000	93,500		608,278	4,617	56.3

Source: Bangladesh Jute Spinners Association.
Note: BJMA = Bangladesh Jute Mills Association; BJMC = Bangladesh Jute Mills Corporation; BJSA = Bangladesh Jute Spinners Association; MT = metric tons.

Table 3.10 Looms in Jute Mills in Bangladesh, 2012

Organization	*Status*	*Loom status*	*Hessian*	*Sacking*	*CBC*	*Other*	*Total*
BJMC	Public	Installed	6,232	3,250	1,157	95	10,734
		Operated	2,966	3,174	558	32	6,730
BJMA	Private	Installed	6,532	5,500	500	390	12,922
		Operated	1,500	3,000	188	215	4,903

Source: Bangladesh Jute Spinners Association.
Note: BJMA = Bangladesh Jute Mills Association; BJMC = Bangladesh Jute Mills Corporation; CBC = carpet backing cloth.

About 40 million people, mostly farmers, depend directly or indirectly on the export of jute fiber, according to Jute Exporters Association estimates (*Al Jazeera English* 2012). In diversified jute products,[18] employment is estimated to be 50,000–100,000 people, although there are no official statistics.

The diversified jute industry relies on extensive institutional public and private sector support in Bangladesh, as illustrated in figure 3.5. Annex 3D provides a summary of support institutions for diversified jute products and their various support activities. The industry also counts a number of stakeholders, including jute farmers and producers, fair trade organizations, local supply outlets, laminating companies, and dyeing and jute mills (table 3.11).

International support for the sector is provided by the International Jute Study Group (IJSG) (www.jute.org), an intergovernmental organization established

Figure 3.5 Institutional Support and Supply Chain Structure for Diversified Jute Products in Bangladesh

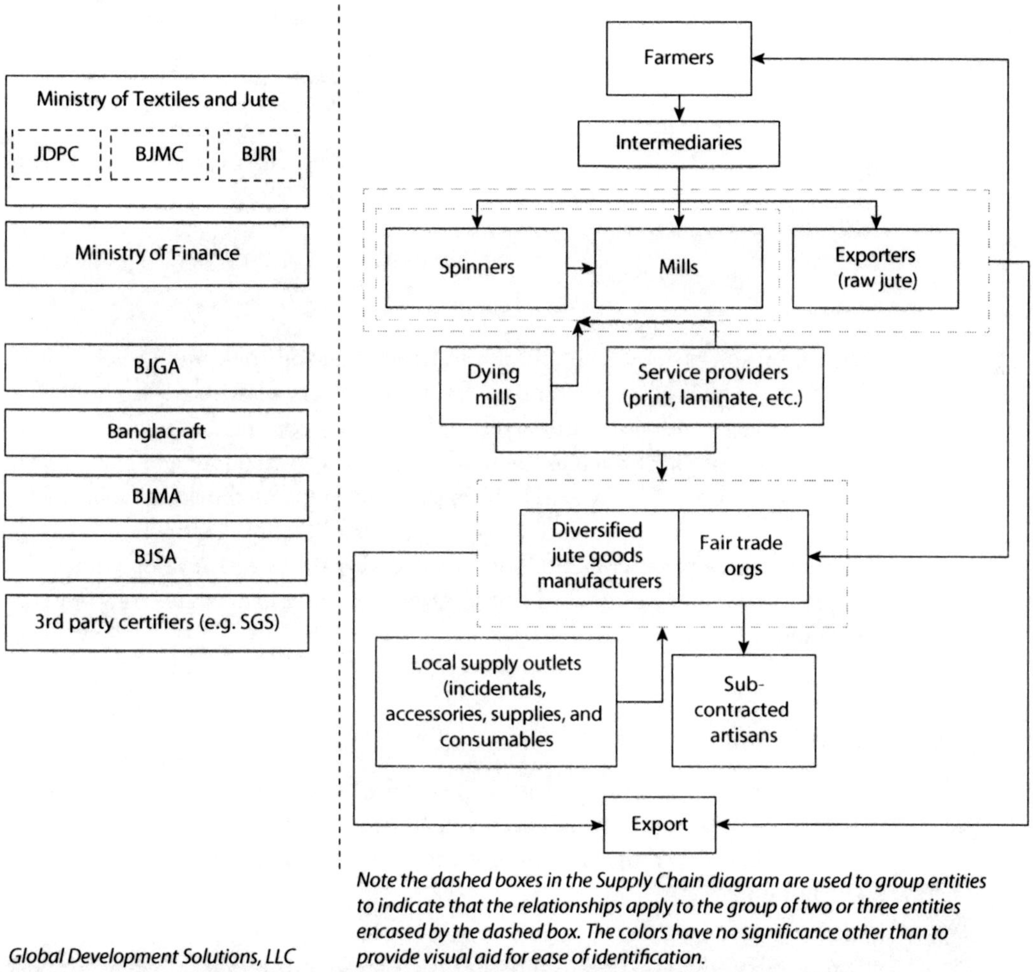

Note: BJGA = Bangladesh Jute Goods Association; BJMA = Bangladesh Jute Mills Association; BJMC = Bangladesh Jute Mills Corporation; BJRI = Bangladesh Jute Research Institute; BJSA = Bangladesh Jute Spinners Association; JDPC = Jute Diversification Promotion Center; SGS = Société Générale de Surveillance.

Table 3.11 Supply Chain Stakeholders and Their Activities for Diversified Jute Products in Bangladesh

Supply chain stakeholders	*Activities*
Jute farmers and producers	Produce (planting, cultivating, harvesting) and process (retting, separating, drying, bundling) jute.
Fair trade organizations	Three such entities contract local artisans, as well as maintain permanent artisans, to produce handicrafts, including jute-based items. They also provide training assistance to jute farmers desiring to become jute artisans.
Local supply outlets	Numerous local suppliers throughout Dhaka and surroundings supply incidentals, chemicals, and dyes to the sector.
Laminating companies	General service providers that are not specialized for laminating jute (17 entities in Dhaka). Export-bound shopping bags are often laminated, as are sacks for the cement industry. In the case of cement sacks, there are mills that have laminating capabilities in-house.
Dyeing mills	Provide services for dyeing jute fabrics and jute yarn.
Screen printers	Silk screen logos and designs onto jute fabrics; commonly required for export-bound shopping bags.
Jute mills	There are approximately 221 jute mills, including spinning mills, throughout the country, which employ approximately 150,000 people.
Intermediaries	Provide the service of collecting jute from farmers and transporting it to mills, spinners, and raw jute exporters.

Source: Global Development Solutions, LLC.

under the auspices of the United Nations Conference on Trade and Development. IJSG meets regularly with members from Bangladesh, India, and the European Union as well as with associate members from other countries to review issues in their collective interest, such as the marketing of diversified jute and harmonized codes for jute products. There have been some attempts by the donor community to expand the sector. For example, in 2010 the UN Common Fund for Commodities awarded US$2 million to a five-year project to develop geotextiles in India and Bangladesh for road construction and other civil engineering applications (*Specialty Fabrics Review* 2010).

Sector Policy

Jute was declared a priority sector according to the government's Industrial Policy Order 2010, implying several incentives for the sector (see box 3.3). Furthermore, in 2011, the government adopted a jute policy pursuing the following major objectives:

- Ensuring production of jute and jute goods according to the consistent demand of local and foreign markets
- Developing land use planning for jute cultivation

Box 3.3 Incentives for the Jute Industry in Bangladesh

Raw jute and jute goods for mills and spinners are granted a subsidy worth 10 percent of the free on board export value. However, this applies specifically to traditional products, raw jute, and yarn. If a manufacturer who does not operate a jute mill of any type exports a jute-based product that is not considered a handicraft, there is no subsidy. An example would be a jute goods producer with no backward integration into the jute processing segment (no milling or spinning) that produces machine-made nursery pots (not considered handicrafts). This is a jute product but the producer does not qualify for the 10 percent jute export subsidy. In addition, the industry benefits from duty drawbacks: a 100 percent value-added tax (VAT) exemption for exports and a 15 percent income tax rate (as opposed to the standard 37.5 percent). For 100 percent exporters of jute, VAT exemptions on gas and energy used in the factory can be applied as a drawback (this takes 3–6 months) or the factory can be approved and VAT is not charged (exemption); and the duty on imported capital equipment is 1 percent (as opposed to the standard 3 percent).

Note: Handicrafts can receive 15–20 percent subsidy but this is not specific to jute; it covers all handicrafts.

- Producing quality jute seed and supplying it to farmers
- Preserving and expanding jute and jute goods markets to help develop a favorable trade balance for the country
- Innovating various diversified jute products and increasing production of diversified jute products
- Ensuring effective networking of all stakeholders related to the jute sector
- Developing and maintaining a jute-related information management system.

The government has passed a mandatory jute packaging law (Law 53 in 2010), but it has yet to be enforced. Local media reported that the law would be enforced starting in August 2013.[19] A diversified jute product manufacturing industry is expected to be set up in Mongla Export Procession Zone at a cost of US$36.94 million. The industrial unit is expected to create employment opportunities for 2,052 people (*Bangladesh Economic News* 2011).

Recent policies aim to support diversified jute products, which have a high probability of success. The handicraft subsector offers a wide variety of market possibilities, ranging from various rugs and carpets (flat weave, braided, plush) to bags of all fashion levels, to toys and Christmas ornaments. In Bangladesh, diversified products have come to light only over the past five or so years and, as such, it is a sector in its infancy. By contrast, India has been developing the diversified jute sector for at least 15 years. Bangladesh has much to do to catch up from the perspective of public policy, including government support programs, availability of formal support institutions, support for market linkages and development, and product diversification.

Integrated Value Chain Analysis for Diversified Jute Products

Product Specification

Shopping bags were chosen for value-chain analysis after consultation with sector stakeholders. Jute bags are a leading product group within diversified jute products and include handbags, shopping bags, promotional bags, wine bags, and other specialty tote bags (photo 3.1). Jute bags were chosen for several reasons. First, they are simple products, do not require large capital investment, and are made by fair trade artisans as well as commercial factories. Second, shopping bag demand is growing and expected to continue based on external market forces.[20] Substitute materials other than jute are available (including cotton, linen, and synthetics such as nylon, woven poly, and nonwoven plastic), but buyers continue to increase orders for jute shopping bags. One large producer of jute shopping bags in Bangladesh states that orders over a two-year period went from 300,000 pieces to 2,000,000 pieces. Shopping bags cover several issues that can arise in the diversified sector. Third, shopping bags require better-quality fabric that is typically laminated, requires some type of printed design (logo, pattern, or otherwise), and may also be dyed. Therefore, several production processes and supply chain dynamics must be considered, which captures the types of analysis required for other diversified products. Finally, value addition of the shopping bag returns a minimum of threefold higher profits over raw jute. For example, one ton of jute can produce 1,500 yards of fabric, which in

Photo 3.1 Examples of Jute Bags and Totes

Source: Global Development Solutions, LLC.

turn can produces 2,300 shopping bags at a profit of approximately Tk 27,600. This profit is 3.9 times greater than profits from the sales of raw jute, which are approximately Tk 5,000–Tk 7,000 (US$61–US$85) per metric ton. The advantage of jute products is that these earnings stay in the country, since the jute is locally sourced and labor is a significant component along much of the jute and jute products value chain.

Shopping bags are always custom made for the buyers, so there is no standard configuration (photo 3.2). The bags can vary on the following: dimensions, color (for truly environmentally friendly bags, buyers will specify natural jute), presence of lamination (approximately 70 percent of bags currently produced in Bangladesh are laminated), the material type (cotton or jute—cotton is most common for export quality bags since it is softer), length of the handles or straps, and screen printing (number of colors, type of ink, design, number of printed sides). The specifications followed for the jute shopping bag in this analysis are as follows:

- Dimensions of 15 × 17 × 7.5 inches
- Laminated inner surfaces
- All panels dyed[21]
- Pigment ink (one color) silk screening on one panel
- Cotton handles with cotton shell encasing cotton rope, 12 inches (two pieces, one for each side of the bag).

Depending on the buyer's requirements, the production process for the jute shopping bag may rely on outsourcing certain processes. The jute fabric is acquired and, if dyeing is necessary, the fabric must be dyed externally at a

Photo 3.2 Two Examples of Jute Shopping Bag Design Features

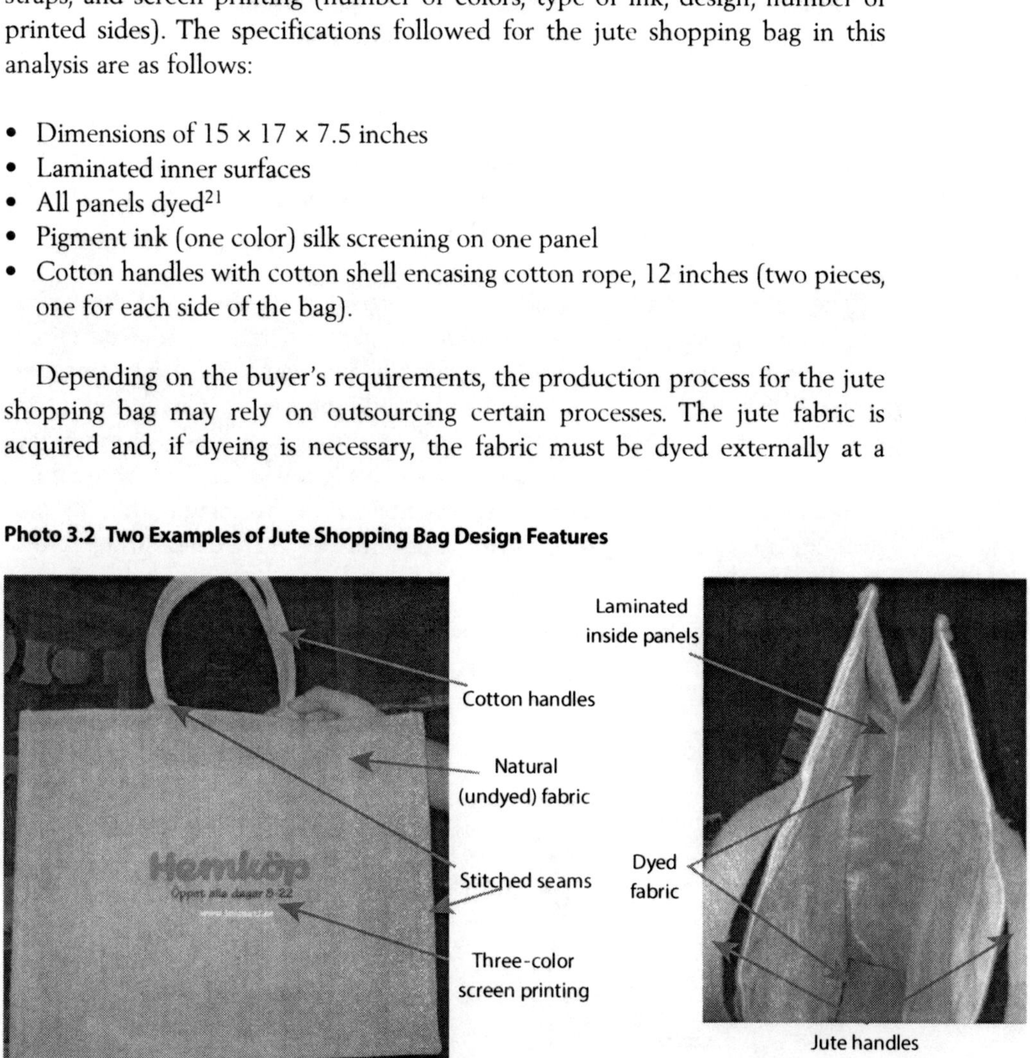

Source: Global Development Solutions, LLC.

dyeing facility.[22] If lamination is required, this too necessarily is outsourced to a laminating facility (there are 17 such facilities throughout Dhaka). The fabric is returned to the shopping bag producer, cut to size, and, if silk screening is required by the buyer, this too is usually outsourced. Virtually all export-bound shopping bags require some form of screen printing. Although in-house printing is possible for some producers, most prefer to send the panels out for printing. While the panels are out, the handles are readied. The panels are returned and then the bag construction (stitching) takes place.

Overall, the process is not capital intensive for the bag producer, although larger investments are required for outsourced services. The only machinery required is sewing machines. Electric scissors are commonly used, particularly by companies, as opposed to individual artisans contracted by fair trade organizations. All the larger capital investments are with the outsourced partners, including jute mills, dyeing facilities, laminating facilities, and screen printing.

Value Chain Analysis

The value chain is fairly simple in that it exhibits no tertiary chains. The primary value chain for the production of this shopping bag is divided into seven major stages, namely: (a) fabric preparation, (b) cutting, (c) screen printing, (d) handle preparation, (e) assembling, (f) finishing and inspection, and (g) packing (figure 3.6).

The simplicity of the value chain can be attributed to the fact that the most complicated processes, dyeing and laminating, are generally outsourced to specialized subcontractors. There are no diversified jute companies laminating their own products. The unit cost of producing a jute shopping bag with the specifications described is Tk 128.2 (US$1.56). According to interviews, these bags take approximately 18–22 minutes to produce. Figure 3.7 depicts the graphical representation of the production process along with the cost buildup for constructing a shopping bag that corresponds with the value chain in figure 3.6.

Figure 3.6 Value Chain Diagram for a Dyed and Laminated Jute Shopping Bag in Bangladesh

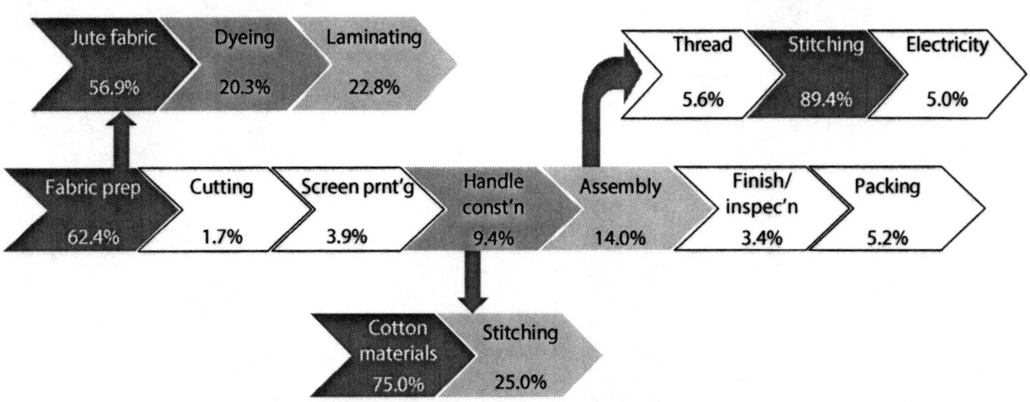

Source: Global Development Solutions, LLC.

Figure 3.7 Production Process and Cost Buildup for Fabrication of a Jute Shopping Bag in Bangladesh

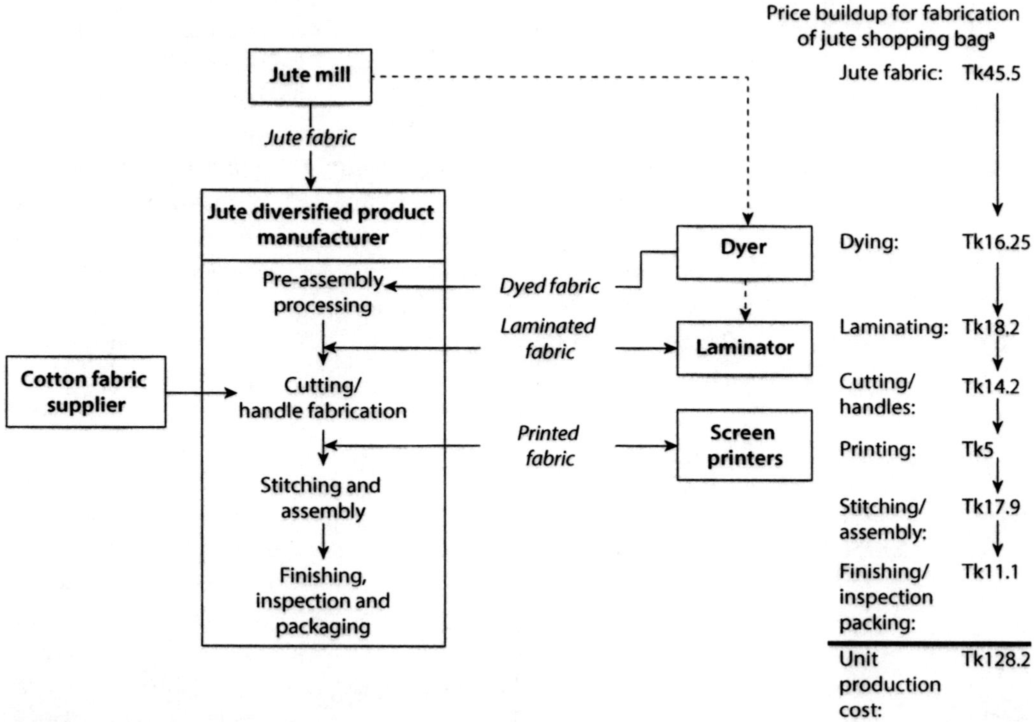

Source: Global Development Solutions, LLC.
a. Cost does not include OH, R&M, and margin.

As seen from the diagram, the fabric can be sent out to the service providers three times: for dyeing, laminating, and screen printing.

In Bangladesh, the two leading cost drivers, fabric and laminating, are particularly uncompetitive when compared with the counterpart pricing in India.[23] Fabric preparation dominates the value chain as it accounts for nearly two-thirds (62.4 percent) of the overall cost of producing the bag. As is generally the case with diversified jute products, the jute fabric itself is the highest cost driver. The cost of the undyed fabric contributes 57 percent to the overall fabric preparation cost. Laminating contributes an additional 23 percent and the cost of dyeing, also outsourced, adds 20 percent to the value chain. In Bangladesh there are 17 laminating companies currently operating in the market. Given the relatively high cost of laminating equipment (approximately US$20,000) and with no incentives to upgrade or purchase equipment in the jute sector, nearly all lamination is outsourced to local subcontractors. Dyeing follows closely behind laminating as the third most costly step in the overall value chain and contributes 12.7 percent overall. Dyeing fees are priced at approximately Tk 25 (US$0.30) per yard. Similar to laminating, dyeing is outsourced to local subcontractors. Another process frequently outsourced to local subcontracts is screen printing (which reportedly is done in-house by some producers, although no cost savings were detected).

Jute fabric in Bangladesh is about 30 percent more costly than similar fabrics in India, while the cost of laminating in Bangladesh is 20 percent over the cost of the same process in India. Furthermore, all stakeholders agree that Indian lamination is far superior in durability and lamination material. Lamination in Bangladesh is either polypropylene or high-density polyethylene, with the one noted exception of cellulose, whereas bag producers claim low-density polyethylene is preferable. Indian equipment accommodates low-density polyethylene and the lamination adheres better and for a much longer period (multiple years as opposed to approximately a year for lamination applied with machines in Bangladesh). The equipment that is generally used in India can cost as much as US$150,000. This is prohibitive for most manufacturers in Bangladesh and the small volume of production would warrant only two facilities operating such equipment.

The second highest value-added process is the cost of assembling the bag, which is the only significant cost driver, taking nearly 90 percent of the assembly process cost. The only other costs involved are thread and electricity, each contributing approximately 5 percent of the cost. Assembly is also the only step in the value chain of the bag producer that consumes any significant electricity. Even with machine cutting for the fabric, the electricity share is only 10 percent compared with the sewing costs. The third highest cost driver is handle preparation, but it contributes less than 10 percent to the overall value chain cost. Cotton material for the construction of the handle accounts for 75 percent of the cost (70 percent of the cotton cost is for the outer shell and 30 percent for the rope). The casing is wrapped around the rope and stitched together. Stitching, the labor component of handle preparation, adds the remaining 25 percent of the cost.

Based on the value chain analysis, the first challenge for diversified jute producers has been competitive sourcing of the original fabric. For small producers, this has been a problem in the past. Many small jute goods producers are located in and around Dhaka, while the closest mill to Dhaka is an hour and a half from the city, making it difficult for small-scale producers to source fabric effectively. In response to this challenge, the Jute Diversification Promotion Center (JDPC) established a consolidation program in 2011 so that fabric is available in Dhaka at the JDPC warehouse. Small producers can now purchase quantities according to their needs from the warehouse rather than having to meet prohibitive minimum orders. Fabric still requires dyeing and the jute goods producers must bring their fabrics to the dyeing mills or mills can deliver fabric to dyeing facilities at a small charge. In general, the elapsed time between procuring the fabric and having the material dyed and laminated is approximately a week.

A tiered supply chain is an essential element for effective and efficient growth of a sector. However, the current supply chain system in Bangladesh revolves mostly around informal structures and relationships between several small-sized players, particularly with respect to dyeing, laminating, and printing. Even if a high volume of high-quality, fine jute fabrics were to become available in the market today, the subcontracting supply chain as illustrated would be unlikely to support the volume and quality of product needed to be competitive with Indian manufacturers.

Limitation of available fabric types is another advantage that Bangladesh concedes to India. For example, in Bangladesh, only a half-dozen or so fabric varieties are readily available on the market, whereas in India the selection covers 50–55 different fabrics. The mindset of the Bangladeshi jute sector, particularly the public sector, is still largely focused on the traditional uses for jute. Specifically, jute continues to be viewed as a basic packing material that does not require a variety of colors, uniform weave, and fabric variety (such as different thicknesses). Recently established private mills, however, are more apt to pursue better equipment and produce diversified fabric. A recent entrant to the market, albeit very small, expressed that his reason for investing in a mill was his inability to find jute-cotton fabric blends. As a result, at a cost of Tk 2,000,000 (US$25,000), this entrepreneur self-financed the establishment of a mill that employs secondhand Chinese machinery capable of weaving 1,000 meters of jute-cotton blend fabric per day.

Only a few mills are experimenting with new fabrics, all in the private sector. For example, there is only one mill that experiments extensively with developing new fabrics and can produce very soft fabrics for fashion items (such as handbags) and very thin fabrics for garments. However, it does not manufacture the fabrics for inventory, so the fabrics are only produced upon a buyer's request. Being specialty fabrics, delivery can take up to one month. Minimum purchase orders of 10,000 yards or greater are required, depending on the type of fabric, which is well in excess of what many small and medium diversified jute product manufacturers require for most consignments. Finally, the mill requires payment in advance. Although high-quality jute fabrics are considered specialty products in Bangladesh, similar products are readily available in India, where there are multiple suppliers of blended and fine jute fabric. In Bangladesh, prospective buyers may not be able or willing to purchase the minimum order, so the fabrics remain difficult to access.

Moreover, the majority of weaving equipment in Bangladeshi mills, particularly in the government mills, is old—up to 70 years. Compounding the age of the machinery in Bangladesh is the fact that the company that manufactured the machines, Dundee (Scotland), went out of business decades ago and spare parts are not available. Spare parts must be custom made in local machine shops. Matching the original parts is difficult and replacement parts are therefore increasingly less reliable. More modern equipment is being used in India and the newer machines are more efficient and are able to weave four times faster than the machines in Bangladesh. All these factors add up to India producing fabric at 30 percent less cost compared with Bangladesh.

The high cost of borrowing (15–18 percent interest rate) and difficulties accessing finance (based on relationships rather than creditworthiness) present significant obstacles to stronger sector performance (production value, export) and new entrants. Restricted access to finance pushes firms to finance growth internally, which contributes to slow growth and slow product diversification. Even with a letter of credit as a guarantee, a local bank will usually provide only 35 percent of the working capital requirement. Entrepreneurs generally must rely on 100 percent internal financing to grow their companies from micro enterprises to small enterprises. One such entrepreneur who was interviewed was able to diversify into weaving with the purchase of an internally funded power loom, but this level of development has taken two decades to attain.

Significant financial support is given to the public sector mills, thereby hurting private sector competitiveness. The government recently announced significant investments in the government-owned mills (BJMC).[24] The producers of diversified jute products may perhaps benefit from more available fabric (it remains to be seen whether some of the subsidy will fund the capacity to produce the higher-quality fabrics needed by the diversified subsector). However, it is anticipated that private sector mills will be hurt by the unfair competition created by the subsidy as the investment is targeted only for the public sector mills. The government has taken some positive steps since 2010 by declaring jute a priority sector. Parliament passed a packaging law (Law 53 of 2010) requiring that all commercial packaging sacks (such as sacks used for sugar, cement, rice, and so forth) be constructed of jute, as opposed to synthetics. Law 53 of 2010 was expected to be enforced from August 2013.

An inefficient customs clearance process at the port creates an additional entry barrier for small entrepreneurs contemplating exports. All companies send a representative to the port when shipping a consignment. Companies claim that without this representative, the consignment is ignored and the goods will not move. Larger, established companies are familiar with the process and can afford to send an employee representative to accompany the shipment, but smaller companies may not have the luxury of sparing an employee capable of performing the task. The smaller company will have to hire a representative to ensure the consignment is properly handled. Not only does this add to uncertainty for the exporter, but hiring representation costs more than sending an employee (sending a company representative from Dhaka to accompany the consignment costs approximately Tk 2,000 (US$25) for the two- to three-day round trip).

Lack of production and trade data and poor access to market information make strategic benchmarking and planning difficult for companies. Interviews with stakeholders along the diversified jute sector indicate continued lack of and access to market information, particularly on available production technology and sources of equipment and technology for upgrading production of basic and complex fabrics. Moreover, there is little to no current, readily available information regarding diversified jute products because of the range of products within diversified jute, inconsistent application and lack of product-specific codes, and an irregular internal sector census that often overlooks non-traditional jute products. Associations track production in their respective subsectors (spinners associations, millers associations, and so forth), but there is no organization effectively tracking the diversified products. JDPC, for example, is not capable of performing this service, yet it is an organization specifically addressing the diversified subsector. As a consequence, Bangladesh as well as jute products are off the radar of many international databases, limiting the country's marketing reach.

Bangladeshi firms will continue to face the threat of new entrants in markets and products. In 2012, Bangladesh and India controlled more than 96 percent of the world jute production; but other countries, including China, Nepal, Uzbekistan, and Vietnam, have had success on a limited scale (40,000 metric tons or less). Given the right conditions, these countries could grow their own indigenous jute rather than importing it. Moreover, although Bangladesh is a leading exporter of jute and jute products, the country has not exploited this position and made Bangladesh synonymous with jute as, say, France is with cheese or Thailand with rice. Despite the versatility of jute, many other materials perform similar functions in common with jute products. For example, although the jute shopping bag is a niche product for Bangladesh, reusable shopping bags of various materials are popular in the global market, including other natural fibers such as cotton or kenaf as well as synthetic materials such as nylon or recycled or laminated plastic. In jute footwear components (for example, espadrille soles exported to be made into finished shoes elsewhere), while the traditional base (sole and midsole wrap) of espadrille soles is jute, substitute materials have been introduced globally to the footwear component market, including hemp rope, synthetic jute, and cork footbeds, threatening Bangladesh's footwear component niche. Substitutes for jute twine include cotton, polycotton, staple fiber polyester, high-tenacity multifilament polyester, tobacco, and sisal.[25]

Conclusions and Recommendations

As the world's second largest producer of jute and the leading producer of high-quality jute, Bangladesh has a unique natural resource advantage toward producing diversified jute products. What is missing is the leap to product design and market links. With its labor cost advantage over China and India and existing export infrastructure, Bangladesh can possibly become an attractive manufacturing hub for diversified jute products. However, antiquated equipment may negate the labor cost advantage. Therefore, investment in modern milling and other equipment is necessary to maximize the cost savings.

Bangladesh needs to develop a clear vision of the future of its jute industry. It also needs to provide the industry with the appropriate level and structure of nondistortionary support.

Currently the JDPC fabric bank stocks fabric for basic diversified products, such as shopping bags, and this can be expanded. A development program in partnership with the private sector can create a fabric bank of higher value-added jute and jute-based fabrics used in handbags and other fashion accessories. The fabrics can be sourced locally in Bangladesh owing to its jute quality, but for this program to be effective, the fabrics need to be priced competitively. The fabric bank will need to remain current in relation to color changes and other global fashion demands. As such, further assistance could include initial market research combined with partnerships with the buying community to track market and fashion trends to help stay on top of international demand.

Customs clearance processes for small exporters increase their overheads. Either small companies need to get together to find a joint solution for customs clearances or customs processes need to become more streamlined so that small firms are not penalized. This will help all small firms (and large ones as well), not just jute firms.

The jute packaging law needs to be enforced. Enforcement will result in increased domestic demand for raw jute and may provide a more stable source of demand for the jute industry. This could improve exports, but the primary concern of policy makers should be total employment and output.

The incentives to public jute mills may hurt the long-term strength of the sector. Subsidies in general are not sustainable. They hurt the private mills, which are arguably more efficient (since they compete without subsidies), and prevent the stronger private mills from becoming larger players. If such subsidies are no longer provided, private mills can expand and could be encouraged to hire from the public sector. This could help keep overall jute mill employment intact. The money saved by government can be used for other support programs, such as more effective research and outreach to farmers and more effective marketing and branding support.

Development partner financing could be considered. Development partner financing to stimulate further research and development in the sector for the development of additional diversified fabrics and to decrease the cost of the currently available high-end fabrics could be useful. The Jute Research Institute, for example, has a pilot project regarding diversified jute fabrics and is exploring collaboration with some garment and textile units for large-scale runs. Fabrics thus developed can also be provided in the fabric bank for diversified jute product producers.

Issues such as marketing, research, and branding could be addressed together with India and Nepal. If the numbers are correct, there is potentially a huge demand for natural fibers like jute, which could be more effectively exploited with a joint approach to marketing and branding. If South Asian countries get together and share marketing and branding costs under a regional approach, this can help all parties. Another approach would be to restrict branding to the two largest production countries and brand "Bengali" jute from Bangladesh and India. Either of these initiatives could be undertaken under the Jute Study Group's mandate. Joint research and development to complement domestic research efforts offers another possibility.

Annex 3A: Potential Jute Sector Classifications

Two-digit code	*Four-digit code*	*Six-digit code*
42: Articles of leather, saddler and harness, travel goods, handbags, articles of gut	4202: Travel goods, handbags, wallets, jewelry cases, etc.	420212: Travel goods, similar containers of plastics or of textile materials 420222: Handbags of plastic sheeting or of textile materials
44: Wood and articles of wood, wood charcoal	4410: Particle board and similar board of wood or other ligneous materials	441090: Of other ligneous materials
46: Manu of straw, esparto, or other plaiting materials, basketware and wickerwork	4601: Plaits etc. and products of plaiting materials	460120: Mats, matting and screens of vegetable materials
53: Vegetable textile fibers nesoi, yarns and woven, etc.	5303: Jute and other text bast fibers nesoi, raw etc. and tow etc.	530310: Jute and other textile bast fibers, raw or retted 530390: Other jute and other textile bast fibers, tow and waste of these fibers
	5307: Yarn of jute and other textile bast fibers nesoi	530710: Yarn of jute or of other textile bast fibers, single yarn 530720: Yarn of jute or of other textile bast fibers, multiple or cabled
	5310: Woven fabrics of jute or other text bast fiber nesoi	531010: Woven fabrics of jute or of other textile bast fibers (unbleached) 531090: Woven fabric of jute/bast fiber, not unbleached/bleached
56: Wadding, felt and nonwovens, special yarns, twine, cordage, ropes and cables and articles	5602: Felt whether or not impregnated, coated, covered or laminated	560229: Felt of other textile materials; not impregnated, coated, covered
	5607: Twine, cordage, rope and cables, coated etc. or not	560710: Twine, cordage, rope and cables of jute or other textile bast fibers
	5609: Articles of yarn like of head 5404/5405 twine or cable nesoi	560900: Articles of yarn, strip or the like of artificial textile materials, rope
57: Carpets and other textile floor coverings	5701: Carpets and other textile floor covering knotted	570190: Carpets and floor coverings, knotted, of other textile materials
	5702: Carpets and other textile floor covering, woven, not tufted or flocked	570239: Carpets and floor coverings of other textile materials, not made up 570249: Carpets and floor coverings of other textile materials, made up
	5705: Carpets and other textile floor covering tufted	570500: Other carpets and other textile floor coverings
58: Special woven or tufted fabric, lace, tapestry, etc.	5805: Hand-woven and needle-worked tapestries	580500: Hand-woven tapestries, needle-worked tapestries
	5806: Nar woven fabrics, other than those of hd 5807	580639: Other narrow woven fabrics of other textile materials
59: Impregnated, coated or laminated textile fabric	5904: Linoleum, floor cover with coat, etc. on a text base	590490
	5905: Textile wall coverings	590500: Textile wall coverings

table continues next page

Annex 3A *(continued)*

Two-digit code	*Four-digit code*	*Six-digit code*
62: Articles of apparel, accessories not knit or crochet	6203: Men's suits, jackets, trousers, etc. and shorts	620319: Men's/boys' suits, of other textile materials, not knitted
63: Made-up textile articles nesoi, needlecraft sets, worn clothing, rags	6305: Sacks and bags of textile material for packing goods	630510: Sacks and bags, of jute or of other textile bast fibers, used for packing goods
64: Footwear, gaiters, and the like	6406: Parts of footwear, insoles, heel cushion, etc.; gaiters, etc., parts	640620: Outer soles and heels, of rubber or plastics
		640699: Parts of footwear, of other materials, other than wood, nes

Source: Foreign-Trade.com.
Note: nes = not elsewhere specified; nesoi = not elsewhere specified or included.

Annex 3B: Potential Diversified Jute Product Classifications

HS code	*Product name*	*Product specifications*
420222	Handbags	With or without handle/shoulder straps
42022230	Handbags and shopping bags	Jute and jute blended fabrics, with or without lamination
42023910	Jewelry box of jute	Jewelry box with outer surface of jute material/fabric or with inner surface of jute material
44103911	Jute particle boards	Flat product manufactured in various dimensions by compressing or extrusion of fragments of jute stocks or other jute materials agglomerated by means of an added binder
46012060	Mats or matting of jute	Woven with plain, stripe, dobby, or jacquard designs; jute mats also can be manufactured by braiding
53101014	Jute canvas (containing 100% by weight of jute)	A plain weave cloth made wholly of jute with double warp and single weft interwoven
53101015	Jute soil saver (containing 100% by weight of jute)	Also known as Geo jute laid on earthen slopes for conservation of soil
53101093	Jute scrim cloth	A plain weave open mesh, light weight fabric (of jute) weighing less than 214 grams/square meter
53109010	Bleached jute	Bleached jute fabric, yarn, or fiber is rendered white by a chemical process
53109011	Decorative fabrics of jute	Nonconventional, value-added jute fabrics made from mute/ blended yarns used for decoration purpose
56022910	Felt of jute not impregnated, coated, covered or laminated	A material formed by entanglement of jute fibers/blends or in union with other materials
56029010	Felt of jute impregnated, coated, covered, or laminated	Felt of jute impregnated, coated, covered or laminated with plastics or rubber coating containing more than 50% jute by weight
56071010	Cordage, cable, rope, and twine of jute	Cordage, cable, rope, and twine of jute
56090030	Articles made up of jute	Jute articles having aesthetic value used for other than industrial and general textiles use
57019011	Carpets of jute	A floor covering having jute yarns or fibers on surface
57019019	Other floor coverings of jute	Jute floor covering fabric woven with plain, striped, dobby, or jacquard designs
57023911	Carpets of jute	Of pile construction, but not tufted or flocked

table continues next page

Annex 3B *(continued)*

HS code	*Product name*	*Product specifications*
57024919	Other floor coverings of jute, of pile construction, made up	Other floor coverings of jute covered by a pile surface
57050031	Of blended jute	Carpets made of jute in blend with other fibers having more than 50% jute by weight
57050032	Of coir jute	Carpets made of jute in blend with coir having more than 50% jute by weight
58050020	Tapestries of jute	A closely woven fabric in which the pattern is developed by colored yarn as warp or as weft or both where jute is more than 50% by weight
58063920	Jute webbing	Heavy-duty jute tape, usually 4–10 centimeters wide
59049010	Floor coverings with jute base	Linoleum, PVC, or other manmade floor covering with jute fabric as backing material
59051060	Jute wall covering	Jute fabric bleached/dyed/designed to cover wall for decoration purposes
62031920	Fashion garments of jute for men/boys	Garments of jute (jute blended or union of jute where jute is the predominant fiber) made of blended or union fabrics of jute used as fashion apparel

Source: Jute Diversified Products Portfolio of Bangladesh, Jute Diversification Promotion Center, 2007.

Annex 3C: Comparative Profile of the Jute Sector in Bangladesh and India, Annual Data, 2007–10

Characteristic		*Bangladesh*	*India*
1.0	Average land area under cultivation (hectares)	464,000	836,000
2.0	Average yield (tons/hectare)	2.32	1.95
	2.1 Average production of jute (million tons)	1.08	1.63
3.0	Number of farm families (millions)	3.5–4	4–4.5
4.0	Average internal consumption of jute (million tons)	0.6	1.8
5.0	Number of jute mills	156	78
6.0	Number of workers employed in jute mills	150,000	370,000
7.0	Average production of jute goods (MT)	592,500	1,705,000
	7.1 Sacking	180,600	1,107,000
	7.2 Hessian cloth	40,490	324,000
	7.3 Carpet backing cloth	11,130	5,000
	7.4 Other (including yarn & twine)	327,970	268,000
8.0	Average internal consumption of jute goods (MT)	100,000	1,489,000
9.0	Average export of jute goods (MT)	487,000	202,000
10.0	Average export value of jute goods (US$, millions)	471	246
11.0	Average export earnings from jute & jute goods (US$, millions)	611.0	65.9

Source: International Jute Study Group.
Note: Data are averages for 2007/08, 2008/09, and 2009/10. MT = metric tons.

Annex 3D: Support Institutions and Their Activities

Institution	*Support activity*
Ministry of Textiles and Jute	• Establishes policy for the sector and oversees JDPC, BJGC, and BJRI

Ministry of Finance	• Through the National Board of Revenue (www.nbr-bd.org), collects taxes and duties including import duties (for materials), export duties (for exports), and VAT.
	  • The Customs Act, 1969 (Act No. IV of 1969) (http://www.wipo.int/wipolex/en/text.jsp?file_id=198651) specifies the authority to levy duty and requirements for drawback but does not specify specific amounts or fees.
	  • The Value Added Tax Act, 2011 (Act No. X of 2011). A 2012 draft is in process (see draft: http://www.nbr-bd.org/vat_pdf/Draft_VAT_Law-2012_English.pdf).

Export Promotion Bureau, Bangladesh, Ministry of Commerce (EPB) (www.epb.gov.bd)	• Established in 1977 as a national export promotion agency under the Ministry of Commerce. • Promotes export trade and improves plans and policies helpful to the sector. • Administered by a board of management comprising members from the public and private sectors. • Makes public statistics on exported products. • Issues Certificate of Origin for exported products.

Jute Diversified Promotions Center (JDPC) (www.jdpc.gov.bd)	• Established in 2002 by the Ministry of Textiles & Jute with assistance from International Jute Organization, UNDP, European Union, and Bangladesh Chamber of Commerce & Industry.
	• Mandated to promote and develop diversified jute enterprises in the private sector, creation of new capacities, and maximization of the existing capacities.
	• Functions:
	  • Provide technical service, market linkage, and organize training and skill development program for entrepreneurship development for micro, small, and medium diversified jute enterprises.
	  • Create awareness among entrepreneurs/weavers/artisans and NGOs about scope and technology advancement for setting up diversified jute production units.
	  • Provide export services (pre- and post-investment services) to poor weavers, artisans, entrepreneurs, etc.
	  • Set up raw materials bank to provide raw materials to small, cottage, micro, and other small NGOs at reasonable price.
	  • Organize local fairs and/or participate in Grameen Melas, Buyer-Seller meets, etc.
	  • Organize workshops for technology dissemination, market information, extension, and promotional services.
	  • Ensure quality of products of the units/enterprises by providing centralized testing facilities, preferably at research institutions.
	• 600 people registered; no membership fee.

Bangladesh Jute Mills Corporation (BJMC) (www.bjmc.gov.bd)	• Division of Ministry of Textiles & Jute • Oversee operations and marketing activities of 27 government-owned jute mills.

table continues next page

Annex 3D *(continued)*

Institution	*Support activity*

Bangladesh Jute Research Institute (BJRI) (www.bjri.gov.bd)	• Established with the Bangladesh government's promulgation of the Jute Act in 1974.
	• Functions:
	  • Promote agricultural, technological, and economic research on jute and allied fibers and their manufactures and disseminate results.
	  • Organize production, testing, and supply of improved pedigree of jute seeds and multiplication, procurement, and their distribution to recognized organizations, selected growers, and such other agencies as may be approved by the BJRI Board.
	  • Set up research centers, substations, pilot projects, and farms in different regions of the country for carrying out research on different problems of jute and allied fiber crops, jute products, and allied materials.
	  • Establish project areas for demonstration of new varieties of jute developed by the institute and train farmers for cultivation of these varieties of jute.
	  • Establish annual reports, monographs, bulletins, and other literature relating to jute research and the activities of the institute.
	  • Organize training of officers and farmers on modern methods of improved cultivation of jute and allied fiber crops and train technical hands for utilization of technological findings.
	  • Do and perform such other activities as may be necessary for the purposes of the Jute Act.

Bangladesh Jute Spinners Association (BJSA) (www.juteyarn-bjsa.org)	• Private sector association established in 1979 to represent the jute spinning sector on various advisory councils and committees of government ministries and departments. • Lobbies government on all matters affecting members, including tax and port issues. • Publishes a monthly bulletin to keep members abreast of sector events, news, and activity, including statistics and policy issues. • 81 members—jute spinning mills producing jute yarn and twine. • Membership fee structure: • One-time registration fee: Tk 200,000 (US$2,440). • Annual fee: Tk 25 (US$0.30) per spindle. • Number of spindles per company ranges from a minimum of 700 to greater than 3,000. • Along with BJGA, is an authorized body for issuing the certificates required for consignments of jute products.
Bangladesh Jute Mills Association (BJMA)	• Private sector association representing 120 jute mills (38 mills with capacity greater than 25 tons/day). • Lobbies government on behalf of members about issues affecting the sector. • Supports new members in acquiring loans by coaching members on how to work with banks. • Arbitrates labor disputes. • Negotiates with the World Bank on behalf of the sector.

table continues next page

Annex 3D *(continued)*

Institution	*Support activity*
	• Infrequently sponsors training for members (one every two or three years). • Publishes annual industry report (includes sector statistics, the list of members, the year's events, and industry news summaries). • One-time registration fee of Tk 50,000 (US$610); annual renewal of fee is Tk 350 (US$4.27) per loom.
Banglacraft (www .banglacrafts.org)	• Registered in 1979; private sector association representing all Bangladesh handicrafts exporters—not specific to jute. Handicraft exporters must go through Banglacraft to receive export subsidy (15–20% for handicrafts).
Bangladesh Jute Goods Association (BJGA)	• Established in 1970 as Bangladesh Jute Goods Exporters Association (has since changed name by dropping "Exporters"), with original purpose to support traders and exporters and help expand the market as well as maintain contacts with foreign chambers of commerce. • No apparent marketing support or international representation, given lack of website. • Membership is not required for jute goods producers, but is required for jute goods exporters (who are not members of BJSA). • One-time registration fee of Tk 14,000 (US$170) and annual membership fee of Tk 4,000 (US$49). • Issues export certification to exporters that allows exporters to obtain GSP from the Export Promotion Bureau and also is to be presented to customs during export. • Has lobbied for the right to issue Certificate of Origin (fee Tk 200 [US$2.44] per document), but has not yet been granted.
3rd party certifiers (Société Générale de Surveillance [SGS], etc.)	• When required by a buyer, SGS tests dyes for banned chemicals (dimethyl fumariate and the AZO group of chemicals).

Source: Global Development Solutions, LLC.
Note: GSP = Generalized System of Preferences; NGO = nongovernmental organization; SGS = Société Générale de Surveillance; UNDP = United Nations Development Programme; VAT = value-added tax.

Notes

1. The jute sector can be viewed in three major categories: (a) raw jute; (b) traditional products (hessian [burlap] cloth, gunnysacks, and carpet backing cloth); and (c) diversified (also known as nontraditional) jute products, including specialty yarns and fabrics.
2. Note that all tons referenced in this chapter are metric tons unless otherwise indicated.
3. FAOSTAT.
4. FAOSTAT.
5. Bluebell Enterprise, www.jutebangladesh.com.
6. Interview with International Jute Study Group.
7. Export Promotion Bureau (EPB) data; http://www.epb.gov.bd/exportdata.php.
8. The Jute Packaging Materials Act of 1987 provides for 100 percent mandatory reservation for jute bags for packaging of sugar and food grain. India provides some other transparent support to its jute sector, including training programs, direct assistance in trade show participation, and effective government research. India provides support

in the form of a minimum support price for raw jute, which benefits farmers but not millers or producers of jute products.

9. Given the diversity of the sector and lack of available HS codes dedicated exclusively to jute, information on specifically the export of diversified jute products is not available from the Export Promotion Bureau.
10. According to *The Financial Express* (July 2, 2012), "Exports to Iran, one of [the] major destinations of Bangladeshi raw jute and jute goods, have almost halved during the period as the country has been facing difficulties in clearing import payments in US Dollar since the UN sanction, the Export Promotion Bureau (EPB) data showed."
11. HS530310: Jute and other textile bast fibers, raw or retted. These three countries are the top importers of raw jute worldwide, together purchasing 90.2 percent by weight and 86.6 percent by value of all globally traded raw jute imports in 2011.
12. According to the environmental group Worldwatch, the United States alone throws away more than 100 billion plastic bags annually and it takes more than 1,000 years for a nonrecyclable plastic bag to break down in a landfill.
13. Plastic bag levies and fees were adopted by Seattle, Washington, in 2008 and by Washington, DC, in 2009. Plastic bag bans were enacted in 30 villages in Alaska in 1998; Oakland, California, in 2007; San Francisco, California, in 2007; and Los Angeles, California, in 2012 (Source: International Jute Study Group).
14. Walmart stores in Citrus Heights, Folsom, and Ukiah, California, charged for plastic bags in June 2010 (Source: International Jute Study Group).
15. International Jute Study Group, "World Jute & Kenaf Statistics: At a Glance: 2012;" http://www.jute.org/IJSG%20Publications/Jute%20&%20kenaf%20Stat%20at%20a%20glance_ijsg.pdf.
16. International Jute Study Group, "World Jute & Kenaf Statistics: At a Glance 2012;" http://www.jute.org/IJSG%20Publications/Jute%20&%20kenaf%20Stat%20at%20a%20glance_ijsg.pdf.
17. Sector stakeholders for raw material include farmers, intermediaries, processors, and exporters; for finished products, stakeholders include spinners, millers, and manufacturers of traditional and diversified jute products.
18. This category excludes farmers and mills; it includes only diversified product production, including footwear, such as espadrilles.
19. Rules designed for mandatory use of jute sacks, *The Daily Star*, June 18, 2013.
20. Although a few large international firms have been purchasing jute shopping bags for the past several years as part of their efforts to position themselves as environmentally friendly, foreign governments have recently been banning disposable plastic shopping bags. Italy and Uganda have already banned plastic bags. The United Arab Emirates declared a ban that took effect January 1, 2013. Canada is scheduled to ban plastics and Japan is considering the same. The European Union as a whole is set to cut usage of plastic bags by 50 percent by 2019 and 80 percent by 2025.
21. Fabric can also be bleached. According to interviews, bleaching costs the same as dyeing.
22. Dyeing is not done at the jute mills, but in some cases the fabric producer will provide the service of getting the fabric dyed. Outsourcing is typical of small millers developing a clientele.

23. The unit cost per yard (48 to 52 inch width) for typical shopping bag fabric is Tk 70 (US$0.85) and a bag of the given dimensions requires 0.65 yard of material. This brings the cost of the jute material used to construct the specified bag of 15 x 17 x 7.5 inches to a total of Tk 45.5 (US$0.55), which comprises more than one-third (35.5 percent) of the cost of the entire value chain, including packing and packaging materials. The unit cost per yard of laminating in Bangladesh varies depending on laminating material, from Tk 15 (US$0.18) for polypropylene to as high as Tk 50 (US$0.61) for cellulose.
24. In 2010/11, the government subsidized mills with Tk 300 crore (US$36.6 million). In 2011/12, the allocation increased to Tk 2,900 crore (US$353.6 million). The allocation for 2012/13 was expected to be Tk 1,700 crore (US$207.5 million). *The Daily Star*, May 11, 2012.
25. Source: Abingoini Packaging Equipment Suppliers, Africa: www.abingoni.com /twine.htm.

References

Al Jazeera English. 2012. "Bangladesh Trade: Iran Sanctions Cripples Jute Business." Television broadcast, September 3.

Bangladesh Economic News. 2011. "Jute Diversified Product Manufacturing Unit to Be Set Up in Mongla EPZ." November 26.

Daily Sun. 2012. "Use of Jute Geotextiles Going On Under UN-Funded Project." May 12.

Dash, Jayajit. 2012. "India Declines to Import Jute Bags from Bangladesh and Nepal." *Business Standard*, September 7.

IJSG (International Jute Study Group). 2012. "World Jute and Kenaf Statistics: At a Glance." IJSG. http://www.jute.org/IJSG%20Publications/Jute%20&%20kenaf%20Stat%20at%20a%20glance_ijsg.pdf.

Specialty Fabrics Review. 2010. "UN Funds Jute Projects in India, Bangladesh." June.

Yusuf, Suhail. 2012. "Bangladeshi Innovators Scoop US Technology Award." SciDevNet, August 7.

CHAPTER 4

Light Manufacturing: Non-Leather Footwear

Glenn Surabian and Yasuo Konishi

Introduction

This chapter assesses the performance of the non-leather footwear value chain in Bangladesh against the backdrop of global competition. The objectives of the value chain analysis are: (a) to review the detailed breakdown of costs and productivity for each selected product and identify the main reasons for the productivity and cost gaps; (b) to identify the most important and common constraints across the value chains; (c) to understand possible practical solutions to address the critical constraints identified; and (d) to benchmark the competitiveness (productivity and costs) of the selected products against competitors (China and India).

The chapter provides a basic description of the sector's value added, domestic market, imports and exports, and employment, followed by a detailed breakdown of the value added for each critical step along the value chain. There is an additional breakdown and analysis of each critical step along the value chain to show the underlying issues for each of these steps, with provision of the breakdown among input, labor, capital, and other costs. The chapter also discusses the quality drivers, such as the quality of key inputs and services at each step of the value chain, the quality of the processing, and the quality of delivery and marketing (time to market).

Sector Profile

Non-leather footwear in Bangladesh takes several forms, including jute-based espadrilles, canvas or rubber tennis shoes, molded polyurethane and polyvinyl chloride (PVC) shoes, and artificial leather shoes (annex 4A).[1] However, according to the Leather Goods and Footwear Manufacturers and Exporters Association of Bangladesh (LFMEAB), espadrilles dominate non-leather footwear exports. The espadrille, a traditional non-leather shoe export of Bangladesh, does not fall neatly into one of the HS codes; as such, trade data specific to espadrilles do not exist. Given the data limitations (box 4.1), the descriptive analysis in this chapter will focus mostly on footwear, with information on non-leather footwear included as much as possible, relying on secondary sources. The value chain analysis will concentrate on espadrilles.

Bangladesh is among the top Asian producers of footwear, with production in 2011 of 276 million pairs and a 1.3 percent world market share. Global production of footwear set a new record in 2011, with an estimated 21 billion pairs produced, an increase of 5 percent over 2010 production volume of

---

Box 4.1 Lack of Proper Product Classification for Non-Leather Footwear in Bangladesh

Manufacturers reportedly categorize espadrilles in Bangladesh trade statistics under the following HS codes (descriptions as per Bangladesh Export Promotion Bureau):

- HS640319: Sports footwear (excluding ski boots, cross-country ski footwear & snowboard boots), with outer soles of rubber, plastic, leather, or composition leather & uppers of leather
- HS640359: Footwear with leather soles and uppers
- HS640419: Footwear (excluding sports footwear), with outer soles of rubber or plastic & uppers of textile material
- HS640520: Footwear with uppers of textile materials, nes
- HS640590: Footwear, nes/other footwear.

There are several important points. First, HS6403 is for leather footwear. A possible explanation for use of these codes is that high-fashion espadrilles sometimes have leather features. Second, with the three legitimate non-leather codes into which the non-leather espadrilles could be classified, producers are not coordinating efforts to be sure they are using a consistent code. Finally, these codes in no way limit the selections to espadrilles. The last three codes (HS640419, HS640520, and HS640590) in particular can cover a vast array of non-espadrille styles. To address the desire for product-specific statistics, the Leathergoods & Footwear Manufacturers & Exporters Association of Bangladesh has lobbied the International Jute Study Group to create an additional category and specific code for espadrilles; the request is pending.

The Bangladesh Bureau of Statistics collects and disseminates data on industrial production of selected industries and the indexes of medium- and large-scale manufacturing industries on a monthly basis. Information is obtained from state-owned manufacturing enterprises as well as major manufacturing enterprises in the private sector. The most recently available industrial production statistics are as of November 2010.[a] Although the report provides data on leather footwear (such as number of pairs produced), it does not provide information on non-leather footwear or the footwear sector as a whole. As such, total Bangladeshi production for the non-leather footwear subsector could not be ascertained.

Note: HS = Harmonized System; nes = not elsewhere specified.
a. http://www.bbs.gov.bd/WebTestApplication/userfiles/Image/keyfinding/key_find_Nov_10.pdf.

---

20 billion pairs. Led by China, with a 60.5 percent market share, world production of footwear by volume is highly concentrated in Asia, with an overall share close to 90 percent, and seven Asian countries counted among the world's top 10 producers (table 4.1). The high labor intensity of most of the industry's production lends itself toward smaller operations. Although large-scale manufacturers operate in the industry, many microenterprises are engaged in footwear manufacturing worldwide. China's dominance in footwear production is primarily attributed to production efficiency that enables higher-volume production across quality and price. India, the number two producer, leverages strengths in producing medium-size orders of midrange leather footwear.[2]

By product segment, women's shoes (excluding athletic) account for the largest share of the world market, with 31.2 percent of industry revenues in 2010, followed by men's nonathletic footwear (24 percent) and athletic shoes (20 percent) (figure 4.1). Particularly in more affluent countries, women are more likely to purchase multiple pairs of shoes; frequent style changes contribute to fragmentation in the footwear industry. Men's footwear has slower changes in styles and often is well suited to mass production in countries with low labor costs. Athletic shoes are largely produced in Asia via a contractor relationship with large athletic footwear companies (such as Nike or Adidas). Rubber and plastic footwear comprised 8.2 percent of industry revenue in 2010 (it has vulcanized, molded, or cemented components; sandals and slippers are separate).

Asia is the largest consumer, purchasing about half of global footwear production volume, followed by Europe (21 percent) and North America (17 percent) in 2011 (APICCAPS 2012). At the country level, China is the world's largest consumer market for footwear in quantity (2.76 billion pairs or 15.9 percent of world consumption), followed by the United States (2.25 billion pairs or 12.9 percent of world consumption) and India (2.20 billion pairs or 12.7 percent

Table 4.1 Top 10 Footwear Producers Worldwide, by Quantity, 2011

Rank	*Country*	*Pairs (millions)*	*World share (%)*
1	China	12,887	60.5
2	India	2,209	10.4
3	Brazil	819	3.8
4	Vietnam	804	3.8
5	Indonesia	700	3.3
6	Pakistan	298	1.4
7	Bangladesh	276	1.3
8	Mexico	253	1.2
9	Thailand	244	1.2
10	Italy	207	1.0
	Other	2,303	12.1
	Total	21,000	100.0

Source: APICCAPS 2012.

of world consumption) (table 4.2). On a per capita basis, the United States topped the list in 2011, with 7.2 pairs per person annually, followed by France (6.7 pairs) and the United Kingdom (5.9 pairs). China consumed 2.0 pairs per person. According to *World Footwear 2012 Yearbook*, Bangladesh produced 276 million pairs and consumed 268 million pairs of shoes in 2011 (APICCAPS 2012), making its per capita consumption 1.7 pairs, similar to that of India.[3]

Figure 4.1 Global Footwear Revenue, by Product Segment, 2010
percent

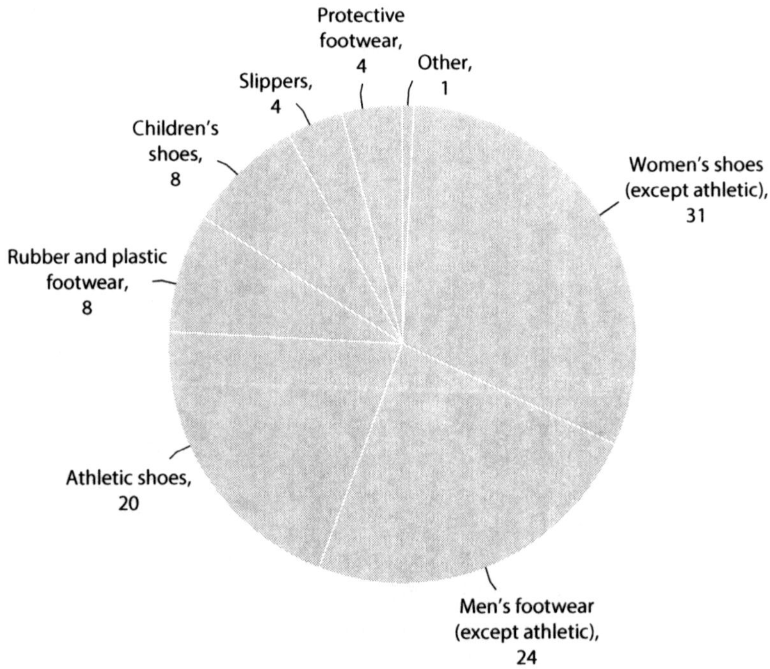

Source: IBISWorld 2010.

Table 4.2 Top 10 Footwear Consumers, by Quantity, 2011

Rank	*Country*	*Pairs (millions)*	*World share (%)*	*Population (millions)*	*Consumption per capita (pairs)*
1	China	2,761	15.9	1,348	2.0
2	United States	2,248	12.9	312	7.2
3	India	2,202	12.7	1,207	1.8
4	Brazil	740	4.3	195	3.8
5	Japan	697	4.0	128	5.4
6	Indonesia	526	3.0	241	2.2
7	Germany	429	2.5	82	5.2
8	France	424	2.4	63	6.7
9	United Kingdom	372	2.1	63	5.9
10	Italy	336	1.9	61	5.5

Source: APICCAPS 2012.

Within the niche espadrilles and jute soles market, Bangladesh apparently commands 90 percent of world production.[4]

China leads in footwear export volume with a market share of 73 percent in 2011, followed by Hong Kong SAR, China, and Vietnam (table 4.3). The number of pairs exported reached nearly 14 billion (APICCAPS 2012). The price per unit (pair) has been rising. By volume, 84 percent of world footwear exports come from Asia. Europe is a distant second, with 11 percent. The leading five Asian countries (China; Hong Kong SAR, China; Vietnam; Indonesia; and Thailand) together contribute 80.5 percent of world export volume. In 2011, the average export price worldwide reached US$7.39, a 27 percent increase over levels 10 years prior. Asian exports have the lowest average global price (less than US$5 per pair), despite a 35 percent increase over the past decade. Europe charges the highest average export price in the world (nearly US$25 per pair), up 56 percent from a decade prior. Among the leading footwear exporters by value, Italy charges the highest price (US$45.32 per pair), followed by Portugal (US$32.00 per pair). At the other end of the scale, China exports at an average price of only US$3.87 per pair.

By value, China has about 40 percent of the world footwear market (table 4.4) and is followed by Italy and Hong Kong SAR, China. In 2011, footwear world exports exceeded US$100 billion for the first time, up 15 percent from 2010. Asia dominates export value, with the top five Asian countries (China; Hong Kong SAR, China; Vietnam; Indonesia; and India) together comprising more than half the world total. Led by Italy, Germany, and Belgium, the top European producing countries together constitute almost a third of world export value.[5]

Leather's share of global footwear exports reportedly has been on the decline and now represents only 16 percent of the volume and 50 percent of the value of worldwide footwear exports. Rubber and plastic footwear has continued to gain share and now represents 56 percent of total global export volume (APICCAPS 2012).

Bangladesh exports mostly leather footwear, although non-leather footwear is growing. Volume data are unavailable in comparable terms with the rest of

Table 4.3 Top 10 Footwear Exporters, by Quantity, 2011

Rank	*Country*	*Pairs (millions)*	*World share (%)*
1	China	10,170	73.1
2	Hong Kong SAR, China	362	2.6
3	Vietnam	316	2.3
4	Italy	229	1.7
5	Belgium	207	1.5
6	Indonesia	206	1.5
7	Germany	194	1.4
8	Netherlands	143	1.0
9	Thailand	141	1.0
10	Spain	130	0.9

Source: APICCAPS 2012.

the world. Footwear exports totaled US$335 million for FY2012, consisting mostly of leather footwear (US$240 million or 71.5 percent); others included non-leather footwear (US$76.5 million or 22.8 percent) and footwear components (such as soles) (figure 4.2). Non-leather footwear exports have grown 142 percent since FY2009 (when exports totaled US$31.5 million) and outpaced growth in footwear export value as a whole, which grew 83 percent for the same period.[6] Information on the number of pairs exported from Bangladesh is not available and does not appear to be tracked by the government of Bangladesh on customs forms or elsewhere. Export volume, as expressed in official statistics from the Export Promotion Bureau of Bangladesh, reflects total kilograms rather than number of pairs, making it difficult to compare Bangladesh's footwear export volume with other countries, since other countries express volume in terms of pairs exported. On a volume (weight) basis, Bangladesh's total footwear exports grew 54 percent, from 14.8 million kilograms in FY2009 to 22.8 million kilograms in FY2011. Exports of non-leather footwear doubled in the same period, from 3.9 million kilograms in 2008/09 to 7.8 million kilograms in FY2011. The breakdown by HS code for all of Bangladesh's footwear exports in FY2012 is presented in annex 4B.

All of Bangladesh's espadrille production is exported. Two of the top exporting categories include the non-leather espadrille codes reportedly used by the non-leather exporters. Collective exports in the three non-leather categories in which espadrilles are reported[7] rose from US$22 million in FY2009 to US$48 million in FY2012 (figure 4.3).[8] Of the leading non-leather footwear categories, Bangladesh's largest export markets are Spain, the Republic of Korea, and Japan (HS640419); Germany, France, and Spain (HS640220); and France, Italy, and Germany (HS640520) (table 4.5).

Table 4.4 Top 15 Footwear Exporters, by Value, 2011

Rank	*Country*	*Exports (US$ millions)*	*World share (%)*	*Average price (US$)*
1	China	39,374	38.3	3.87
2	Italy	10,376	10.1	45.32
3	Hong Kong SAR, China	5,317	5.2	14.70
4	Vietnam	5,123	5.0	16.20
5	Germany	4,392	4.3	22.66
6	Belgium	4,172	4.1	20.16
7	Indonesia	3,227	3.1	15.65
8	Netherlands	2,933	2.9	20.55
9	Spain	2,870	2.8	22.04
10	France	2,409	2.3	30.18
11	Portugal	2,091	2.0	32.00
12	India	1,421	1.4	12.61
13	United Kingdom	1,400	1.4	15.90
14	Romania	1,391	1.4	24.35
15	Brazil	1,296	1.3	11.47

Source: APICCAPS 2012.

Figure 4.2 Bangladesh's Footwear Exports, FY2008–FY2012

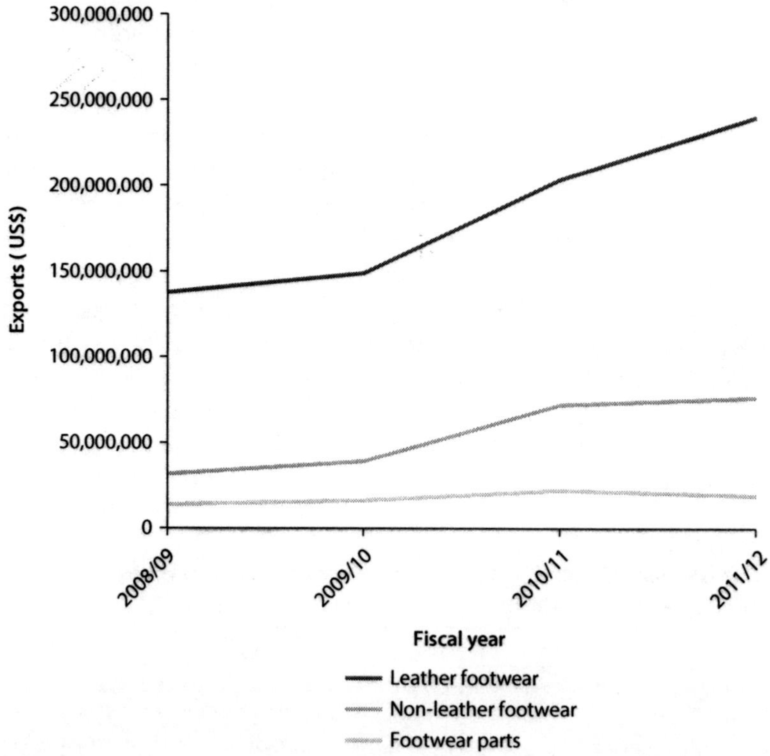

Source: Global Development Solutions, LLC, analysis of data provided by Export Promotion Bureau, Bangladesh.

Figure 4.3 Bangladesh's Exports of HS640419, HS640520, and HS640590, Including Espadrilles, FY2008–FY2012

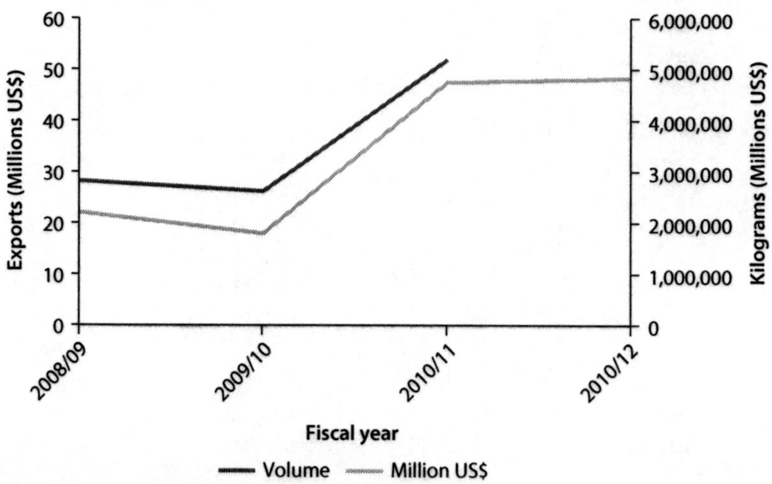

Source: Export Promotion Bureau, Bangladesh.

Regionally, Europe imports the most footwear by value and volume (table 4.6), followed by North America, which is fueled by the U.S. market. As of 2011, the United States was the world's largest footwear buyer, importing 2.3 million pairs worth US$23 billion, representing 22 percent of world market share (tables 4.7 and 4.8). The next leading countries by import quantity are Japan (619 million pairs and 6.0 percent of world import value) and Germany (593 million pairs and 5.8 percent of world value). After the United States, the top importing countries by value are Germany (US$8.7 billion or 8.4 percent of world value) and France (US$6.5 billion or 6.3 percent of world value). In 2007 (the latest year for which import data are available), imports of footwear from Bangladesh totaled US$45.6 million, comprised of leather footwear (US$6.4 million or 14.0 percent), non-leather footwear (US$18.0 million or 39.4 percent), and footwear parts (US$21.3 million or 46.6 percent).[9] Bangladesh reimported US$79,228 in leather footwear, US$16,540 in non-leather footwear, and US$2.2 million in footwear parts, primarily HS640620 (outer soles and heels of rubber or plastic).

Table 4.5 Top 10 Export Markets for Bangladeshi Non-Leather Footwear, Selected Categories, FY2012

	Country	*Exports (US$)*	*Share (%)*
HS640419: Other footwear with outer soles of rubber or plastic and uppers of textile materials			
1	Spain	17,082,560	54.5
2	Korea, Rep.	4,515,405	14.4
3	Japan	3,728,338	11.9
4	France	2,885,626	9.2
5	China	1,062,092	3.4
6	Belgium	758,677	2.4
7	Russian Federation	340,275	1.1
8	Brazil	240,399	0.8
9	Senegal	237,392	0.8
10	Taiwan, China	157,564	0.5
	Other	352,262	1.1
	Total	31,360,591	100.0
HS640220: Footwear of rubber or plastic, upper straps assembled to sole by plugs			
1	Germany	3,440,954	27.6
2	France	3,303,951	26.5
3	Spain	2,836,426	22.7
4	Mexico	898,328	7.2
5	Netherlands	548,033	4.4
6	United Kingdom	442,712	3.5
7	Belgium	357,738	2.9
8	Greece	288,129	2.3
9	Brazil	110,038	0.9
10	Italy	82,733	0.7

table continues next page

Table 4.5 Top 10 Export Markets for Bangladeshi Non-Leather Footwear, Selected Categories, FY2012 *(continued)*

	Country	*Exports (US$)*	*Share (%)*
	Other	161,961	1.3
	Total	12,471,003	100.0
HS640520: Footwear with uppers of textile materials, nes			
1	France	1,343,734	24.2
2	Italy	1,267,486	22.8
3	Germany	857,533	15.5
4	Spain	801,083	14.4
5	United Kingdom	474,348	8.5
6	Belgium	406,365	7.3
7	Portugal	97,882	1.8
8	Sweden	75,065	1.4
9	United States	65,792	1.2
10	Turkey	39,926	0.7
	Other	119,109	2.1
	Total	5,548,323	100.0

Source: Export Promotion Bureau, Bangladesh.
Note: HS = Harmonized System; nes = not elsewhere specified.

Table 4.6 Global Footwear Imports, by Continent, 2011

Continent	*Value (US$, millions)*	*Share (%)*	*Pairs (millions)*	*Share (%)*	*Average price (US$)*
Europe	51,351	49.4	4,078	39.6	12.63
North America	27,990	26.9	2,736	26.6	10.23
Asia	17,899	17.2	2,205	21.4	8.12
South America	3,053	2.9	382	3.7	7.99
Africa	2,108	2.0	724	7.0	2.91
Oceania	1,629	1.6	167	1.6	9.75
Total	104,030	100.0	10,300	100.0	

Source: APICCAPS 2012.

Table 4.7 Top 10 Footwear Importers, by Quantity, 2011

Rank	*Country*	*Pairs (millions)*	*World share (%)*
1	United States	2,302	22.4
2	Japan	619	6.0
3	Germany	593	5.8
4	France	480	4.7
5	United Kingdom	455	4.4
6	Hong Kong SAR, China	425	4.1
7	Italy	358	3.5
8	Spain	354	3.4
9	Russian Federation	256	2.5
10	Netherlands	245	2.4

Source: APICCAPS 2012.

Table 4.8 Top 15 Footwear Importers, by Value, 2011

Rank	*Country*	*Value (US$, millions)*	*World share (%)*	*Average price (US$)*
1	United States	23,245	22.3	10.10
2	Germany	8,717	8.4	14.69
3	France	6,506	6.3	13.55
4	Italy	5,662	5.4	15.83
5	United Kingdom	5,169	5.0	11.35
6	Japan	5,062	4.9	8.17
7	Hong Kong SAR, China	4,850	4.7	11.40
8	Russian Federation	3,940	3.8	15.39
9	Netherlands	3,465	3.3	14.14
10	Spain	2,977	2.9	8.42
11	Belgium	2,322	2.2	11.89
12	Canada	2,089	2.0	12.72
13	Austria	1,596	1.5	21.42
14	Korea, Rep.	1,536	1.5	13.29
15	Switzerland	1,402	1.3	18.72

Source: APICCAPS 2012.

Key Market Drivers and Options for Growth

Bangladesh's non-leather footwear is currently in the non-luxury niche. Therefore, changing consumer attitudes bode well for demand for Bangladeshi shoes. As noted at the World Footwear Conference in November 2011, the global production of footwear is expected to reach 30 billion pairs by 2024, a 150 percent increase over production levels in 1994 of 12 billion pairs (Lee 2011). Demand for high-priced European-manufactured footwear is expected to fall as consumers pare spending in light of tight economic conditions. Demand from several countries, including China, India, the Russian Federation, and parts of the Middle East, for high-end and mid-priced manufactured footwear is expected to be flat in the near term.[10]

International trade of footwear is expected to continue to grow as the supply chain for footwear manufacturing becomes increasingly globalized and high-income countries continue to outsource production to lower-cost countries. As labor costs as well as currency values in China rise and the country moves toward higher-value manufacturing, footwear brands and buyers are shifting production toward lower-cost manufacturing in Asia and, to a lesser extent, Africa. In the near term, China and India are expected to continue their role as the largest producers, although there may be a gradual global shift away from manufacturing in China as international footwear firms seek lower-cost labor. Vietnam's emergence among the top three exporters (by quantity) illustrates how China has become vulnerable to competitors. Bangladesh can be an attractive manufacturing hub because of its competitive labor rates and existing export infrastructure. India's production thus far has been primarily for domestic consumption, as is the case with some other populous countries producing mainly for their internal market (Lee 2011).

Once considered peasant footwear, designer espadrilles are now widely available in many modern interpretations. Although the popularity of espadrilles has ebbed and flowed (boosted notably by Hollywood stars sporting espadrilles in numerous movies and TV shows), today espadrilles are considered a summer staple whose natural material has become synonymous with warm-weather fashion.[11] Espadrille designs include slingback, peeptoe, wedge, and platform styles, sold by value-priced as well as luxury global design houses, such as Burberry, Ferragamo, Marc Jacobs, and Missoni. Espadrilles may retail for more than US$400 per pair, albeit these high-end espadrilles have leather components.[12] The common denominator in all is the jute (or jute rope-like) sole or wrapped midsole. Currently, none of these extremely high-end espadrilles are fully assembled in Bangladesh, although they may be manufactured in countries such as Brazil, France, Italy, or Spain or use Bangladeshi components. One espadrille company in Bangladesh reported to have exported more than one million pairs of completed espadrille subassemblies (jute midsole with vulcanized rubber outsole) to France in the past year, with orders increasing yearly.

Leather's share of the global footwear market is on the decline, for environmental and other reasons. In 2001, leather footwear exports represented approximately 62 percent of value and 34 percent of volume, but by 2011, exports of leather footwear had declined to 50 percent of value and 16 percent of volume (APICCAPS 2012). Reasons for leather's decline include reduced supply caused by drought, increasing cost of animal feed, growing concerns about the ethical treatment of animals, and the adverse environmental effects of the tanning process. Some of these issues resonate in Bangladesh, where the safety and health of workers are major concerns. It is reported that leather workers get little safety training and most tannery workers suffer from diseases resulting from chemical exposure. The same sources report that hundreds of tanneries dump thousands of cubic liters of toxic waste, including cancer-causing chromium, into the Buriganga, the region's main river and central water supply (Chua 2011). As the health and environmental repercussions of tanning become known worldwide, there may be a backlash against use of leather in all products, including footwear, which would benefit the non-leather footwear segment.

Awareness about green fashion is also rising and bodes well for non-leather footwear.[13] Green fashion currently occupies a sliver of the apparel market (less than 1 percent of industry sales), but it is growing. According to Marshal Cohen, chief industry analyst at market research firm NPD Group, 18 percent of consumers are aware that eco-fashion exists, up from 6 percent four years ago (Kuchment 2008). Although most environmentally friendly fashion—whether made from organic cotton, recycled material, or in adherence to fair trade principles—comes at a price premium, there are signs that greener apparel is entering the mainstream and is available at competitive prices.[14] Non-leather footwear emphasizes nonanimal materials and healthy, natural products. In addition to jute, eco-friendly footwear materials globally include cotton (conventional and organic), peace silk (a process that lets silkworms live out their full life cycle) (Kuchment 2008), non-leather composites, cork, hemp, natural rubber, and recycled materials like reclaimed wood, rubber inner tubes and tires, and even a microfiber made from discarded television screens (Yoneda 2010). Cork in particular has triumphed in the non-leather footwear segment under the tutelage of the Portuguese cork industry, which actively sought alternative uses for cork as wine manufacturers turned to synthetic stopper materials (box 4.2). The Portuguese cork case presents competition for Bangladesh as well as an example of how a concerted effort in research, development, and marketing can lead to innovation and success in the eco-friendly niche of footwear.

Box 4.2 Cork: A Study in Footwear Innovation

Starting in the mid-1990s, a number of wine brands switched from cork to alternative wine bottle closures. This shift threatened to affect the cork industry and the economy of Portugal (where 50 percent of all cork originates). The Portuguese Cork Association, research organizations, and the private sector collaborated to develop alternate uses of cork, including construction materials and fashion, while building Portugal's cork brand beyond traditional uses. Today, products including fashion accessories of cork now constitute €40 million (US$54 million) or 8.6 percent of the value of Portuguese cork exports (2010).[a]

An example of a basic wedge sole of cork, similar in style to that made of jute and ethylene vinyl acetate (EVA) foam in Bangladesh, is depicted in photo B4.2.1. The sole provides a lightweight, durable, comfortable, and eco-friendly shoe foundation. Another example includes vegan (nonanimal product) shoes incorporating virgin and/or recycled cork (photo B4.2.2). The shoe uses 35 percent cork in the midsole, a cork-wrapped footbed, hemp, and recycled polyester for the strip and a natural and synthetic rubber blend outsole. Similar to jute footwear, the sole reportedly will mold and conform to the shape of the wearer's feet. By recognizing its natural resource endowments and applying creative design and marketing strategies while promoting the virtues of environmental sustainability, Portugal was able to launch a cork footwear industry within a short time and realize significant economic benefits.

Photo B4.2.1 Cork Sole for Wedge-Heel Shoe

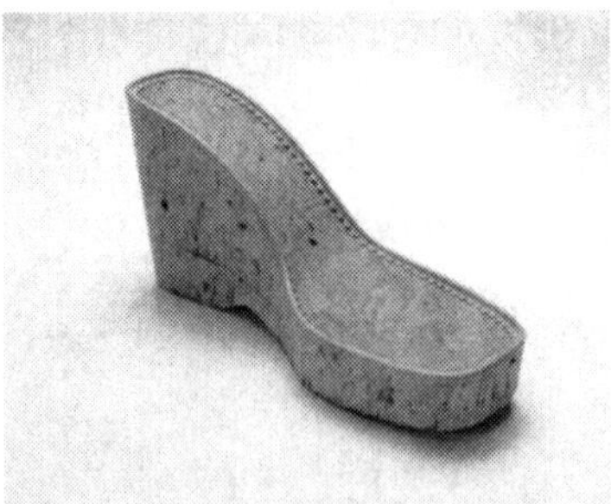

Source: Portuguese Cork Association.
a. APCOR 2011.

Photo B4.2.2 Men's Cork and Hemp Flip Shoe

Source: http://www.orthoticshop.com/sole-casual-flip-flops-mens.html.

With the Generalized System of Preferences (GSP), Bangladesh espadrille manufacturers have an advantage over the Chinese in European markets, but not in the United States. Given Bangladesh's status as a least-developed country, Bangladesh benefits from GSP privileges in most major markets (including Australia, Canada, the European Union, Japan, Korea, and New Zealand) and as such has zero import duty. However, non-leather footwear exports to the United States are subject to an import duty of 36 percent[15]—the leading country in terms of footwear import quantity and value (APICCAPS 2012). Currently, 99 percent of all footwear sold in the United States is imported, of which more than 80 percent is imported from China, a country that has no GSP privileges in the United States.[16] Bangladesh manufacturers report strong competition from China when vying for U.S. market share, with the long-established Chinese offering a greater variety of styles and materials (amounting to one-stop shopping) and faster delivery.[17]

Institutional and Regulatory Environment, Market Structure, and Supply Chain

According to LFMEAB, there are four companies (recently down from five) in Bangladesh that export non-leather shoes.[18] Of these four, three can be classified as large firms (more than 250 permanent employees, assets of at least US$122,000) with the fourth company on the cusp between medium and large. All four companies boasted strong annual sales growth of over 20 percent for the past several years. A fifth manufacturer, and most recent entrant, exited the espadrille market in 2011, but it continues to operate in the footwear sector.[19] The sector also includes a multitude of small and micro companies that are available to the larger firms during peak season. These smaller entities may be an individual working from home or a group of individual producers coordinated by a contractor (acting either as a subcontractor to the large companies to handle peak season overflow or directly filling local orders for simple shoes, such as PVC/PU shoes and sandals). By the nature of its organization, it is not possible to quantify the number of entities in the subsector, although overall worker estimates in the non-leather footwear sector were quoted at around 30,000 people.[20]

There is no current foreign direct investment (FDI) in the espadrille sector, but export processing zones (EPZs), particularly in Chittagong, have received FDI in non-leather footwear. Some foreign assistance has been provided to local espadrille manufacturers in the past. For example, a private French company assisted one of the manufacturers in setting up its espadrille manufacturing operations. The espadrille producer purchased machinery in France and the French company aided in setting up and training. Although there is no EPZ specifically for footwear, there are footwear companies (not specifically non-leather) in the three EPZs, as shown in table 4.9. However, espadrille producers and representatives from the Bangladesh Export Processing Zones Authority indicate that espadrilles are not produced by companies operating

Table 4.9 Footwear Manufacturers in Bangladesh EPZs, 2012

	Name of firm	*Location*	*Type*[a]	*Employment*
1	M/s Cosmos Shoes Ind. Ltd.	Chittagong EPZ	A	565
2	M/s Patenga Footwear Ltd.	Chittagong EPZ	A	782
3	M/s QSM BD Ltd.	Chittagong EPZ	A	436
4	M/s Young One Shoes Accessories Ltd.	Chittagong EPZ	A	1,057
5	M/s Young One Shoes Ind. Ltd.	Chittagong EPZ	A	6,593
6	M/s Papella Ltd.	Chittagong EPZ	B	420
7	M/s Excelsior Shoes Ind. Ltd.	Chittagong EPZ	B	1,413
8	M/s MS Shoes Ind. Ltd.	Chittagong EPZ	C	89
9	Bangladesh Pou Hung Industrial	Karnaphuli EPZ, Chittagong	A	1,477
10	Paolo Footwear (BD) Ltd.	Karnaphuli EPZ, Chittagong	A	912
11	Xin Chang Shoes (BD) Limited	Karnaphuli EPZ, Chittagong	A	1,036
12	M/s Savar Industry (Pvt) Ltd.	Dhaka EPZ	C	229

Source: Bangladesh Export Processing Zones Authority.
Note: BD = Bangladesh; Pvt = private.
a. Type: A = 100 percent foreign owned; B = Bangladesh and foreign investor joint venture; C = 100 percent Bangladeshi owned.

in the EPZ. Nonetheless, industries tend to form informal clusters in geographic areas where labor with relevant skills and know-how is concentrated. For example, the Comilla EPZ is in close proximity to a large concentration of espadrille producers.

There is limited focus on non-leather footwear from public and private institutions. The institutional support and supply chain structure as well as roles and responsibilities of various participants in non-leather footwear in Bangladesh are detailed in figure 4.4 and tables 4.10 and 4.11. LFMEAB was established in 2003 and lobbies for policies and regulations that support its members, which include leather and non-leather footwear companies. Its official mandate omits reference to non-leather footwear, although it has jurisdiction over such products through the government requirement that non-leather footwear export certificates be generated by LFMEAB. Moreover, a non-leather footwear member serves on the board of the association. The association undertakes no apparent marketing activities on behalf of its members. There is no evidence of support provided to the non-leather footwear sector by donors or nongovernmental organizations.

Footwear (leather and non-leather) was designated a priority sector by the government of Bangladesh in 2009. As such, the sector is entitled to the following benefits: (a) bonded warehouse facilities; (b) 100 percent duty drawback for reexported inputs; (c) 1.5 percent income tax (compared with 15 percent for nonpriority sectors); and (d) tax-free import of capital equipment. In addition, leather footwear exports receive a 12.5 percent export subsidy targeted toward the export of finished leather goods. In reality, the duty drawback is not much for espadrilles, considering the high local content of the shoes (greater than 75 percent). However, vertically integrated manufacturers that operate jute mills receive a 10 percent jute export subsidy as processors of jute. This can affect a potential entrant into the sector, if it does not operate a jute-processing mill.

In the international arena, Bangladesh is absent from membership in the International Footwear Conference (Lan 2012). At the global level, institutions such as the World Footwear Congress and the International Footwear Conference meet periodically (every three years and every year,

Figure 4.4 Institutional Support and Supply Chain Structure for Non-Leather Footwear in Bangladesh

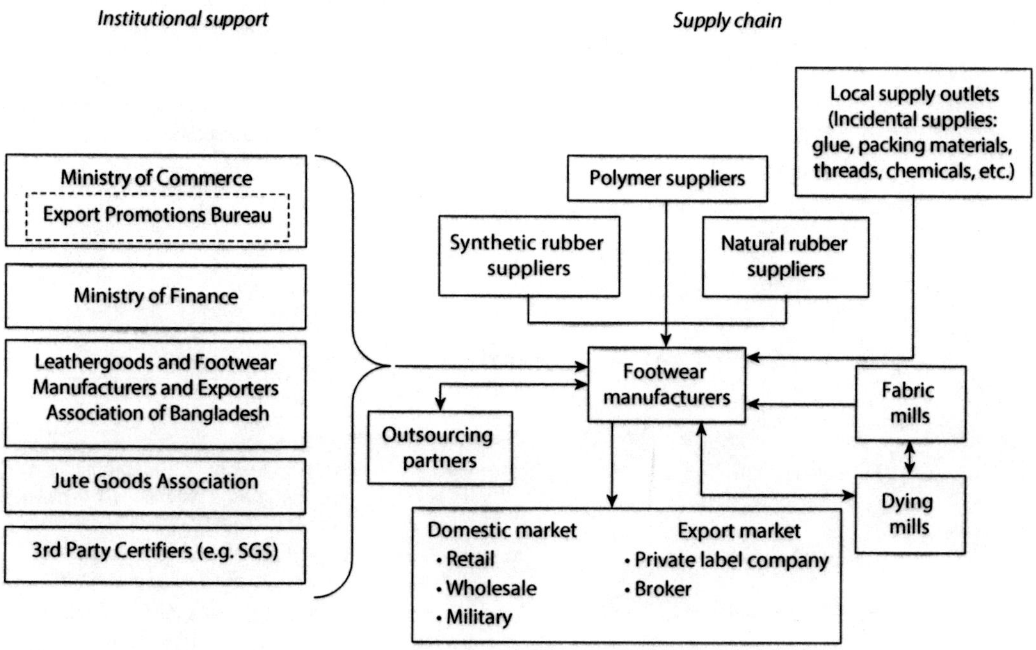

Source: Global Development Solutions, LLC.
Note: SGS = Société Générale de Surveillance (http://www.sgs.com/).

Table 4.10 Specific Support Institutions and Their Support Activities for Footwear

Institution	*Support activity*
Leathergoods & Footwear Manufacturers & Exporters Association of Bangladesh (LFMEAB) (www.lfmeab.org)	Established in 2003, the stated aim of the association is to "establish a healthy business environment for a close and mutually beneficial relationship between the local manufacturers and exporters of leather footwear and leather goods and foreign buyers."
	Member companies include: footwear (32), leather goods (12), and espadrille and others (3).[a] Membership is not required for footwear producers, but it is required for footwear exporters.
	There is a one-time registration fee of Tk 23,000 (US$240) and the annual membership fee is also Tk 23,000.
	The association is the only authorized body for issuing the certificates required for each consignment (shipment) of footwear export:

table continues next page

Table 4.10 Specific Support Institutions and Their Support Activities for Footwear *(continued)*

Institution	*Support activity*
	Export Certificate (Tk 300 or US$3.65)
	Realization of Export Certificate (Tk 300)
	Generalized System of Preferences (GSP) Certificate (as needed, for exports to the European Union and other GSP markets) (Tk 300).
Jute Goods Association (JGA)	Given that jute is a significant component of some non-leather shoes, some footwear manufacturers are members of the JGA so that they can receive support regarding quality control of jute raw material. Further, two of the four espadrille producers are jute millers as well and as such are members of either the Bangladesh Jute Spinners Association or the Bangladesh JGA. Jute processors are entitled to a 10 percent export subsidy on their jute products and the certification for these exports is provided by either one of these two associations.
3rd party certifiers	When required by a buyer, SGS tests dyes for banned chemicals (dimethyl fumariate and the AZO group of chemicals).

Source: Global Development Solutions, LLC.
Note: SGS = Société Générale de Surveillance (http://www.sgs.com/).
a. LFMEAB, http://www.lfmeab.org.

Table 4.11 Supply Chain Stakeholders and Their Activities

Supply chain stakeholders	*Activities*
Footwear producers	As described in section above
Outsourcing partners	Provide services to main producers but do not produce entire shoes. For example, in the case of espadrilles, partners will glue and stitch the upper to the subassembly.
Local supply outlets	Numerous suppliers throughout Dhaka and surroundings supply incidentals, chemicals, and dyes to the sector.
Natural and synthetic rubber suppliers	While there are said to be about 100 natural rubber suppliers within the Dhaka vicinity, synthetic rubber is available from about a dozen suppliers. Synthetic rubber is imported; natural rubber is indigenous.
Fabric mills	There are approximately a dozen local fabric mills from which companies can source canvas. If necessary, producers claim they can also import the canvas directly, although this is not practiced.
Dying facilities	Canvas can be sourced gray or colored. If it is gray, the producer will color the fabric as necessary. One of the significant problems in the non-leather footwear sector is the inability to dye small amounts of fabric. Footwear producers claim that a minimum order of 5,000 meters is required.

Source: Global Development Solutions, LLC.

respectively) to discuss industry issues. The International Footwear Conference meets annually in an Asian country. All member countries of the conference currently are Asian (China; Hong Kong SAR, China; India; Indonesia; Japan; Korea; Malaysia; the Philippines; Taiwan, China; Thailand; and Vietnam).

Integrated Value Chain Analysis for Non-Leather Footwear

Espadrilles have been identified by LFMEAB as the only type of non-leather footwear being exported in significant quantity from outside the EPZs.[21] What is termed by the sector as the "basic shoe" (in photo 4.1, second from right, lower row) was recommended by producers as a proxy to represent the sector for value chain analysis. Espadrilles traditionally are a casual, flat shoe, but increasingly can be found in high heel or wedge fashion styles. They usually have a cotton canvas or jute fabric upper and flexible sole made of rope or rubber material. The natural golden color found in high-quality jute is a major design feature of modern espadrilles.

As a producer of high-quality jute, Bangladesh has become a manufacturing center for premium quality jute soles and complete espadrilles. The shoe design originated in the Pyrenees (Spain and France), but today espadrilles are made in full or in part in several countries. It is possible that much or most of the world's total production of complete espadrilles is manufactured in Bangladesh,[22] while manufacturers in France, Italy, and Spain import jute soles from Bangladesh to finish espadrilles in those countries. Complete espadrilles are also manufactured in Argentina, Bolivia, Colombia, Paraguay, and República Bolivariana de Venezuela.

The manufacturing process for espadrilles is generally complex. The soles are created by machine-braiding jute twine[23]; these braids then are manually formed into the shape of the sole, pressed to form the final shape, and then completed with vertical stitching (photo 4.2). Rubber is vulcanized with chemicals, cut into slugs, fitted into the sole forms, and then hot pressed onto the jute to serve as the outer sole. When making a wedged heel, ethylene vinyl acetate (EVA) foam or

Photo 4.1 Sample Espadrille Styles

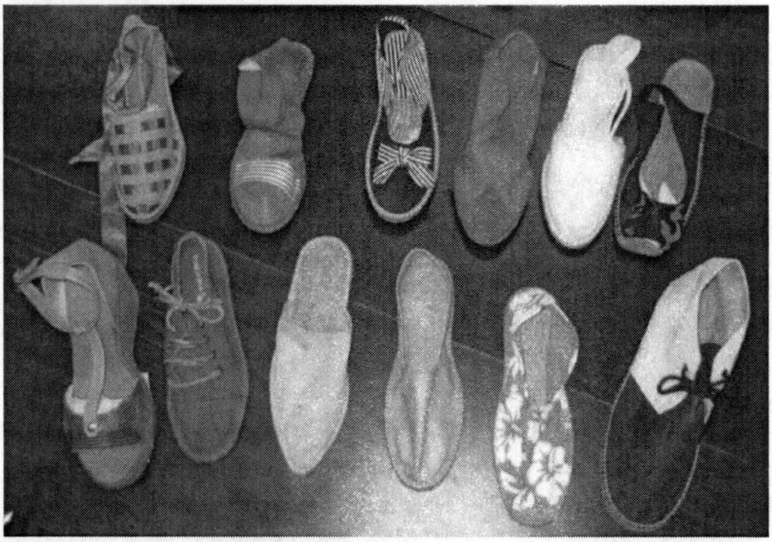

Source: Global Development Solutions, LLC.

Photo 4.2 Comparing Jute Soles of Different Quality

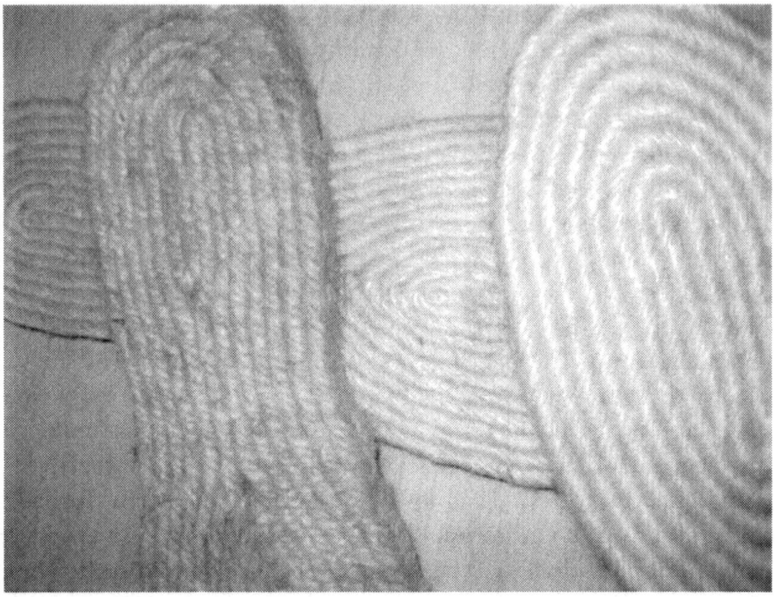

Source: Global Development Solutions, LLC.
Note: Different grades of jute were used for producing each of the soles. The sole on the left is of the lowest quality. Notice color variation with specs of black, gray, and brown (remnants of bark) and fuzziness around the edges. The underlying sole is of good quality but not as good as the sole on the right. The sole on the right has the bright golden glow that is indicative of high-quality jute.

wooden heels (wood is not used in Bangladesh) are glued in place and more jute braids are wrapped around the wedge to complete the soles. Uppers of different styles are then built (typically glued and then stitched) onto the subassembly. Decorative stitching or accessories may be incorporated to complete the espadrille. The basic shoe uses the same rubber sole mold for the right and left feet, while the high-fashion espadrilles require different molds for each foot, as well as for multiple sizes (photo 4.3). Generally, high-fashion espadrilles require as many as 20 different molds per style. For example, molds for six different sizes of one style would require an investment of Tk 2 million (US$25,000). However, the life expectancy of a mold is 18–20 years, and the mold can be used with a variety of upper designs and fabrics. High-fashion designs fetch upward of US$6.50 per pair, with some styles as much as US$25 (free on board [FOB]). Basic espadrilles generally sell for an FOB price of less than US$2.

The unit cost of producing an espadrille in Bangladesh is approximately Tk 105 (US$1.28) per pair, excluding margins and the cost of transportation to port. Given the unpredictable cost fluctuation associated with electricity and fuel costs, it is common practice for manufacturers to include an additional 10 percent contingency cost as part of the production cost. Including the contingency cost, the production cost of basic espadrilles ranges between Tk 114 and Tk 120 (US$1.39–US$1.46) per pair. Each pair of basic espadrilles takes 10–14 minutes to produce. The primary value chain for the production of espadrilles is divided into five major stages: subassembly, upper preparation, mounting, finishing and inspection, and packing (figure 4.5).

The value chain analysis suggests that raw material is the primary cost driver for the production of espadrilles in Bangladesh. Subassembly accounts for nearly 60 percent of the total value chain for the production of an espadrille. Further breakdown of the value chain for subassembly shows that jute preparation and the midsole and outer sole account for more than 97 percent of subassembly costs. As figure 4.5 indicates, raw material inputs, namely jute and rubber, account for more than 75 percent of the total subassembly cost. The second highest cost associated with espadrille production is the preparation of uppers, which accounts for nearly 25 percent of the total production cost. Similar to the subassembly, the breakdown of the upper preparation costs points to input material as the highest cost driver in the value chain.

Photo 4.3 Espadrille Shoes and Features

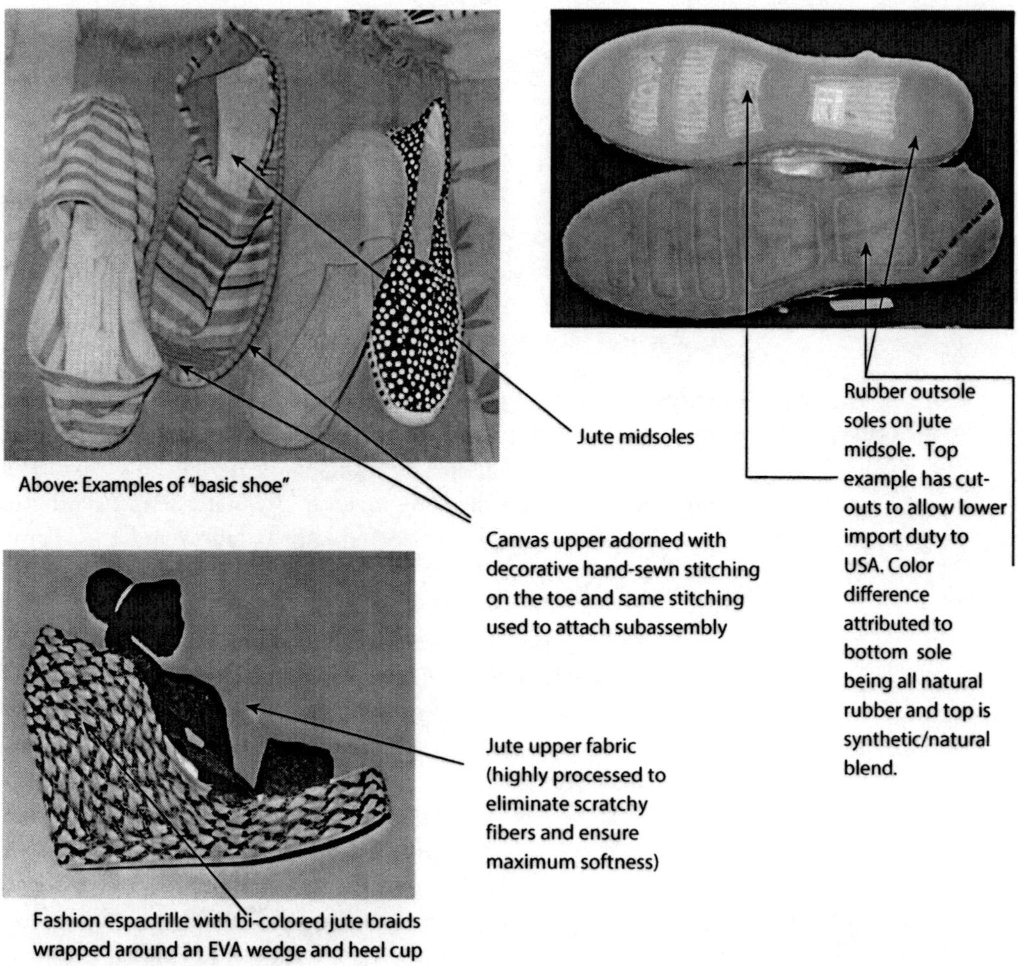

Global development solutions, LLC

Figure 4.5 Value Chain for Basic Shoe (Espadrille)

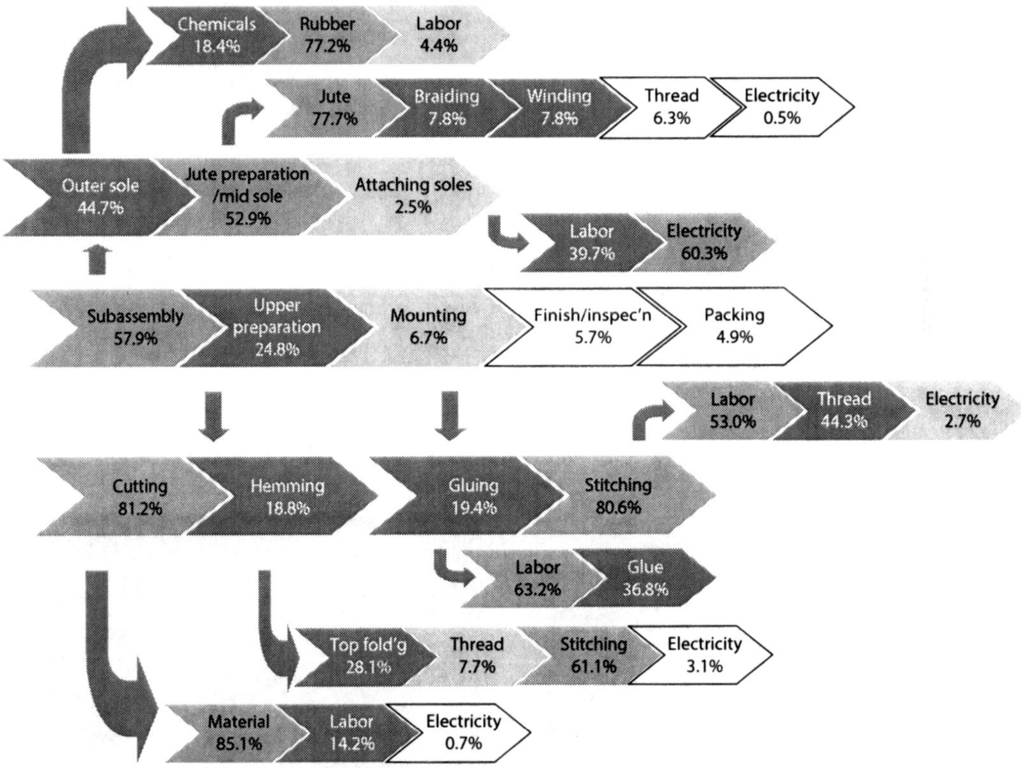

Source: Global Development Solutions, LLC.

Buyers generally specify the type of material, color, and ratio of imported synthetic to natural rubber to be used for the rubber soles, but overall espadrilles are made of 75–100 percent locally available material. Raw materials used in producing the basic espadrille shoe include jute, natural and synthetic rubber, thread for the subassembly, and cotton canvas fabric and thread for the upper.[24]

- A pair of jute midsoles requires approximately 250 grams of jute yarn at a cost of Tk 90–Tk 100 (US$1.10–US$1.22) per kilogram. Upper fabric is often dyed to order given customer color requirements, so, with the exception of standard traditional colors (those not subject to style trends, such as black), it is not typically stockpiled.
- The cost of upper fabric ranges widely according to style, but a basic espadrille requires approximately 0.1 square meter of dyed fabric at a cost of about Tk 18 (US$0.23) per pair. Dyes, if purchased by the footwear producer as opposed to purchasing dyed fabric, typically are sourced from China and Germany and, when required, are tested by a third-party certifier (such as SGS) for banned substances such as dimethyl fumariate, and the AZO group of chemicals.

Testing costs US$63 per color and is done at the request of the buyer and does not occur for all orders. Depending on the purchase contract, the cost of testing can be paid by the buyer or the footwear manufacturer or the cost is shared.

- The third major raw material for the production of basic espadrilles is rubber. Generally, buyers specify the ratio of synthetic and natural rubber to be used. Synthetic rubber is imported at a cost of approximately Tk 457 (US$5.57) per kilogram and natural rubber is available through the local market at a cost of about Tk 300 (US$3.66) per kilogram. The production of a basic espadrille requires approximately 0.125 kilogram of rubber per pair at a cost of approximately Tk 21 (US$0.26).[25]

The labor cost advantage over China—combined with locally available jute, fabric, and rubber—creates a substantial competitive advantage for Bangladesh's manufacturers over its largest market rival, China. Labor costs across the production and packing process add 23.5 percent (US$0.33) to the total cost of espadrille production. The monthly salary for unskilled factory workers is approximately Tk 4,000 (US$49), while skilled workers earn Tk 9,000–Tk 12,000 (US$73–US$146). These wages in the footwear sector are comparable to those earned in Vietnam and are markedly lower than those in China—ranging from 14 percent (high end of the range for unskilled workers) to 33 percent (low end of the range for skilled workers) of Chinese wages (see table 4.12). A large producer may have 450 permanent employees with as many as 1,200 shop floor workers per shift, working three shifts per day during the peak production season (August–March). There is a low average supervisor-to-worker ratio (1:40), given that the reported in-line defect rate and client rejection rates are low (less than 1.5 percent). According to interviews, line supervisors practice spot in-line rework.

Espadrille manufacturing is not a utility-intensive process, but the industry suffers from erratic electricity supply. The production process for a basic espadrille consumes only Tk 1.5 (US$0.018) of electricity per pair.[26] The bulk of this electricity cost (60 percent) is attributed to the process of hot pressing the rubber onto the jute to form the subassembly. However, the country's power supply is erratic. Thus, many firms rely on generators, which leads to increased production costs. Specifically, load-shedding can occur anywhere from one to four hours

Table 4.12 Wage Comparisons, Selected Countries
US dollars

Labor	*China*	*Vietnam*[a]	*Ethiopia*	*Tanzania*	*Bangladesh*
Skilled	286–562	119–140	41–96	160–200	109–146
Unskilled	237–488	78–93	16–33	80–140	49–73

Source: Global Development Solutions, LLC.
Note: With the exception of Bangladesh, all data were collected in 2011, reflecting average worker wages in the leather shoe manufacturing sector in each of the countries indicated.
a. Data for Vietnam reflect assembly cost only.

each day, requiring producers to rely on generators at a cost of approximately Tk 1,830 (US$22.32) per hour to operate a 500 kilovolt generator.[27] When the generators are running heavily, which was reported to be every other hour during the summer months in 2012, the cost of electricity increases by two to three times and the total electricity bill per pair was approximately US$0.054. Although the operating cost of a generator is generally manageable for most producers, the initial investment cost and access to finance to purchase a generator is generally prohibitive for small producers.

There are frequent retroactive electricity rate hikes. Four rate hikes took place in the six months from April to September 2012. The latest hike was in March 2014, when the average retail tariff for small industries and commercial users increased by 8.14 and 6.49 percent, respectively. According to the Bangladesh Power Development Board, these increases are still not enough to cover the cost of power generation, so enterprises expect the rates to continue to rise. Given the gap between cost and prices of electricity, such hikes can be expected. However, the lack of predictability of rate hikes makes cash flow and financial planning difficult for producers.

Large firms rely on local subcontractors to meet demand during the high season. They produce as much as 1.5 million pairs of basic espadrilles and 150,000 pairs of various high-fashion espadrilles throughout the year. Since most of these orders are received during the peak season, a short period of time, producers must regularly rely on local subcontractors. Examples of this are sewing uppers onto the completed sole subassembly (performed manually) or sewing elaborate decorations (such as sequins and beads) onto uppers. Although the current subcontracting structure with individuals and microenterprises creates employment opportunities for local workers, the informal nature of the relationship and the lack of a structured subcontracting supply chain inhibit producers from responding effectively to large production orders. The bulk of this outsourcing is received by individuals working from homes or through representatives of a group of such individuals. Alternatively, the larger company brings these smaller shoemakers onto its premises on a temporary contract. If a smaller company has a desire to participate more independently in the sector, it is possible to purchase completed sole subassemblies and perform the remainder of the necessary work—upper cutting, folding, hemming, stitching, and finishing—to complete a shoe.

Footwear manufacturers must compete for access to fabric from domestic producers in a competitive and tight market. As a major exporter of ready-to-wear garments, demand for textile fabric in Bangladesh is high, not only from domestic garment producers, but also from foreign markets, which account for more than three times the demand compared with domestic demand for knit and woven fabric. For example, the projected demand for fabric in 2014–15 was estimated to be about 15,712 million meters, of which 4,123 million meters were expected to be absorbed by the domestic market. Moreover, as of 2009, there were 363 spinning and 1,131 weaving mills operating in Bangladesh (table 4.13), producing fabrics to meet the growing

Table 4.13 Textile Production Capacity in Bangladesh

Process	*Mills*	*Equipment*	*Production capacity*
Spinning	363	9.36 million spindles	1.7 billion kilograms
Weaving	1,131	48,659 shuttle looms	2 million meters
Dyeing and finishing	359		6 million meters equivalent

Source: Chowdhury 2009.

domestic and export demand. However, in the absence of further investment, given the current installed capacity, the country could face a shortfall of more than 6,455 million meters by 2014–15.

As a consequence, footwear manufacturers are required to have a minimum order size of 5,000 meters of fabric. This amount of fabric can produce as many as 35,000 pairs of basic espadrilles. But the average order size received by large producers ranges from 15,000 to 20,000 pairs per consignment, thus creating a challenge for producers to figure out what to do with the remaining material. Canvas fabric used in making espadrilles is seldom incorporated into a shoe in its natural color. Colors are critical when considering apparel of all kinds, particularly in the fashion-conscious, international women's footwear market. Fashion is, however, fickle and colors change year to year. Thus, producers must only purchase what they need to fill their orders.

Espadrille producers in Bangladesh have been confined to selling basic espadrilles at the low end of the market, given the challenges associated with timely access to special-order dyed fabrics. However, high-fashion designs fetch three to 12 times the value of a basic espadrille. China, by contrast, is more prevalent in fashion because there are many fabric producers and dyed material fabric is readily available in virtually any quantity desired. Interviews with manufacturers suggest that even if a particularly unique color is not available, it can be produced within one week in China. It is this fact that lends China a competitive advantage over Bangladesh in the U.S. market.

Footwear manufacturers point to further challenges in the supply chain. First, there is no forum in which footwear and fabric manufacturers can discuss upcoming trends and fabric needs. As a consequence, there is no systematic approach to supply and stock management in the fabric-to-footwear supply chain. Second, in the absence of up-to-date intelligence on market demand and trends in key markets, particularly in the EU market, nearly all the orders received by Bangladesh footwear manufacturers occur during trade shows. With a 90-day order-to-delivery window from EU footwear buyers, this leaves little advance notice for fabric manufacturers to plan their production once they receive an order from footwear manufacturers. As a result, delivery of fabric takes as long as 60 days, thus regularly leaving footwear manufacturers to subcontract production rather than optimizing their own production facility.

These and several other factors help prevent existing espadrille producers from diversifying their product mix to the high-value and more lucrative fashion market. These factors include (a) absence of advanced intelligence on demand

and market trends; (b) short-notice orders for fabrics resulting in slow fabric delivery, inducing footwear manufacturers into a piecemeal subcontracting situation with individual producers; and (c) no dynamic supply chain between fabric producers and espadrille manufacturers, because they cannot plan production schedules in advance.

Small companies face entry barriers. Jute-based products receive an export subsidy of 10 percent but espadrilles cannot collect this subsidy as long as they are classified along with the general footwear sector. Two of the four major espadrille producers have backward links to the jute-processing sector. This allows these companies to take advantage of the 10 percent jute export subsidy, thus providing them with a built-in advantage over new entrants that do not have an integrated operation in the jute sector. Unless new market entrants also operate jute mills (either spinning or weaving), they face a 10 percent cost disadvantage against existing market players. The two companies that are not vertically integrated are the longest-standing companies in the espadrille sector and, as such, have a well-established client base that is unwilling to switch to a lower-cost producer. This market and policy structure creates a barrier to all new entrants that are not vertically integrated with the jute sector. It is an example of incentive policies having unintended entry barriers.

Duty drawback and/or subsidy payments can take up to a year, contributing to cash flow pressures for new entrants. However, in the case of espadrilles, considering that local content is greater than 75 percent, producers often do not make the effort to claim the duty drawback. Manufacturers claim that the delay is so long that the amount is not significant enough to expend the effort in applying for the drawback. In addition, financing is not easy for potential entrants. It seems to be generally available to those with a preestablished banking relationship; relationships initially are established through personal or political connections and are not dependent on viable business plans or creditworthiness.

Trade logistics constraints hurt exporters' efficiency. Most trade documents continue to be processed manually. This causes inefficiency, given multiple inspections, and encourages bribes to complete document stamps and signatures. Most companies must send a representative to the port when shipping a consignment. Without this representative, companies indicate that the consignment is ignored and the goods will not move. Moreover, including travel time, it takes a company representative two to three days to clear a consignment in person at the port, at a cost of about Tk 2,000 per consignment. From the export perspective, the average order size for large producers is between 15,000 and 20,000 pairs per consignment, but the loading capacity of a 20-foot container is approximately 28,000 pairs. As a consequence, exporters must identify consolidated shipping opportunities to minimize shipping costs, which generally requires time and resources.

Foreign travel limitations create difficulties for accessing international supply chain networks and participating in international trade shows outside Bangladesh. Travel visas reportedly are difficult to obtain unless the traveler has a history of international travel. This limits marketing ability and skews participation toward existing firms and new entrants with international travel history. Moreover, the cost of attending conferences and trade shows in dominant shoe import markets (such as Europe) is high. Despite footwear being declared a priority sector, Bangladesh had no representation at the 31st International Footwear Conference held in March 2012 in the Philippines—reportedly the largest gathering of major Asian shoe manufacturers.

A concerted country-level marketing effort is needed to attract foreign investors and buyers to relocate manufacturing from China to Bangladesh. However, lack of production and trade data makes strategic benchmarking and planning difficult and causes Bangladesh to be off the radar of many international databases, limiting the country's marketing reach. There is little to no current, readily available information regarding the non-leather footwear subsector for the following reasons: (a) espadrille exports are categorized across several different HS codes, making it impossible to track the total volume of espadrille exports and (b) export data continue to be tracked by weight rather than pairs, making it impossible to conduct relevant market analysis.

Policy Recommendations

Bangladesh is highly competitive in the espadrille market and this could be a major niche area in the future, providing a substantial number of low-skilled to highly skilled jobs. To enhance competitiveness, Bangladesh could reduce and eliminate its own policy distortions, including removing entry barriers, and capitalize on the trend toward non-leather footwear. It can encourage further local value added and move into higher-quality and higher-value product markets. Policy actions in this context should be seen together with those for diversified jute products.

The government should move toward a more neutral policy regime that does not discriminate between types of raw material or by extent of vertical integration. The government provides subsidies to leather footwear exporters and for exports of jute mills. However, espadrille manufacturers that are not integrated into jute weaving or spinning do not get this subsidy. The government should conduct a review of all cash and other fiscal incentives, with a view to providing a more coherent, transparent, and predictable set of incentives. The incentives should incorporate a firm sunset clause, so that industry, while enjoying certainty of the regime, can plan to work without the incentives.

Market research and advocacy should be supported to spur extended use of jute in footwear, including through development partner support.[28] The non-leather footwear sector can benefit from a wide array of colorful uppers, particularly in moving toward higher value-added espadrilles. Although at present the uppers for virtually all espadrilles are of cotton canvas, market research in selected target countries with high purchasing volume of espadrilles (such as the European Union, Japan, and the United States) can help to determine consumer response to diversified jute fabric uppers for espadrilles, particularly higher-fashion designs. Ongoing market research can help manufacturers anticipate fashion trends for designs, colors, and patterns. Advocacy tools can help to encourage consumers in key import markets to rely increasingly on natural and environmentally friendly fibers such as jute. These are areas where development partners can help Bangladesh, potentially also bringing other exporting countries into the alliance to help expand market demand.

Exporters should be helped to link up with buyers and the international supply chain. This can potentially be a partnership among the private sector, development partners, and the Export Promotion Bureau.

Corresponding with the proposal for jute fabrics in the jute products section, support could be envisaged for fabrics for espadrille uppers. The analysis presented in this chapter indicates that the fabric constraint could be a critical one for expanding production and entering higher-value segments. Creative ways to overcome this constraint are needed, including encouraging private sector cooperative solutions, or a government-supported fabric bank.

Some of these proposals possibly could be supported by a dedicated non-leather footwear marketing board, provided that it is set up under strict conditions with an expiry clause if it does not perform according to its performance agreement. Its mandate could include the following tasks:

- Promote awareness of Bangladesh's non-leather footwear manufacturing capabilities to external markets.
- Act as an information conduit regarding global trends and fashions, upcoming trade fairs, and similar international functions.
- Be authorized to issue export certificates.
- Brand Bangladesh as the up-and-coming source for non-leather footwear, particularly espadrilles, and introduce canvas tennis shoes and similar items such as hand-sewn canvas moccasins (for example, canvas boat shoes).
- Help proactively organize non-leather footwear buyers' missions to Bangladesh.
- Help bring attention and support to the non-leather subsector, which currently is part of LFMEAB, where its needs are overshadowed by those of leather footwear.
- Manage the marketing portal and provide recommendations for constituents' web designs.

Annex 4A: Footwear Classifications

In examining the global footwear market, this analysis references the Harmonized Commodity Description and Coding System (HS), as noted in tables 4A.1 and 4A.2. Generally, the four-digit HS codes fall along the lines of waterproof (HS6401), rubber and plastic (HS6402), leather (HS6403), textile (HS6404), and other (HS6505). But in practice, at the six-digit level, the HS codes note a combination of leather and non-leather materials, confounding the issue of leather versus non-leather footwear classification.

Table 4A.1 Harmonized Commodity Description and Coding System for Footwear

Two-digit code	*Four-digit code*	*Six-digit code*
64: Footwear, gaiters and the like, parts thereof	6401: Waterproof footwear, outer sole & upper of rubber or plastic, bonded sole (not fixed to sole nor assembled)	640110 Waterproof footwear incorporating a protective metal cap
		640191 Waterproof footwear covering the knee
		640192 Waterproof footwear covering the ankle
		640199 Other waterproof footwear with outer soles, uppers of rubber or plastic
	6402: Footwear nes, outer soles and uppers of rubber or plastics	640211 Ski boots, cross-country ski footwear
		640219 Other sports footwear, outer soles and uppers of rubber or plastic
		640220 Footwear with upper straps assembled to the sole by means of plugs
		640230 Other footwear, incorporating a protective metal toe cap
		640291 Other footwear covering the ankle
		640299 Other footwear with outer soles and uppers of rubber or plastic
	6403: Footwear, outer sole rubber, plastic, or leather and leather upper	640311 Ski boots, cross-country ski footwear, uppers of leather
		640319 Other sports footwear, uppers of leather
		640320 Footwear with outer soles and uppers of leather
		640330 Footwear made on a base or platform of wood, uppers of leather
		640340 Other footwear, incorporating a protective metal toe cap
		640351 Footwear with outer soles and uppers of leather, covering the ankle
		640359 Other footwear with outer soles and uppers of leather
		640391 Footwear, covering the ankle, with uppers of leather
		640399 Other footwear with uppers of leather
	6404: Footwear, outer sole rubber, plastic, or leather and textile upper	640411 Sports footwear with outer soles of rubber or plastic
		640419 Other footwear with outer soles of rubber or plastic
		640420 Footwear with outer soles of leather or composition leather
	6405: Footwear, nes	640510 Other footwear with uppers of leather or composition leather
		640520 Other footwear with uppers of textile materials
		640590 Other footwear
	6406: Parts of footwear; insoles, heel cushion, etc.; gaitors, etc., parts	640610 Uppers and parts thereof, other than stiffeners
		640620 Outer soles and heels, of rubber or plastic
		640691 Parts of footwear, of wood
		640699 Parts of footwear, of other materials, other than wood

Source: Foreign-Trade.com.
Note: nes = not elsewhere specified.

Table 4A.2 Non-Leather Footwear Classifications

HS code	*Product*
6401	Waterproof footwear, outer sole & upper of rubber or plastic, bonded sole (not fixed to sole nor assembled)
6402	Footwear nes, outer soles and uppers of rubber or plastic
640411	Sports footwear with outer soles of rubber or plastic and uppers of textile materials
640419	Other footwear with outer soles of rubber or plastic and uppers of textile materials
640520	Footwear, nes/other footwear with uppers of textile materials
650590	Footwear, nes/other footwear

Source: Foreign-Trade.com.
Note: nes = not elsewhere specified.

Annex 4B: Bangladesh Footwear, All Categories, FY2012

	Total exports		*Leather*		*Non-leather*	
HS code and description	*US$*	*Total (%)*	*US$*	*Total (%)*	*US$*	*Total (%)*
6401: Waterproof footwear, outer sole/upper of rubber/plastic upper not fixed to sole	*53,681*	*0.0*	—	*0.0*	*53,681*	*0.1*
640110: Waterproof footwear, outer sole/upper of rubber/plastic, metal toe cap	33,231	0.0	—	0.0	33,231	0.1
640192: Waterproof footwear, outer sole/upper of rubber/plastic covering ankle not knee, nes	20,294	0.0	—	0.0	20,294	0.0
640199: Waterproof footwear, outer sole/upper of rubber or plastics, nes	156	0.0	—	0.0	156	0.0
6402: Footwear nes, outer soles and uppers of rubber or plastic	*22,612,918*	*7.1*	—	*0.0*	*22,612,918*	*34.7*
640212: Ski boots, snowboard boots, all rubber/plastic	27,818	0.0	—	0.0	27,818	0.0
640219: Sports footwear, outer soles and uppers of rubber or plastic, nes	4,779,139	1.5	—	0.0	4,779,139	7.3
640220: Footwear of rubber or plastic, upper straps assembled to sole by plugs	12,471,003	3.9	—	0.0	12,471,003*	19.2
640291: Footwear, outer soles/uppers of rubber or plastic, covering ankle, nes	958,477	0.3	—	0.0	958,477	1.5
640299: Footwear, outer soles/uppers of rubber or plastic, nes	4,376,481	1.4	—	0.0	4,376,481	6.7

table continues next page

Annex 4B *(continued)*

HS code and description	*Total exports*		*Leather*		*Non-leather*	
	US$	*Total (%)*	*US$*	*Total (%)*	*US$*	*Total (%)*
6403: Footwear, upper of leather	*233,983,490*	*73.9*	*233,983,490*	*97.5*	*—*	*0.0*
640312: Ski boots, snowboard boots, uppers of leather	5,000,169	1.6	5,000,169	2.1	—	0.0
640319: Sports footwear, other than ski, outer sole of rubber/plastic//leather & upper of leather	23,137,594	7.3	23,137,594	9.6	—	0.0
640320: Footwear, outer sole/upper of leather, strap across the instep/ and big toe	41,546,085	13.1	41,546,085	17.3	—	0.0
640340: Footwear, outer sole of rubber/plastic/leather, uppers of leather with metal toe cap	692,980	0.2	692,980	0.3	—	0.0
640359: Footwear, outer soles and uppers of leather, nes	117,375	0.0	117,375	0.0	—	0.0
640391: Footwear, outer soles of rubber/plastic uppers of leather covering ankle, nes	7,864,854	2.5	7,864,854	3.3	—	0.0
640399: Footwear, outer soles of rubber/plastic uppers of leather, nes	155,624,432	49.2	155,624,432	64.8	—	0.0
6404: Footwear, upper of textile material	*40,220,805*	*12.7*	*3,321,530*	*1.4*	*36,899,275*	*56.7*
640411: Sports footwear with outer soles of rubber or plastic & uppers of textile materials	5,538,684	1.8	—	0.0	5,538,684	8.5
640419: Footwear other than sports, with outer soles of rubber/plastic & uppers of textile materials	31,360,591	9.9	—	0.0	31,360,591**	48.2
640420: Footwear with outer soles of leather and uppers of textile materials	3,321,530	1.0	3,321,530	1.4	—	0.0
6405: Footwear, nes	*19,596,588*	*6.2*	*2,684,739*	*1.1*	*5,548,323*	*8.5*
640510: Footwear with uppers of leather or composition leather, nes	2,684,739	0.8	2,684,739	1.1	—	0.0
640520: Footwear with uppers of textile materials, nes	5,548,323	1.8	—	0.0	5,548,323***	8.5
640590: Footwear, nes	11,363,526****	3.6	n.a.	n.a.	n.a.	n.a.
Total	**316,467,482**	**100.0**	**239,989,759**	**100.0**	**65,114,197**	**100.0**

Source: Global Development Solutions, LLC, analysis of data provided by Export Promotion Bureau, Bangladesh.
Note: — = not available; n.a. = Not applicable.
*Top category, non-leather footwear
**Second highest category, non-leather footwear
***Third highest category, non-leather footwear
****Breakdown between leather and non-leather cannot be determined

Notes

1. For the purposes of this chapter, non-leather footwear falls into the following HS categories: HS6401, HS6402, HS640411, HS640419, HS640520, and HS650590.
2. Global Industry Analysts, Inc., http://www.prweb.com/releases/footwear_sports_leather/athletic_footwear/prweb9101683.htm.
3. Assuming Bangladesh's population is 156 million (2010).
4. "Espadrilles Made in Spain France Bangladesh China," November 12, 2005: http://espadrille.blogspot.com.
5. Commodity Trade Statistics Database, United Nations Statistics Division; http://comtrade.un.org/.
6. Export Promotion Bureau, Bangladesh.
7. HS640419, HS640520, and HS640590.
8. Export Promotion Bureau, Bangladesh. Data for FY2012 did not indicate volume transacted, only U.S. dollar value; thus, the volume comparison cannot be made.
9. Commodity Trade Statistics Database, United Nations Statistics Division.
10. Global Industry Analysts, Inc., http://www.prweb.com/releases/footwear_sports_leather/athletic_footwear/ prweb9101683.htm.
11. Its style has garnered praise, such as: "Nothing says summer like a good pair of espadrilles.... These rope-soled beauties are a staple in any Fashionista's wardrobe." And: "If there is one shoe that screams summer, it's the espadrille."
12. Zappos.com.
13. Although undefined officially, green fashion broadly can include eco-friendly materials (for example, organic, recycled, nonpetroleum based, non-PVC, vegetable dyes), vegan or nonanimal materials (for example, non-leather, animal-free adhesives), earth-friendly manufacturing (for example, use of hydro or solar power or overall minimized use of electrical- or fuel-powered machinery, as with handmade products), socially responsible manufacturing or marketing (for example, fair trade, nonsweatshop, no child labor, ethical treatment of workers, living wage, buy-one-give-one) and more.
14. Global companies such as Toms (United States), Beyond Skin (United Kingdom), Vegan Wares (Australia), Vegetarian Shoes (United Kingdom), Novocas (Portugal), Bourgeois Boheme (United Kingdom), Simple Shoes (United States), Neuaura Shoes (Brazil), Olsen Haus (United States), and Cri de Coeur (United States) are among the recent entrants with success in the green fashion footwear niche. For example, Toms launched in 2006 with a buy-one-give-one model and sold one million pairs in 2010 and two million pairs in 2012.
15. If the textile content is less than 50 percent of the sole that comes in contact with the ground, then the U.S. duty is 36 percent. If the textile content is greater than or equal to 50 percent, then the U.S. duty is reduced to 8 percent. For what is termed the basic espadrille shoe (the proxy non-leather shoe style used in the value chain analysis section), manufacturers have large cut-outs in the sole when selling to the United States. This generally is not possible with fashion espadrilles, however.
16. American Apparel and Footwear Association, https://www.wewear.org/aafa-on-the-issues/category/?CategoryId=96.
17. With GSP prospects for its footwear uncertain, Bangladesh's exports to the United States may possibly be helped by the Affordable Footwear Act, legislation

moving through the U.S. Congress that seeks to end import tariffs on footwear (American Apparel and Footwear Association, https://www.wewear.org/aafa-on-the-issues/category/?CategoryId=96). If this occurs, it will also benefit China and other exporting countries.

18. This does not include companies located in export processing zones (EPZs), since those companies are not represented by LFMEAB. The only EPZ with non-leather shoe manufacturers is located in Chittagong.
19. From 2008 to 2011, three new market entrants were unable to compete and have since left the market.
20. Bangladesh institutes a census of manufacturing industries, which is supposed to be collected monthly and yearly and classified by manufacturing sector activities following the Bangladesh Standard Industrial Classification at the four-digit level. The most recent information on the Bangladesh Bureau of Statistics website is for November 2010 and is incomplete, having only tracked leather footwear manufacturers.
21. Non-leather footwear in Bangladesh takes several forms, including jute-based espadrilles, canvas or rubber tennis shoes, molded polyurethane and PVC shoes and sandals, and artificial leather shoes.
22. Wikipedia article on Espadrille (http://en.wikipedia.org/wiki/Espadrille).
23. There are some designs that do not use braided jute midsole but, instead, use a jute fabric wrapped around an EVA or wood wedge.
24. Higher fashion (that is, higher value added) espadrilles produced in Bangladesh may include jute uppers, midsoles of various materials, EVA (wedge heels), accessories such as beads and sequins, cotton strapping, or leather accents. Wood is not a material used in Bangladesh.
25. This cost reflects a synthetic-to-natural rubber ratio of 1:3.
26. This reflects a combination of on- and off-grid electricity costs.
27. A 500 kilovolt generator requires 30 liters of diesel fuel per hour to operate with a fuel cost of Tk 61 per liter. However, diesel fuel continues to be subsidized by the government. For example, during FY2012, on average, the cost per liter of diesel was Tk 71, but it was sold at a price of Tk 51 (BIDS and IISD 2012).
28. Alternatively, the mandate of sector associations or the chambers of commerce could be expanded to conduct targeted market research on behalf of their constituents.

References

APCOR (Portuguese Cork Association). 2011. *Cork Yearbook 2011*. http://www.apcor.pt/userfiles/File/Publicacoes/anuario2011.pdf.

APICCAPS (Components and Leather Goods Manufacturers' Association). 2012. *World Footwear 2012 Yearbook*. http://www.apiccaps.pt/c/document_library/get_file?uuid=7d10300e-b8e0-40ae-b9be-246e4327714c&groupId=10136.

BIDS and IISD (Bangladesh Institute of Development Studies and International Institute for Sustainable Development). 2012. "A Citizen's Guide to Energy Subsidies in Bangladesh." http://www.bids.org.bd/files/ffs_bangladesh_czguide.pdf.

Chowdhury, A. H. 2009. *Future Prospects of Bangladesh's Raw Cotton and Textile Industry*. Ministry of Textiles and Jute, Government of Bangladesh.

Chua, Jasmin Malik. 2011. "Are Bangladesh's Toxic Leather Tanneries Killing Their Workers?" *Ecouterre*, February 18. http://www.ecouterre.com/are-bangladeshs-toxic-leather-tanneries-killing-their-workers.

IBISWorld. 2010. *Global Footwear Manufacturing: C1321-GL*. IBISWorld Industry Report, IBISWorld, Inc. http://www.just-style.com/store/samples/2010_IBISWorld%20Global%20Style%20Sample%20Industry%20Report.pdf.

Kuchment, Anna. 2008. "Sense and Sensibility." *The Daily Beast*, April 5. http://www.thedailybeast.com/newsweek/2008/04/05/sense-and-sensibility.html.

Lan, Percy. 2012. "Report on the 31st International Footwear Conference." *Peditimes*, March 12. http://www.peditimes.com/specialreport/2012-06-19/1.html.

Lee, Steve. 2011. "The World Footwear Market: Facts, Figures and Perspectives." Presentation at the World Footwear Congress, Rio de Janeiro.

Reuters. 2012. "Bangladesh Hikes Electricity Prices by 15 Percent." Reuters, September 20. http://www.reuters.com/article/2012/09/20/bangladesh-power-price-idUSL4E8KK51520120920.

Yoneda, Yuka. 2010. "Olsenhaus Eco-chic Vegan Shoes Made from Recycled TVs!" *Inhabitat*, February 28. http://inhabitat.com/olsenhaus-eco-chic-vegan-shoes-made-from-recycled-tvs.

CHAPTER 5

Value Chain Analysis for Polo Shirts

Christine Elbert, Nebiyeleul Gessese, and Yasuo Konishi

Introduction

The objective of this chapter is to assess the performance of the garment value chain in Bangladesh in the context of strong international competition. Critical to the value chain analysis (VCA) is the identification of the best product proxy to represent the garment sector in Bangladesh as well as in comparison with other countries. Polo shirts were selected as a proxy because of the product standardization in the apparel industry and across countries. Although many variants of the polo exist, a comparatively standard specification for polo shirts can be found globally in numerous garment manufacturing locations. Thus, the VCA data are benchmarked against a similar product produced in China, Vietnam, and Ethiopia to identify competitive gaps in the production process in Bangladesh. China and Vietnam are, like Bangladesh, among the top Asian apparel exporters. Ethiopia serves as a proxy for garment production in Africa, which is emerging as a lower-cost textile and apparel production base relative to Asia.

The prospects for Bangladesh's apparel manufacturing can be viewed in the context of the rapid growth of Asian manufacturers over the past two decades as well as shifts in socioeconomic trends that affect apparel demand. China controls a dominant share of apparel manufacturing for export, while Bangladesh and Vietnam are strong but relatively new entrants to the global apparel trade, and Ethiopia has yet to achieve significant apparel exports. China's share of global apparel exports may erode further as it shifts to higher value-added manufacturing in other industries, thus driving wages higher, and as the country retains apparel production to satisfy increasing domestic demand.

Sector Profile: The Apparel Industry in Bangladesh

The ready-made garment (RMG) industry is a strategic sector for Bangladesh. In 2012, it provided 3.6 million direct jobs, 13 percent of gross domestic product (GDP), and more than 75 percent of foreign exchange earnings. Most other manufacturing sectors in Bangladesh, by and large, have not been able to create jobs and generate export revenues of any significant scale since the country's independence over 40 years ago. Over the past two decades, starting from the early 1980s, Bangladesh has built a strong reputation centered on price advantage via low-cost labor and investment incentives; production capacity, particularly within export processing zones (EPZs, box 5.1); and satisfactory quality levels, especially in value and mid-market price point segments. Going forward, the price advantages may erode somewhat as new entrants are able to offer labor at an even lower cost, although Bangladesh looks to retain its capacity advantage for the time being. Bangladesh has not made marginal advancements

---

Box 5.1 Export Processing Zones in Bangladesh

The Bangladesh Export Processing Zones Authority (BEPZA) has devised several incentives to attract export processing zone (EPZ) investors, including the following:

- Clarity of law and regulations pertaining to investment and operations
- Fixed and favorable tariffs, enabling attraction of investment and financial and business planning
- Infrastructure facilities, including allegedly more consistent electricity supply versus that available to manufacturers outside the EPZs
- Proximity to ports, reducing lead time in getting product to market
- Ready-constructed factory space
- Custom bonded areas
- Infrastructure facilities, including utilities
- Administrative facilities, including expedited at-factory customs clearance
- Fiscal and nonfiscal incentives for investment, including tax exemption for several years (varies by date of establishment); duty-free import of construction materials, machinery, equipment, and spare parts; duty-free import and export of raw materials and finished goods; Generalized System of Preferences facility available; and duty- and quota-free access to major markets, including Australia, Canada, the European Union, and Norway.

In addition, BEPZA is a signatory of the Multilateral Investment Guarantee Agency and the International Centre for Settlement of Investment Disputes, as well as a member of the World Intellectual Property Organization and the Overseas Private Investment Corporation.

Through 2011/12, BEPZA reported annual investment of US$339.3 million, cumulative investment of US$2.457 billion, annual exports of US$4.212 billion, and cumulative exports of US$29.643 billion (table 5.1). To date, 35 countries (including Bangladesh) have invested in EPZ facilities. As of May 2012, the largest investors were Bangladesh (US$555.4 million), the Republic of Korea (US$518.8 million), and China (US$310.9 million). Among the more than 20 industries operating in the EPZs in Bangladesh, garments are the dominant industry and represent 24.9 percent of enterprises, 32.9 percent of

box continues next page

Box 5.1 Export Processing Zones in Bangladesh *(continued)*

investment, and 56.5 percent of employment (Bangladesh Export Processing Zones Authority). Major U.S. and European apparel brands manufactured in Bangladesh EPZs include Nike, Reebok, H&M (Sweden), Gap, Wal-Mart, Kmart, Ospig (Germany), Mother Care (United Kingdom), Lee, Wrangler, Dockers, Tommy Hilfiger, Adidas, American Eagle, North Face, and Timberland. Production may be by direct factory investment or via third-party outsourcing. Many foreign buyers have strengthened their sourcing base by shifting toward direct sourcing and opening local offices in Dhaka and Chittagong.

The oldest EPZ in Bangladesh is the Chittagong EPZ, which had its first investment in FY1984 and reported cumulative investment of US$960.2 million through FY2012 (table 5.1). Chittagong EPZ also is the largest employer and reported 9,822 local employees, or 29 percent of total EPZ employees of 33,598, for FY2012, followed by neighboring Karnaphuli EPZ, which employed 7,049 or 21 percent of total EPZ employees. Chittagong EPZ also dominates exports and contributed US$1.884 billion or 44.7 percent of FY2012 total EPZ exports and 50.8 percent of cumulative exports since the EPZs were established. Although today the majority of Bangladesh's apparel manufacturing occurs outside the EPZs, they are still popular with foreign investors (map B5.1.1).

Map B5.1.1 Bangladesh Export Processing Zones

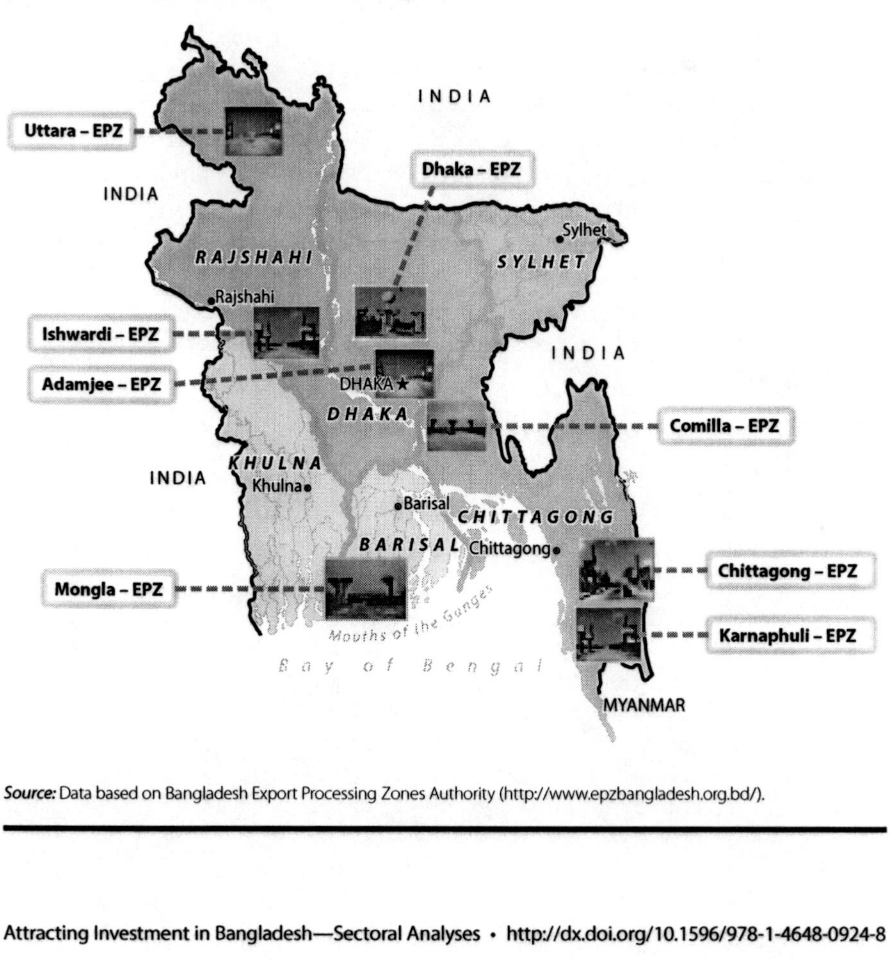

Source: Data based on Bangladesh Export Processing Zones Authority (http://www.epzbangladesh.org.bd/).

in production of high-end apparel segments, which require greater labor skill and higher technology, two areas in which Bangladesh is weak. For Bangladesh, opportunities for growth in the apparel manufacturing sector lie in enhancing the productivity of existing production value chains without adversely impacting social welfare in the sector, which has become a critical issue. The country's concentration of exports in one industry subjects Bangladesh to greater risk; as exports are diversified, it will be even more critical that apparel manufacturing productivity be enhanced.

The RMG sector is the largest manufacturing sector employer in Bangladesh. Since Bangladesh has made a concerted effort to develop the garment manufacturing sector, the number of RMG factories has grown steadily, reaching about 5,600 factories in FY2013 (but declining subsequently, to about 4,300 in FY15, even as output continues to grow), and 4 million employees (figure 5.1). Employment has also grown steadily, from 1.8 million in FY2002 to 3.6 million in FY2010, and 4 million in FY2015. At the same time, the scale and size of RMG factory operations has grown, with RMG factory employment averaging 300 workers per factory in FY1984 and growing to approximately 714 garment workers per factory in FY2014. Bangladesh's capacity compares favorably with that of other Southeast Asian RMG suppliers; for example, in 2011, Indonesia, Vietnam, and Cambodia had approximately 2,450, 2,000, and 260 factories, respectively, compared with Bangladesh's 5,150 (McKinsey & Company 2011).

Of the estimated 3.6 million employees in the Bangladesh Garment Manufacturers and Exporters Association (BGMEA) member factories in 2011, about 80 percent (around 2.9 million) were women. The industry has been credited with not only with providing employment, but also empowering women and economically disadvantaged populations in general. For example,

Figure 5.1 Bangladesh Garment Industry Factories and Employment, FY1984–FY2011

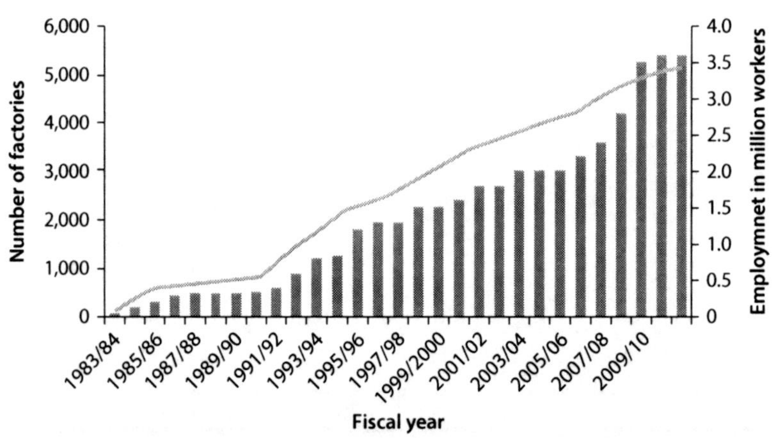

Source: Bangladesh Garment Manufacturers and Exports Association (http://www.BGMEA.com.bd).

BGMEA provides scholarships to the children of garment workers, vocational training, distribution of food at a subsidized price during Ramadan, and medical centers. Medical treatment includes HIV/AIDS awareness instruction and reproductive health services.[1] Still, worker safety and welfare remains a critical issue, as evidenced by several fires since 2007 that resulted in the deaths of more than 500 garment workers. Although growth to date has been impressive, the RMG industry will be challenged to expand in the future. Bangladesh's price advantage will be eroded by increased costs associated with labor and worker welfare compliance related to national and international pressures.

The yarn, fabric, and dyeing-printing-finishing mills of the primary textile sector are an important source of employment and a critical link in the supply chain. According to the Bangladesh Textile Mills Association (BTMA), which represents private sector mills, approximately four million people are employed at BTMA member mills and more than US$5.1 billion has been invested in these mills (annex 5E provides details on mill type and operating capacity and annex 5F provides information on the quantity and capacity of textile and garment units overall). BTMA mills fulfill 100 percent of Bangladesh's domestic fabric and yarn requirements, 50 percent of the cotton woven fabric requirements of the export-oriented garment subsector, and over 95 percent of the yarn and fabric requirements of the export-oriented knitwear subsector. According to BTMA, the value addition is around 35–40 percent in woven RMG and around 70 percent in knit RMG. Domestic weaving mills supply around 40 percent of woven fabrics for export-oriented RMG. Fabric requirements are increasing at 20 percent per year.

Bangladesh has eight designated EPZs (table 5.1). The largest of these by land area is Karnaphuli Export Processing Zone, which spans 222.4 hectares, while the largest by building size is Dhaka EPZ, which provides 108,850 square meters of factory space (annex 5A). Karnaphuli EPZ and Chittagong EPZ are in close proximity (6 kilometers or less) to Chittagong Port, the largest and most active seaport in Bangladesh, and together provide 85,495 square meters of factory building space. Although more consistent electricity supply is cited as a benefit of EPZs, they have no designated power supply, unlike water and gas providers (annex 5A). This gap in infrastructure leaves no party accountable when the power supply fails. In addition, lack of adequate infrastructure makes companies outside EPZs less competitive.

Garment companies in Bangladesh's EPZs are comparable in size to firms in China and Vietnam, where medium- to large-size firms dominate the apparel manufacturing sector.[2] By contrast, apparel manufacturing in Ethiopia is less concentrated, with 91 percent of enterprises considered small. In Bangladesh, garment industry firms located in EPZs had an average of 1,848 employees in May 2012,[3] making these firms large and comparable to Chinese and Vietnamese apparel manufacturers. As in BGMEA member factories, employment in garment firms outside EPZs ranges between 300 and 500 for small firms and 500 and 1,000 for medium-size firms. The majority (approximately 80 percent) of the sector's workforce in Bangladesh, China, and Vietnam is female, while

Table 5.1 Bangladesh Export Processing Zones: Investment, Employment, and Exports

	Investment				*Employment*			*Exports*			
Export processing zone (EPZ)	*First FY reported*	*Annual FY2012 (US$, millions)*	*Cumulative from first FY reported through FY2012 (US$, millions)*	*Total (%)*	*First FY reported*	*Annual FY2012 (average number of local employees, from first FY reported)*	*Total (%)*	*First FY reported*	*Annual FY2012 (US$, millions)*	*Cumulative from first FY reported through FY2012 (US$, millions)*	*Total (%)*
Adamjee	2006	34.6	164.2	7	2006	4,861	14	2006	207.3	560.6	2
Chittagong	1984	101.7	960.2	39	1984	9,822	29	1984	1,883.8	15,062.6	51
Comilla	2002	20.1	156.6	6	2002	1,935	6	2002	148.4	712.3	2
Dhaka	1994	77.2	863.1	35	1994	2,595	8	1994	1,614.5	12,584.4	42
Ishwardi	2005	17.9	67.7	3	2005	2,593	8	2005	41.5	82.9	0
Karnaphuli	2007	81.8	217.1	9	2007	7,049	21	2008	245.1	489.0	2
Mongla	2002	0.1	5.2	0	2001	948	3	2002	54.2	128.8	0
Uttara	2002	6.0	22.7	1	2002	3,795	11	2007	16.0	22.7	0
Total		339.3	2,457.0	100		33,598	100		4,210.8	29,643.3	100

Source: Global Development Solutions, LLC, analysis of Bangladesh Export Processing Zones Authority data (http://www.epzbangladesh.org.bd/).

Ethiopia has a majority male apparel employee base (58 percent). In Bangladesh, China, and Vietnam, the garment sector generates millions of jobs, while in Ethiopia in 2012 fewer than 10,000 people were employed in the sector. Looking at export value per employee (and ignoring production for domestic consumption), in 2012, China dominated productivity with US$31,227 per worker, 5.1 times that of Bangladesh and 2.7 times that of Vietnam. Based on this indicator, Vietnam is twice as productive as Bangladesh, while Ethiopia is only 57 percent as productive as Bangladesh (table 5.2).

Multiple problems persist in Bangladesh's cotton-to-garment processing chain. The supply chain structure for apparel manufacturing in Bangladesh is illustrated in figure 5.2. It includes garment producers, outsourcing partners producing yarn for fabric manufacturers, local suppliers of accessories, dyeing facilities, and fabric mills. The problems include the raw cotton imports that take many days to clear customs, the inadequate energy and power supply that leads to higher production cost and lower capacity utilization, and the relatively low-skilled labor force that reduces productivity (see figures 5.2 and 5.3).

Bangladesh, similar to China, Ethiopia, and Vietnam, maintains various input and output subsidies or rebates to encourage industrial production and exports. In Bangladesh, support includes subsidies, mainly to mills because of the costs they incur from cotton import price volatility, coupled with tax reductions on import of chemicals, machinery and equipment, and spare parts for effluent treatment plants. In addition, enterprises in EPZs receive tax holidays, duty-free import of machinery and equipment, and duty-free import and export of raw materials and finished goods, among other benefits. (Several institutions provide other support for the textile and garment sector in Bangladesh and are summarized in annex 5B.) In China, apparel exporters are given a 16 percent rebate on the exported price of apparel to compensate for the value-added tax (VAT) that manufacturers pay on inputs; this enables flexibility in pricing when negotiating with foreign buyers.[4] In Vietnam, electricity prices are controlled and generally

Table 5.2 Snapshot of the Apparel Sector in Bangladesh, China, Ethiopia, and Vietnam

Key comparative indicators	*Bangladesh*	*China*	*Ethiopia*	*Vietnam*
Total exports (US$)	21.8 billion	143.3 billion	34.0 million	13.9 billion
Companies operating in the sector	5,150	52,828	436	3,174
Small	n.a.	13.2%	91.1%	26.8%
Medium	n.a.	54.0%	1.6%	55.0%
Large	n.a.	32.8%	7.3%	18.2%
Estimated number of workers in sector	3,600,000	4,587,000	9,746	1,194,310
Male	20%	20%	58%	17%
Female	80%	80%	42%	83%
Export value per employee (US$)	6,069	31,227	3,485	11,609

Sources: Data compiled by Global Development Solutions, LLC. Bangladesh data from personal interviews; data for China, Vietnam, and Ethiopia from Global Development Solutions, LLC study "Competitive Africa: The Value Chain and Feasibility Analysis Module" (GDS n.d.).

Note: Bangladesh data as of 2012; China, Vietnam, and Ethiopia as of 2011. n.a. = not available.

Figure 5.2 Supply Chain Structure, Bangladesh Apparel Manufacturing

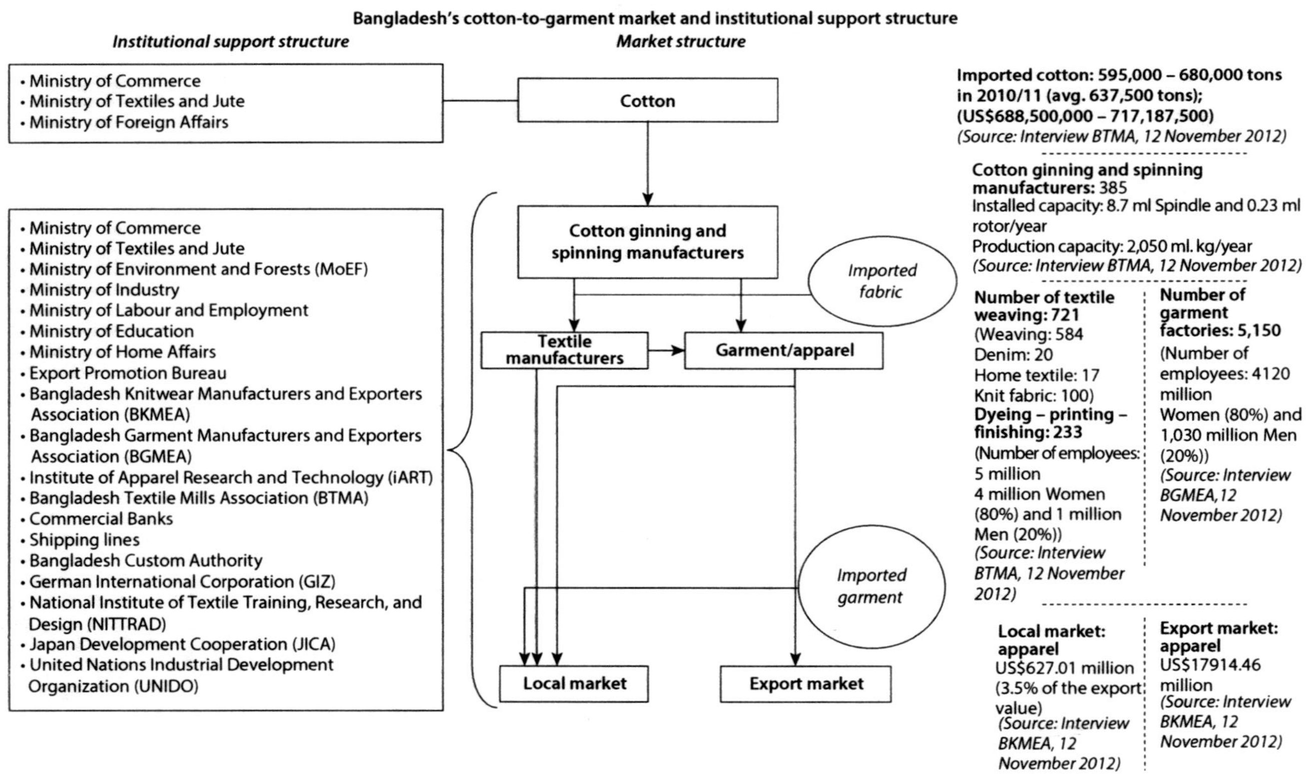

Source: Global Development Solutions, LLC.

Figure 5.3 Bangladesh's Cotton-to-Garment Processing Roadmap

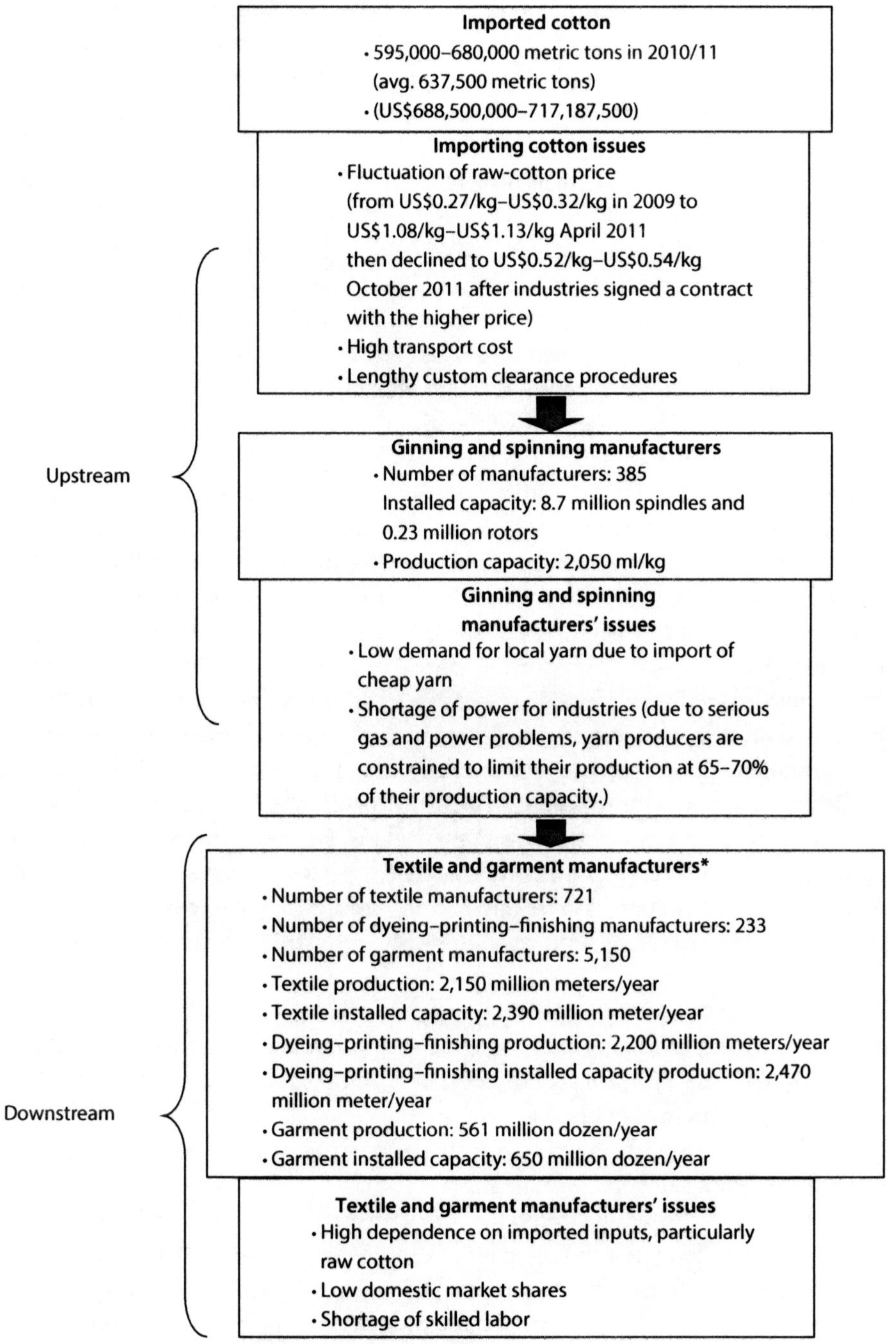

Source: Global Development Solutions, LLC.
Note: Mfs = manufacturers; ml = milliliter; kg = kilogram.
a. BTMA interview (November 12, 2012).

subsidized; industry can access electricity at low prices and generally at rates on par with household consumers without paying premiums for load factors. Ethiopian apparel manufacturers do not enjoy support at such levels and generally face a range of taxes and levies that increase their costs of doing business. Garment exporters working under EPZ status are exempt from duties on inputs and get VAT refunds.

The government of Bangladesh recently adopted a new textile policy, applicable only to textile mills, to replace the textile policy enacted in 1995.[5] The main objective of the new policy is to adapt and reshape the textile sector in light of changes in the global textile industry. The policy emphasizes research and development of technologies, production of value-added multiple items, domestic production of cotton, human resources development, technical support, and fiscal incentives to sustain growth of the textile sector. Moreover, customs procedures will be simplified, waivers will be given on the import of dyes and chemicals, and the waiver on imports of textile machinery should continue. The policy provides for export-oriented textile mills to be licensed to utilize bonded warehouse facilities to import raw materials, chemicals, and accessories at zero tariffs. Moreover, BTMA has been empowered to recommend the renewal of bonded warehouse licenses for its member mills. With regard to cotton waste, the minimum export price has been raised to US$4.50 per kilogram from US$1.6 per kilogram (BTMA 2011). Ten percent of the production of EPZ industrial units and 20 percent of the production of outside units would be cleared for sale in the local market, subject to payment of government taxes and duties as applicable.

International apparel firms increasingly are involved in social and safety initiatives to support third-party garment manufacturers in Bangladesh. This follows several safety and other worker welfare incidents. Some buyers have announced social and safety initiatives, but these have not been adopted industrywide. Further, international buyers are not necessarily willing to pay for the cost of compliance. Private sector support to the RMG industry includes the following:[6]

- Encouraging the government to raise the minimum wage
- Implementing fire safety measures, including training films on safety and fire prevention, fire safety inspections, formal remediation plans, accountability, and reports made publicly available
- Funding of a support program to pay factory employees for missed work days because of fire safety remediation
- Providing vendors with accelerated access to capital for safety improvements
- Operating vocational training centers to upgrade garment workers' technical skills as well as to educate them as to their rights and responsibilities
- Establishing a helpline for female workers exposed to violence and discrimination;
- Providing subsidized health care for workers and their families
- Continuing engagement with the government of Bangladesh, U.S. government, and International Labour Organization to promote comprehensive change and develop industrywide solutions.

Integrated Value Chain Analysis for Polo Shirts

This section analyzes the state of the value chain for polo shirts in 2012 (see annex 5C). Polo-style shirts are the focus of this chapter, as they represent a value-added apparel product with more complex production than simpler products such as T-shirts. In addition, the basic polo shirt model is somewhat standardized globally, thus facilitating the comparison of Bangladeshi productivity with other apparel-producing countries. What is termed by the sector as the "basic polo" was recommended by producers as a proxy to represent the sector for VCA. To facilitate comparison across countries, product standards were sought. The sample product is 100 percent cotton, has a weight of 250–270 grams, and is designed to be worn by men. Other features and specifications are shown in figure 5.4.

A polo shirt, also known as a golf shirt or a tennis shirt, is a T-shaped shirt with a collar, a placket with typically two or three buttons, and an optional pocket. Polo shirts usually are made of knitted (rather than woven) cloth, typically of cotton, but also less commonly may be made of silk, merino wool, or synthetic fibers. In examining the global apparel manufacturing market, the analysis in this chapter references the Harmonized Commodity Description and Coding System (HS) as noted in annex 5D. The primary HS codes for apparel are HS61 (articles of apparel and clothing accessories—knitted or crocheted) and HS62 (articles of apparel and clothing accessories—not knitted or crocheted). Although global apparel broadly may include articles of plastic, rubber, leather, or fur skin,[7] such articles are outside the scope of the analysis. Used garments (for example, HS6309: Worn clothing and other worn textile articles) are excluded from the analysis. Within HS61, the analysis more closely examines HS610910 (T-shirts, singlets, other vests, knitted or crocheted, of cotton), under which cotton polo-style shirts are exported, according to BGMEA. There is no dedicated HS code for the polo-style shirt; thus, the production and export value and volume of polo shirts specifically cannot be ascertained for Bangladesh or globally.

Figure 5.4 Polo Shirt Features and Technical Specifications

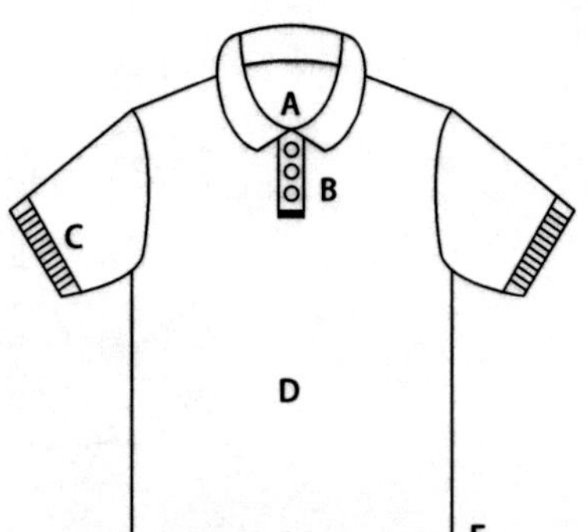

A. Collar of 46 cm
B. 3-button placket of 15 cm by 3.5 cm
C. 21 cm sleeves with banded cuffs
D. Body of 100% pique cotton
E. Split bottom

Source: Interview with textile expert at Global Development Solutions, LLC.
Note: cm = centimeters.

Value Chain Analysis

The unit cost of producing a basic polo-style shirt in Bangladesh compares favorably with the unit cost in China. The VCA reveals that the unit cost in Bangladesh is approximately US$3.46 (Tk 283.72) per shirt, excluding margins and the cost of transportation to port (figure 5.5), against US$3.93 per shirt in China (figure 5.6) and US$3.06 per shirt in Ethiopia (figure 5.7). Although a polo shirt costs only US$0.39 to manufacture in Vietnam (figure 5.8), the VCA for

Figure 5.5 Polo Shirt Exports Value Chain: Savar, Bangladesh

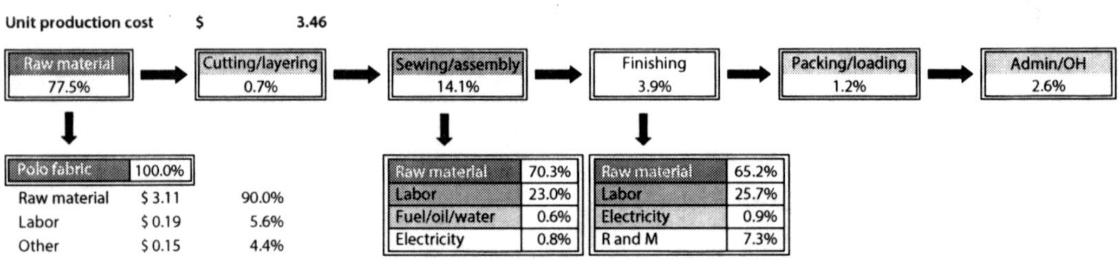

Source: Analysis by Global Development Solutions, LLC.
Note: The highest cost contribution is indicated in blue, the second highest in orange, and the third highest in green. Skilled:unskilled worker ratio not available for Bangladesh. OH = overhead. R and M = repair and maintenance.

Figure 5.6 Polo Shirt Exports Value Chain: Guandong, China

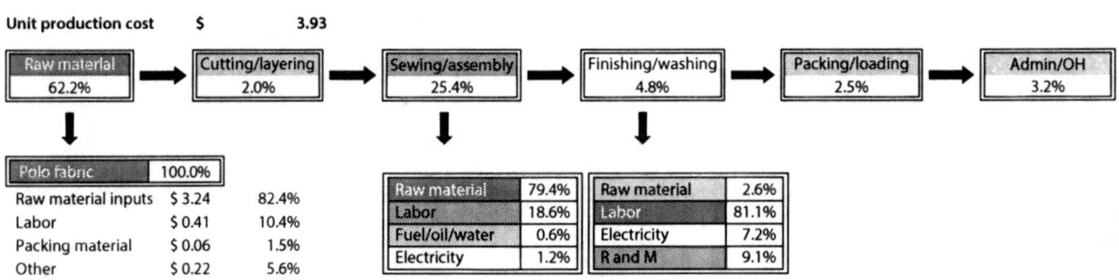

Source: Analysis by Global Development Solutions, LLC.
Note: The highest cost concentration is indicated in blue, the second highest in orange, and the third highest in green. OH = overhead; R and M = repair and maintenance.

Figure 5.7 Polo Shirt Exports Value Chain: Addis Ababa, Ethiopia

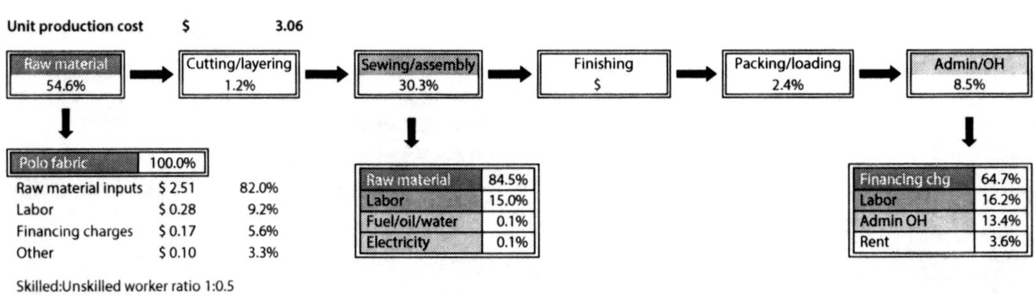

Source: Analysis by Global Development Solutions, LLC.
Note: The highest cost contribution is indicated in blue, the second highest in orange, and the third highest in green. OH = overhead; R and M = repair and maintenance.

Figure 5.8 Polo Shirt Exports Value Chain: Hai Duong, Vietnam

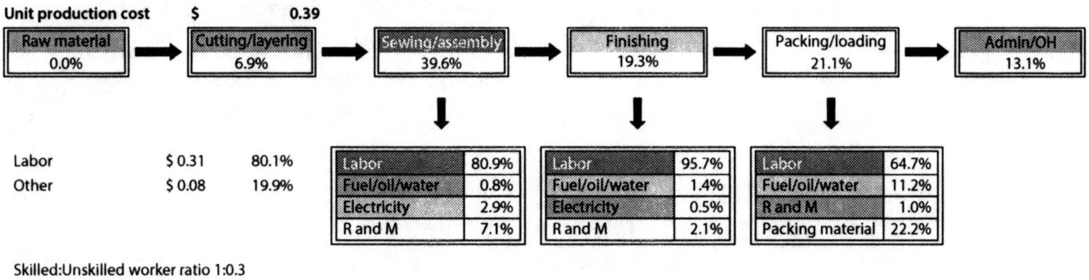

Source: Analysis by Global Development Solutions, LLC.
Note: The highest cost contribution is indicated in blue, the second highest in orange, and the third highest in green. OH = overhead. R and M = repair and maintenance.

Vietnam is not directly comparable to that of Bangladesh, China, or Ethiopia. Vietnam's apparel production is dominated by the cut-make-trim (CMT) process and as such Vietnamese manufacturers do not incur the cost of raw materials, including fabric, which is the most expensive component in making polo shirts.

The highest cost component in polo shirt production is fabric in Bangladesh, China, and Ethiopia. The primary value chain for the production of polo shirts is divided into six major stages: (a) raw material; (b) cutting and layering; (c) sewing and assembly; (d) finishing; (e) packing and loading; and (f) administrative cost and overhead. Figures 5.5–5.8 show the value chains for Bangladesh, China, Ethiopia, and Vietnam. For the top three stages in the primary value chain, a secondary value chain is provided that details contributions to the cost of the respective stage. The secondary chain components shown in the figures are limited to the top four contributing categories. For each chain, the highest cost contribution is indicated in blue, the second highest in orange, and the third highest in green. Raw material (fabric) is the highest cost component in polo shirt production in Bangladesh, China, and Ethiopia, representing 77.5, 62.2, and 54.6 percent of total costs, respectively. Bangladesh's textile sector that supplies fabric to the garment subsector relies mainly on imports of raw cotton. China and Ethiopia produce cotton domestically. Ethiopian garment makers import the fabric for polo production, since the locally sourced fabric is of inferior quality and not competitively priced. There is no cost of fabric for Vietnam manufacturers using the CMT process.

The second highest cost component in polo shirt production for Bangladesh, China, and Ethiopia is sewing and assembly, which represents 14.1, 25.4, and 30.3 percent of total costs, respectively. In all three countries, the cost of accessories is high and amounts to 70.3, 79.4, and 84.5 percent, respectively, for Bangladesh, China, and Ethiopia. In China, labor for the sewing and assembly stage is 18.6 percent of total costs, compared with 23 percent in Bangladesh. Other components, such as repair and maintenance (R&M) and electricity, contribute negligible costs to this stage for China and Bangladesh.

The third highest production cost in Bangladesh and China is for finishing, at 3.9 percent of total cost in Bangladesh and 4.8 percent in China. In Bangladesh, the largest contributor at this stage is raw material (65.2 percent of finishing cost), followed by labor (25.8 percent) and R&M (7.3 percent). For China, labor contributes 81.1 percent of finishing costs, followed by R&M (9.1 percent) and electricity (7.2 percent). In Ethiopia, the third highest cost is administration and overhead, which contributes 8.5 percent of polo shirt production costs. Nearly two-thirds (64.7 percent) of overhead costs are financing charges, exacerbated by low access to finance. For Bangladesh and China, other stages, such as cutting and layering, packing and loading, and administration and overhead, are the least expensive components of polo shirt manufacturing and collectively contribute 4.2 percent and 7.7 percent to total production cost, respectively. In Ethiopia, cutting and layering, finishing and packing, and loading are the least expensive components and total 6.6 percent of production cost.

Raw materials (fabric, collar, thread, labels, buttons, consumables, and so forth) are the most costly aspect of polo shirt production in most countries. Bangladesh, China, and Ethiopia are no exception; raw materials constitute roughly 90 percent of polo manufacturing cost in Bangladesh, 84 percent in China, and 83 percent in Ethiopia (table 5.3). The fabric for the body of the shirt is the highest proportionate contributor to raw material cost at 86 percent of the total raw material cost in Bangladesh, and 78 percent of the total raw material cost in China and Ethiopia. The absolute value of polo shirt material is highest for Bangladesh as well, at US$2.68 per shirt versus US$2.65 for China and US$1.70 for Ethiopia.

Manufacturing Polo Shirts in Bangladesh

In most cases, polo shirt manufacturers in Bangladesh import raw cotton. In a few cases, they also import yarns from abroad, but this is much more expensive than importing raw cotton. The cost of knitting in-house or outsourced to other factories is virtually the same, Tk 8 (US$0.10) per kilogram of yarn in both cases. The cost breakdown for producing yarn in-house is shown in table 5.4. However, outsourcing saves the investment cost for knitting machinery. Taking waste and

Table 5.3 Raw Material Input Cost Comparison for Polo Shirts: Bangladesh, Ethiopia, and China

Cost	*Bangladesh*	*China*	*Ethiopia*
Raw material inputs as a percentage of value chain	90	84	83
Total cost of raw material inputs/shirt	$3.11	$3.41	$2.17
Fabric			
US$ cost/shirt	$2.68	$2.65	$1.70
Percentage of total input	86	78	78
Other inputs			
US$ cost/shirt	$0.43	$0.76	$0.47
Percentage of total input	14	22	22

Source: Global Development Solutions, LLC.

Table 5.4 Cost of In-House Knitting

Cost factor	*Cost (Tk/polo)*	*Cost (US$/polo)*
Operator	0.0500	0.0006
Helper	0.0350	0.0004
Feeder man	0.1000	0.0012
Master	0.1000	0.0012
Supervisor	0.0700	0.0009
Loader	0.0400	0.0005
Electricity	0.3000	0.0037
Fuel	0.1200	0.0015
Cleaner	0.0400	0.0005
Extra	0.1000	0.0012
Depreciation	7.2300	0.0893
Total	8.1850	0.1010

Source: Interviews by Global Development Solutions, LLC.

losses into account, a 250-gram polo shirt requires 300 grams of yarn. A factory with a daily output of 5,000 polo shirts requires about six jersey machines, at a cost of Tk 2,200,000 (US$27,161) per machine. Such a factory, therefore, could avoid an investment cost of more than Tk 13,194,900 (US$162,900) by delivering raw cotton to outsourced knitting factories and paying only a service charge of Tk 8 (US$0.10) per kilogram of yarn. The cost of raw cotton is Tk 42.12 (US$0.52) per kilogram.

Manufacturers of polo shirts dye the yarn at a cost of Tk 98 (US$1.21) per kilogram, after which the yarn is converted into finished fabric at a cost of Tk 438.21 (US$5.41) per kilogram. The fabric is then taken to the cutting and sewing section, followed by finishing, inspection, packing, and delivery to store.

Most polo shirts are destined for export at a free on board (FOB) price of Tk 388 (US$4.80) per polo. Only about 3 percent of total production is sold in the local market, at Tk 340 (US$4.20) per polo at the factory gate and Tk 500 (US$6.17) retail. The selling prices are based on the market and are therefore similar among producers. However, the cost of production varies greatly among garment manufacturers and depends on variables including age and quality of machinery and factory-specific wages.

According to interviews with manufacturers, the commercial costs of exporting are about 3 percent of the CMT cost of the polo shirt. Manufacturers obtain about 20 percent profit margin on CMT of the polo shirt. Figure 5.9 depicts polo shirt manufacturing as a flowchart—from raw material procurement to production to export.

Productivity of Manufacturing Polo Shirts in Bangladesh

The Bangladeshi labor productivity rate of 13–27 polo shirts per person per day is substantially lower than the 18–35 pieces per person per day achieved by similar factories in China.[8] A major driver of the globalization of apparel

Figure 5.9 Manufacturing Polo Shirts in Bangladesh

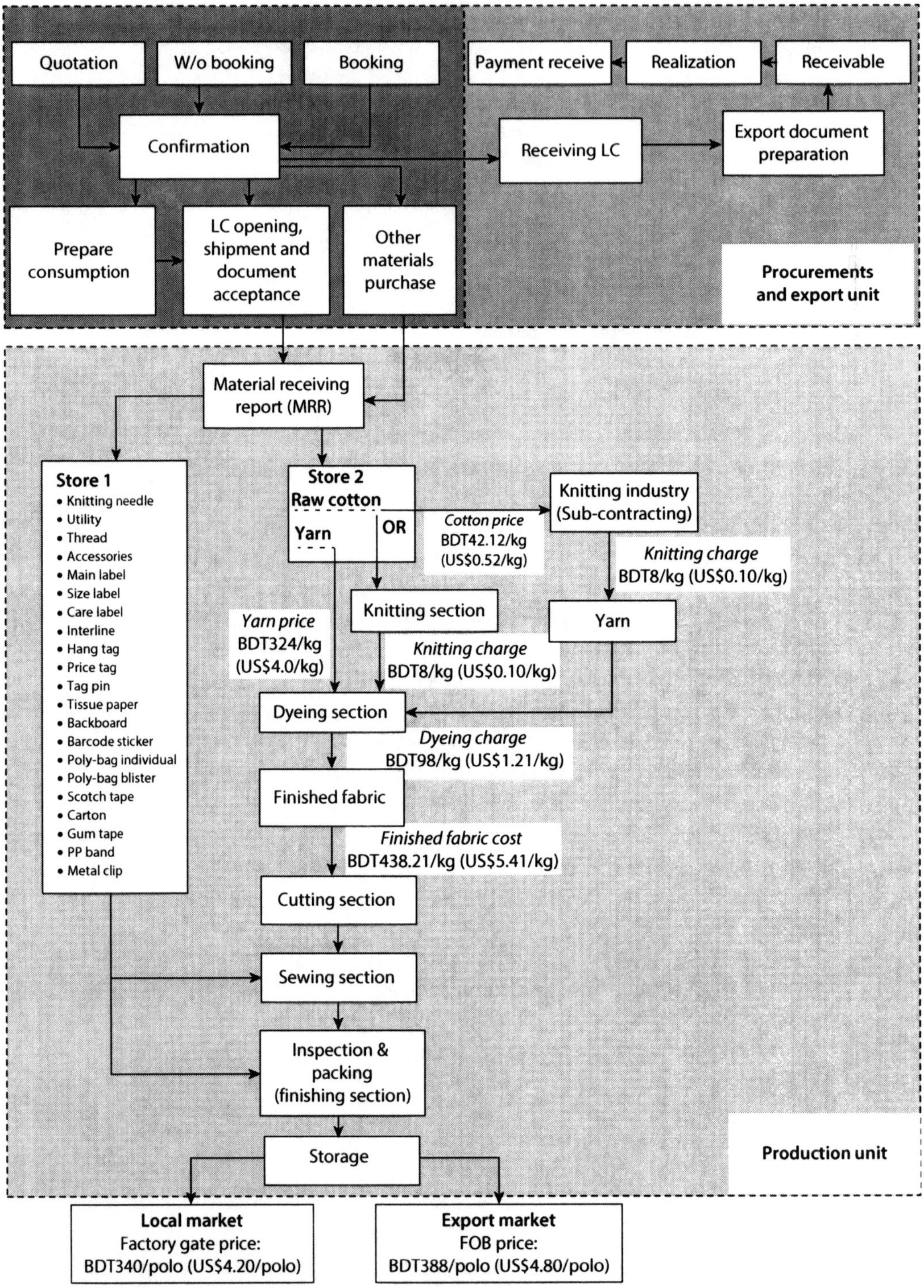

Source: Global Development Solutions, LLC.
Note: FOB = free on board; kg = kilogram; LC = letter of credit; w/o = without.

manufacturing is the ability to access low-cost labor. Moreover, the labor skills required in the garment sector generally are lower than those required for other industries, decreasing the barriers to entry in establishing apparel outsourcing or direct investment. When touting investment, Bangladesh promotes its comparative wage advantage, which is quite low relative to the region and particularly to China, the current world leader in apparel manufacturing and exports (figure 5.10, wage comparisons for 2014). According to Bangladesh Export Processing Zones Authority (BEPZA), in 2010, wage rates in Vietnam were nearly twice as high and in China nearly 10 times as high as those in Bangladesh (the gap has narrowed as of 2014, but is still very high). At US$26–US$48 per month for unskilled labor, Ethiopian wages for polo shirt production are more in line with those of Bangladesh.

Bangladesh's minimum wage rates are set by the government, not the employing companies, and minimum wages are higher in the EPZs than outside the EPZs. Wage rates vary by skill level; as of 2014, wages ranged from US$39 per month for an apprentice, to US$48 per month for a helper, US$61 per month for an operator worker, and US$109 per month for a highly skilled worker. Work weeks reportedly are 48 hours per week, six days per week. Unions are permitted under the new labor law; however, its implementation is slow. Turnover is high, with few workers staying longer than a few years. According to international media, on average only a quarter of the workforce actually receives the minimum wage (Vidal 2012), although BGMEA claims that through its oversight, the minimum wage is paid in 99.99 percent of all factories.[9]

Relative to Asian competitors, there is clear room for improvement for Bangladesh in rejects, wastage, and labor absenteeism. In examining polo shirts as a proxy for the apparel sector, Bangladesh's capacity utilization is slightly lower

Figure 5.10 Monthly Minimum Wages in Selected Countries, 2014
US dollars

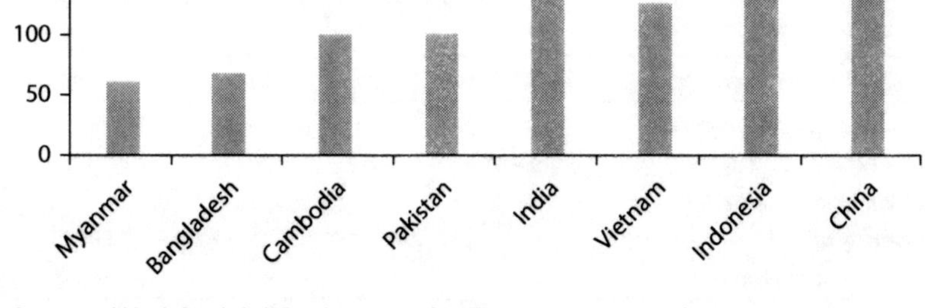

Source: World Bank: Bangladesh Development Update October 2014, using data from www.wageindicator.org

than that of Vietnam and China, and significantly higher than that of Ethiopia (see annex 5H). However, Bangladesh's in-factory average product rejection rates (4–8 percent) were higher—the result of lower-skilled labor. Relative to Bangladesh, Chinese and Vietnamese enterprises had lower labor absenteeism rates, although absenteeism is a significant issue in Ethiopia. Bangladesh's labor inefficiency (including lower skill levels, lower motivation, absenteeism, and high turnover) and production inefficiency (for example, waste and reject rates) have been documented in the value chain study by Global Development Solutions (GDS n.d.). Technical efficiency can be measured by wastage, reject rates, labor absenteeism, and capacity utilization (table 5.5).

Moreover, garment manufacturers in Bangladesh suffer from the high cost and poor quality of electricity. On-grid costs range from US$0.07 to US$0.10 per kilowatt hour (kWh). More important, the percentage of time off-grid per month is approximately 30 percent, which is two to three times higher than in competing countries (see annex 5G, table 5G.1 for details). Off-grid generating costs are as high as US$0.26 per kWh, again substantially higher than competitors in Asia and Africa.

The time it takes to import inputs is a major complaint of textile manufacturers. They believe that the delay erodes general textile and garment competitiveness since it affects the entire supply chain. On average, based on the requisite steps, procedures, and logistics, it takes 68.2 days (range 61.5–75 days) to import inputs from the date of obtaining a valid trade license. Because some activities can be performed concurrently, there is room for major improvements, provided the various parties involved (freight forwarders, transitors, customs authorities, transports, shipping lines, and others) can work more closely together. Details of importing inputs are summarized in annex 5G, table 5G.2.

The World Bank Garment Firm Survey 2011 noted that the lead time (number of days from order receipt to delivery) in Bangladesh is much longer than that in India or China, with an average 88 days in Bangladesh but only 40–60 days in China and 50–70 days in India (World Bank 2011a). The difference was attributed chiefly to inefficiency at the Port of Chittagong, where it reportedly takes 4.5 days to turn around a ship of 800 20-foot equivalent units (TEUs) versus 8–12 hours in Singapore.[10] In addition, the narrow Dhaka-Chittagong Highway slows apparel shipments (Haroon 2012). Long lead times for imported

Table 5.5 Efficiencies in Capacity Utilization, Waste, Rejects, and Absenteeism
percent

Polo shirt manufacturing	*Bangladesh*	*China*	*Ethiopia*	*Vietnam*
In-factory product rejection	4–8	2–3	2–5	1–3
Product rejection by client	0–3	0	1–3	0–1
Production waste/scrap	5–12	5–10	10–11	1–7
Capacity utilization	73–80	60–85	55–70	80–95
Labor absenteeism rate	0.3–3	1	6–12	0.3–2

Source: Global Development Solutions, LLC.

Table 5.6 Comparative Business Environment Competitiveness Rankings

Metric	*Bangladesh*	*China*	*Ethiopia*	*Vietnam*
Ease of doing business (of 185)	129	91	127	99
Ease of getting electricity (of 185)	185	114	94	155
Global competitiveness (of 144)	118	29	121	75

Sources: World Bank 2012; World Economic Forum 2012.

inputs and exported products are impediments to sector growth. (See annex 5G, tables 5G.3 and 5G.4 for import and export transport costs.)

Bangladesh performs poorly in terms of the overall business environment, which affects the country's manufacturing competitiveness. According to the 2012 World Bank Doing Business Indicators (World Bank 2012), Bangladesh ranked 129th, while China, Ethiopia, and Vietnam had rankings of 91st, 127th, and 99th, respectively (table 5.6). Although none of the four countries scored highly for ease of getting electricity, an important component for any manufacturing, Bangladesh was the worst of all 185 countries evaluated. Despite more competitive wages, Bangladesh and Ethiopia scored well below China and Vietnam in the World Economic Forum Global Competitiveness Index, in which Bangladesh, China, Ethiopia, and Vietnam ranked 118th, 29th, 121st, and 75th, respectively, of 144 countries.

Global Apparel and Cotton Markets

Apparel Market

In 2011, the Americas and Europe were the largest consumers of apparel, but future growth will likely be driven by emerging economies. The global apparel retail industry grew by 3.7 percent in 2011 to reach a value of US$1.2 trillion (MarketLine 2012). The apparel retail industry consists of men's wear, women's wear, and children's wear, including active wear, casual wear, essentials, formalwear, occasion wear, and outerwear. It includes RMGs (ready-to-wear or mass-produced) and custom-made (tailored) fashion. Women's wear is the largest segment of the global apparel retail industry and accounted for US$603.8 billion or 51.2 percent of total retail apparel revenue in 2011, followed by men's wear, with US$377.8 billion or 32.1 percent, and children's wear, with US$197.1 billion or 16.7 percent (MarketLine 2012). The Americas and Europe together account for more than 70 percent of global apparel retail sales (table 5.7).[11] The global apparel retail industry is forecast to reach US$1.4 trillion by 2016, fueled in particular by consumer demand in emerging markets (MarketLine 2012). The industry is experiencing significant trends, including the following: (a) increased consolidation among retailers; (b) proliferation of private brands; (c) proliferation of lifestyle and quick fashion brands; (d) increased outsourcing through third-party manufacturers; (e) increased raw material and labor costs; and (f) increased pressure to demonstrate social and environmental responsibility in the supply chain.

Table 5.7 Global Apparel Retail Sales, by Region, 2011

Region	*Value (US$, millions)*	*Percent of total*
Americas	423,199.2	35.9
Europe	412,136.9	35.0
Asia-Pacific	305,163.7	25.9
Middle East and Africa	38,192.7	3.2
Total	1,178,692.5	100.0

Source: MarketLine 2012.

Competition in garment manufacturing is more than just a function of low-cost labor. The supplying countries and firms that are best able to adjust to the trends are anticipated to succeed in the global clothing supply chain. China's dominance of global apparel manufacturing illustrates the importance of adaptability to industry trends. China currently commands the greatest share of global apparel exports, despite rising labor costs and currency appreciation, which have caused many to question China's ability to remain competitive. However, despite higher labor costs than much of the apparel-producing world, China's production efficiencies allow it to export clothing at prices below world averages, as noted in table 5.8. A country must be able to compete on various levels to capture market share.

Bangladesh is the third largest exporter of apparel, after China and Hong Kong SAR, China. Global apparel exports exceeded US$355 billion in 2011. The top 10 exporting countries commanded more than 80 percent of total export value, with the top three countries alone capturing 53 percent of global apparel exports. China led the rankings with US$143.2 billion or 40.3 percent of world exports, followed distantly by Hong Kong SAR, China (US$23.2 billion or 6.5 percent) and Bangladesh (US$21.8 billion or 6.1 percent) (table 5.9). Vietnam made the top 10, ranking sixth, with US$13.9 billion in exports and a 3.9 percent share. Although the top 10 exporters were evenly split in number between Asia and Europe, Asian exporting nations comprised 75 percent of the export value of the top 10 countries.

Bangladesh's apparel exports are evenly split between knitwear (HS61) and woven wear (HS62) products. According to Bangladesh's Export Promotion Bureau (EPB) data, exports of HS62 totaled US$9.6 billion in FY2012. Bangladesh's total apparel exports were US$19.1 billion in FY2012 (figure 5.11),[12] an increase of 55 percent from US$12.3 billion in FY2009. The share of apparel in Bangladesh's total exports ranged from 74 to 79 percent during FY2001 to FY2011 (table 5.10).

Bangladesh is the third largest knitwear exporter in the world, after China and Turkey, according to the Bangladesh Knitwear Manufacturers and Exporters Association (BKMEA). The major product categories of apparel exported over the years are noted in table 5.10. The most recent data available indicate that products with the largest export value were T-shirts and other casual shirts (US$4.7 billion) and trousers (US$4.2 billion). Although all product categories have grown tremendously, the greatest increase in terms of value over the past decade has been observed in the T-shirt and polo shirt categories (+760 percent),

Table 5.8 Comparative Prices for Select Categories of Knit Apparel, China and the World, 2009–11

HS61: Articles of apparel and clothing accessories, knitted or crocheted		*2011 world exports (US$, billions)*	*World exports to world (including China), exported unit value (US$/ton)*				*China exports to world, exported unit value (US$/ton)*				*Difference in unit value, China/world (%)*
HS Code	*Product label*		*2009*	*2010*	*2011*	*Average 2009–11*	*2009*	*2010*	*2011*	*Average 2009–11*	
611030	Sweaters, pullovers, sweatshirts, waistcoats (vests), of manmade fibers	17	38,453	20,402	22,625	20,370	39,483	14,868	17,753	18,026	−12
611020	Sweaters, pullovers, sweatshirts, waistcoats (vests), of cotton	19	22,260	20,801	23,261	16,580	35,043	14,457	18,023	16,881	2
610910	T-shirts, singlets, other vests, of cotton	23	25,944	22,389	23,082	17,854	30,162	13,639	16,748	15,137	−15
610990	T-shirts, singlets, and other vests, of other textile materials	11	37,036	24,765	24,103	21,476	43,793	16,262	18,867	19,731	−8
610462	Women's or girls' trousers, breeches, of cotton	6	25,404	15,738	16,348	14,373	28,755	11,070	13,755	13,395	−7
611120	Babies' garments and accessories, of cotton	5	14,197	16,899	15,492	11,647	13,455	13,379	17,195	11,007	−5
610510	Babies' garments and accessories, of cotton	5	33,804	25,800	26,661	21,566	42,836	15,549	18,661	19,261	−11
610711	Men's or boys' underpants, briefs, of cotton	3	25,922	15,514	18,947	15,096	32,869	11,300	13,498	14,417	−4
610610	Women's or girls' blouses, shirts, of cotton	4	28,391	25,677	22,979	19,262	39,664	16,138	19,662	18,866	−2

Source: UN Comtrade.

Note: Categories shown represent the top 10 products in HS61 world exports and 50 percent of the total value of HS61's world exports of US$187 billion in 2011.

Table 5.9 Top 10 Apparel-Exporting Countries, 2011

Rank	*Country*	*Value (US$, millions)*	*Percent of global exports*
1	China	143,238.43	40.3
2	Hong Kong SAR, China	23,170.62	6.5
3	Bangladesh	21,848.83	6.1
4	Italy	21,398.68	6.0
5	Germany	19,895.61	5.6
6	Vietnam	13,865.24	3.9
7	India	13,744.74	3.9
8	Turkey	13,512.77	3.8
9	France	10,110.76	2.8
10	Belgium	8,465.05	2.4
	Other	66,078.26	18.6
	World	355,328.98	100.0

Source: United Nations Statistical Division.
Note: Data shown are for classifications HS61 and HS62.

Figure 5.11 Bangladesh's Apparel Exports, July 2008–June 2012

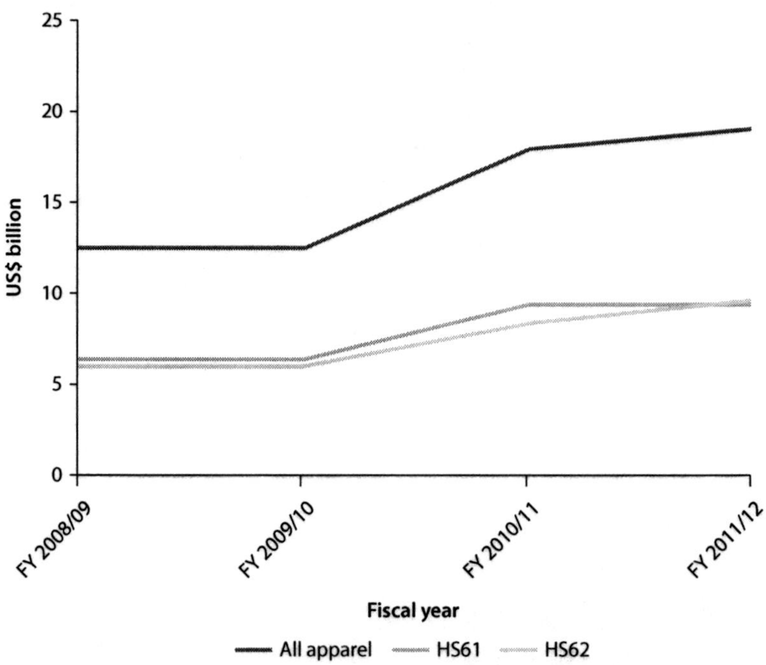

Source: Global Development Solutions, LLC, analysis of data provided by the Export Promotion Bureau.
Note: The fiscal year runs from July to June.

followed by trousers (+554 percent). Over the past decade, knitwear's share of total apparel exports rose significantly, from 30.8 percent in FY2001 to 46.3 percent in FY2011 (table 5.11).

For knitwear and woven wear, the leading buyers of Bangladesh's apparel were Germany, the United Kingdom, and the United States in FY2012 (table 5.12).

Table 5.10 Major Apparel Items Exported by Bangladesh, Selected Years
US$, millions

Fiscal year	*Shirts*	*Trousers*	*Jackets*	*T-shirts (including polo)*	*Polo shirts (est.)*	*Sweaters*
1996	807.66	112.02	171.73	366.36	109.91	70.41
1999	1,043.11	394.85	393.44	471.88	141.56	271.70
2002	871.21	636.61	412.34	546.28	163.88	517.83
2005	1,053.34	1,667.72	430.28	1,349.71	404.91	893.12
2008	915.60	2,512.74	1,181.52	2,765.56	829.67	1,474.09
2009	1,000.16	3,007.29	1,299.74	3,065.86	919.76	1,858.62
2010	993.41	3,035.35	1,350.43	3,145.52	943.66	1,795.39
2011	1,566.42	4,164.16	1,887.50	4,696.57	1,408.97	2,488.19

Source: Bangladesh Textile Mills Association, interview, November 12, 2012.

The top export markets for Bangladesh reflect traditional apparel consumers. Together these three markets represented 53 percent of all of Bangladesh's apparel exports. Within Bangladesh's apparel exports, the products are fairly concentrated: the top 10 products comprised 77 percent of total apparel exports and the top three alone comprised 50.5 percent in FY2012. The dominant categories in FY2012 were HS610910, HS620342, and HS611090, as shown in table 5.13.

Bangladesh was the second largest exporter of polo shirts in 2011, after China, reflecting its cost advantage worldwide. Polo shirts do not have a designated product category, so their contribution to Bangladesh's exports could not be ascertained with certainty. According to BTMA, polo shirts are exported under the code HS610910 (T-shirts, singlets, and other vests of cotton, knitted), the largest apparel category for Bangladeshi exports. Approximately 30 percent of that category is attributable to polo shirts. Leading export partners in FY2012 for HS610910 include Germany (21.1 percent of the category), the United Kingdom (9.9 percent), and France (9.4 percent) (table 5.14). For calendar year 2011, exports of HS610910 were US$5.2 billion for China, US$4.1 billion for Bangladesh, US$1.6 billion for India, US$535.8 million for Vietnam, and US$16.6 million for Ethiopia (table 5.15). At a price of US$2.75 per shirt, Bangladeshi production value is in line with that of Vietnam (US$2.82 per shirt). Bangladesh has a cost advantage over India (US$3.48 per shirt) and Ethiopia (US$4.03 per shirt), but not China (US$2.24 per shirt).[13]

Bangladesh's apparel exports have benefited from duty-free access to the European Union via the Generalized System of Preferences (GSP) privileges accorded to least-developed countries (LDCs) (European Parliament 2011). In addition to the European Union, Australia, Canada, Japan, and Norway provide duty-free, quota-free market access for Bangladesh's exports. However, the European Union adopted a new GSP on October 31, 2012, effective January 1, 2014 (European Commission 2012). The updated GSP is designed to extend privileges to fewer countries with greater need and uses criteria such as per capita income and economic diversification. A "GSP+" program was developed

Table 5.11 Annual Apparel Exports of Bangladesh, FY2001–FY2011

	Knitwear exports				*Woven exports*				*Total apparel exports*		
Fiscal year	*Value (US$, millions)*	*Annual change (%)*	*Share of apparel exports (%)*	*Share of Bangladesh exports (%)*	*Value (US$, millions)*	*Annual change (%)*	*Share of apparel exports (%)*	*Share of Bangladesh exports (%)*	*Total apparel (US$, millions)*	*Total Bangladesh exports (US$, millions)*	*Apparel as share of total exports (%)*
2001	1,496.23	0.0	30.8	23.1	3,364.20	—	69.2	52.0	4,860.43	6,467.30	75.2
2002	1,459.24	−2.5	31.8	24.4	3,124.56	−7.12	68.2	52.2	4,583.80	5,986.09	76.6
2003	1,653.83	13.3	33.7	25.3	3,258.27	4.28	66.3	49.8	4,912.10	6,548.44	75.0
2004	2,148.02	29.9	37.8	28.3	3,538.07	8.59	62.2	46.5	5,686.09	7,602.99	74.8
2005	2,819.47	31.3	43.9	32.6	3,598.20	1.70	56.1	41.6	6,417.67	8,654.52	74.2
2006	3,816.98	35.4	48.3	36.3	4,083.82	13.50	51.7	38.8	7,900.80	10,526.20	75.1
2007	4,553.60	19.3	49.4	37.4	4,657.63	14.05	50.6	38.2	9,211.23	12,177.90	75.6
2008	5,532.52	21.5	51.7	39.2	5,167.28	10.94	48.3	36.6	10,699.80	14,110.80	75.8
2009	6,429.00	16.2	52.1	41.3	5,918.51	14.54	47.9	38.0	12,347.51	15,565.19	79.3
2010	6,483.29	0.8	51.9	40.0	6,013.43	1.60	48.1	37.1	12,496.72	16,204.65	77.1
2011	9,482.06	46.3	52.9	41.4	8,432.40	40.23	47.1	36.8	17,914.46	22,924.38	78.1

Source: Bangladesh Garment Manufacturers and Exporters Association.

Table 5.12 Top Bangladeshi Apparel Export Markets, FY2012

Rank	*Country*	*Exports (US$)*	*Category (%)*
HS61: Articles of apparel, accessories, knit or crochet			
1	Germany	2,039,968,240	21.5
2	United Kingdom	1,103,299,153	11.6
3	United States	1,013,949,065	10.7
4	France	855,179,290	9.0
5	Spain	660,730,730	7.0
6	Italy	571,463,391	6.0
7	Canada	401,815,066	4.2
8	Netherlands	325,277,455	3.4
9	Belgium	320,456,338	3.4
10	Denmark	318,718,652	3.4
	Other	1,875,532,927	19.8
	Total	**9,486,390,307**	**100.0**
HS62: Articles of apparel, accessories, not knit or crochet			
1	United States	3,515,450,981	36.6
2	Germany	1,358,921,611	14.2
3	United Kingdom	1,026,772,149	10.7
4	Canada	473,039,424	4.9
5	France	416,724,096	4.3
6	Spain	410,390,819	4.3
7	Italy	291,151,747	3.0
8	Japan	239,994,652	2.5
9	Belgium	238,609,018	2.5
10	Turkey	231,196,876	2.4
	Other	1,401,084,957	14.6
	Total	**9,603,336,331**	**100.0**

Source: Export Promotion Bureau, Bangladesh.

Table 5.13 Top Bangladeshi Apparel Export Products, FY2012

Rank	*Commodity*	*Trade value (US$)*	*Share of apparel exports (%)*
1	610910: T-shirts, singlets and other vests, of cotton, knitted	4,490,119,742	23.5
2	620342: Men's/boys' trousers and shorts, of cotton, not knitted	3,664,075,946	19.2
3	611090: Pullovers, cardigans & similar articles of other textile materials, knitted	1,494,196,580	7.8
4	620462: Women's/girls' trousers and shorts, of cotton, not knitted	1,433,020,567	7.5
5	620520: Men's/boys' shirts, of cotton, not knitted	1,109,860,373	5.8
6	611020: Pullovers, cardigans and similar articles of cotton, knitted	665,959,561	3.5
7	610510: Men's/boys' shirts, of cotton, knitted	624,230,712	3.3

table continues next page

Table 5.13 Top Bangladeshi Apparel Export Products, FY2012 *(continued)*

Rank	*Commodity*	*Trade value (US$)*	*Share of apparel exports (%)*
8	620590: Men's/boys' shirts, of other textile materials, not knitted	598,850,315	3.1
9	620349: Men's/boys' trousers and shorts, of other textile materials, not knitted	312,535,433	1.6
10	620333: Men's/boys' jackets and blazers, of synthetic fibers, not knitted	299,770,305	1.6
	Other apparel	4,397,107,102	23.0
	Total apparel exports	19,089,726,638	100.0

Source: Export Promotion Bureau, Bangladesh.
Note: Based on six-digit categories within HS61 and HS62.

Table 5.14 Bangladesh's Leading Export Partners, HS610910 Including Polo Shirts, FY2012

Rank	*Country*	*Export value (US$)*	*Share of total exports (%)*
1	Germany	946,422,134	21.1
2	United Kingdom	443,273,668	9.9
3	France	423,400,995	9.4
4	Spain	355,280,721	7.9
5	United States	315,604,931	7.0
6	Italy	267,873,727	6.0
7	Belgium	197,496,286	4.4
8	Denmark	191,945,214	4.3
9	Netherlands	188,747,245	4.2
10	Canada	176,781,081	3.9
	Other	983,293,742	21.9
	Total	4,490,119,742	100.0

Source: Export Promotion Bureau, Bangladesh.

Table 5.15 Comparative Exports, HS610910 Including Polo Shirts, 2011

Country	*Export value (US$)*	*Number of units*	*US$/unit*
China	5,196,067,671	2,323,048,282	2.24
Bangladesh	4,129,423,647	1,499,087,388	2.75
India	1,637,401,752	470,321,877	3.48
Vietnam	535,824,379	189,812,266	2.82
Ethiopia	16,611,059	4,123,741	4.03

Source: United Nations Statistical Division (unstats.un.org/).
Note: Values are based on mirror data and therefore CIF price, not FOB.

to accord greater benefits to countries that ratify and implement international conventions on core human and labor rights, the environment, and good governance. Prospective beneficiary countries must apply for new GSP+ benefits. Current GSP preferences will be phased out at the country or product level via a graduation mechanism for LDCs with extremely successful export sectors (such as textiles) that no longer need GSP to successfully penetrate world markets. However, if a specific group of products accounts for more than 50 percent of total GSP-covered exports, the group cannot be graduated as a whole, because doing so could disrupt the main pillar of an economy. Furthermore, Bangladesh benefits from the European Union's Everything But Arms initiative, which provides LDCs with duty-free, quota-free access to the European market for all products except arms and ammunition. Like Bangladesh, China, Ethiopia, and Vietnam are current GSP beneficiaries, but their future status has yet to be determined.

Bangladesh's apparel is considered "sensitive" by the United States and as such is not covered under the U.S. GSP program (and this was the case even before the post–Rana Plaza suspension of Bangladesh's GDP privileges). In 2006, the Office of the United States Trade Representative (USTR) accepted a GSP new country practice petition from the American Federation of Labor and Congress of Industrial Organizations (AFL-CIO) regarding workers' rights in Bangladesh.[14] The petition alleged a number of labor practice problems in the EPZs, the RMGs sector, and the shrimp processing sector. In April 2009, a high-level delegation from Bangladesh, along with private sector representatives from the garment, apparel, and shrimp sectors, as well as the AFL-CIO, testified before the GSP Subcommittee regarding improvements in the labor environment. The USTR is evaluating country progress on matters raised in the petition and has not made a decision on Bangladesh's GSP eligibility yet. As a result, exported apparel from Bangladesh, like other exporting countries, such as China, faces tariffs in the United States ranging from 0 to 32 percent.[15] However, the majority of Ethiopian apparel exports to the United States are duty-free under the African Growth and Opportunity Act (AGOA). Even with this incentive, Ethiopia only exported US$10 million in apparel to the United States in 2011.

The United States is Bangladesh's most important single-country trading partner. Bangladesh is the fourth largest apparel exporter to the United States, which takes about a quarter of Bangladesh's exports. In 2011, Bangladesh's U.S. exports topped US$4.9 billion, with more than 90 percent as articles of clothing in the form of woven apparel (US$3.4 billion), knit apparel (US$1.0 billion), textile products (US$186 million), and headgear (US$120 million). From the U.S. perspective, although Bangladesh is a small trading partner (currently the 57th largest goods trading partner),[16] it is the fourth largest apparel exporter to the United States after China, Vietnam, and Indonesia. Apparel exports to the United States grew 65 percent in the five years from 2005 (US$2.4 billion) to 2010 (US$3.9 billion).

Cotton Markets

Apparel prices are highly dependent on the prices of underlying raw materials and price volatility can squeeze margins of manufacturers or global apparel companies, depending on contract terms. Typically, raw materials account for 25–50 percent of the cost of producing a garment, while labor contributes another 20–40 percent, depending on product complexity (Bruemmer 2011).

Cotton prices rose considerably between September 2010 and July 2011 and hit a 150-year high in February 2011 (figure 5.12) after bad weather in major cotton-producing countries reduced harvests, causing a ripple effect in the prices of yarn, fabric, and apparel in the manufacturing supply chain. Apparel brand firms reacted by raising consumer retail prices as much as possible and reducing the cotton content of clothing and substituting alternate materials.

Cotton production is highly concentrated in a handful of countries. The top five producers (China, India, the United States, Pakistan, and Brazil) are responsible for nearly 80 percent of 2011 world production (table 5.16). While the

Figure 5.12 Five-Year Price Volatility of Cotton, October 2007–October 2012

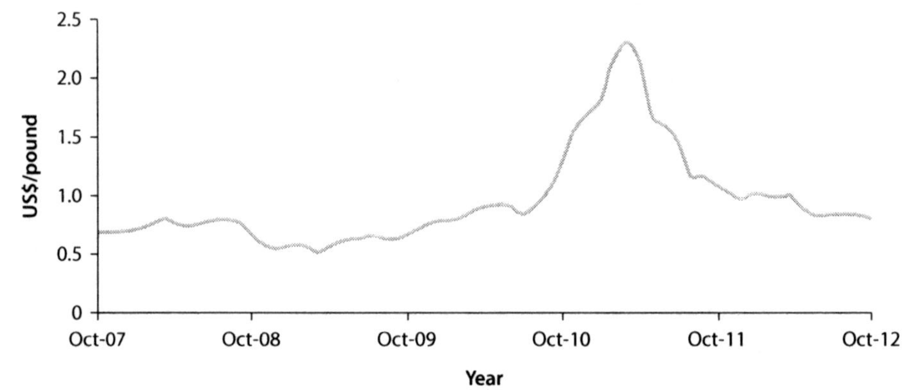

Source: Index Mundi, http://www.indexmundi.com/.
Note: The trend is based on the monthly price for cotton, Cotlook "A Index," middling 1-3/32 inch staple, cost and freight (CFR) Far Eastern ports.

Table 5.16 Stock of Top Cotton Producers, Ranked by 2011 Production
480-pound bales, thousands

Rank	*Country*	*Beginning stocks*	*Production*	*Imports*	*Total supply*	*Mill use*	*Exports*	*Ending stocks*	*Share of world production (%)*
1	China	10,603	33,100	24,533	68,236	38,000	55	30,181	27.1
2	India	10,074	27,500	600	38,174	19,950	10,500	7,724	22.5
3	United States	2,600	15,573	19	18,192	3,300	11,714	3,350	12.8
4	Pakistan	2,732	10,600	1,000	14,332	10,100	1,150	3,057	8.7
5	Brazil	7,906	8,700	29	16,635	4,000	4,792	7,993	7.1
6	Australia	2,550	5,500	—	8,050	40	4,642	3,518	4.5
7	Uzbekistan	1,148	4,200	—	5,348	1,350	2,500	1,498	3.4
8	Turkey	1,722	3,440	2,382	7,544	5,600	300	1,724	2.8
9	Turkmenistan	899	1,400	—	2,299	600	750	949	1.1
10	Greece	321	1,330	20	1,671	130	1,000	491	1.1
NR	Bangladesh	842	75	3,150	4,067	3,200	—	857	n.a.

Source: U.S. Department of Agriculture-Foreign Agriculture Service website, as reported by the National Cotton Council of America.
Note: Data are based on the marketing year, which runs from August to July. Bangladesh is not ranked; data provided for comparison.
— = not available.

United States exported 75 percent of its production, China retained all production and supplemented quantities further through imports to meet the significant demands of its milling and apparel manufacturing sectors. Bangladesh, Ethiopia, and Vietnam are not among the top 30 cotton producers, producing only 75,000, 95,000, and 23,000 480-pound bales in 2011, respectively.[17]

Bangladesh is unique among major textile producers in that it is wholly dependent on imported cotton and thus incurs greater risk in terms of price volatility and supply interruption. The dominant consumers of cotton are mills, which create fabric from the raw material. Two-thirds of global cotton use by mills is concentrated in China, India, and Pakistan. Of the total cotton milled in 2011, China led with 38 million 480-pound bales (37.8 percent of total world milling), followed by India with 19.8 percent and Pakistan with 10.0 percent. Bangladesh ranked seventh in cotton mill use, with 3.2 million bales and 3.2 percent of world cotton mill quantity (table 5.17). Vietnam ranked in the top 10 for cotton milling, taking 10th place with 1.65 million bales or 1.6 percent of total cotton mill quantity. Although Ethiopia does mill its domestic cotton, the quantities are not sufficient to register among the top 30 cotton milling countries. In addition to supplying the Bangladeshi apparel manufacturers, Bangladesh's mills export fabric, to the tune of US$30.9 million in FY2012.[18]

The United States is the world's leading cotton exporter; it exported 11.7 million 480-pound bales or 26.4 percent of world export volume in 2011. Major cotton export markets for the United States include China, Mexico, and Turkey. The United States then imports processed cotton products, including apparel, household goods, and fabric. Other major cotton exporters include India, with 23.6 percent of world exports, and Brazil, with 10.8 percent of world exports (table 5.18). The top three countries together account for 60.8 percent of world cotton exports.

Bangladesh is the second largest importer of cotton. The world's leading apparel producers rank highly among cotton importers, with the top 10 importers

Table 5.17 Top 10 Cotton Millers, 2011

Rank	*Country*	*Mill use (480-pound bales x 1,000)*	*Share of world mill use (%)*
1	China	38,000	37.8
2	India	19,950	19.8
3	Pakistan	10,100	10.0
4	Turkey	5,600	5.6
5	Brazil	4,000	4.0
6	United States	3,300	3.3
7	Bangladesh	3,200	3.2
8	Indonesia	1,900	1.9
9	Mexico	1,700	1.7
10	Vietnam	1,650	1.6

Source: U.S. Department of Agriculture-Foreign Agriculture Service website, as reported by the National Cotton Council of America.
Note: Data are based on the marketing year, which runs from August to July.

Table 5.18 Top 10 Exporters of Cotton, 2011

Rank	*Country*	*Exports (480-pound bales x 1,000)*	*Share of world exports (%)*
1	United States	11,714	26.4
2	India	10,500	23.6
3	Brazil	4,792	10.8
4	Australia	4,642	10.5
5	Uzbekistan	2,500	5.6
6	Pakistan	1,150	2.6
7	Malaysia	1,023	2.3
8	Greece	1,000	2.3
9	Turkmenistan	750	1.7
10	Mali	625	1.4

Source: U.S. Department of Agriculture-Foreign Agriculture Service website, as reported by the National Cotton Council of America.
Note: Data are based on the marketing year, which runs from August to July.

Table 5.19 Top 10 Importers of Cotton, 2011

Rank	*Country*	*Imports (480-pound bales x 1,000)*	*Share of world imports (%)*
1	China	24,533	55.7
2	Bangladesh	3,150	7.1
3	Turkey	2,382	5.4
4	Indonesia	1,975	4.5
5	Vietnam	1,625	3.7
6	Thailand	1,263	2.9
7	Korea, Rep.	1,170	2.7
8	Malaysia	1,125	2.6
9	Mexico	1,000	2.3
10	Pakistan	1,000	2.3

Source: U.S. Department of Agriculture-Foreign Agriculture Service website, as reported by the National Cotton Council of America.
Note: Data are based on the marketing year, which runs from August to July.

dominated heavily by Asian manufacturers. In 2011, China led in cotton imports by quantity, with 24.5 million 480-pound bales and 55.7 percent of global cotton imports. Bangladesh came in second place, with 3.2 million bales and 7.1 percent of world import quantity. Vietnam ranked in the top five, with 1.6 million bales and 3.7 percent of cotton imports by quantity (table 5.19). The top three countries together purchase 68.2 percent of all cotton traded globally. Ethiopia was not among the top 30 cotton importers.

Bangladesh has diversified its sources of cotton imports. Although in the past nearly all of Bangladesh's cotton imports came from Uzbekistan, Bangladesh now purchases about 33 percent of its cotton from Uzbekistan, 28 percent from India, 12 percent from Africa, and 9 percent from Turkmenistan, with the remaining 12 percent coming from other countries (Ahsan 2012). Cotton lint was Bangladesh's second largest commodity import by value in 2010, totaling US$794.4 million and 401,258 tons.[19] That same year, China's cotton lint imports totaled US$6.1 billion or 3,052,246 tons and Vietnam's cotton lint imports totaled US$600.6 million or 305,212 tons.

Disruption in cotton supply is a serious risk for Bangladesh. Although not a major trading partner in cotton for Bangladesh, China still can impact Bangladesh's cotton supply as the largest producer and importer of cotton. For example, in recent years, China has stockpiled significant quantities of Indian cotton, prompting the government of India to ban cotton exports to all markets for two consecutive seasons, driving up world prices. As China utilizes its cotton reserve rather than importing cotton, cotton prices may decline because of decreased demand, exposing Bangladesh to price risk for its cotton imports. Additional supply risk comes from the fact that Uzbekistan ships most of its cotton through Iranian ports, which are subject to a U.S. embargo. Possible measures to mitigate this risk include: (a) government-to-government agreements with major suppliers to guarantee supply; (b) the creation of a national reserve of raw cotton to ensure uninterrupted supply and stabilize the local market; (c) increased domestic cotton cultivation; and (d) further diversified sources, such as African countries, where there may be less geopolitical risk.

Key Market Drivers and Options for Growth

Although clothing is an essential item, in general total worldwide spending on apparel is largely discretionary and as such is dependent on population and consumer income levels as well as consumer sentiment. Consumers are influenced by fashion trends and a desire to signal social status. The recent economic downturn slowed but did not deter apparel industry growth. Although global sales grew only 1.5 percent from 2007 to 2008, they grew 3.7 percent from 2010 to 2011 (MarketLine 2012).

Several countries have moved into the low-price manufacturing space, including Bangladesh, Indonesia, the Philippines, and Vietnam, and, to a lesser extent, Cambodia and Sri Lanka. As labor costs and currency values in China rise and the country moves toward higher-value manufacturing, apparel brands and buyers are shifting production toward lower-cost manufacturing in Asia and, to a lesser extent, Africa. Purchasing officers increasingly are seeking alternate sourcing markets, given rising labor costs and shortages in China. Particularly for the RMG industry, entry-level positions are unskilled and workers who develop skills can command higher wages in other industries. And in China, production focus is shifting from exports to serving the quickly growing, more profitable domestic market.

Bangladesh will gain from becoming recognized as a socially responsible producer. International apparel companies increasingly are focusing on social and environmental responsibility in their supply chain, to appease customer and investor demands and to ensure operational sustainability. Particularly for publically traded companies, disclosure is no longer limited to financial statements. Rather, disclosure now involves integrated reporting that reflects the commercial, social, and environmental context within which the entity operates and demonstrates organizational stewardship under corporate social responsibility parameters (Pawlicki 2012). Moreover, vendors are increasingly subject to supply chain vendor code of conduct requirements, under which companies must disclose environmental, social, and governance information. In some cases, companies must have this information verified by a third party to supply large retail organizations. Consumer demand is another significant driver of sustainability reporting, as customers are showing a decided preference for socially and environmentally responsible products, and companies that offer these products can command a price premium. Several certification programs have been developed to enable companies to demonstrate best practices in the areas that are important to their stakeholders. Finally, companies must comply with various federal and state regulatory and legislative requirements, such as the recent Securities and Exchange Commission release on conflict minerals and the California Transparency in Supply Chains Act, which focuses on fair trade practices.

However, Bangladeshi apparel manufacturers have been troubled by issues related to working conditions. More than 600 workers have died in Bangladeshi garment factory fires over the past five years. In 2010, three people were killed and scores injured as more than 20,000 EPZ garment workers rioted over wages in Dhaka and Bangladesh (AsiaNews 2010). Most factory buildings in Bangladesh lack fire escapes, sprinklers, and other modern safety equipment. Fires and other incidents have prompted companies to cancel orders. In response, international apparel brands have pledged major improvements to safety. In March 2012, PVH, the company that produces Tommy Hilfiger, announced a US$1–US$2 million commitment to enforce safety reforms demanded by labor groups, including an independent fire inspector and public reports about safety conditions (ABC News 2012). In October 2012, Gap Inc. made similar pledges in the multi-million dollar range to improve building and fire safety standards across the company's approved third-party garment manufacturing factories in Bangladesh (Gap Inc. 2012).

International apparel brands continue to press the government, factory owners, and other stakeholders to improve conditions. Illustrating the significance of corporate social responsibility in the supply chain, executives of 30 global apparel brands and retailers convened in Dhaka in November 2012 to discuss a mutually beneficial path toward sustainable development in the apparel and footwear sectors. These companies represented US$5.8 billion or 30.4 percent of Bangladesh's RMG exports in FY2012. Issues of concern included minimum wages, a sustainable factory model, factory compliance, worker welfare, and safety and infrastructure development (Islam 2012). With all the international support, Bangladesh has the opportunity to transform its RMG sector into a model for sustainable development and cement customer relationships in the process.

Conclusions and Recommendations

Investing in the skill levels of workers will enable Bangladesh to increase efficiency in the near term, decrease wastage, realize cost savings, and use resources more efficiently. Over the longer term, improvements in product quality may eventually enable Bangladesh to target higher-value apparel segments that require more complex production processes. Skill building should not be limited to line workers, but should also involve management to develop the talent needed to run effective and efficient international garment manufacturing enterprises. Realization of this goal is complex and involves many stakeholders from firms, institutions, and government.

Labor issues (wages, workplace safety, and compliance with labor standards) can generate major reputational risk for Bangladesh's overall garment exports and will need to be carefully managed. Labor standards and safety issues can affect future exports and Bangladesh's overall reputation in the exporting sector. Concerns have been heightened recently, following a series of fatal incidents, and the government has been pressured to take a number of measures to improve workers' safety. International buyers and governments have reacted strongly to these events (box 5.2). On June 27, 2013, the United States suspended GSP trade privileges for Bangladesh over concerns about safety problems and labor rights violations in the garment industry. Minimizing the chances of further tragedies in the garment and export sectors in Bangladesh has become a precondition for sustained export growth. Whatever measures the government will implement under domestic and international pressure, the important issue will be enforcement and commitment to ensure better and safer practices. The government needs to demonstrate its seriousness by providing leadership on this front, partly to convince the European Union and the United States, the major players post–Rana Plaza. In doing this, it will need to partner with the domestic and international private sectors.

Strengthening labor relations will help Bangladesh improve productivity via the quality and quantity of output, retain a supply of trained labor, and retain its international customer base while maintaining competitiveness. Labor relations directly affect productivity and the ability to deliver customer orders under agreed contract terms. Garments cannot be produced if the workers are on strike and productivity suffers if the workers have high turnover, absenteeism, or are

Box 5.2 Rana Plaza Momentum for Reforms: Implementation Will Be Key

The fallout from the April 24, 2013, collapse of the eight-story Rana Plaza multipurpose building in Savar, Dhaka, has had domestic and international repercussions. The death toll exceeded 1,100, mostly female garment workers who worked on the upper floors of the building in several garment factories supplying about 30 Western clothing retailers. Analysis suggests that the building was not built to code; was not fit to sustain the additional weight of the three highest floors, which were added after the original building was built; and was not suited to carry the weight of people and equipment that a garment factory requires or to withstand the vibrations of the back-up generators that were installed in the upper-floor factories. A few people have been jailed for complicity in this situation, including the building owner and

box continues next page

Box 5.2 Rana Plaza Momentum for Reforms: Implementation Will Be Key *(continued)*

some factory owners (who urged factory workers to return to their work places a day after large cracks were found in the building and a structural engineer pronounced the building to be unfit for use) and others have been suspended, including public officials who authorized the building's construction.

In the meantime, international clothing retailers that source products in Bangladesh as well as the European Union are paying more attention to ensure safety compliance and improve supply chain transparency. The Accord on Fire and Building Safety (http://bangladeshaccord.org), consisting of more than 180 global apparel brands (mostly European), has agreed on a legally binding plan to inspect all Bangladeshi garment factories that supply the companies, and publicly disclose the names of these factories as well as inspection reports and agreed remediation measures. As of September 2014, 1,103 factories had been inspected, resulting in the highlighting of 52,605 safety issues. The brands also agreed on 500 corrective action plans (CAPs) with the factory owners. The inspection reports and CAPs are being published online.

A group of 26 American retailers, which have formed the Alliance for Bangladesh Worker Safety, announced a non-binding five-year initiative, developed with the help of the Bipartisan Policy Center. This initiative seeks to improve factory safety in the Bangladeshi garment industry[a] by inspecting 100 percent of Alliance member factories, developing common safety standards, sharing inspection results transparently, and ensuring that all alliance factories actively support the democratic election and successful operation of Worker Participation Committees in each factory. Until March 2015, the Alliance had conducted initial inspections of 580 factories (100 percent), of which 19 have been partially or fully closed. Almost 300 CAPs have been finalized with the factories. The Alliance plans to complete final inspection (after implementation of remediation measures) of all these factories by July 2017.

As initial inspection of all the factories has been completed, international buyers can move toward implementation of remediation measures and coordinate among themselves while doing so, to help minimize additional burden and the possibility of remediation fatigue among factory owners. Financing of the remedial work is also becoming a growing concern, as in some cases buyers are allegedly not getting involved as promised.

Although Bangladesh is still considered the leading apparel sourcing destination alternative to China, its popularity as a top destination for sourcing in the next five years dropped after the Rana Plaza incident, leading to order cancellations of around US$110 million from 37 factories, according to a newspaper report.[b] The potential impact on Bangladesh's garment industry, which accounts for almost 80 percent of export earnings, and therefore on gross domestic product, could be significant. Under pressure to respond to the Savar tragedy, the Government of Bangladesh has made considerable progress in improving labor safety and working conditions by amending the Labor Law, revising the minimum wage for garment workers from Tk 3,000 (US$38) to Tk 5,300 (US$68), and strengthening the labor inspection system. The government has also inspected 282 factories that are not under the purview of the Western initiatives. While there is progress in improving workplace compliance, more needs to be done to fulfill the commitment of raising it to international standards.

a. "Reuters Insight Inspection Intensifies Bangladesh Garment Industry's Woes," *The Bangladesh Chronicle*, June 27, 2014.
b. "Safety Compliance a Make or Break for Many Garment Factories," *The Dhaka Tribune*, April 30, 2014.

otherwise unmotivated to maintain or enhance productivity and product quality. Two tangible actions that will strengthen labor relations are the following:

- *The creation of worker groups* (associations, unions, and so forth) with the explicit support of government and industry. The government has stated that it will allow worker groups, but in practice formation and participation has been discouraged and requests for reform ignored. The groups will be effective only if they are permitted to form independently and are recognized as legitimate by industry stakeholders. Trading partners such as the United States, the largest importer of global apparel and a major market for Bangladesh, have expressed concern regarding lack of worker associations and made reduction in tariffs conditional on the establishment of such groups and the development and enforcement of regulations related to workers' rights. Thus, if effective worker groups were formed, Bangladesh could realize significant economic benefits.
- *The enactment and enforcement of policies related to worker compensation*. This is a tricky area for the government to get involved in, since it should normally be left to the private sector. However, there is a history of government involvement in garment sector wages through minimum wage promulgations, set through a negotiation process between workers and the private sector, with the government as a kind of arbiter. Given this, and the renewed recent concerns about worker conditions, the government's current involvement in setting minimum wages appears to be warranted. As recommended in the World Bank's recent report on exports, a more regular cost-of-living adjustment may reduce the frequency of labor unrest (World Bank 2012). In the past, minimum wages were adjusted with lags of 10, 12, and four years. An annual setting of minimum wages, although not a guarantee of industrial peace, may impact worker behavior and expectations in a positive way. Poor and lagged implementation of minimum wages has often triggered labor unrest and the government can help ensure that the lag between wage awards and implementation is minimal. The longer-term goal should be for wage negotiations to be conducted more autonomously as part of a more credible labor relations process.

Bangladesh could increase its competitiveness by reengineering import and export logistics. Significant reductions in import and export times will help Bangladesh participate in fast fashion cycles and better meet customer inventory management needs. Without improvement, Bangladesh will be stuck in the low-value garment basics segment and have no ability to utilize its existing production capacity for higher-value garments. The bottlenecks for import and export affect the textile and garment sectors and are for the most part beyond the control of the manufacturers. Resolving this issue involves government import and export policy improvements. The operations of logistics providers, such as customs authorities, transporters, shipping lines, maritime service providers, and insurance providers, need to be streamlined.

Improved power reliability would reduce manufacturing costs, increase productivity, increase capacity utilization, better utilize human resources and capital assets, and increase overall competitiveness by speeding production and attracting greater sector investment. These improvements require direct government intervention and significant public and private investment. Where possible, green power options should be encouraged.

Bangladesh should strengthen institutions for research and development and capacity building. This will help the industry maintain its competitiveness with existing apparel manufacturing countries and new entrants and encourage best practices in garment manufacturing to be applied sectorwide. Leveraging technology can improve production efficiency and help move the sector beyond low labor costs as the sole means to profitability. Technology can also help Bangladesh adapt to the rapidly changing needs of fashion buyers. On the human resources side, increasing skills will improve the quality of products and increase resource efficiency. Strengthening institutional capacity requires the support and involvement of firms, institutions, and government, and will be enhanced by collaboration with supply chain partners.

Annex 5A: Bangladesh's Export Processing Zones: Location, Physical Size, and Utility Infrastructure

										Utility services[a]					
										Water		Gas		Electricity	
EPZ	Location	Proximity to ports	Zone area (ha)	Number of industrial plots	Size of each plot (m^2)	Land rent (US$/$m^2$/month)	Space of standard factory building (m^2)	Number of buildings	Factory building rent (US$/$m^2$/month)	Water supply	Storage capacity (million liters/day)	Tariff (Tk/m^3)	Gas supply	Tariff (Tk/m^3)	Power supply	Tariff (Tk/kWh)
Adamjee Export Processing Zone	Adamjee Nagar, Shiddirgonj, Narayanganj	15 km from Dhaka city center, 40 km from Hazrat Shahjalal Airport, 255 km from Chittagong Port	118.62	307	2,000	2.20	42,737	n.a.	2.75	Own water supply system	n.a.	22.43	Titas Gas Transmission & Distribution Co., Ltd.	6.45	11 kv, 3 phase, 50 cycles/second	6.11
Chittagong Export Processing Zone	South Halishahar	3.1 km from sea port, 5.5 km from main business center, 11.3 km from Shah Amanat International Airport, Chittagong	183.37	502	2,000	2.20	65,809	15	2.75	Chittagong WASA	7.26	22.43	Bakhrabad Gas System, Ltd.	6.45	11 kv, 3 phase, 50 cycles/second	6.11

table continues next page

Annex 5A *(continued)*

											Utility services[a]					
											Water		Gas		Electricity	
EPZ	Location	Proximity to ports	Zone area (ha)	Number of industrial plots	Size of each plot (m^2)	Land rent (US$/$m^2$/month)	Space of standard factory building (m^2)	Number of buildings	Factory building rent (US$/$m^2$/month)	Water supply	Storage capacity (million liters/day)	Tariff (Tk/m^3)	Gas supply	Tariff (Tk/m^3)	Power supply	Tariff (Tk/kWh)
Comilla Export Processing Zone	Comilla old airport area	167 km from Chittagong port, 97 km from Dhaka	108.28	213	2,000	2.20	29,450	n.a.	2.75	Own water supply system	n.a.	22.43	Bakhrabad Gas System, Ltd.	6.45	11 kv, 3 phase, 50 cycles/second	6.11
Dhaka Export Processing Zone	Savar	35 km from Dhaka city center, 25 km from Hazrat Shahjalal Airport, 304 km from Chittagong Sea Port	146.09	442	2,000	2.20	108,850	17	2.75	Own water supply system	n.a.	22.43	Titas Gas Transmission & Distribution Co., Ltd.	6.45	11 kv, 3 phase, 50 cycles/second	6.11
Ishwardi Export Processing Zone	Pakshl, Pabna	10.6 km from Ishwardi Airport, 220 km from Dhaka, 280 km from Mongla port, 110 km from Rajshahi Airport, 484 km from Chittagong Port	124.99	158 (100 in Phase1)	2,000	1.25	18,000	n.a.	1.60	Own water supply system	n.a.	22.43	Paschimanchal Gas Company, Ltd.	6.45	11 kv, 3 phase, 50 cycles/second	6.11

table continues next page

Annex 5A *(continued)*

										Utility services[a]						
										Water			Gas		Electricity	
EPZ	Location	Proximity to ports	Zone area (ha)	Number of industrial plots	Size of each plot (m^2)	Land rent (US$/$m^2$/month)	Space of standard factory building (m^2)	Number of buildings	Factory building rent (US$/$m^2$/month)	Water supply	Storage capacity (million liters/day)	Tariff (Tk/m^3)	Gas supply	Tariff (Tk/m^3)	Power supply	Tariff (Tk/kWh)
Karnaphuli Export Processing Zone	North Potenga and Halishahar	6 km from Chittagong Port, 10 km from main business center of Chittagong, 9 km from Shah Amanat International Airport, Chittagong	222.42	254	2,000	2.20	19,686	n.a.	2.75	Chittagong WASA and own water treatment plant	n.a.	22.43	Bakhrabad Gas System, Ltd.	6.45	11 kv, 3 phase, 50 cycles/second	8.36 (peak), 5.35 (off peak)
Mongla Export Processing Zone	Mongla Port area, Bagerhat	105 km from Jessore Airport, 397 km from Dhaka, 664 km from Chittagong Port	186.21	124	2,000	1.25	9,000	n.a.	1.60	Fresh water from Public Health Engineering Department and own supply network	n.a.	22.43	Not available	n.a.	11 kv, 3 phase, 50 cycles/second	6.11

table continues next page

Annex 5A *(continued)*

											Utility services[a]						
											Water			Gas		Electricity	
EPZ	*Location*	*Proximity to ports*	*Zone area (ha)*	*Number of industrial plots*	*Size of each plot (m^2)*	*Land rent (US\$/m^2/month)*	*Space of standard factory building (m^2)*	*Number of buildings*	*Factory building rent (US\$/m^2/month)*	*Water supply*	*Storage capacity (million liters/day)*	*Tariff (Tk/m^3)*	*Gas supply*	*Tariff (Tk/m^3)*	*Power supply*	*Tariff (Tk/kWh)*
Uttara Export Processing Zone	Shongalshi, Nilphamari	18 km from Syedpur Airport, 401 km from Dhaka, 650 km from Chittagong Port, 586 km from Mongla Sea Port	85.79	202	2,000	1.25	12,400	n.a.	1.60	Own water supply system	n.a.	22.43	Not available	n.a.	11 kv, 3 phase, 50 cycles/second	6.11

Source: Bangladesh Export Processing Zones Authority.
Note: n.a. = not available.
a. Utilities will be charged at the current Tk:US\$ exchange rate.

Annex 5B: Support Institutions and Their Activities

Institution	*Support activity*
Ministry of Commerce	Establishes policy for the sector
Ministry of Finance	• Through the National Board of Revenue (www.nbr-bd.org), collects taxes and duties, including import duties (for materials), export duties (for exports), and VAT. • The Customs Act, 1969 (Act No. IV of 1969) (http://www.wipo.int/wipolex/en/text.jsp?file_id=198651) specifies the authority to levy duty and requirements for drawback but does not specify specific amounts or fees. • The Value Added Tax Act, 2011 (Act No. X of 2011). There is a 2012 draft in process (see draft: http://www.nbr-bd.org/vat_pdf/Draft_VAT_Law-2012_English.pdf).
Export Promotion Bureau, Ministry of Commerce, Bangladesh (www.epb.gov.bd)	• Established in 1977 as a national export promotion agency under the Ministry of Commerce. • Promotes export trade and improves plans and policies helpful to the sector. • Administered by a board of management comprising members from the public and private sectors. • Compiles public statistics on exported products. • Issues Certificate of Origin for exported products.
Bangladesh Garment Manufacturers and Exporters Association (BGMEA) (www.bgmea.com.bd)	• Represents the export-oriented woven, knit, and sweater garment manufacturers and exporters of Bangladesh. • Created to establish a healthy business environment and mutually beneficial relationship among manufacturers, exporters, and importers, thus ensuring steady growth in the foreign exchange earnings of the country. • Issues Utilization Declaration to exporters and monitors exports. • Plays a strong role to lead the industry in concurrence with the government, which BGMEA lobbies to promote the sector. • Promotes garment worker welfare and safety, manufacturer compliance with wage regulations, and vocational training programs. • Headquartered in Dhaka, with a regional office in Chittagong. • Operates the BGMEA Institute of Fashion and Technology, established in 2000 and which provides certificates, diplomas, and short courses in fashion design and garment merchandising.
Bangladesh Knitwear Manufacturers and Exporters Association (www.bkmea.com)	• Formed in 1996 to promote the knitwear sector, the largest export earning sector of the country. • Promotes Bangladesh's knitwear and diversity export markets to ensure better market access. • Works with national and international stakeholders, including the International Apparel Federation, Global Alliance for Fair Textile Trade, and American Manufacturing Trade Action Coalition. • Signed memorandum of understanding with GTZ in 2005 and Metro Group in 2010 to enhance productivity and social compliance of member factories, including centralized health and daycare. • Committed to child-free labor. • Currently 1,700 knitwear manufacturer and exporter members.
Bangladesh Textile Mills Association (BTMA) (www.btmadhaka.com)	• Registered in 1983, BTMA is the national trade organization of the primary textile industry, such as yarn manufacturing, fabric manufacturing, and dyeing-printing-finishing mills of Bangladesh under the private sector. • Current membership totals 1,364 mills and includes 383 yarn mills (28%), 743 fabric mills (55%), and 238 dyeing-printing-finishing mills (17%).

table continues next page

Annex 5B *(continued)*

Institution	*Support activity*

Bangladesh Export Processing Zones Authority (www.epzbangladesh.org.bd)	• Established in1983 to promote foreign direct investment and local investment, develop backward and forward linkages, generate employment, transfer technology, upgrade skills, and develop management capabilities.
	• Manages and oversees operations of the EPZs of Bangladesh.
	• Provides land or factory buildings in customs bonded areas, infrastructure, administrative facilities, and fiscal and nonfiscal incentives for investment.
	• Current activity includes:
	  • Eight EPZs, located in Chittagong, Dhaka, Mongla, Ishwardi, Comilla, Uttara, Adamjee, and Karnaphuli
	  • 352 registered entities (205 or 58% with 100% foreign ownership, 49 or 14% as joint venture, and 98 or 28% as 100% local venture)
	  • 35 countries invested, including Bangladesh
	  • More than 30 industries, including textile, woven, and knitted fabrics and garments and garments accessories.

Private sector	• In addition to making direct investments, several international apparel companies provide training, safety instruction, and other assistance to the sector in the interest of sector development.

Source: Global Development Solutions, LLC.
Note: EPZ = export processing zone; VAT = value-added tax.

Annex 5C: The Value Chain Analysis

The VCA provides a complete framework within which to assess, for the selected product value chain, the relative performance of each sector in terms of productivity and costs as well as to identify the main factors impeding growth and competitiveness. VCA in particular highlights the critical importance of industry-specific factors (for example, product market regulations and market failures) that tend to be overlooked by traditional cross-cutting approaches.

More specifically, the objectives of the VCA are to:

- Review the detailed breakdown of costs and productivity for the selected product and identify the main reasons for the productivity and costs gaps
- Identify the most important and common constraints across selected product value chains
- Generate insights into possible practical solutions for addressing a critical mass of the identified constraints
- Benchmark the competitiveness (productivity and costs) against Asian and African competitors in a representative sample of polo value chains.

Once the product selection was made, the work proceeded in parallel across the polo shirt value chains in the following analytical phases:

- *Basic description.* The analysis provides a basic description of the selected product value chain in terms of value added, domestic market, imports and exports, and employment.

- *Cost breakdown of the selected products.* The analysis provides a detailed breakdown of the value added for each critical step along the value chain. Furthermore, each critical step along the value chain is provided with an additional breakdown and analysis to show the underlying issues for each of these steps and provide the breakdown among input, labor, capital, and other costs.
- *Quality drivers of the selected products.* Understanding quality drivers in respective supply chains is essential, as it greatly influences the capacity of countries to compete and move up the value chain. Quality drivers include the quality of key inputs and services at each step of the value chain, the quality of the processing, as well as the quality of delivery and marketing (for example, time to market).
- *Productivity analysis and benchmarking.* In the case of polo shirts, the productivity analysis and benchmarking encompasses the efficiency dimension (for example, the number of polo shirts assembled per eight hours of work or the capacity utilization of the machines). Specifically, the VCA for polo shirts is benchmarked against a similar product produced in China, Ethiopia, and Vietnam. The productivity analysis also includes:
  - Benchmarking the performance of Bangladeshi polo shirt producers with Asian and African competitors by highlighting the major productivity differences at the operational level. Determining the relative importance of factors, such as scale, capacity utilization, waste levels, supplier relations (backward and forward linkages), and quality issues with the end product (as revealed by price differences in competitive markets).
  - Benchmarking the costs of Bangladeshi polo shirt producers with Asian and African competitors along the full spectrum of value-adding activities from inputs sourcing, manufacturing, and assembly to delivery of product in the market.

Based on the results of the VCA, the main constraints and respective recommendations are established by estimating the relative impact of key impediments on the productivity and costs of respective value chains in Bangladesh. In the case of polo shirts, the synthesis and recommendation stage integrates findings from productivity, cost, and other relevant benchmarks from China, Ethiopia, and Vietnam obtained from VCAs conducted previously by Global Development Solutions, LLC.

Source: Global Development Solutions, LLC team.

Annex 5D: Apparel Classifications

Table 5D.1 Apparel Classifications

Two-digit code	*Four-digit code*
61: Articles of apparel and clothing accessories—knitted or crocheted	6101: Men's or boys' overcoats, etc., knit or crocheted
	6102: Women's or girls' overcoats, etc., knit or crocheted
	6103: Men's or boys' suits, ensembles, etc., knit or crocheted
	6104: Women's or girls' suits, ensembles, etc., knit or crocheted
	6105: Men's or boys' shirts, knit or crocheted
	6106: Women's or girls' blouses and shirts, knit or crocheted
	6107: Men's or boys' underpants, pajamas, etc., knit or crocheted
	6108: Women's or girls' slips, pajamas, etc., knit or crocheted
	6109: T-shirts, singlets, tank tops, etc., knit or crocheted
	6110: Sweaters, pullovers, vests, etc., knit or crocheted
	6111: Babies' garments and accessories, knit or crocheted
	6112: Track suits, ski suits and swimwear, knit or crocheted
	6113: Garments, knit, etc., coated, etc., rubber, plastic, etc.
	6114: Garments nesoi, knitted or crocheted
	6115: Pantyhose, socks, and other hosiery, knit or crocheted
	6116: Gloves, mittens, and mitts, knitted or crocheted
	6117: Made-up clothing accessories nesoi, part, etc., knit, etc.
62: Articles of apparel & clothing accessories—not knitted or crocheted	6201: Men's or boys' overcoats, cloaks, etc., not knit or crocheted
	6202: Women's or girls' overcoats, cloaks, etc., not knit or crocheted
	6203: Men's or boys' suits, ensembles, etc., not knit or crocheted
	6204: Women's or girls' suits, ensembles, etc., not knit or crocheted
	6205: Men's or boys' shirts, not knitted or crocheted
	6206: Women's or girls' blouses, shirts, etc., not knitted or crocheted
	6207: Men's or boys' undershirts, etc., not knitted or crocheted
	6208: Women's or girls' slips, etc., not knitted or crocheted
	6209: Babies' garments and accessories, not knitted or crocheted
	6210: Garments, of felt, etc., or fabric impregnated, etc.
	6211: Track suits, ski suits, and swimwear, not knit etc.
	6212: Bras, girdles, garters etc., knitted, etc. or not
	6213: Handkerchiefs
	6214: Shawls, scarves, mufflers, mantillas, veils, etc.
	6215: Ties, bowties, cravats, not knitted or crocheted
	6216: Gloves, mittens, and mitts, not knit or crocheted
	6217: Made-up clothing accessories nes, garments, etc. parts nes

Source: Foreign-Trade.com.
Note: nes = not elsewhere specified; nesoi = not elsewhere specified or included.

Annex 5E: Private Sector Mills Capacity

Table 5E.1 Private Sector Textile Mills in Bangladesh

Type of mill	*Number of BGMA member mills*
Yarn manufacturing	373
Ring spinning	97
Ring spinning with open-end capacity	195
Rotor or open-end	51
Synthetic yarn mills	30
Fabric manufacturing	703
Woven	561
Denim	21
Home textiles	18
Knit fabrics	103
Dyeing, printing, finishing	230
Total mills	1,306

Source: Bangladesh Textile Mills Association.

Table 5E.2 Private Sector Textile Mills Capacity in Bangladesh

Spindle capacity	8,700,000
Rotor/open-end	23,000
Yarn manufacturing capacity (kg)[a]	1,700,000,000
Number of shuttle-less looms	17,000
Number of shuttle looms	13,000
Fabric manufacturing capacity (Mtr)	2,000,000,000
Fabric processing capacity (Mtr)	2,000,000,000
Raw material requirements (bales)	7,600,000
Raw cotton (bales)[a]	7,500,000
Raw cotton imported or consumed (bales)[a]	4,000,000
Raw cotton source	United States, Australia, Commonwealth of Independent States, Russian Federation, India, Pakistan, China, Central America, Africa
Type of raw cotton imports	1 1/8", 1 1/6", 1/32", 1 5/32", etc.
Other raw material used	Polyester, viscose, and acrylic staple fiber, chief and pet-chips, cotton waste, and waste cotton Yarn 5–10 counts (for knit and woven) Synthetic and filament yarn All kinds of cotton and knit fabrics

Source: Bangladesh Textile Mills Association.

a. Subject to 100 percent capacity utilization. kg = kilograms, Mtr = material testing reactor, " = inch.

Annex 5F: Capacity of Textile and Garment Units in Bangladesh

	Subsector	*Number of units*	*Installed capacity*	*Annual production capacity*
1	Spinning	385	8.7 million spindles 0.23 million rotors	2,050 million kilograms
2	Weaving or fabric manufacturing	721	17,250 shuttleless 13,500 shuttle	2,150 million meters
	1. Weaving	584	2,390 million meters	
	2. Denim	20		
	3. Home textile	17		
	4. Knitting	100		
3	Dyeing-printing-finishing	233	2,470 million meters	2,200 million meters
4	Export-oriented garment industry	5,150	650 million dozen	561 million dozen

Source: Bangladesh Textile Mills Association (Interview November 12, 2012).

Annex 5G: Productivity of Manufacturing Polo Shirts in Bangladesh

Table 5G.1 Benchmarking Key Variables for the Production of Polo Shirts

Benchmarking data sheet: Polo shirts		*China*	*Vietnam*	*Ethiopia*	*Bangladesh*	*Note*	*Notes*
1.0	***Average spoilage and reject rates***						
1.1	In-factory product rejection	2%–3%	1%–3%	2%–5%	4%–8%		
1.2	Production rejection by client	0%	0%–1%	1%–3%	0%–3%		
2.0	***Average waste and losses***						
2.1	Production waste, scrap (fabric-to-polo, weight)	5%–10%	1%–7%	10%–11%	5%–12%		
2.2	Losses (theft)	–	0%	0%	0%–1%		
3.0	***Electricity***						
3.1	On grid (cost/kWh)	$0.13	$0.07	$0.05–$0.06	$0.07–$0.10	a	High cost and poor quality of electricity
3.2	Off grid (cost/kWh)–self generated	–	$0.10	$0.07	$0.26		
3.3	Percent of time off grid/ month	0%–10%	7%–10%	10%–16.7%	30%		
4.0	***Water***						
4.1	Cost (US$/m^3)	$0.59–$0.61	$0.31–$0.45	$0.06	$0.27–$0.31	b	
5.0	***Fuel and oil***						
5.1	Cost (US$/liter)	$0.87–$0.96	$0.36–$0.87	$0.89–$0.93	$0.65	c	

table continues next page

Table 5G.1 Benchmarking Key Variables for the Production of Polo Shirts *(continued)*

Benchmarking data sheet: Polo shirts		*China*	*Vietnam*	*Ethiopia*	*Bangladesh*	*Note*	*Notes*
6.0	***Productivity and efficiency***						
6.1	Range of labor productivity (polos): pieces/employee/day	18–35	8–14	7–19	13–27		Relatively high labor productivity rate despite high in-house rejection rate but less productive than China
6.2	Average labor productivity (polos): pieces/employee/day	25	12	11	20		
6.3	Electricity usage: on-grid (kWh/1,000 pieces)	49–196	132–344	40–98	74		
6.4	Electricity usage (US$/1,000 pieces)	$6–$24	$8–$25	$2–$6	$7		
6.5	Water usage (m^3/1,000 pieces)	3–14	3–15	16–37	0.58		
6.6	Water usage (US$/1,000 pieces)	$2–$8	$1–$7	$1–$2	$2.25		
6.7	Fuel and oil usage (liters/1,000 pieces)	0.5–5	1–13	1–13	5.81		
6.8	Fuel and oil usage (US$/1,000 pieces)	$1–$5	$1–$13	$0.73–$12.28	$3.78		
6.9	Transport (US$/km-ton)	$0.27–$0.30	$0.12–$0.25	$0.03–$0.19	$0.20		
7.0	***Factory***						
7.1	Capacity utilization	60%–85%	80%–95%	55%–70%	73%–80%		
7.2	Installed capacity (pieces/day)	357–2,000	3,200–77,000	1,000–4,156	2,500–3,000		
7.3	Labor absenteeism rate (%)	1%	0.3%–2%	6%–12%	0.3%–3%		
7.4	Average salary/wage/month						
7.5	Skilled (US$)	$311–$370	$119–$181	$37–$185	$54–$68		
7.6	Unskilled (US$)	$237–$296	$78–$130	$26–$48	$33–$41		
7.7	Days of operation/month	26–28	26	25	26		
7.8	Working hours/day	9–10	8	7.5	8		
7.9	Average age of major equipment (years)	1.1–2.5	4–13	3–13	5–10		
8.0	***Exported output (finished primary product)***						
8.1	Direct export without consolidator/broker	0%–25%	97%–100%	0%–100%	90%–100%		
8.2	Indirect export through local consolidator	75%–100%	–	0%–27%			
8.3	Indirect export through overseas consolidator	0%	–	0%			

table continues next page

Table 5G.1 Benchmarking Key Variables for the Production of Polo Shirts *(continued)*

Benchmarking data sheet: Polo shirts	*China*	*Vietnam*	*Ethiopia*	*Bangladesh*	*Note*	*Notes*
9.0 Domestically sold output (finished primary product)						
9.1 Direct sales to wholesalers/ retailers without consolidator	0%	0%–3%	0%–80%	10%		
9.2 Direct sales through own outlets/shops/ showrooms	0%–25%	0%	0%–30%			
9.3 Indirect sales through local consolidator/trader	0%	0%	0%–10%			
10.0 Unit production cost (US$/piece)						
10.1 Unit production cost	$3.93–$4.33	$0.39–$0.55	$1.98–$3.21	$3.46		Competitive with polo shirts of similar quality produced in China
10.2 Export VAT rebate	$0.74–$0.79					Immediate rebate
11.0 Average selling price (US$/piece)						
11.1 Factory gate	$4.97–$5.36	–	$3.19–$8.89	$4.20		
11.2 Wholesale	$5.18–$5.58	–	$3.19–$9.33			
11.3 FOB price	$5.38–$5.80	$0.80–$1.42	$2.95–$3.41	$4.80		

Source: Global Development Solutions, LLC.

Note: Data shown for EPZ and non-EPZ factories. Bangladeshi EPZs represent about 30 percent of total apparel production. EPZ = export processing zone; FOB = free on board; kWh = kilowatt hour; m = meter, km = kilometer; VAT = value-added tax; – = not available.

a. Most EPZs charge Tk 6.11/kWh (US$0.07/kWh). Karnaphuli EPZ charges Tk 8.36 ($0.10) peak and Tk 5.35 (US$0.07) off peak.

b. All EPZs charge Tk 22.43/m^3 (US$0.27/$m^3$). Most have their own water supply systems and some are supplied by the local water authority (exclusively or as supplement to EPZ system).

c. EPZs are on natural gas and the tariff is Tk6.45/m^3 (US$0.08/$m^3$).

Table 5G.2 Procedures, Fees, and Time Lapse during Input Import Process

	Import procedure or step	*Fees*	*Time required*	*Responsible or issuing authority*	*Remarks*
1	Obtain valid trade license for foreign trade	US$600–US$700 (avg. US$650 deposit)	1–2 days (avg. 1.5 days)	Chief Control of Import and Export with the approval of Board of Investment	
	Develop confidence of the bank		3 months		
2	Terms of sale agreed between Bangladesh importer and foreign exporters. Importer applies for indemnity letter: an official request for foreign exchange for import trade.	US$100	3–4 days (avg. 3.5 days)	Commercial bank or any other bank	
2	Importer presents copies of pro forma invoice. Photocopy of valid trade licenses for foreign trade/investment/ industry, tax identification number certificate.	15% of document value	1 day	Commercial bank or any other bank	
3	Insurance certificate.	0.6%–1% of document value	0.5 day	Insurance company	
4	Importer presents application for L/C.	US$15–US$20 (avg. US$17.50)	1–2 days (avg. 1.5 days)	Commercial bank or any other bank	Bank issues account number for importing customer.
5	Importer's bank sends its irrevocable L/C to foreign exporter's bank and requests confirmation.	0.4%–0.5% of document value (avg. 0.45%)	1 day	Commercial bank or any other bank	Effectively this is the order for import of inputs.
6	Letter of confirmation along with the irrevocable L/C sent to foreign exporter (optional).		3–4 days (avg. 3.5 days)	Correspondent	
7	Foreign exporter reviews carefully all conditions in the L/C. Its freight forwarder is contacted to make sure that the shipping date can be met. If the exporter cannot comply with one or more of the conditions, the customer is alerted at once.		5 days	Correspondent	
8	The foreign exporter arranges with their freight forwarder to deliver the goods to the appropriate port or airport.		15–30 days (avg. 22.5 days)	Exporter	To be processed within valid period as indicated by exporter.

table continues next page

Table 5G.2 Procedures, Fees, and Time Lapse during Input Import Process *(continued)*

	Import procedure or step	*Fees*	*Time required*	*Responsible or issuing authority*	*Remarks*
9	The foreign exporter (or their freight forwarder) presents the documents, evidencing full compliance with the L/C terms, to the confirming bank. A foreign exporter that has sold to a Bangladesh importer on L/C basis should present to the bank these five sets of documents: original sets of clean bill of lading, shipping document, packing list, commercial invoice, and certificate of origin.		10–25 days (avg. 17.5 days)	Foreign exporter	
10	The confirming bank reviews the documents. If they are in order, the documents are sent to the importer's bank for review and then transmitted to the importer.	0.25%–0.5% document value (avg. 0.37%)	2–3 days (avg. 2.5 days)	Courier and bank	If confirmation is required from a bank other than the foreign exporter's bank, the buyer pays 0.3% of the document value.
12	Importer gives all relevant documents to local freight forwarder (transitor) for clearing, upon delegation to accomplish loading and customs-related issues.	US$20–US$50 (avg. US$35)	2–4 days (avg. 3 days)	Freight forwarder	Time-consuming transit documentation.
13	Clearing and release of the goods from customs.	US$250 per container	1 weeks	Customs officer	
13	Material or container is transported overland to Dhaka for customs clearance.	US$170–US$340 (avg. US$255)	2 days		
14	Material or container waits at customs for inspection.	US$170–US$350 (avg. US$260)	4 days	Transport and customs	Clearance.
15	Material is transported to importer's warehouse.	US$160–US$300 (avg. US$230)	Few hours	Importer	
	Total		**61.5–75 days (avg. 68.2 days)**		

Source: Interviews by Global Development Solutions, LLC.
Note: L/C = letter of credit.

Table 5G.3 Cost of Transportation and Related Services from Chittagong to Dhaka for Imports

		Cost (Tk)		*Cost (US$)*	
	Cost item	*20-foot container*	*40-foot container*	*20-foot container*	*40-foot container*
1	Port handling	3,515.4	5,273.1	43.4	65.1
2	*Inland transportation*				
	Trailer	28,350	44,550	350	550
	Rail	32,400	44,550	400	550
3	*Empty container*				
	Trailer	17,820	20,250	220	250
	Rail	4,050	6,480	50	80
3.1	*Demurrage*				
	Free time—four days				
	First seven days	486	972	6	12
	Second seven days	972	1,944	12	24
	Til delivery	1,944	3,888	24	48
3.2	Deposit (returnable)	145,800	291,600	1,800	3,600

Source: Interviews by Global Development Solutions, LLC.

Table 5G.4 Cost of Transportation and Related Services from Dhaka to Chittagong for Exports

		Cost (Tk)		*Cost (US$)*	
	Cost item	*20-foot container*	*40-foot container*	*20-foot container*	*40-foot container*
1	Port handling	3,515.4	5,273.1	43.4	65.1
2	*Inland transportation*				
	Trailer	28,350	44,550	350	550
	Rail	12,150	26,325	150	325
3	*Empty container*				
	Trailer	17,820	20,250	220	250
	Rail	4,050	6,480	50	80
3.1	Demurrage	nil	nil	nil	nil
3.2	Deposit (returnable)	145,800	291,600	1,800	3,600

Source: Interviews by Global Development Solutions, LLC.

Annex 5H: Apparel Sector in China, Ethiopia, and Vietnam

China

Notwithstanding the current difficulties caused by the global economic recession, China remains the single most important player in the global apparel trade (figure 5H.1). More than 18 million people were employed in the cotton, textiles, and apparel industries in 2009. An estimated 4.6 million people worked in the apparel sector in 2009,[20] mainly young women. As with most

Figure 5H.1 Cotton-to-Garment Market and Institutional Support Structure, China

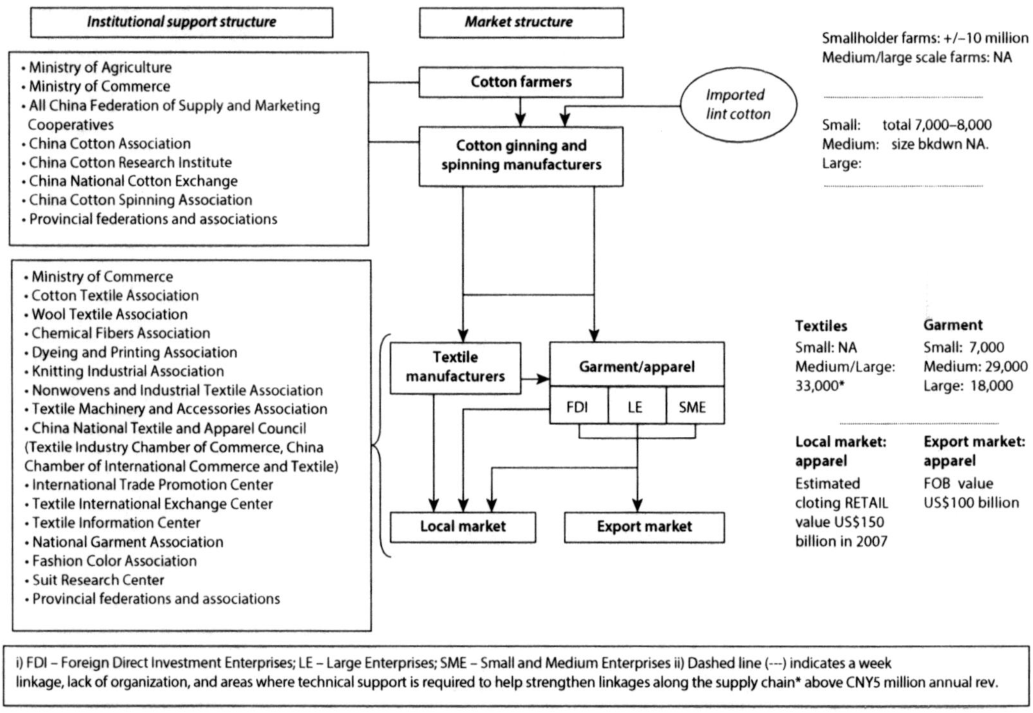

Source: Global Development Solutions, LLC.

light manufacturing sectors in the country, the Chinese apparel industry operates in a fairly efficient supply chain characterized by competitively priced and locally available raw materials, accessories, and other inputs. The apparel sector in China is based mainly on the east coast (Guangdong, Zheijang, and Jiangtsu provinces). Most factories are within "special economic zones." They predominantly are privately owned and foreign investment is common. In Guangdong Province, over 60 percent of garment factories are owned by companies based in Hong Kong SAR, China, or Taiwan, China.

The year 2009 was a disappointing one for the Chinese apparel sector: apparel exports fell by 11 percent compared with 2008 amid a generally negative unit price environment (table 5H.1). China's 2009 apparel exports were more than US$100 billion; they constituted a third of the yearly global trade in apparel and were roughly 10–15 times higher in value compared with other top exporters in the sector (Bangladesh, India, Turkey, and Vietnam).[21]

The biggest challenge to China's apparel industry is that abundance and competitive prices increasingly are more difficult to attain in light of the evolving labor environment. Although some social compliance measures have been introduced,[22] the working conditions in the apparel industry in China generally are unfavorable to workers. Practically no freedom of association (and thus no independent trade

Table 5H.1 Export Volume and Number of Enterprises in China's Apparel Sector, 2007–09

Total exports	*2007*	*2008*	*2009*
Volume (million pieces)	30	30	26
Value (Y billion)	783	815	728
Value (US$, billions)	115	120	107
Main countries or regions of destination	Germany; Hong Kong SAR, China; Japan; United Kingdom; United States		
Estimated number of companies operating in the sector	*Number of companies*	*% of total*	*Ave. no. of employees/firm*
Small	6,976	14	150
Medium	28,526	56	350
Large	17,326	34	500
Subtotal	*51,370*	100	337

Source: China Statistical Yearbook Database (http://www.stats.gov.cn/english/statisticaldata/yearlydata/).

associations) is allowed in the country. Garment workers—most of whom are migrants—move between industries to improve their wages and working conditions. For garment firms in China, this labor movement often means high labor turnover rates (up to 85 percent in some parts of Guangdong) and increasing labor costs (US$200–US$300 monthly wages for unskilled labor in 2010, up 10–20 percent from 2009). Firms must increasingly turn down favorable orders.

Ethiopia

Ethiopia's textile sector grew to become the biggest contributor to GDP and one of the largest employers in the country. The socialist government (1974–91) allocated more land for cotton production, nationalized existing textile and apparel firms, and built large textile factories to supply yarn and fabric. Inefficiencies of the command economy led to the sector falling into neglect as technology became outdated and international standards could no longer be met. As a result, the cotton farming and apparel sectors ended up producing well below capacity. However, revitalization has taken effect over the past decade as factories have been privatized and foreign investment has entered. The sector has attracted US$3 million in foreign investments, mainly from the United States, Italy, and Turkey. Ethiopian apparel exports have been growing steadily from less than US$4 million in 2002. In 2009, the sector employed an estimated 9,746 workers—58 percent male and 42 percent female—and accounted for 7.1 percent of the country's industrial production. Small companies are prevalent and in 2009 employed approximately 91 percent of the apparel labor force (see table 5H.2).

Advantages for the apparel sector in Ethiopia are low labor wages, a local supply of raw materials, and preferential access for Ethiopian exports to the United States under the AGOA until 2015. Total apparel exports from the approximately 40 AGOA member African countries reached US$903.21 million in 2011; of this, Ethiopia contributed US$9.967 million.[23] As of the fiscal year ending in June 2010, apparel exports totaled US$12 million, which comprised 0.72 percent of the country's total exports for the period.[24] Key products for the

Table 5H.2 Employment Statistics for Ethiopia's Apparel Sector

Company size	*Estimated number of companies*	*Companies by size (%)*	*Number of employees*	*Average number of employees*
Small	397	91.1	1,961	5
Medium	7	1.6	343	49
Large	32	7.3	7,442	233
Total	436	100.0	9,746	

Source: Central Statistical Authority.

Table 5H.3 Apparel Production and Trade Statistics, Ethiopia, 2009

Measure	*Domestic production*	*Domestic demand*	*Total imports*	*Total exports*
Volume (pieces)	17,543,075	132,467,738	117,734,080	2,809,417
Value (US$)	10,937,533	73,079,213	72,546,928	10,405,248

Sources: Global Development Solutions, LLC; Ethiopian Customs Authority; Ministry of Trade and Industry.

year were polo shirts (4,219,250 pieces), T-shirts (5,424,750 pieces), sportswear (2,411,000 pieces), work clothes (1,845,000 pieces), and uniforms (2,152,500 pieces). Major export destinations were the United States (11.4 percent), Italy (10 percent), the Netherlands (5.1 percent), Germany (3.9 percent), Belgium (3.2 percent), and the United Kingdom (1.9 percent).

Ethiopia's apparel imports, primarily from China, outweigh domestic production by approximately 7:1 (table 5H.3). The total import value is over 99 percent of domestic demand; yet import volume is 88 percent of demand, suggesting that domestically produced items are less costly than imported goods. Export figures suggest that the price per piece is much higher than for products imported or sold in the domestic market. Thus, higher quality items likely are being exported from Ethiopia. These trends have been repeated for at least three years since 2007.

However, a major drawback is that Ethiopia is landlocked. This, compounded by the weak transportation and communication links, presents problems for efficient exports, especially considering the high importance of time-to-market in the global apparel market. Further, and most significantly, while local raw material (cotton) is available, the inability of the textile sector to produce fabric in sufficient quantity and quality for use in export apparel completely offsets the advantage of having locally grown cotton.

The major stakeholders in the Ethiopian textile and garment sector are small farm holders, collectors (merchants), private commercial farms, state farm enterprises, ginneries, and textile and garment manufacturers. They are supported by development partners, including the United Nations Industrial Development Organization, the United States Agency for International Development, and the Food and Agriculture Organization of the United Nations. Other support comes from technical and vocational training (TVET) institutions, universities, sector associations, and government institutions (see figure 5H.2).

Figure 5H.2 Ethiopia's Cotton-to-Garments Market and Institutional Support Structure

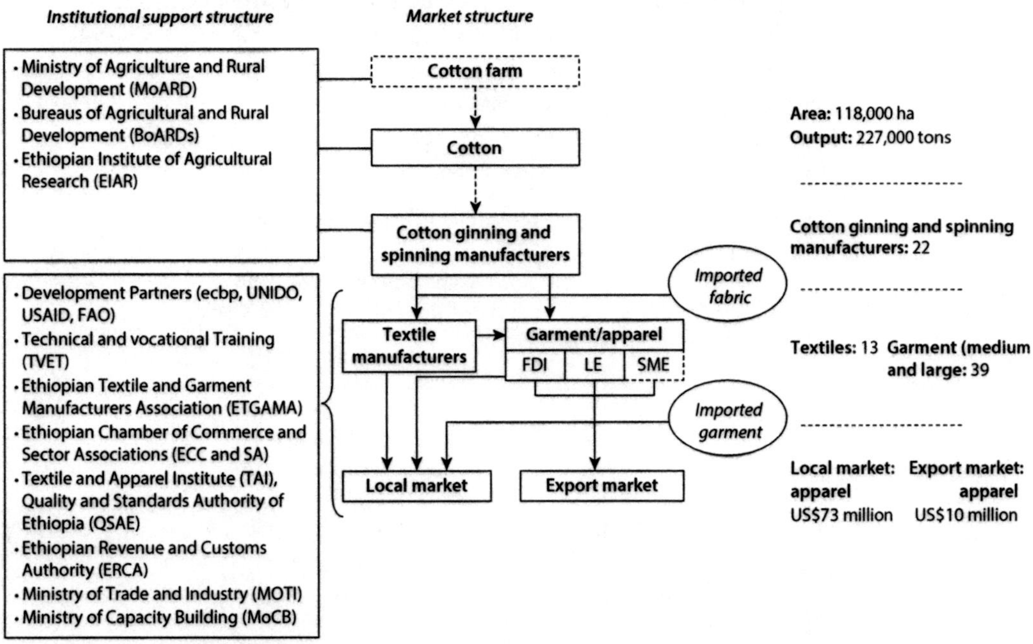

Notes: i) FDI – Foreign Direct Investment Enterprises; LE – Large Enterprises; SME – Small and Medium Enterprises
ii) Dash line (- - -) indicates a weak linkage, lack of organization, and areas where technical support is required to help strengthen linkages along the supply chain

Source: Global Development Solutions, LLC.

The Ethiopian apparel sector receives extensive institutional support. The Ethiopian Ministry of Trade and Industry determines policy and strategy and leads and supports the industrial development of the country. The Textile and Apparel Institute is a specialized institute under the Ministry of Trade and Industry and has the task of promoting the textile and garment subsector. The Textile and Apparel Institute is responsible for human resource development, technology transfer for industrial development, marketing support, and research and development activities. The Ministry of Agriculture and Rural Development leads the development of cotton as a major input for the textile industry. Regional developments, extension services, and training are promoted and organized through the Bureaus of Agricultural and Rural Development. Under the guidance of the Ministry of Education, seven TVET centers in textile occupations have been selected countrywide in connection with the establishment of textile and garment clusters: Addis Ababa, Adwa, Awassa, Bahir Dar, Dire Dawa, Kombolcha, and Nazreth. However, Bahir Dar University Textile Department is the only educational institution where textile education is provided at the university level. The Ministry of Capacity Building, together with development partners, aims to build capacity in priority sectors of the Ethiopian economy. The Cotton Growers Association and the Ethiopian Textile and Garment Manufacturers Association share a role in the developmental activities of the textile and garment sector in Ethiopia. The latter was established in 2003 and represents the majority of Ethiopia's textile mills and garment factories.

Multiple problems persist along the cotton-to-garment processing chain in Ethiopia. Starting from the farm level and all the way up to garment assembly, productivity and capacity utilization are not optimal, technology is generally obsolete, and dependence on imported inputs is high (see figure 5H.3).

Figure 5H.3 Ethiopia's Cotton-to-Garments Processing Roadmap

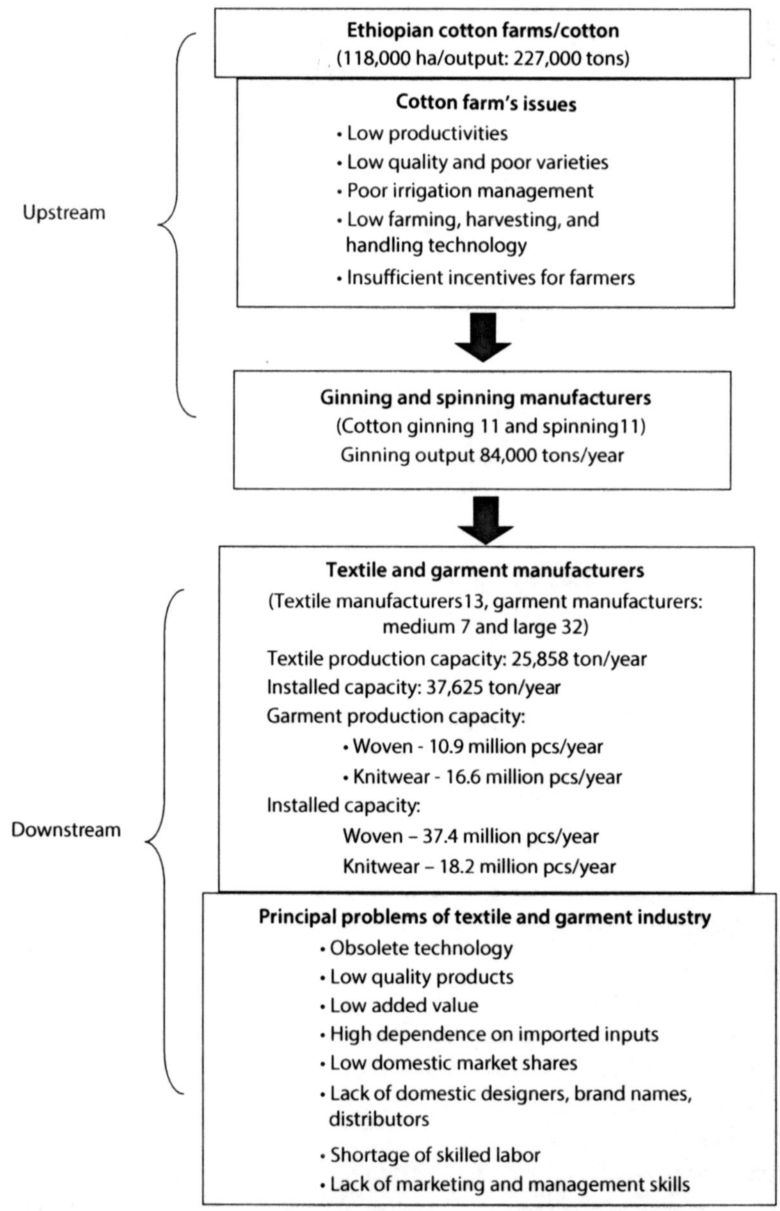

Source: Global Development Solutions, LLC.

Box 5H.1 Fabric Shortage for Garment Manufacturers in Ethiopia

There is a dire shortage of fabric for garment manufacturers in Ethiopia as only a single textile factory is functioning. All others are dysfunctional for several reasons, including lack of working capital, mismanagement, problems with sourcing of raw materials, and other technical and nontechnical problems. The only operating textile factory used this opportunity to increase its prices for fabric by 45 percent in 2010. More price increases may drive away customers. Garment producers are currently preordering fabrics, especially knits, and are holding inflated inventories, because of long lead times from the sole local producer in the face of high demand. One private sector garment producer claimed that he had to use his "connections" to buy an adequate quantity of fabric. But he is suffering from a shortage of working capital because of the money tied up in fabric inventory.

Source: World Bank 2011b.

From interviews with people in the textile sector, the general consensus is that the performance of the existing textile mills in Ethiopia is relatively poor and the sector is not in a position to produce world-class competitive fabric due to the following major factors: (a) the low level of technology used, (b) lack of skilled labor, and (c) financial constraints in acquiring adequate technology and operating at high capacity (box 5H.1).

Greenfield investments in the sector, however, are numerous. The aggregate level of investments, at different stages of development, registered by the Investment Agency of Ethiopia since 1992, is given in table 5H.4. In 2010 alone, approximately 23 textile and garment projects were registered by the agency; the projects are in various stages.

Vietnam

The apparel industry led Vietnam's exports in 2009. It had turnover of US$9.1 billion and employed about 1.2 million workers in 3,174 officially registered small, medium, and large enterprises (table 5H.5).[25] Currently, Vietnam's apparel products account for roughly 2.7 percent of the world's total market share. The main importers of Vietnam's apparel are the United States (55 percent), the European Union (20 percent), and Japan (10 percent). In the domestic market, during the first half of 2010, garment and textile producers grew at 15–18 percent. According to the Vietnam Textile and Garment Group (Vinatex), local apparel manufacturers reported a rise in export orders, with prices rising 10–15 percent year-on-year amid the global economic recovery. Of the 3,174 enterprises, 587 (18.5 percent) are partially or wholly foreign-owned enterprises, 2,539 (80.0 percent) are Vietnamese-owned nonstate enterprises, and 48 (1.5 percent) are state-owned enterprises.

Accompanying the impressive growth achieved by the apparel industry are challenges that continue to threaten the competitiveness of the sector (see figures 5H.4 and 5H.5). The biggest hurdle to maintaining competitiveness in the

Table 5H.4 Summary of Licensed Textile and Garment Investment Project, by Investment Type and Status, 1992–September 30, 2010

Investment type		*Domestic*	*Foreign*	*Public*	*Grand total*
Implementation	No. of projects	38	20	—	58
	Capital (US,$ thou-sands)	27,198	60,835	—	88,033
	Perm. empl.	4,475	1,296	—	5,771
	Temp. empl.	943	828	—	1,771
Operation	No. of projects	36	51	5	92
	Capital (US$, thou-sands)	127,696	79,263	15,308	222,266
	Perm. empl.	7,668	9,170	1,241	18,079
	Temp. empl.	429	3,315	20	3,764
Preimplementation	No. of projects	416	145	2	563
	Capital (US$, thou-snads)	259,124	388,297	15,547	662,968
	Perm. empl.	44,869	29,215	1,415	75,499
	Temp. empl.	20,762	20,081	184	41,027
Total	No. of projects	490	216	7	713
	Capital (US$, thou-sands)	414,018	528,394	30,855	973,267
	Perm. empl.	57,012	39,681	2,656	99,349
	Temp. empl.	22,134	24,224	204	46,562

Source: Ethiopian Investment Agency.

Table 5H.5 Enterprises in the Apparel Sector in Vietnam, 2010

Size category	*Number of enterprises*	*Percent of total*	*Number of employees*
Small	851	26.8	<10
Medium	1,745	55.0	10–200
Large	578	18.2	>300
Total	3,174	100	

Source: Vinatex, Interview, August 2010.

world market is Vietnam's high dependence on imported inputs. Currently, an estimated 80–95 percent of production relies on imported material (primarily from China; Taiwan, China; and the Republic of Korea). For example, during the first seven months of 2010, the sector imported US$3.18 billion worth of cloth (up 34.3 percent from the previous year), US$1.47 billion worth of apparel and footwear materials and accessories (up 35.4 percent from the previous year), US$620 million worth of fiber (up 47.5 percent), and US$362 million worth of cotton (up 98 percent). Global prices for cotton more than doubled in 2010, placing even more downward pressure on profits for the apparel sector in Vietnam.

The second challenge faced by the sector is the slow transformation of the sector from CMT to original design manufacturing (ODM). The CMT production modality generally is considered to be suboptimal among Vietnamese policy makers. However, it has served Vietnam well, particularly in the context of employment creation, developing a skilled and semiskilled labor force, and contributing to the economic growth of the country. CMT has also given

Figure 5H.4 Vietnam's Cotton-to-Garments Processing Roadmap

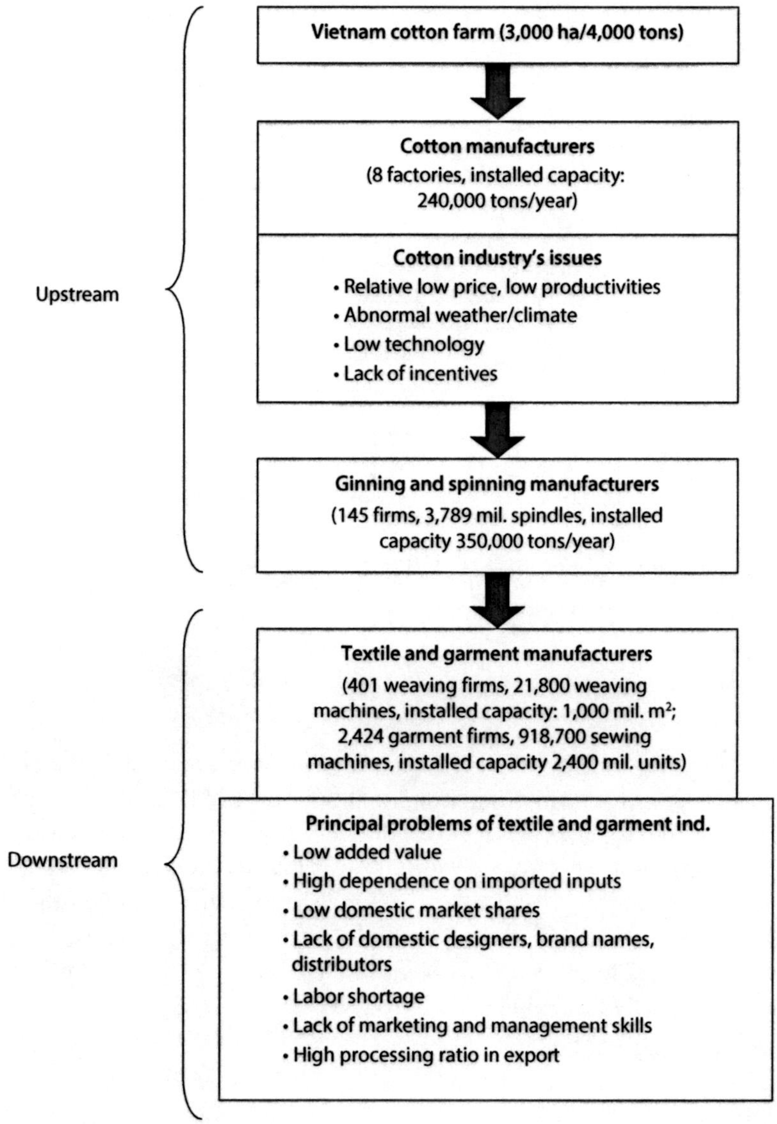

Source: Global Development Solutions, LLC.

garment producers opportunities to strengthen operational and management capacity without committing scarce resources and taking risks. To realize a fully integrated value chain from the production of cotton to finished fabric under ODM, vast amounts of investments, technical know-how, and technology are required. With this noted, however, Vinatex invested D15.3 billion (or US$0.8 billion) in the production of fiber, cotton, and dye, but growth in the sector far outpaced the level of investments made by state and private enterprises along the entire value chain.

Figure 5H.5 Vietnam's Cotton-to-Garment Market and Institutional Support Structure

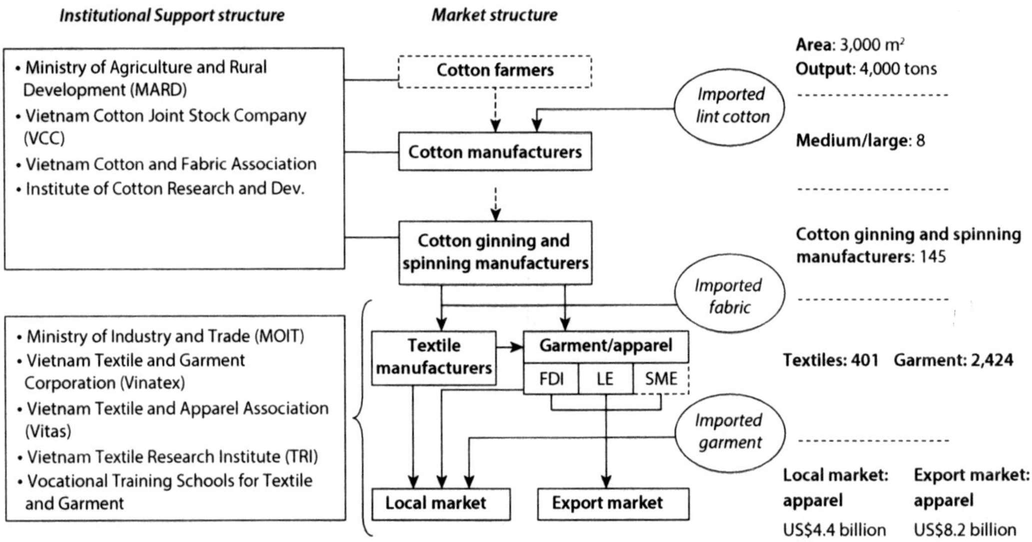

Notes: i) FDI – Foreign Direct Investment Enterprises; LE – Large Enterprises; SME – Small and Medium Enterprises
ii) Dash line (- - -) indicates a week linkage, lack of organization, and areas where technical support is required to help strengthen linkages along the supply chain

Source: Global Development Solutions, LLC.

The third challenge faced by the sector is the shortage of skilled and semi-skilled labor. Even with a starting salary at D2 million to D3.5 million (US$104–US$181) per month, enterprises have a difficult time hiring workers, particularly in urban and peri-urban areas where factories currently are located. The government is encouraging the relocation of factories to rural areas through the development of specialized processing zones, but according to Vinatex, the labor shortage was likely to exceed 10 percent in 2010. As such, the apparel sector in Vietnam is basically low value-added production.

Notes

1. Leading Bangladesh to Prosperity," http://www.BGMEA.com.bd.
2. Medium-size firms are 85 percent and large firms are 75 percent of the sector.
3. Derived from Bangladesh Export Processing Zones Authority data as of May 2012 (http://www.epzbangladesh.org.bd/).
4. The rebate rates and the list of items that qualify for export rebates change frequently depending on policy makers' assessments of various trends, such as the global price outlook, local market developments, and so forth.
5. The policy was expected to be endorsed by the Cabinet by the end of November 2012.

6. H&M and Gap Inc. data. See, for example, http://about.hm.com/AboutSection/en/About/Sustainability/Commitments/Responsible-Partners/Beyond-Monitoring.html; http://www.gapinc.com/content/gapinc/html/csr/bangladesh.html and http://gapinc.com/content/attachments/gapinc/Bangladesh.pdf.
7. HS categories for these items include HS392620: Articles of apparel and clothing accessories of plastic; HS4015: Articles of apparel and accessories of unhard vulcanized rubber; HS401590: Articles of apparel and clothing accessories of vulcanized rubber; HS4203: Articles of apparel and accessories of leather and composition leather; and HS4303: Articles of apparel, etc., of fur skin.
8. However, given the competitive labor rates, the unit production cost per polo shirt produced in Bangladesh (US$3.46/piece) has the potential to be competitive (with respect to quantity and quality) with similar operations in China (US$3.93–4.33/piece).
9. BGMEA at a Glance, www.bgmea.com.bd/home/pages/aboutus.
10. More than 90 percent of import and export activity in Bangladesh is done through the Port of Chittagong.
11. "Americas" is defined as North America and South America (MarketLine 2012).
12. Bangladesh's fiscal year runs from July to June.
13. Because of the lack of Bangladeshi export data in the UN Comtrade database after 2007, mirror data from trading partners were used. Therefore, the values noted reflect cost, insurance, and freight (CIF), not FOB prices for all countries listed in table 5.14. HS610910 includes many styles of shirts and therefore unit prices may not be comparable, given that each country will have a different product mix within HS610910. Thus, the unit value is intended only as a general indicator and not indicative of polo shirts in particular.
14. The United States has repeatedly raised concerns regarding possible changes in rules that currently allow international shipping companies to operate as 100 percent foreign-owned companies in Bangladesh. U.S. officials have stated that such a policy would have a negative effect on foreign investment in Bangladesh by creating uncertainty and imposing increased costs on local apparel exporters.
15. Product-wise customs duties for the United States can be found at http://hts.usitc.gov.
16. U.S. Trade Representative and U.S.–Bangladesh Trade Facts, U.S. Embassy (Bangladesh), www.bdembassyusa.org/uploads/US%20-%20BD%20trade.pdf.
17. United States Department of Agriculture, as noted on IndexMundi.com.
18. Export Promotion Bureau, Bangladesh. (Data obtained during interview by Global Development Solutions, LLC.)
19. FAOSTAT, http://faostat.fao.org.
20. According to the Chinese Statistical Yearbook Database (http://www.stats.gov.cn/english/statisticaldata/yearlydata/).
21. Excluding the European Union and intra-European Union trade.
22. An example is the CSC9000t Code of Conduct for the textile and apparel industry, which was introduced in 2005 by the China National Textile and Apparel Council. The code is still new and proportionally only a few firms are involved. CSC9000t is neither compulsory nor independently verified.

23. AGOA.info, http://www.agoa.info/index.php?view=.&story=news&subtext=1718.
24. Ministry of Trade and Industry.
25. According to Vietnam's General Statistics Office and Vinatex.

References

ABC News. 2012. "Workers Die at Factories Used by Tommy Hilfiger." March 21.

Ahsan, Quamrul. 2012. "Sourcing Cotton: Geopolitical Risks for Bangladesh." *The Financial Express*, May 3. http://www.thefinancialexpress-bd.com/more.php?news_id=128445&date=2012-05-03.

AsiaNews. 2010. "Garment Workers Riot over Wages in Chittagong, Three Dead, Dozens Injured." December 13, http://www.AsiaNews.it.

Bangladesh Export Processing Zones Authority. http://www.epzbangladesh.org.bd/.

Bruemmer, Claudia. 2011. "Rising Cost of Cotton Affects Clothing Manufacturers." *Top Ten Wholesale News*, February 17. http://www.toptenwholesale.com/news/rising-cost-of-cotton-affects-clothing-manufacturers-3595.html.

BTMA (Bangladesh Textile Mills Association). 2011. *Report of the Board of Directors of BTMA for 2011*. http://www.btmadhaka.com/Image/Directors%27%20Report-11-final.pdf.

European Commission. 2012. "The EU's New Generalised Scheme of Preferences (GSP)." Factsheet. http://trade.ec.europa.eu/doclib/docs/2013/february/tradoc_150582.pdf.

European Parliament. 2011. "Regulation (EU) No 512/2011, Amending Council Regulation (EC) No 732/2008." *Official Journal of the European Union*, May 31. http://trade.ec.europa.eu/ doclib/docs/2011/may/tradoc_147958.pdf.

Gap Inc. 2012. "Gap Inc. Announces Comprehensive Building and Fire Safety Action Plan for Bangladesh Apparel Facilities." Press Release, October 2. http://gapinc.com/content/gapinc/html/media/pressrelease/2012/med_pr_GapInc_Announces_Building_Fire_Safety_Action_Plan100212.html.

GDS (Global Development Solutions, LLC). n.d. "Competitive Africa: The Value Chain and Feasibility Analysis Module." http://www.gds-llc.com/index.php?competitive,africa,the,value,chain,and,feasibility&art=92.

Haroon, Jasim Uddin. 2012. "WB Survey Finds BD Lead Time Higher." *The Financial Express*, November 17.

Islam, Siddique. 2012. "30 Global Brands, Retailers in City to Establish Sustainable Factory Model." *The Financial Express*, November 11.

MarketLine. 2012. "Global Apparel Retail, MarketLine Industry Profile." http://www.marketline.com/.

McKinsey & Company. 2011. "Bangladesh's Ready-Made Garments Landscape: The Challenge of Growth."

Pawlicki, Amy. 2012. "Emergence of Social Stock Exchanges and Other Market Drivers of Sustainability." *AICPA Insights*, November 19.

Vidal, John. 2012. "Are Export Processing Zones the New Sweatshops, or Drivers of Development?" *The Guardian*, April 30.

World Bank. 2011a. "World Bank Garment Firm Survey 2011." World Bank, Washington, DC.

———. 2011b. "Competitive Africa: The Value Chain and Feasibility Analysis Module." World Bank, Washington, DC. http://www.gds-llc.com/index.php?competitive,africa,the,value, chain,and,feasibility&art=92.

———. 2012. *Doing Business 2012: Doing Business in a More Transparent World.* Washington, DC: World Bank.

World Economic Forum. 2012. *The Global Competitiveness Report 2012–2013*. Geneva: World Economic Forum.

CHAPTER 6

The Pharmaceutical Sector in Bangladesh

Nadeem Rizwan and Sanjay Kathuria

Introduction

In the early post-independence period in Bangladesh, multinational companies (MNCs) dominated the pharmaceutical sector. Eight leading multinational companies enjoyed 75 percent of the total domestic market (BTC 2010), producing vitamins, enzymes, and cough syrups locally and importing other essential drugs from their sister units located abroad. The National Drug Policies (NDPs) of 1982 and 2005 helped the formation and growth of a domestic pharmaceutical sector. Under NDPs, multinational companies could no longer produce vitamins, enzymes, and cough syrups. Only local companies were allowed to produce them. MNCs were restricted to producing injectable vitamins for local supply. Furthermore, contract manufacturing by Bangladeshi companies for multinationals was prohibited.[1] The policy restricted importation of a pharmaceutical product or a close substitute as long as the pharmaceutical product was being produced in the country. As a result of these restrictions, several multinational corporations sold their companies to local entrepreneurs. This led to the formation of local pharmaceutical companies and an increase in domestic production. Bangladesh, which was once a drug-importing country, became a drug-exporting country by the late 1980s.

Although the industry has been able to meet the bulk of domestic needs, it has not done well on the export front, despite being long held up as a major export prospect. Under the Trade Related Aspects of Intellectual Property Rights (TRIPS) agreement, signed by all members of the World Trade Organization (WTO) in 1995, low- and middle-income countries agreed to honor product patents for drug manufacturing after 2005. Least-developed countries (LDCs) like Bangladesh were exempted from its obligations until 2016. This gave Bangladesh an edge over countries like India and Brazil during 2005–15, wherein it could legally reverse-engineer patented pharmaceutical products and sell them in its domestic market as well as export to other countries (mostly LDCs) where the product patents were not recognized. However, exports have been low and stagnant, while countries like India have emerged as major players in the generics market.

This chapter looks at the current status of the sector, exports, trade policy, and the regulatory framework for pharmaceuticals. Does export development need a different policy regime from the one that has prevailed since the 1980s? Any strategy will need to factor in the TRIPS exemptions that are due to end sooner or later (by 2016, or later if extended for LDCs, or earlier, if Bangladesh graduates from LDC status).

Current Status

Bangladesh is almost self-sufficient in manufacturing pharmaceuticals. In 2011, 97 percent of the country's needs were met by domestic manufacturers (including locally based MNCs) and the rest was imported (Beximco Pharmaceuticals 2011). The imported drugs are mostly specialized pharmaceutical products like vaccines, anti-cancer drugs, and essential lifesaving drugs. Industry insiders believe that this ratio might shift further in favor of the local producers as some of the large domestic firms are preparing to manufacture these drugs in-house.

Pharmaceutical manufacturing generally consists of two steps (World Bank 2008). Manufacturing of active pharmaceutical ingredients (APIs), the first step, is a highly sophisticated, technically demanding chemical and biochemical fermentation and synthesis process. Firms can either manufacture their own APIs or purchase them on the open market. Commodity API manufacturing tends to be a high-volume, low-margin business based extensively on scale economies and large, dedicated manufacturing lines. Smaller manufacturers therefore have limited opportunities to compete globally. The second step is the drug's final formulation. Unlike the chemical business of API production, final formulations belong to the manufacturing sector. During this process, firms mix APIs and excipients (other nonactive ingredients); press the mixture into pills, tablets, or solutions; and then package the product for the consumer market. Final formulations are equally as complex as API manufacturing, but require different skills. Because firms can produce 50 or more products in a single plant with adaptable equipment, economies of scale are less important for final formulations than for API manufacturing.

Bangladesh's pharmaceuticals industry does not have any significant capability for research or sophisticated production. It mainly produces final formulations of branded generics[2] from imported APIs. There is virtually no research and development (R&D) activity, and so capacity for reverse engineering patented drugs is limited. Bangladesh's pharmaceutical production is import intensive, as raw materials like API, packaging, and materials are imported from abroad. Around 50 percent of total pharmaceutical imports come from China, 30 percent from India, and the rest from other countries (Dhaka Chamber of Commerce and Industry 2007). According to 2007 estimates, manufacturers are producing about 450 generic drugs for 5,300 registered brands, which have 8,300 different forms of dosages and strength

(UNCTAD 2011).[3] The wide range of generic products includes anti-ulcerants, flouroquinolones, anti-rheumatic, nonsteroid drugs, non-narcotic analgesics, antihistamines, and oral anti-diabetic drugs. About 85 percent of the drugs sold in Bangladesh are generics and 15 percent are patented drugs (BRAC EPL 2012). This structure differs significantly from the international market, as the large R&D-based MNCs tend to dominate the world market rather than generic firms.

Bangladesh's API capacity is insignificant. APIs are a significant part of the manufacturing cost of a drug. Approximately 80 percent of the APIs are imported[4] and 75–80 percent of the imported APIs are generic (World Bank 2008). At present, there are 21 companies in Bangladesh manufacturing 41 APIs (IDLC 2011). However, the manufacturers mainly run the final chemical synthesis stage with API intermediaries, instead of the complete chemical synthesis.

The domestic pharmaceutical market is highly concentrated and has been growing steadily. According to the Directorate General of Drug Administration (DGDA), there are currently 274 pharmaceutical companies in Bangladesh. Among these firms, 67 are termed as "nonfunctional" or "suspended." The companies include medium to large Bangladeshi companies with international links, specialized subsidiaries of MNCs, and a number of small companies. However, the top 10 firms (all of which are locally owned) hold 67.6 percent of market share, while the top MNCs hold only 9.1 percent of the total market (IDLC 2011). In the past five years, the domestic pharmaceutical market has experienced robust growth and has almost doubled in value to more than US$1 billion (table 6.1). This owes to the growth in the market and rising health care spending (table 6.2), improving access to health care, and an increase in new types of illnesses.

Pharmaceutical companies employ the highest number of white collar workers in Bangladesh (Bhuiyan, Sultana, and Sultana 2011). Pharmaceutical manufacturing is a capital-intensive and technically challenging industry where skilled labor is essential. Around 115,000 workers are employed in this sector, of which 58.6 percent work in management and 41.4 percent work in production. Only 2.1 percent of the total work force in this industry is female (BTC 2010).

Table 6.1 Size and Growth of Bangladesh's Pharmaceutical Market, 2007–12

Year	*Market size (Tk billions)*	*Growth (%)*
2007	44.0	15.8
2008	47.0	6.9
2009	54.9	16.8
2010	68.0	23.8
2011	84.0	23.6
2012[a]	106.1	26.2

Sources: Bangladesh Association of Pharmaceutical Industries; Square Pharmaceuticals 2012.
a. Figures for 2012 are estimated.

Table 6.2 GDP and Health Care Expenditure in Bangladesh, 2005–10

Year	*GDP (US$, billions)*	*Total health care expenditure (US$, billions)*
2005	60.3	1.9
2006	61.9	2.1
2007	68.4	2.4
2008	79.6	2.7
2009	89.4	3.0
2010	100.3	3.5

Source: World Bank, World Development Indicators.

DGDA is mandated with controlling prices for 209 essential medicines. The pricing of all other pharmaceutical products is based on the indicative value-for-money price. The maximum retail price is broken down into trade price (75.5 percent), wholesale commission (2.3 percent), retail commission (12.0 percent), and value-added tax (VAT; 12.5 percent). Imported finished products are priced by adding a fixed percentage of markups to the cost and freight price to arrive at the maximum retail price. The breakdown for the imported products includes trade price (88.89 percent) and retail commission (11.11 percent) (UNCTAD 2011). Prices of Bangladeshi generics are among the lowest in the world (*Forbes Asia* 2013).

Export of Pharmaceuticals

By the late 1980s, Bangladesh had become a drug exporting country, but exports have stagnated (table 6.3) and are a small share of production. Bangladeshi pharmaceutical exports totaled US$69.2 million in FY2014, only 0.2 percent of total export earnings. The bulk of export earnings owe to Novartis/Sandoz.[5] Exports comprise only around 8 percent of the total production of the local pharmaceutical companies that are exporting.[6] Currently, the world generic market is around US$130 billion, with India holding roughly a one-fifth share.

As of 2008, Bangladesh was exporting pharmaceuticals to more than 70 countries, but mostly to the less regulated markets. Bhutan, Kenya, Myanmar, Nepal, and Vietnam are examples of such markets. Bangladeshi pharmaceuticals are also exported to two other types of markets, but to a much lesser extent. One is the semi-regulated or moderately regulated market, like Malaysia, the Russian Federation, and Tanzania. However, the biggest market in generics is the United States, which is very strictly regulated. Australia and the United Kingdom are also strictly regulated markets in which Bangladeshi exports are minimal. Only a select few firms have the proper accreditation and they export only a few products. The largest barriers for Bangladesh's entry into regulated markets are lack of manufacturing facilities, which cost at least US$50 million each, and lack of know-how (World Bank 2008).

Table 6.3 Pharmaceutical Exports from Bangladesh, 2005/06–2011/12

Fiscal year	*Exports (US$, millions)*	*Share of total exports (%)*
2006	27.5	0.3
2007	28.2	0.2
2008	43	0.3
2009	46	0.3
2010	41	0.3
2011	44	0.2
2012	48	0.2

Source: Export Promotion Bureau.

Exporting pharmaceutical products is challenging. Each country has its own product regulations, registration requirements, language requirements, cultural preferences, national packaging requirements, and industry protection mechanisms. Sales on the global market are quite competitive with firms from around the world vying for business. Furthermore, initiating exports requires a significant investment in money, time, and paperwork to register the product in the target country. Because generic products are branded in less regulated markets, pharmaceutical firms also need to make significant investments in sales and marketing. Testing and certification investments are also critical. All these investments are made without a guarantee of future sales.

Various factors in the industry have prevented Bangladesh's pharmaceutical exports from growing as hoped. Perhaps the expectations for the industry were too high.[7] The industry is inherently a capital-intensive one, where quality of production and highly sanitized conditions are at a premium. Additional investments need to be made for the export market to guarantee quality and provide certification. The share of labor in total production cost is low and this is even more so when the cost of APIs is included in the overall cost of production. Moreover, the incentives created by policy (as opposed to exhortations by policy makers) have led to a private sector focus on import substitution. Thus, the industry did not focus on the capacity to reverse engineer to take advantage of the TRIPS waiver.

Other factors that affect exports include weak enforcement of quality regulations and strict foreign exchange controls. The lax enforcement of regulations has allowed local companies to fall below the standards necessary for the more strictly regulated export markets. Strict foreign exchange controls deter firms from undertaking critical activities to increase exports. These activities include receiving certification from foreign regulatory authorities, using consulting services to advise on best practices in manufacturing, and having drug samples tested. Obtaining permission to transfer large amounts of foreign currency is a lengthy and cumbersome process that is creating a non-tax barrier for exports. Lack of an API production facility means that Bangladesh has to rely on imported APIs for formulation and, although it is not insurmountable, this could create a handicap vis-à-vis companies in countries that have in-house or in-country API production.[8]

Trade Policy for Pharmaceuticals

Import Policy

Pharmaceutical firms are subject to a special low-tariff regime for outputs and inputs. This is because of the special dispensation under the Drug Policy (the Drug Control Act of 1982 restricted imports and capped prices) to keep domestic prices low but with strong controls on competing imports. The effective rate of protection (ERP) in the pharmaceutical sector is apparently very low, ranging from –0.5 percent to about 20 percent, provided that the output tariff of 0 to 5 percent is the one actually levied. However, once the tariff equivalence of import controls is taken into account,[9] ERPs could be much higher (see Kathuria and Malouche 2016, chapter 2, on trade policy).

The import regime consists of banned items, restricted items, and freely importable items. Importation of final products of medicines and vaccines is based on a list of importable items published in the government gazette by DGDA. The procedures for importation are facilitated by creating a "block list" of imports for each recognized pharmaceutical company approved by the Director of DGDA. The block list describes the raw material, packaging material, value, and quantity according to the annual production plans of the pharmaceutical companies. The list is usually prepared as part of product registration. Companies importing raw materials have to present an import invoice and analysis report of the quality, value, and quantity for each import. The analysis report of the raw materials must be certified by DGDA or be prepared by a government-approved preshipment inspection agent (Ministry of Commerce 2012).

Export Policy

The pharmaceutical sector has been among the highest priority sectors of Bangladesh's export policy since 2006. Highest priority sectors are entitled to income tax exemption for export earnings, export credit at reduced rates, assistance in marketing in overseas markets through participating in export fairs, and so on. In addition, the government reduced or exempted duties on some capital machinery and raw materials imported for the use of pharmaceutical production.[10] The sector also enjoys a tax holiday and duty drawback scheme. The export policy of 2012–15 doubled the value of samples allowed to be sent by the pharmaceutical industry to overseas buyers to US$60,000 a year. The World Bank (2012) estimates the ERP for the drugs that are exported to be mildly negative (0 to –0.5 percent).

Regulatory Framework and Standards

The Directorate General of Drug Administration, under the Ministry of Health and Family Welfare, is the drug regulatory authority of the country. DGDA supervises and implements all prevailing drug regulations in the country and regulates all activities related to import, procurement of raw and packing material, production and import of finished drugs, export, sale, and pricing of all kinds of medicine. DGDA has 37 offices in 36 districts, including the head office located in Dhaka. There are two drug testing laboratories under DGDA—one in Dhaka and the other in Chittagong.

Despite extensive rules, the pharmaceutical market remains underregulated because of the lack of capacity of the regulatory authority. The primary responsibility for drug quality control lies with the manufacturers and the top firms have their own quality control mechanisms. However, DGDA has to ensure the quality, efficacy, and safety of pharmaceutical products through the implementation of relevant legislation, via its monitoring and supervision functions. Although DGDA was upgraded from "department" to "directorate general" status after the adoption of the revised NDP 2005, it continues to suffer from funding, staffing, and technical competence constraints.

DGDA is severely understaffed, given the rapidly growing pharmaceutical market, large number of registered products, and large population size (USAID and SIAPS 2013), and the enforcement of standards suffers. As of September 2014, there were 370 personnel vacancies at different levels, against which 226 had been filled. The World Health Organization (WHO) promotes current good manufacturing practice (cGMP) regulations[11] for high-quality production of medicines in low- and middle-income countries and NDP 2005 seeks to enforce it. The responsibility of assessing cGMP compliance lies with DGDA. With limited human resources, and staff not sufficiently trained in recent developments in quality control, compliance is difficult to test and enforce. Local inspectors have been found to be less stringent compared with international inspectors and DGDA has issued some questionable cGMP certifications.[12] To overcome this issue, some pharmaceuticals firms are adhering to different manufacturing quality standards, like the Therapeutic Goods Administration of Australia and the United Kingdom's Medicines and Healthcare Products Regulatory Agency; other firms are operating below cGMP standards. This is preventing the use of a harmonized global standard in drug regulation.

The drug testing laboratories have insufficient capacity. Testing of drugs is required for evaluating preregistration and the quality of post-marketed drugs and medicines. The two laboratories under DGDA have extremely limited capacity with inadequate staffing and equipment. According to the United Nations Conference on Trade and Development (2011), there are three technical staff members in the Chittagong Laboratory and eight in the Dhaka Laboratory. There is neither a central reference laboratory nor any independent contract research organizations in the country. Companies that export to international markets have their products tested and certified in established laboratories in other countries.[13]

Infrastructure support for the regulatory body is insufficient. For example, DGDA does not have its own office building in Dhaka. District offices are rented and logistical support for district-level staff is inadequate. Proper office facilities, such as Internet connections and computers, are also lacking (DGDA 2012). There is no electronic system to maintain an updated register. DGDA does not have a specialized lawyer to handle the legal aspects of violations of standards and regulations. Such drawbacks have led to an ineffective supervisory system, in which a situation of medicines and commodities that are substandard or lacking has become part of the health system.

DGDA's effectiveness is further constrained by the complexities of multiple administrative bodies and committees involved in the relevant regulatory processes. The recommendation for registration of drugs by DGDA comes from the Drug Control Committee. The National Drug Advisory Council advises on implementation of NDP and promotion of local pharmaceutical industries. There is also a Pricing Committee (which approves pricing decisions on medicaments) and a Standing Committee for Procurement and Import of Raw Materials and Finished Drugs (GTZ 2007). Adding to this structure, the National Research Ethics Committee is responsible for reviewing all clinical trials of medicinal substances and advises DGDA to ensure that the drugs available in the country fulfill the necessary requirements for safety, quality, and efficacy. There is a clear public health need for this governance structure to be reconciled with the changes introduced since 2005 (UNCTAD 2012).

The industry does not have any bioequivalence testing facility, which is mandatory for product registration in high-income markets. For a generic final formulation to be approved for import into a regulated market and some moderately regulated markets, the drug needs to be tested for bioequivalence—that is, comparability studies on healthy volunteers between the brand and generic drugs. Bangladeshi firms that want to export have to send drug samples to an internationally recognized bioequivalence laboratory abroad, which costs around US$50,000–US$60,000 per sample. This increases costs and makes exports less competitive. In addition, stringent regulations on sending foreign currency abroad further complicate the process.

TRIPS and Bangladeshi Pharmaceuticals

WTO's Agreement on Trade Related Aspects of Intellectual Property Rights requires all signatories to legislate 20-year patent protection for pharmaceutical products into their domestic law (box 6.1). TRIPS is a framework for intellectual property protection with minimum agreed standards. Although signatory countries must meet its requirements through legislation, TRIPS provides significant flexibility.

LDCs, including Bangladesh, are not obligated to legislate patent rights for pharmaceutical products until 2016. LDCs were not required to participate in the mailbox program or give exclusive marketing rights for any drugs during the period in which patent protection is not provided.[14] Therefore, until 2016, LDCs need not provide any patent protection or they may choose to provide less patent protection than required by TRIPS (or more if they so desire). In fact, many LDCs have implemented full TRIPS patent protection or expanded TRIPS-plus patent protection in advance of the 2016 deadline. However, in June 2013, the TRIPS Council of the WTO decided to allow LDCs to delay implementation of

Box 6.1 TRIPS Implementation in LDCs in Africa

Twelve least-developed countries (LDCs) in Africa are members of the Organisation Africaine de la Propriété Intellectuelle (OAPI), which was created on March 2, 1977, under the Bangui Agreement, to introduce a uniform law on intellectual property (IP) and to create a common industrial property office. The member countries are: Benin, Burkina Faso, Central African Republic, Chad, Equatorial Guinea, Guinea, Guinea-Bissau, Mali, Mauritania, Niger, Senegal, and Togo. OAPI serves as the national office of industrial property and the central authority for documentation and information regarding intellectual property in the member states. The 1999 revision to the Bangui Agreement made OAPI compatible with the Trade Related Aspects of Intellectual Property Rights (TRIPS) Agreement, including all categories of intellectual property rights covered by the TRIPS Agreement. In some cases, OAPI is even considered as TRIPS-plus.

Some countries have been reforming their IP laws largely based on TRIPS standards (although not complete yet). Revision of the existing legislation and issuance of new laws in areas where there were none are the two areas where reforms are taking place. For example, Uganda issued its trademarks act in 2010, trade secrets protection act in 2009, copyright and neighboring rights act in 2006, and patents amendment act in 2002; The Gambia put in place an industrial property act in 2007, a copyright act in 2004, and industrial property regulations in 2010; Burundi enacted its 2009 industrial property law and the 2005 copyright and related rights act; Djibouti did the same with its industrial property act in 2009 and copyright and neighboring rights act in 2006; and Rwanda enacted its IP laws in 2009. The IP policy of Rwanda clearly pronounces the role of IP in its economic development and outlines needs and priorities as well as the challenges Rwanda faces.

The European Union's Economic Partnership Agreements (EPAs) IP section is mainly based on TRIPS standards with some "TRIPS-plus" provisions. As part of ongoing EPA negotiations with the East African Community, four LDC members—Burundi, Rwanda, Tanzania, and Uganda—initialed a framework EPA on November 28, 2007, and are now negotiating a comprehensive regional EPA. Similarly, an interim EPA was signed by the European Union and Lesotho, Madagascar, and Mozambique in 2009.

Source: Merso 2013.

the TRIPS Agreement until July 1, 2021, except for pharmaceutical products. LDCs can assess their situation and may request an extension in 2016 with respect to pharmaceutical products.

Moreover, should public health issues arise, the WTO framework allows significant flexibility to all WTO members. WTO's declaration of 2001,[15] while maintaining the importance of the TRIPS agreement, recognized the need for flexibility in matters of public health, including the right of each WTO member to grant compulsory licenses.

In terms of exports, however, TRIPS appears to be less and less relevant for Bangladesh. Although TRIPS provides some limited export advantages to Bangladesh, these are offset by the pace and competitiveness of Indian and Chinese firms (World Bank 2008). In both countries, companies can produce drugs at highly competitive prices, even with the higher costs associated with buying patented APIs or paying royalties. If Bangladesh wants to make any major inroads into the world market, especially the large regulated markets, it will have to develop inherent competitive strength and not rely on the remaining transition window provided by TRIPS.

Bangladesh has a stronger pharmaceutical manufacturing base than almost all other LDCs, but this has not been associated with strong export performance. Future growth of the industry will need to rely much more on better regulatory enforcement, competition, and foreign direct investment (FDI), which would also be helpful for exports.

Prospects

Bangladesh's pharmaceutical industry has some advantages. The industry has matured in its own right. It has the ability to formulate generic medicine. Although the availability of less expensive, highly skilled labor like pharmacists and biologists is not a deciding factor, it is an added advantage. Labor costs in the industry are approximately 20–30 percent lower than in India (World Bank 2008).

The global generics market is forecast to expand. Globally, generics are growing at twice the rate of brand-name drugs. The patent expiry of several major blockbuster drugs worth US$150 billion between 2010 and 2017 will fuel the growth of the global generic pharmaceuticals markets (Frost and Sullivan 2011). In addition, the global expansion in health care systems and rising health care costs will help grow the generic market from US$242 billion in 2012 to US$400 billion to US$430 billion. Half of this increase is expected to come from low-cost generics.

Like in other sectors, such as shipbuilding, differences in domestic and export products are inimical to building scale and, equally important, confidence in the capability of Bangladesh's industrial sector. Working to international norms and standards is important not only for exports, but, more important, for consumer safety. Hence, a key focus of policy has to be on standards and enforcement. These and other issues are outlined in the following section.

Policy Options

Improvement in Bangladesh's regulatory functioning is of extreme importance for increasing exports (annex 6A). Strict regulatory environments are associated with higher-quality drugs. So far, Bangladeshi manufacturers have worked under a lax regulatory regime, without WHO prequalification for any product. Common perceptions of the country and questions regarding the local quality-control system are posing challenges for exporters. Initiatives should focus on building DGDA into an effective regulatory body by providing the agency with the necessary facilities, staff, and authority. Institutional measures should be investigated to increase transparency and provide inspectors with incentives to find, report, and fine low-quality manufacturing. Many governments have satisfactorily appointed a semi-autonomous regulatory authority. The authority's independence promotes a professional discharge of responsibilities. The case of Zimbabwe shows that a self-financing drug regulatory agency can act independently, even when the government appoints the staff (World Bank 2008).

Capacity building of the regulatory body will help harmonize quality standards. For example, the Pharmaceutical Inspection Convention and Pharmaceutical Inspection Co-operation Scheme (jointly referred to as PIC/S, http://www.picscheme.org/) are two international instruments that link countries and pharmaceutical inspection authorities. Together they provide active and constructive cooperation in the field of good manufacturing practices (GMP). When a regulatory authority applies to become a member of PIC/S, a detailed assessment is undertaken to determine whether the authority has the capacity and competence necessary to apply an inspection system comparable to that of current PIC/S members. This assessment includes an examination of the authority's inspection and licensing system, quality system, legislative requirements, inspector training, and so forth. It is followed by a visit from a PIC/S delegation to observe inspectors carrying out actual GMP inspections. There is an annual fee of SwF 8,100 (US$8,600) for PIC/S members. There are currently 43 participating regulatory authorities. In addition to improved quality standards, other benefits of PIC/S membership are export facilitation and enhanced market access for all the member countries. In addition, some non-PIC/S authorities (such as in Colombia) accept GMP certification from PIC/S participating authorities.

To ensure quality standards for the export market, Bangladesh needs to modernize its drug testing laboratories and establish bioequivalent testing facilities.[16] There is a need to develop accredited laboratories and clinical setups to conduct bioequivalent tests to ensure that drugs meet globally accepted standards. Domestic bioequivalence testing facilities could help reduce costs and time delays and potentially help open up regulated markets, even for manufacturers of medium size. As for testing labs, government approved and internationally accredited independent private testing laboratories could provide drug monitoring and quality services. These private labs could have industry representatives from associations, academics, civil society, and a government representative as their board members.

Deregulation in foreign exchange controls and capital investment is also critical for the growth of Bangladesh's pharmaceutical exports. Pharmaceuticals require heavy investments to comply with global standards. Receiving certification from the regulatory authorities of other countries, hiring consulting services to create best-practice manufacturing, and bringing and sending drug samples for testing require several foreign exchange transactions, currently subject to stringent government regulations. Transferring foreign currency for business purposes is a time-consuming, cumbersome process that involves monetary and nonmonetary costs. Deregulating the foreign exchange regime would reduce these costs and make pharmaceuticals more competitive. In addition, entering regulated or semi-regulated markets through registering products and acquiring various certifications is a lengthy process. And current regulations do not allow domestic companies to invest abroad except on a very lengthy, case-by-case basis. This can be changed (see Kathuria and Malouche 2016, chapter 7, on trade finance).

Gradual introduction of competition may improve the quality of products. Bangladeshi pharmaceutical firms operate in a highly protected environment. The near absence of foreign competition in the domestic pharmaceutical market may actually be hampering the pharmaceutical industry's aspirations to become a major global supplier of high-quality, competitively priced drugs (UNCTAD 2012). Bangladesh should consider opening up its domestic pharmaceutical market to global competition, allowing FDI through joint ventures to begin with. Similarly, import restrictions should be gradually lifted, to benefit the consumer with greater choice of drugs and induce domestic firms to compete not only on price, but also in quality terms. This could help reduce the market share of spurious drugs that are clearly a major problem in Bangladesh, provided that it is accompanied by a major initiative to improve the drug testing and certification infrastructure.

Clear strategy, planning, and transparency are needed to enter API production. The government of Bangladesh has wanted to establish an API park since 2008, but plans are moving slowly. API production requires scale economies and Bangladesh may find it difficult to compete internationally in APIs. However, there are some options here. FDI-based tie-ups with Indian or Chinese firms that manufacture API competitively can help. Further analysis is needed to determine which APIs Bangladesh could produce on a scale relevant to the Bangladeshi environment and still be price competitive. As water treatment plants and waste management are expensive operations, common effluent treatment facilities would be beneficial. To produce APIs, ensuring the quality of education and human resources and a supply of skilled labor in the chemistry and engineering fields would need particular attention.

Annex 6A: Action Matrix for Bangladesh's Pharmaceutical Sector

Proposed recommendation	*Responsible government unit*	*Timeline (short, medium, long term)*	*Implementation complexity*	*Expected impact*	*Comments*
Capacity building of DGDA	Ministry of Health and Family Welfare	Short	Low	High	World Bank is supporting a capacity-building program under the Health Sector Development Program. USAID is also supporting DGDA under its SIAPS program.
Modernization of drug testing laboratories	Ministry of Health and Family Welfare	Short	Low	High	World Bank with the technical assistance of the World Health Organization is currently working on converting the Dhaka drug testing laboratory into a modernized National Testing Laboratory.

table continues next page

Annex 6A *(continued)*

Proposed recommendation	*Responsible government unit*	*Timeline (short, medium, long term)*	*Implementation complexity*	*Expected impact*	*Comments*
Development of bioequivalence testing laboratory	Ministry of Health and Family Welfare	Medium	Medium	Medium	Analysis of laboratory construction and operational costs is required to determine if a domestic laboratory could offer internationally acceptable bioequivalence services at competitive cost.
Deregulation of foreign exchange controls	Ministry of Finance/ Bangladesh Bank	Medium	High	Medium	Kathuria and Malouche 2016, chapter 7, on trade finance has some detailed suggestions.
Increased competition through opening up the market to imports and FDI	Ministry of Health and Family Welfare	Long	High	High	Consensus among the stakeholders is required. It remains to be seen if the vision of the government regarding the pharmaceutical sector as the National Drug Policy of 2012 will be finalized. In the long term, more domestic competition will be essential not only for exports but, more important, for consumer welfare and public health.

Note: DGDA = Directorate General of Drug Administration; FDI = foreign direct investment; SIAPS = System for Improved Access to Pharmaceuticals; USAID = U.S. Agency for International Development.

Notes

1. In 2005, the National Drug Policy was revised and the ban on Bangladeshi companies manufacturing under contract and license for multinationals was lifted.
2. A generic drug is identical or bioequivalent to a branded drug in all respects, including safety, strength, and quality, as it has the same chemical composition.
3. These are estimates from 2007. These figures have not been updated, as there was no new survey.
4. Interviews with pharmaceutical companies confirmed this figure.
5. Novartis is an MNC operating in Bangladesh. World Bank (2008) presents this fact and it has been confirmed from interviews conducted with local and multinational companies, including Novartis.
6. Bangladesh Association of Pharmaceutical Industries conveyed this estimate in the Pharma Expo 2013, February 23–25.
7. Source: field interviews with pharmaceutical companies.
8. Source: field interviews with local pharmaceutical companies.
9. It would be speculative to put any number on the effective output protective tariff, although import bans under the Drug Policy imply that effective tariffs

(when compared with other subsectors where bans do not exist) on generic or brand name drugs produced locally are on the high side.

10. The 2012/13 budget reduced the total tax burden for 46 essential items of pharmaceutical manufacture from 38–59 percent to 3 percent. In the 2012/13 and 2011/12 budgets, duties were withdrawn or reduced on machinery such as air handling units, heating ventilation, cartridge filters, sandwich panels, and leucocyte filters.
11. cGMP certification is provided to a facility for a certain product if it meets the standards for base materials, premises, equipment, processes, documentation, training, and personal staff hygiene. These standards are quite general; their implementation determines their actual stringency.
12. Although many organizations use the same WHO standards, there may be great differences among various inspecting agencies.
13. Source: interviews with local firms.
14. According to TRIPS articles 70.8 and 70.9, countries without patent protection had to create a "mailbox" to receive patent applications. Between 1995 and January 1, 2005, 13 countries, including India, used this provision and allowed patent applications to be filed, although the decision on patenting could be deferred.
15. http://www.wto.org/english/thewto_e/minist_e/min01_e/mindecl_trips_e.htm.
16. With financing by the World Bank and technical assistance from WHO, the drug testing laboratory in Dhaka (which has been declared the National Testing Laboratory) has been renovated and modernized.

References

Beximco Pharmaceuticals. 2011. *Annual Report 2011*. Beximco Pharmaceuticals, Dhaka.

Bhuiyan, A., M. Sultana, and S. Sultana. 2011. "Analysis of Pharmaceutical Industry of Bangladesh." *Bangladesh Research Publications Journal* 5: 142–56.

BRAC EPL Stock Brokerage Ltd.2012. "An Overview of the Pharmaceutical Sector in Bangladesh." BRAC EPL. http://www.bracepl.com/brokerage/research/1337161382An%20Overview%20of%20the%20Pharmaceutical%20Sector%20in%20Bangladesh%20%28May%202012%29.pdf.

BTC (Bangladesh Tariff Commission). 2010. "An Analysis of Assistance to the Pharmaceutical Industry." BTC, Dhaka.

DGDA (Directorate General of Drug Administration). 2012. *Annual Report, 2011–12*. DGDA, Dhaka.

Dhaka Chamber of Commerce and Industry. 2007. "Bangladesh: Supply and Demand Survey on Pharmaceutical and Natural Products." Dhaka Chamber of Commerce and Industry. http://legacy.intracen.org/docman/oeve11926.pdf.

Forbes Asia. 2013. "Window on a Different Dhaka." *Forbes Asia*, January.

Frost & Sullivan. 2011. "Generic Pharmaceutical Market—A Global Analysis." Frost & Sullivan. http://www.frost.com/sublib/display-report.do?id=M74E-01-00-00-00.

GTZ (Deutsche Gesselschaft für Technische Zusammenarbeit). 2007. "Study on the Viability of High Quality Drugs Manufacturing in Bangladesh." GTZ, GmbH. http://www.unido.org/fileadmin/user_media/Services/PSD/BEP/en-high-quality-drugs-bangladesh-2007.pdf.

IDLC Finance Limited. 2011. "Research Report: Pharmaceutical Industry of Bangladesh." IDLC, Dhaka. http://www.idlc.com/sector_coverage/1332567100Research%20Report%20on%20Pharmaceutical%20Sector%20of%20BD-Initiation,%20June%2028,%202011.pdf.

Kathuria, Sanjay, and Mariem Mezghenni Malouche, eds. 2016. *Strategies to Strengthen Bangladeshi Competitiveness: Thematic Assessments*. Washington, DC: World Bank.

Merso, F. 2013. "IP Trends in African LDCs and the LDC TRIPS Transition Extension." Policy Brief 16. International Centre for Trade and Sustainable Development.

Ministry of Commerce. 2012. *Import Policy Order 2012–2015*. Dhaka: Government of Bangladesh.

Square Pharmaceuticals. 2012. *Annual Report 2011–2012*. Square Pharmaceuticals, Dhaka. http://www.squarepharma.com.bd/financial-reports/spl_annual-report_11-12.pdf.

UNCTAD (United Nations Conference on Trade and Development). 2011. "Case Study 2 on Bangladesh." In *Local Production of Pharmaceuticals and Related Technology Transfer: A Series of Case Studies by the UNCTAD Secretariat*, 57–88. New York: United Nations. http://www.who.int/phi/publications/Local_Production_Case_Studies.pdf.

———. 2012. *Investment Policy Review*. New York: United Nations.

USAID and SIAPS (United States Agency for International Development, and System for Improved Access to Pharmaceuticals and Services). 2013. "Strengthening the Pharmacovigilance System in Bangladesh." DGDA with support from the SIAPS Program, funded by USAID and the U.S. Food and Drug Administration. http://siapsprogram.org/2013/02/11/strengthening-the-pharmacovigilance-system-in-bangladesh/.

World Bank. 2008. "Public and Private Sector Approaches to Improving Pharmaceutical Quality in Bangladesh." Bangladesh Development Series Paper 23, World Bank, Washington, DC.

———. 2012. "Bangladesh: Assessment of Effective Rates of Protection-Survey of Manufacturing Enterprises." World Bank, Washington, DC.

CHAPTER 7

Accelerating the Development of IT-Enabled Services

Atdhe Veliu and Glenn Surabian

Introduction

The information technology (IT) sector in Bangladesh is considered by the public and private sectors to have high growth potential. The industry employs an estimated 70,000 people and generates an estimated US$400 million in annual revenues. The majority of IT firms report software development and maintenance to be their core business. However, the outsourcing of IT-related business processes generates more revenue in the industry than software development. Such outsourcing is formally known as information technology–enabled services (ITES)–business process outsourcing (BPO), or ITES-BPO. The value of exports from the formal software and ITES-BPO sector in 2013 was US$101.63 million, a relatively low amount compared with other countries in the region. Despite high expectations, the sector remains a marginal contributor to Bangladeshi exports. Nevertheless, several recent developments have raised hopes for the sector in the near future: exports are on the rise and multinational corporations are investing in research and development (R&D) centers in the country. In light of these developments, ITES-BPO was selected as a service sector for value chain analysis.

Sector Profile: ITES-BPO

Outsourcing is a well-understood management process that was first used by multinational corporations in the 1990s. It has been used increasingly by a range of companies of all sizes ever since. Outsourcing basically involves contracting out to third parties business functions and processes that companies no longer want to perform themselves, because of perceived or real disadvantages in costs, risks, and other aspects of business performance and competitiveness.

Business functions and processes that are outsourced to or purchased from third parties include the following:

- *Manufacturing*. Multinationals frequently outsource many manufacturing processes to third parties. This type of outsourcing may involve transfer of employees or assets from the contracting manufacturer to its contractor or business partner.[1]
- *Information technology*. Information technology outsourcing (ITO) has one main objective: to reduce the cost of IT systems or site or data centers.[2] This constitutes one of the largest outsourcing segments.
- *Information technology–enabled services*. ITES involves outsourcing a vast array of business processes. As with other forms of outsourcing, ITES can take place in the same or proximate geographies or countries. When the contracting firm and its contractor or service provider are from nearby countries, the outsourcing is commonly called nearshoring. In cases where the contracting firm and the contractor are in countries separated by large distances or time zone differences, the outsourcing is called offshoring.[3] The bulk of ITES outsourcing takes place within or in the vicinity of key outsourcing countries (the United States and European countries): only 30 percent of the estimated US$464 billion BPO industry in 2011 was composed of offshored services. India dominates the offshore market, capturing a 40 percent share, followed by China (30 percent) and the Philippines (10 percent).[4] In terms of segments (verticals), financial industry ITES contributes approximately 17 percent to global outsourcing, followed by the telecom sector (16 percent) and consumer goods and services (15 percent).

Worldwide spending for IT and BPO (including hardware, engineering, and R&D) exceeded US$1.7 trillion in 2011, a growth of 5.4 percent over 2010 (figure 7.1). Software products, IT services, and BPO services continued to lead the spending, accounting for more than US$1 trillion (63 percent) of the total market. In terms of the maturity of various segments of the BPO industry, services such as document management, customer services, and application development and maintenance are reaching maturity, whereas banking, insurance, and procurement BPO are at the phase of rapid growth. Life sciences, health care, and utilities BPO are in the early stage of growth (see box 7.1).

In Bangladesh, more than 1,000 software and ITES companies are registered, employing about 70,000 people and generating an estimated US$400 million in annual revenues.[5] About two-thirds of the firms are small, employing 10–30 people. In addition, there are an estimated few hundred unregistered small companies doing software and ITES-BPO business for local and international markets. Another 5,000 people are estimated to be working as freelancers. Many firms provide a range of software and ITES-BPO services at the same time (see table 7.1 for more details). Approximately half the officially registered companies provide a range of ITES-BPO services, including data and form processing, graphic and website design, content management, and others.

Figure 7.1 Worldwide IT and BPO Expenditures
US$, billions

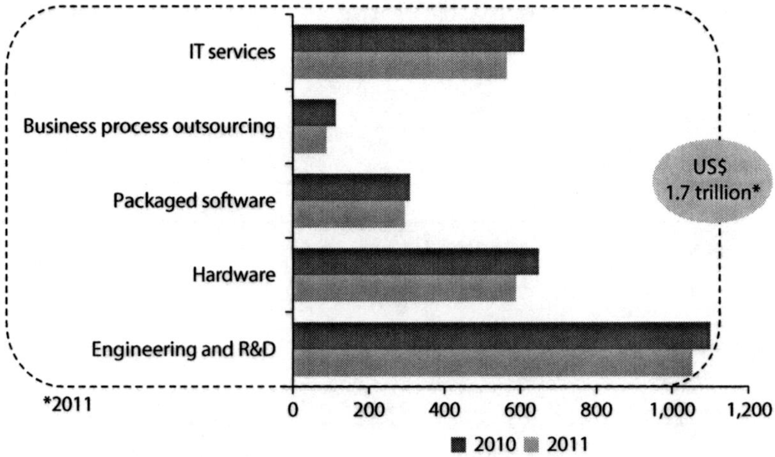

Source: Original data from Gartner, IDC, complied by NASSCOM. Available at NASSCOM's website, http://www.nasscom.org/global-sourcing.

Box 7.1 IT-Enabled Services Product Segments

IT-enabled services (ITES) generally can be divided as follows:

Outsourcing of strategic, knowledge-based business processes, typically known as knowledge process outsourcing (KPO). Outsourcing of legal, patent, and similar services can also be generally classified under KPO, although sometimes it is classified separately as legal process outsourcing. The offshore KPO market was worth an estimated US$8 billion in 2011 (over 60 percent of the market was captured by India).

Outsourcing of transactional, nonstrategic business processes, commonly referred to as business process outsourcing (BPO). Since Internet and other IT technology is involved, in varying degrees, in the delivery of all transactional business processes, BPO services in this category are often referred to as ITES-BPO[a] They include the following:

- Procurement, inventory, transport, and logistics functions. Commonly referred to as procurement outsourcing, these are supporting functions related to the supply chain of a firm—from inventory ownership, procurement, and management to distribution of final product to consumers.
- Back-office processes. These include finance, accounting, human resources, and other general administration processes.
- Front-office business processes. These include selling, marketing, customer relations, and similar business processes.

a. ITES-BPO and BPO are overlapping terms. It is generally difficult to find BPO processes in which delivery does not depend on information technology. Throughout this report, ITES-BPO is used.

Table 7.1 Overview of the IT and ITES-BPO Industry in Bangladesh, 2011

Details	*Units*
Number of firms (IT and ITES-BPO) (no. of which exporting)	800+ (160+)
Number of people employed in the industry (IT and ITES-BPO)	30,000
Industry revenue (IT and ITES-BPO)	US$250 million
Industry revenue, ITES-BPO only (% of total)	US$140 million (56%)

Business specialization by type of service (BASIS members)

Type of service	*Percent of firms*
Customized application development and maintenance	76
ITES-BPO	50
E-commerce or web services	45
Product development	18
Mobile application or content provider	17
IT/infrastructure management/system integration R&D services	11/7/3/3

Business distribution by employment size (BASIS members)

Number of employees	*Percent of firms*
10–30	64
30–50	16
50–100	12
100+	8

Business specialization by revenue (BASIS members)

Annual revenue (US$)	*% of firms*
1–60,000	43
60,000–180,000	26
180,000–600,000	17
600,000+	14

Officially reported exports (IT and ITES-BPO), 2006–12

Fiscal year	*2007*	*2008*	*2009*	*2010*	*2011*	*2012*
US$ millions	26.08	24.09	32.91	35.36	45.31	70.81

Source: Compiled by Global Development Solutions, LLC, from BASIS data.
Note: BPO = business process outsourcing; IT = information technology; ITES = information technology–enabled services; R&D = research and development.

The industry has generated limited exports in the past, but several recent developments have raised hopes for the sector. Officially reported exports grew from US$26 million in fiscal year 2005–06 (FY2006) to US$45 million in FY2011 and jumped to US$71 million in FY2012, a 56 percent increase over the previous year. These export figures do not include an estimated US$20 million to US$30 million in annual exports generated by freelancers or informal companies that are not captured by the official records. BASIS estimates that 160 IT and ITES-BPO companies are involved in exports. The industry has recently gained new multinational members: Samsung opened its R&D center in 2010, employing more than 200 engineers; BASIS also reports that LG, IBM, and AMD are in the process of exploring setting up similar centers; and more than 30 joint ventures have been established in Dhaka to provide offshore services to clients in international markets.[6]

Globally, Indian firms and the Indian industry in general are the world leaders in ITES-BPO and provide useful insights into key drivers for growth at the firm and industry levels. Although ITES-BPO firm and industry growth in other countries may not necessarily follow the exact path and growth phases of the Indian industry, some characteristics of the Indian success story are present in major BPO-exporting countries like China, the Philippines, and others. Boxes 7.2 and 7.3 describe key drivers and dynamics of growth at the industry and firm levels that may provide useful insights for the ITES-BPO sector in Bangladesh.

Box 7.2 Growth Phases of the Indian BPO Industry

First Wave: Company-Owned (Captive) Units Pioneer BPO in India

Company-owned units (commonly known as captives), such as American Express, General Electric, Citibank, and AOL, etc., triggered the trend of outsourcing back-office operations and call center services to India. In essence, multinational captives put the country on the world's business process outsourcing (BPO) map and paved the way for many banks, insurance companies, airlines, and manufacturing companies to set up back-office service centers in India. Industry linkages between captives and local firms grow and set the stage for the second wave.

Second Wave: Venture-Funded New Companies

After having learned business processes and gained industry experience from interactions with captives and other players in the industry, several small firms led by experienced professionals start operations with the help of venture capital funds.

Third Wave: Leading IT Services Companies Enter BPO

Capitalizing on synergies with the software services business and the ability to leverage their high-end physical infrastructure and management bandwidth, large information technology (IT) services companies venture into information technology–enabled services (ITES). Consolidation of the market starts, with smaller players merging with each other and larger companies for economies of scale.

Fourth Wave: Domain- or Industry-Specialized BPOs

Niche players in industry or specific business processes set up BPO businesses. Many of these players with experience in the domestic market start offering offshore BPO services. Generalized large BPO players now focus on "verticalizing" their competencies and structures by specific industry domain: financial industry, telecom, knowledge process outsourcing, etc.

box continues next page

Box 7.2 Growth Phases of the Indian BPO Industry *(continued)*

Lessons for Bangladesh

- Put Bangladesh on the world BPO map by attracting captives.
- Attract captives by providing what captives need to invest in offshore BPO centers: good labor talent pool and good infrastructure (IT connectivity and good intellectual property, IT security framework, and good business environment).
- Leverage the presence of captives to boost domestic industry growth by providing dedicated industry funding (venture or other capital).
- Make continuous business environment improvements to encourage business growth and specialization.

Source: Compiled by Global Development Solutions, LLC. Indian industry growth information adapted from PriceWaterhouseCoopers 2005.

Box 7.3 BPO Service Models under Rising Performance Expectations

"The importance of picking the right deal structure in offshoring is critical in light of the long-term strategic implications it has on cost savings and performance quality. The choice can be a difficult one—between pursuing a captive model, doing a BOT (build operate transfer), doing a joint venture with a supplier, or going straight to the supplier for a direct services relationship [third party model]. The deciding factors depend broadly on the level of flexibility that an organization is willing to assume and the degree of control that it wishes to exert on the overall operations. [Surveyed Indian BPOs] state that there is no one "most suitable" model that exists in the industry, stemming from the fact that the requirements, expectations and risk appetite of clients vary significantly…

The third-party offshore model has witnessed considerable activity over the past few years, a direct consequence of the emergence of world-class service providers with significant critical mass. Respondents stated that the preference for this model may be attributed to the shorter payback period (between 6 months to a year) and lower exit costs. In addition, clients believe that the third party models hold the maximum potential of leveraging economies of scale—thereby reducing costs and maximizing efficiencies. However, the nature of work outsourced is typically noncore and noncritical, in light of a perceived lower level of data security."[a]

Independent of the service model chosen, industry research shows three firm performance trends that may provide valuable lessons for Bangladesh. "First, while clients rated their [Indian] offshore partners (captives or third parties) highly on process performance, they want providers to offer more than just labor cost-savings. In the first few years of offshoring, clients tend to focus on cost benefits and on provider's ability to maintain quality levels comparable to those at onshore sited. Given the availability of skilled talent and lower wage rates, most [Indian] offshore partners can meet these initial expectations relatively easily and therefore generate

box continues next page

Box 7.3 BPO Service Models under Rising Performance Expectation *(continued)*

high levels of client satisfaction. Within two to three years, however, as clients become accustomed to the cost savings, they begin to look for productivity benefits and service delivery innovations…

[Second] a significant spread in performance [exists] between leading outsourcing providers and the rest of the pack…

[Third] companies whose management devotes substantial time and effort to streamlining and 'industrializing' their processes, for example, outperform their peers. Also, since reducing attrition rates is the key to keeping costs low and quality high, providers that innovate in the areas of recruitment, training, and people management tend to deliver better value as well."[b]

Lessons for Bangladesh

- Remove bottlenecks that hamper the ability of Bangladeshi business process outsourcing (BPO) to provide good quality of service, most notably the poor Internet connectivity and the poor quality of electricity.
- Support the industry with a steady supply of educated and talented labor.
- Encourage the emergence of specialized training institutions that can help the industry in workforce training.
- With this support in place, the industry can focus on providing increased productivity and service delivery innovations.
- To date, it is impossible for Bangladeshi BPOs to focus fully on service innovations and quality, because they have more immediate practical bottlenecks that they have to deal with on a daily basis: Internet and electricity outages, talent finding, etc.

Source: Compiled by Global Development Solutions, LLC.
a. PriceWaterhouseCoopers 2005.
b. Assocom/McKinsey, "Benchmarking India's Business Process Outsourcers," 2005.

Supply Chain

The supply chain of an ITES-BPO exporter is to a large extent based on labor arbitrage, at least to begin. Outsourcing companies typically aim to transform as many fixed costs as possible into variable costs without jeopardizing their competitiveness as measured by product or service quality and customer satisfaction. Nowhere is this more evident than in ITES-BPO that, by and large, involves transformation of outsourcing companies' labor-intensive fixed costs into variable costs. Work associated with back office, front office, or other business processes is cheaper to do in countries with low labor costs compared with high-income countries. In Bangladesh, industry interviews indicate that labor arbitrage opportunities are by and large limited to the low value-added BPO segments (data entry and rule-based processing). This is because most of the available labor force has limited soft skills, such as English language proficiency, general knowledge of personal computers and information and communications technology (ICT), and communication skills, among others—see figure 7.2. Workers with the managerial

Figure 7.2 ITES-BPO Sector Supply Chain, Bangladesh

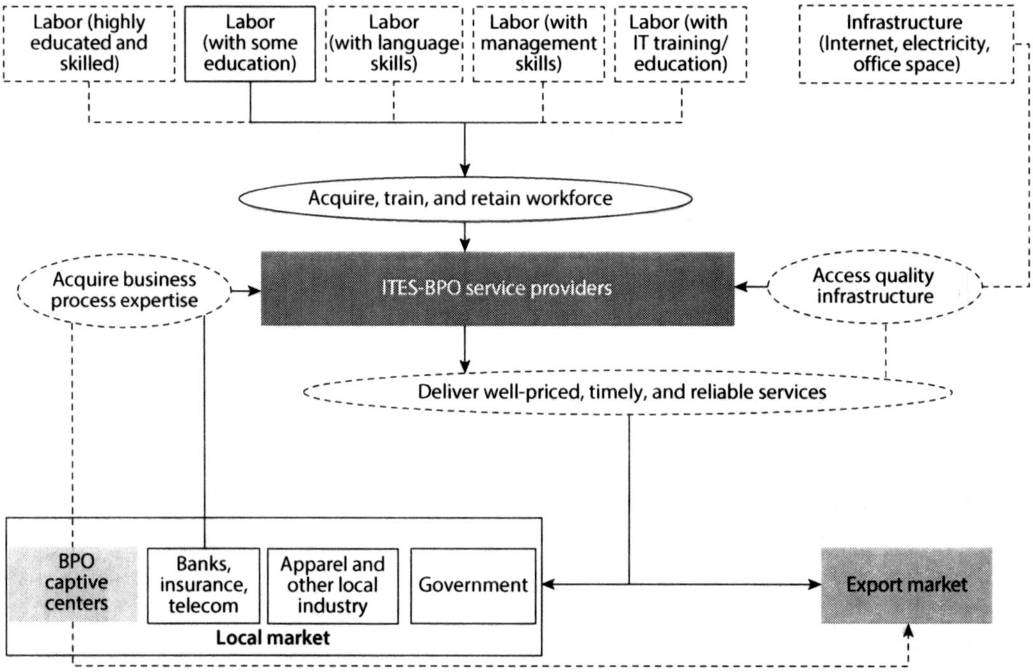

Source: Global Development Solutions, LLC.
Note: Dashed lines indicate underdeveloped parts of and relationships in the supply chain. IT = information technology; ITES-BPO = information technology–enabled services–business process outsourcing.

and business skills required for mid- and upper-level supervisory duties are also in short supply, perhaps more so.

The current state of infrastructure is the next key component in the supply chain of ITES-BPO service exporters. From the perspective of BPO clients, outsourcing a business process only makes sense if the provider delivers services in a timely and reliable manner. As illustrated in the supply chain in figure 7.2, Bangladeshi BPO service providers report major difficulties in building quality and reliability reputations with foreign clients because their delivery of services is interrupted by poor Internet connectivity and supply of electricity. Without major improvements in the quality of basic infrastructure, labor or other cost arbitrage will not be enough to make the Bangladeshi ITES-BPO industry attractive internationally. Bangladesh would only be attractive for the most basic data entry and similar low-risk business processes.

Bangladeshi ITES-BPO service providers operate in a supply chain without any captive BPO centers. Service providers need to have domain-specific knowledge of business processes to supply BPO services in finance, human resources, insurance, procurement, or any other outsourcing field. Lessons from successful ITES-BPO supply chains in countries like the Philippines and India suggest that local BPO service providers obtain vital business process knowledge through business relationships with captive BPO centers. Bangladesh has a competitive disadvantage because it is not able to acquire business process knowledge and expertise directly from captive BPO centers. Providers must acquire business process expertise from local clients in the banking, insurance, telecom, and similar service sectors, or directly from international clients abroad. Acquiring expertise and specialization through these channels is slow and arduous, as Bangladeshi ITES-BPO firms have discovered.

Captive BPO centers—those set up and owned by multinational corporations—are a critical source of business process information for local BPO service providers. American Express, General Electric, British Airways, Citibank, and hundreds of other multinational corporations own BPO centers in the Philippines, India, and other countries. Moreover, depending on where they are in the trajectory of the build-operate-transfer business model, foreign-owned captives become deeply embedded in local BPO supply chains. Many linkages along cross-ownership, subcontracting, vertical industry specialization, and other lines emerge between captives and local BPO centers. This way, local BPOs not only gain deep understanding of business processes in a range of industries, but also grow together with captive centers through third-party business relationships (see table 7.2 for third-party service delivery trends of captive centers in the Philippines).

In the absence of captive centers, Bangladeshi BPOs must create market demand on their own, which is extremely difficult. In India, for example, captive units dominate the ITES-BPO industry; in 2005, they accounted for over 65 percent of the value of the work offshored to India.[7] Captive centers are also generally involved in developing local managerial and other talent; this option generates considerable cost-savings compared with the parent firms sending over their expatriate managers. Furthermore, with current technologies, parent companies adopt virtual training methods that generate additional savings and at the same time accelerate staff development in the countries where they operate their captive centers. Deep familiarity with the parent company's business processes is a major advantage in outsourcing and Bangladesh suffers in this respect. Table 7.3 summarizes and ranks the status of captive centers in the Philippines.

Table 7.2 Third-Party Service Delivery Trends of Multinationals in the Philippines

Trend	*Surveyed parent companies of BPO captives (%)*
Move low-skill, high-volume to third-party provider	19
Gradually shift to a third-party provider	6
Explore third-party options	13
Gradually shift to a pure captive	6
None	56

Sources: BPAP and Hewitt 2010.
Note: BPO = business process outsourcing.

Table 7.3 Status of ITES-BPO Captives in the Philippines

	Importance		
Indicator	*Rank 1*	*Rank 2*	*Rank 3*
Drivers for adopting a captive strategy	End-to-end process control	Arbitrage	Quality
Country advantages	Talent profile and costs	Infrastructure	Business environment
Priority areas for development	Increase headcount	Develop capabilities	Increase efficiencies
Common alternative or competing locations	India	China	Malaysia
Key challenges during setup	Human capital issues	Legal, facilities	Project execution and team deployment
Key investment areas	IT infrastructure	Skill enhancements	Process improvements

Source: BPAP and Hewitt 2010.
Note: IT = information technology; ITES-BPO = information technology–enabled services–business process outsourcing.

Supporting Institutions and Policies

BASIS is the key private sector body directly involved with supporting ITES-BPO industry in the country.[8] Founded in 1997, BASIS today has nearly 500 member companies and the following reported objectives: domestic and international market development, capacity building and member service development and delivery, advocacy, and social contribution. In terms of domestic and international market development, some success has been achieved through regular trade fairs, business-to-business meetings, and other similar activities organized by BASIS. However, few contracts and business leads have materialized through such avenues. In the area of advocacy, BASIS is active in raising regulatory and other issues with policy makers, the media, and other stakeholders. Its most recent activities involve raising regulatory and policy issues with the Ministry of Information and Communication Technology in relation to Internet bandwidth pricing, lobbying for a minimum 80 percent allocation in all government procurement for local software and ITES companies, and funding for ICT employment creation through skills development programs.

Capacity building and member service development are other areas where BASIS is generating tangible results for the industry. In July 2012, BASIS inaugurated the BASIS Institute of Technology and Management (BITM). The key objective of BITM is to increase the supply of technical and managerial training and resources needed for the IT and ITES industry. Interviews with BASIS suggest that every year an estimated 8,000–10,000 IT engineering graduates enter the labor market, but this is still low compared with China, India, and other major exporters of IT and ITES-BPO. Moreover, the skill set (including technical, language, and other skills) of IT and other graduates entering the labor market is generally insufficient to meet industry requirements. For example, ITES-BPO exporters do not necessarily need workers with IT education as much as they need workers with the language and other soft skills required to understand and deliver business process services. BITM aims to address these gaps by training university graduates through a service delivery model. The model combines training programs, coaching, workshops, and certification for individuals as well as organizations (see table 7.4 for details).

The government gave new impetus to the ICT industry with its "Digital Bangladesh by 2021" agenda in 2009. Digital Bangladesh is an ambitious policy agenda that envisions utilization of ICT as a pro-poor tool, "to eradicate poverty, establish good governance, ensure social equity through quality education, health care and law enforcement for all and prepare the country for climate change" (GOB 2010). The government also updated the ICT Policy 2009 and ICT Act 2009, which represent the current strategic and policy framework for the ICT sector in the country. ICT Policy 2009 has a comprehensive list of objectives across a wide range of areas, from social equity, health care, and the environment to employment generation, export growth, and support for the ICT sector (table 7.5). It includes a specific policy objective related to improving access to finance for software and ITES companies. In late 2011, the Ministry of Information and Communication Technology was established to spearhead ICT policy implementation.[9] Giving the ICT industry priority is a powerful message by the government and can lead to positive returns if implemented in a strategic manner.

Table 7.4 BASIS Institute of Technology and Management

Objectives	• To equip university graduates with the skills required to secure employment within ICT industry—locally and abroad • To provide existing ICT professionals and users a platform to get additional managerial, technical, and soft skills and best practices to help raise their level of performance • To extend opportunities to academic partners to increase their portfolio of training, and engage with ICT sector stakeholders
Course delivery models	• 3–6 month diploma training • 1–2 month certificate training • 1–2 week training programs • 3–5 day workshops • 1–2 day coaching by consultants (for C-level) • Customized training, certification, or accreditation for individuals and organizations
Roadmap	*Short term (0–6 months)* • Establish relationships with cooperating agencies • Conduct identified training (1,000 students in 2012) *Medium term (6–24 months)* • Develop affiliation with internationally recognized training partners • Engage with ICT industry as a resource pool of qualified candidates • Create and implement assessment capability • Scale up training to 2,000 students per year *Long term (24 months+)* • Develop research capability • Set up regional BITM centers, capacity of 5,000+ students per year

Source: BASIS.
Note: BASIS = Bangladesh Association of Software and Information Services; BITM = BASIS Institute of Technology and Management; ICT = information and communications technology.

Table 7.5 ICT Policy 2009, Bangladesh

Objectives	*Details*
Support for ICT	• Ensure reliable and cost-effective power. • Improve Internet availability and reliability. • Create supportive legal framework for protection of intellectual property, online document sharing, and transactions and payments. • Build ICT infrastructure facilities in educational institutions. • Decentralize ICT growth outside the capital. • Improve education quality in IT, mathematics, and English.
Employment generation	• Provide incentives for investment in local ICT industry. • Build institutional capacity for producing greater numbers of ICT professionals. • Standardize skills for local ICT industry. • Facilitate global employment of a skilled ICT workforce. • Provide financial assistance to ICT professionals for skills development.
Strengthening exports	• Develop strong marketing, promotion, and branding for Bangladeshi ICT products and services in global markets. • Ensure access to finance for promising software and ITES companies. • Develop and maintain reliable ICT infrastructure. • Provide incentives to increase exports and create industry-friendly policy and an enabling environment. • Foster innovation through research and development to improve quality, process, technology, domain, value chain, and niche markets.
Education and research	• Assess skills of ICT professionals and meet gaps with targeted trainings. • Encourage closer collaboration between academia and industry. • Extend the reach of ICT literacy throughout the country by incorporating ICT courses in secondary education and technical and vocational education. • Enhance the quality and reach of education at all levels with a special focus on mathematics, science, and English. • Ensure ICT literacy for all in public service and in all levels of education.
Productivity	• Encourage e-commerce, e-payments, and e-transactions.
Universal access	Within five years, extend universal connectivity, Internet, and IP telephony to all citizens in all parts of the country. Extend Internet backbone infrastructure to all district headquarters immediately at the same access cost as in the capital. Make IP-based telecommunications ubiquitous and affordable by all.
Social equity	Bridge the digital divide for lower-income groups, ethnic minorities, women, and persons with disabilities and special needs. Facilitate citizens' participation in local and national government and policy making.
Integrity	Ensure the use of the country's official language, Bangla, in all ICT activities. Ensure transparency and accountability in government service delivery, interconnectivity/data sharing across government offices, and availability of all public information through electronic means.
Health care	Improve management of health care delivery system. Improve community awareness of and access to health care facilities for all, including difficult-to-access areas. Promote a special emphasis on child and maternal health.
Environment	Adopt environmentally friendly green technologies. Promote environmental protection through the use of ICT tools and ICT-based disaster warning and management technologies. Ensure safe disposal of toxic wastes from use of ICT.

Source: Compiled by Global Development Solutions, LLC, from public policy documentation.
Note: ICT = information and communications technology; IP = intellectual property; IT = information technology; ITES = information technology–enabled services.

Unfortunately, ICT Policy 2009 is wide ranging, lacks prioritization, and is poorly implemented. The policy has guidelines for budgetary allocation, which, not surprisingly, are not implemented.[10] The general perception in the industry is that government ICT policy each year recycles the same initiatives without major action and financial commitment to back them up. Annual budgets have for many years emphasized establishment of high-tech parks, setting up a second submarine telecommunication cable, and many related initiatives that by and large are considered by the industry as paper-based policies only. Finally, according to the industry, there are 306 action items in ICT Policy 2009 for which various agencies have been designated as key or supporting implementing agencies. Although some agencies, most notably Bangladesh Bank, have implemented or started to implement some action items during the past three years (including e-commerce and a national payment gateway), many other initiatives, such as special education loans for ICT graduates and technology parks, remain unaddressed. Recently, the Cabinet approved the National ICT Policy 2015, but this has not yet been approved in Parliament.

IT and ITES benefit from a number of preferential policies. IT and ITES-BPO firms had exemptions from income taxes that were set to expire in 2015; the industry called for extension of this relief until 2018. The industry enjoys various value-added tax exemptions for some imported hardware, software, and related service purchases. Moreover, an estimated 20 IT and ITES firms have been provided access to grade-A office space at preferential prices at the government-owned Janata Tower premises in central Dhaka. The industry can also use the Equity Entrepreneurship Fund (EEF), a venture capital fund offering equity support and managed by the Bangladesh Bank, in place since 2001. An estimated 40–50 IT and ITES companies have made use of roughly US$10 million in the past 10 years, but according to the industry, bureaucratic procedures have made access to this fund difficult.

However, tax exemptions do not seem to apply to items that are frequently purchased by ITES-BPO companies. Most notably, Internet connections sourced from local service providers are taxed at 15 percent. Import tariffs on ICT-related products and accessories are also considered too high by the private sector. Microphones, headphones, and related accessories used by providers of voice-related BPO services have a tariff of 25 percent. Optical fiber cable imports face tariffs of 12 percent; UPS/IPS backup devices have a tariff of 5 percent; and modems, routers, and similar networking equipment have a tariff of 3 percent. If duties protect a particular sector and hurt a sector that is potentially large and promising, then such duties need to be looked at carefully (see Kathuria and Malouche 2016, chapter 2, on trade policy). For example, it appears that protection of the domestic manufacturer of optical fiber cable may be hurting the rest of the sector (see box 7.4).

The industry suffers from stringent foreign exchange regulations and inflexible payment regimes. There are several restrictions. According to Foreign Exchange Circular No. 15,[11] foreign exchange intermediaries can remit on behalf of IT and

Box 7.4 Increased Duties for Optical Fiber Cables in Bangladesh

In 2011, the National Board of Revenue (NBR) increased the import tariff on optical fiber cable (OFC) from 3 to 12 percent. According to NBR officials, this action was based on the Ministry of Industry's recommendations to "protect the domestic manufacturers of optical fiber cable." In fact, the country has only one OFC manufacturer, the government-owned Bangladesh Cable Shilpa Limited (BCSL). BCSL started OFC manufacturing in July 2011. According to NBR officials, import tariffs had to be increased because "BCSL had to pay up to 25 percent duty on import of raw materials for OFC production while the private-sector importers were paying only 3 percent duty on import of finished OFC." According to BCSL, "the prices of OFC are competitive in comparison of world market. BCSL is maintaining high and world standard quality with imported high quality raw materials. BCSL hopes about 70 percent of the present market demand in Bangladesh will be fulfilled from its factory production. These OFC will play an important and vital role for implementing 'Digital Bangladesh' program as a commitment of the Prime Minister."

However, interviews with private sector stakeholders, including Internet service providers (ISPs), suggest that a level playing field could be achieved by reducing tariffs on raw materials for OFC production rather than hiking tariffs on the end product (finished OFC). According to industry representatives, this policy reduces the ability of ISPs to provide Internet access at more affordable rates to business and residential clients, and contradicts the strategic objective of Digital Bangladesh to increase access to affordable information and communications technologies in the country.

Sources: Interviews, Global Development Solutions, LLC. Quotes from *New Age* Online Edition, http://www.newagebd.com/, and from the BCSL website, http://www.bcsl.gov.bd.

ITES firms only up to US$10,000 in a calendar year for fees related to software registration, domain registration or hosting, server maintenance, and similar fees. The industry would benefit if this limit was increased to at least US$50,000 per year and if the list of eligible expenditures was expanded to include technical training fees, Web advisement and listing fees, and conference and event registration fees. The maximum allowable foreign exchange outward remittances for technical services are 6 percent of the previous year's sales[12] and permission from the Board of Investment is required for each transaction. These rules restrict the scope of business. Finally, IT and ITES companies cannot purchase or renew softcopy downloadable software licenses through a letter of credit. As a result, IT and ITES companies face problems when they want to import software through the Internet in legal ways. Allowing letter of credit payment for nonphysical software purchases would facilitate doing business, by making transactions easier and reducing the use of illegal software and licenses.

Access to loans for small and medium enterprises (SMEs) is one of the biggest challenges for the ICT sector. ITES-BPOs, with the exception of large ones, are generally unable to access credit easily. Most of them have limited physical collateral, which prevents them from accessing credit. The situation would likely improve with policy support to facilitate access to specialized credit facilities such as the EEF or other government- or donor-based SME financing facilities. Two key initiatives that can improve access to finance exist, but success has been limited so far:

- *The Equity Entrepreneurship Fund.* According to BASIS, access to EEF for its members has been limited since it was introduced in 2002. This is because of problems with the setup of EEF, including improper tools for valuation of assets and fund repayment policies. EEF is poorly implemented by the Investment Corporation of Bangladesh, especially in proposal evaluation, fund disbursement, supervision, and monitoring and evaluation. The industry called for a special committee with representatives from Bangladesh Bank, the Investment Corporation of Bangladesh, and BASIS to review and address key problems with access to EEF by IT and ITES companies.[13]
- *The Donor SME Loan Facility.* In May 2011, the Japan International Cooperation Agency (JICA) established an SME loan facility with Bangladesh Bank. Industry representatives suggest that this facility should be extended to its members and to the ICT sector at large. BASIS has lobbied for the Bangladesh Bank to allocate a portion of the JICA fund to the IT sector. In addition, there are calls from the industry for the unused portions of EEF to be utilized (as a loan guarantee fund) for collateral-free SME funding.

Value Chain Analysis: ITES-BPO

The range and variety of business process services sourced or traded in the international marketplace is extremely wide; a full review of such services is beyond the scope of this chapter. For the purpose of this analysis, ITES-BPO services can be broadly classified as shown in figure 7.3. In Bangladesh, the majority of ITES-BPO providers operate in the lower end of the BPO pyramid, offering services from data capturing and transcription to some level of problem solving and basic voice services. Up to 2011, Bangladesh did not export any basic voice services, but according to a recent study, some revenues (US$2 million) were generated in 2011 (ITC and KPMG 2012).[14] The bulk of revenue and exports, however, remains in the areas of basic data capturing and rule-based processing. This section provides value chain analyses for the typical data capturing and rule-based processing BPO services provided in Bangladesh: (a) vectorization data processing (image processing) and (b) accounting rule-based processing of data (invoices and similar data). In addition, a third, higher value-added, value chain of industrial engineering BPO services is discussed.

The general steps involved in delivering basic data- and rule-based BPO services are as follows:

- *Data reception.* Once specific process requirements are analyzed and deliverables are agreed with the client, BPO service providers receive and store the data, typically via e-mail or through upload to designated servers.

Figure 7.3 Value Pyramid of BPO Services in Bangladesh

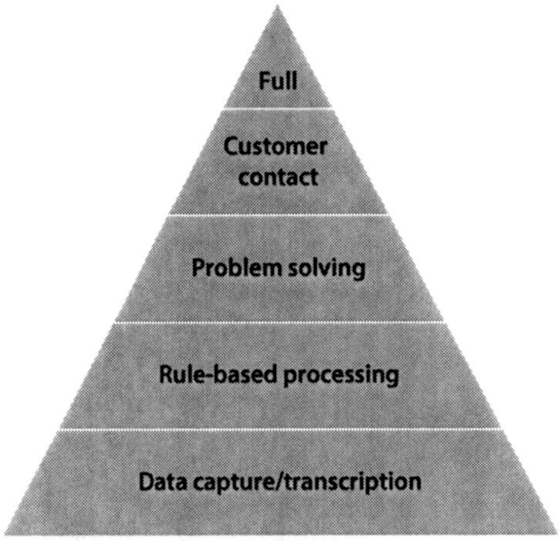

Full process outsourcing and knowledge services: Activities with deep domain knowledge not governed by standard rules; end-to-end transaction and business process services with voice support; research, engineering, legal.
Specialized voice: Complicated interactions that cannot be fully scripted and that require domain knowledge; customer service or help desk, credit card collections, selling.
Basic voice: Scripted problem-solving activities requiring minimal training; operations help desk, telesales, sales order processing, channel support, collections.
Rule-based processing: Data processing and decision making based on domain-specific rules, codes, and guidelines; insurance claims, accounts payable, loan processing, and similar back-office processes.
Basic data: Relatively uncomplicated data processing activities; data entry of applications, enrollments, and other data into databases; data conversion from one format to another; data reconciliation between different databases and similar basic tasks.

Source: Compiled by Global Development Solutions, LLC, from industry sources.

- *Data entry and integration.* Once data are received, they are entered and integrated into BPO service providers' IT-based data systems. For some service providers, such as those providing image-processing and graphic design vectorization services, this step is relatively straightforward and does not involve any major effort. Images that need to be processed are sorted and then delivered to image-processing staff for data processing and vectorization (conversion from one image format to another—see figure 7.4). For invoice and other back-office processing, data entry is generally the most labor-intensive task.
- *Data processing or coding.* Once data are entered into their database(s), BPO service providers proceed with data processing, commonly referred to in the industry as data coding. This coding is not software coding. It represents codification of data according to the specific rules, codes, and guidelines of a given business process domain. An example is classifying all accounts receivable or payable invoices into proper accounting codes or numbers.
- *Data quality control and delivery.* Once the data are processed and controlled for quality, they are delivered to the client via e-mail or uploaded to client-designated addresses and servers.

Value Chain Analysis for Image-Processing BPO Services

Bangladeshi BPO service providers typically provide the three most basic graphic design services that are referred to here as vectorization services: clipping path, layer masking, and vector conversion (typically a raster-to-vector conversion of bitmap raster dots into drawings with smooth vector lines).[15] Interviews suggest an estimated average cost of US$0.94 per processed image.[16] The highest costs

Figure 7.4 Sample ITES-BPO Service Process

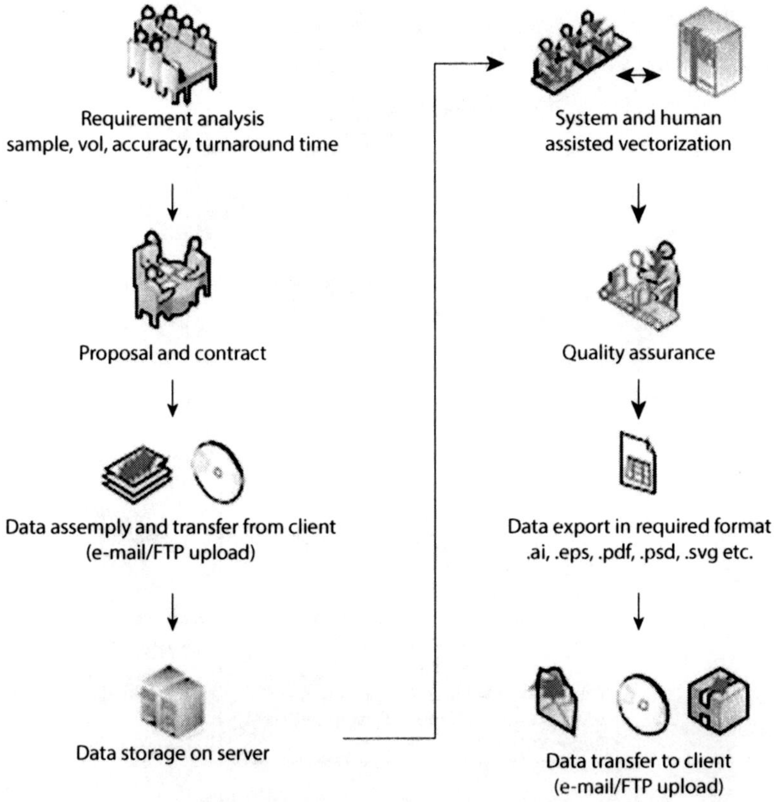

Source: Abacus Data Systems, http://www.abacusdatasys.com/data-services/data-entry.html.

associated with providing image-processing BPO services include data image processing (54 percent), administration and overhead (22 percent), and delivery and quality control of processed images (11 percent).

The value chain analysis shows that ITES-BPO companies run a business model based on labor arbitrage (figure 7.5). In this particular example, the cost of labor dominates the highest cost component of the value chain, data or image processing (78 percent). A typical worker in firms operating in the basic data entry BPO segment in Bangladesh earns US$100–US$250 per month. Mid- and higher-level managers earn US$600 or more. The workers are generally young (in their early twenties), have 10–12 years of education in total, and come from Dhaka and its peri-urban areas (see the example employee profile in table 7.6).

Workers with industry-specific skills and education in graphic design are often not readily available in the market. Moreover, young workers seeking employment in the data entry BPO industry often have limited ICT and general personal computer knowledge. Before entrusting them with any work, firms typically train workers first on basic ICT skills and then on image-processing

Figure 7.5 Image-Processing BPO Service Exporter, Value Chain Analysis, Bangladesh

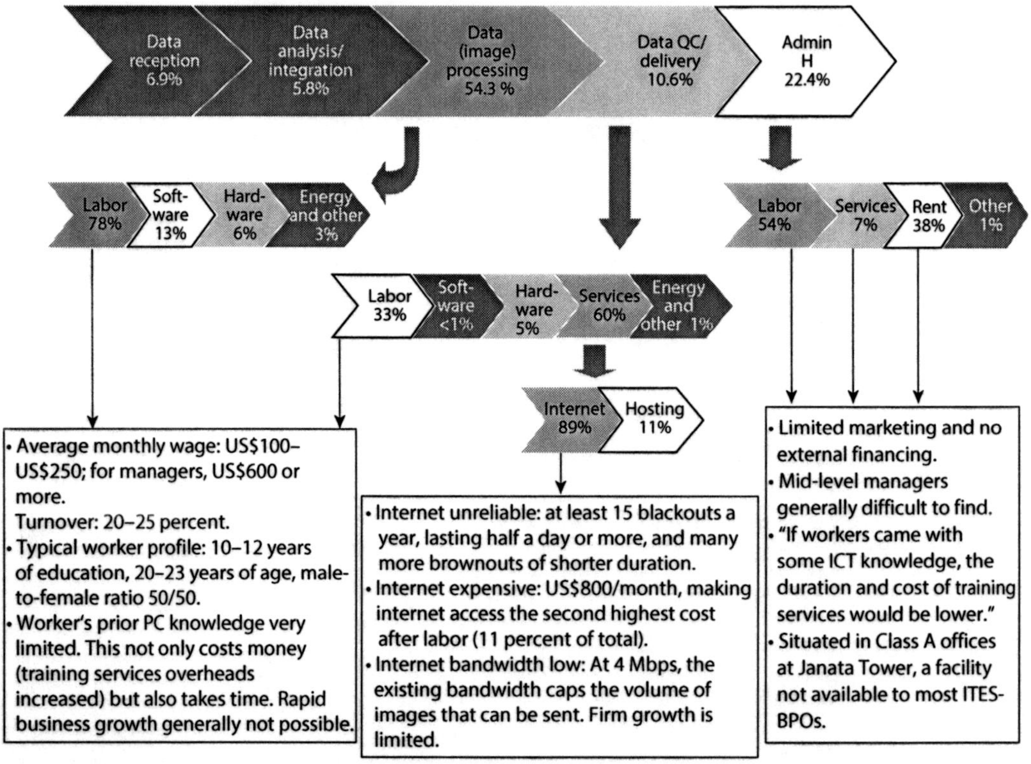

Source: Global Development Solutions, LLC.
Note: Mbps = megabits per second.

Table 7.6 Sample Employee and Trainer Profiles, Graphic Design SME, Dhaka

Category	*Employee profile*	*Trainer profile*
Age	20–23	32
Education	10–12 years	MA in management
Industry experience	None	4–5 years
ICT or PC literacy	None/limited	High
English language skills	Limited	Good
Training duration per course	65–80 hours	

Source: Interviews, Global Development Solutions, LLC.
Note: ICT = information and communications technology; PC = personal computer; SME = small and medium enterprise.

techniques or other basic data and software use processes. Small firms typically hire training services from individual training consultants, who themselves may not necessarily be trained in graphic design. Training consultants are typically educated in management, marketing, and similar fields (see table 7.7 for sample trainer profiles). It generally takes small firms three to six months to train workers. Basic ICT skills are later complemented by specific business process skills, including graphic design skills like clipping paths and layer masking. A longer time is needed to train workers on more complex skills like raster-to-vector and similar graphic design skills. Some services, such as catalog design, are not provided by SMEs. According to interviews with SMEs, this is because training the workforce in complex graphic design skills is expensive and economically not justifiable, especially considering the employee turnover rate of 20–25 percent.

According to industry professionals, the failure of the education system to provide a workforce with basic ICT skills effectively caps how much and how fast graphic design SMEs can grow. Table 7.8 illustrates that most Bangladeshi graphic design BPO exporters mainly offer lower-value graphic design services of basic to moderate complexity. In this context, basic data-processing BPOs would greatly benefit from a better-educated workforce in general and an ICT-literate labor force in particular.

Basic data-processing BPOs typically need a labor force that comes out of secondary schools and colleges that can then be trained. In this respect, Bangladesh has one of the poorest records of any country competing in the BPO market and major improvements are needed to improve ITES-BPOs' access to an educated workforce. Bangladesh's performance on literacy rates and secondary school enrollment is extremely poor (see table 7.9).

Table 7.7 In-House Training of Staff, Graphic Design Skills, Bangladesh

Graphic design service/skill	*In-house training period*
Clipping path	3–4 months
Layer masking	+6 months
Raster to vector	+8 months
Image manipulation	+1 year
Catalog/web design/template conversion	No training in house

Source: Interviews, Global Development Solutions, LLC.

Table 7.8 The Scope and Cost of Graphic Design BPO Services in Bangladesh
US dollars

Graphic design service complexity	*Clipping path*	*Layer masking*	*Raster to vector*	*Image manipulation*	*Catalog/web design/ template conversion*	*Creative design*
Basic	0.9	1.5	2	5+	10–12	Generally not outsourced
Moderate	1.5–2	4–6	5–6	50+	100+	
Complex	3–5	7–10–12	7–10–20	100+	150+	

Sources: Interviews, Global Development Solutions, LLC.
Note: The table shows BPO market prices per image (US$), lower value (left) to higher value (right). Typical BPO services provided by Bangladeshi firms are highlighted in grey. BPO = business process outsourcing.

Table 7.9 Benchmarking Literacy and Enrollment Rates in Bangladesh and Comparator Countries, 2011
percent

Country	*Secondary school enrollment*	*Adult literacy*
Sri Lanka	90	91
Philippines	82	95
Egypt, Arab Rep.	81	66
China	76	93
Malaysia	70	92
Vietnam	70	93
India	59	62
Bangladesh	**44**	**56**
Pakistan	33	55

Source: Data compiled by Global Development Solutions, LLC, from UNESCO, http://www.uis.unesco.org/Library/ Documents/human-development-report-education-2011-en.pdf.

For ICT literacy, the national ICT Policy 2009 goals stipulate, among others, the following objectives in the area of education:

- Boost ICT tools at all levels of education.
- Extend the reach of ICT literacy throughout the country by incorporating ICT courses in secondary, technical, and vocational education.
- Encourage closer collaboration between academia and industry.
- Ensure that all universities provide education with global ICT standards.

Overhead costs are dominated by the cost of administrative and managerial labor (54 percent), followed by rent (38 percent) and training and marketing services (7 percent). Interviews suggest that firms consider the high administrative labor costs to be reasonable in international terms (table 7.10). The interviewed companies are concerned about the poor quality of managerial labor and the poor quality of locally available research and training services. According to industry representatives, major improvements are needed in the education system to increase the quality of managerial and other labor available in the marketplace, especially considering that pressure on skilled professionals to emigrate to countries with higher wages is considerable. The local availability of specialized training services is extremely low (table 7.11).

Bangladesh is among the least-developed countries in ICT development. In the ICT Development Index for 2010 released by the International Telecommunications Union, which measures computer, Internet, and other ICT penetration per household,[17] Bangladesh was ranked 137 of 154 countries. Moreover, it is slipping further behind over time (table 7.12).

Internet costs are a heavy burden on ITES-BPO SMEs and can result in delivery costs that resemble those of manufacturing value chains. Internet services comprise approximately 50 percent of the total cost of delivering services to clients. Internet connectivity is needed for data reception and data delivery and,

Table 7.10 Benchmarking Compensation Costs in Bangladesh and Comparator Countries, 2011
US dollars

	National averages (US$ per year)			
Country	*BPO analyst*	*Accountant*	*IT programmer*	*Country average*
Sri Lanka	4,104	5,977	8,996	1,584
Bangladesh	**4,200**	**6,000a**	**7,800**	**1,440**
Philippines	4,653	8,121	11,371	1,524
India	5,451	10,123	10,170	1,620
China	9,121	10,156	23,576	4,716
Malaysia	10,398	14,271	33,704	6,708
United Kingdom	28,679	45,434	44,297	32,769

Sources: A.T. Kearney, Competitive Benchmarking: Sri Lanka Knowledge Services, http://www.atkearney.com/ paper/-/asset _publisher/dVxv4Hz2h8bS/content/competitive-benchmarking-sri-lanka-knowledge-services/10192.
a. Interviews, Global Development Solutions, LLC.

Table 7.11 Benchmarking the Quality of Education and Training Services in Bangladesh and Comparator Countries, 2012

Country	*Quality of management schools (rank)*	*Local availability of specialized research and training services (rank)*
United Kingdom	6.1 (1)	5.9 (5)
Malaysia	5.0 (26)	5.4 (17)
India	4.9 (33)	4.3 (59)
Sri Lanka	4.8 (38)	4.3 (63)
Philippines	4.7 (39)	4.3 (62)
China	4.2 (68)	4.4 (55)
Bangladesh	**3.9 (91)**	**2.8 (137)**

Source: Compiled by Global Development Solutions, LLC, from World Economic Forum Global Competitiveness Report 2012–2013, http://www.weforum.org/issues/global-competitiveness.
Note: Scale: 1 = poor, 7 = excellent, among the best in the world. Rank: 1 = highest ranked country, 144 = lowest ranked country.

when these activities are included, Internet costs contribute 11 percent to the total cost structure of the representative image-processing SME being discussed. Although data reception and delivery is by and large automated and done electronically, the value chain structure of ITES-BPO service providers more closely resembles manufacturing value chain structures that involve costly transportation and delivery of physical goods. This is because Internet access in Bangladesh is costly. Notwithstanding the fact that Internet service prices are decreasing, BPO SMEs spend US$10,000–US$14,000 per year to secure a relatively modest Internet connection bandwidth (table 7.13).

In addition to and despite its high price, the quality of Internet services is poor. First, Internet network failures are common. At least once and up to three times a month, the Internet connection is not available for six to eight hours. Shorter duration failures of a few hours are more frequent. One of the key

Table 7.12 Benchmarking ICT Development in Bangladesh, 2008 and 2010

Economy	*ICT index rank, 2008*	*ICT index rank, 2010*
Korea, Rep.	1	1
Poland	41	38
Brazil	62	64
Vietnam	91	81
Philippines	95	92
Sri Lanka	106	105
India	117	116
Nigeria	125	122
Nepal	137	134
Bangladesh	**135**	**137**
Tanzania	141	138
Ethiopia	150	150
Chad	151	152

Source: Compiled by Global Development Solutions, LLC, from International Telecommunications Union, http://www.itu.int/ITU-D/ict/publications/idi/.
Note: ICT = information and communications technology.

Table 7.13 Internet Service Prices in Bangladesh, 2010–13
US dollars

Year	*US$/Mbps/month*	*VAT (%)*	*US$/Mbps/month*	*Annual fee for maximum available bandwidth of 5 Mbps (US$)*
2010	525	15	604	36,225
2012	150–200	15	173–230	10,350–13,800
2013[a]	85	15	98	5,880

Sources: Interviews, Global Development Solutions, LLC.
Note: ISP = Internet service provider; ITES-BPO = information technology–enabled services–business process outsourcing; Mbps = megabits per second; VAT = value-added tax.
a. Reported price negotiated with ISPs for 2013 by some ITES-BPOs, generally larger firms.

reasons for Internet network failures is that there is only one international submarine cable. For image-processing BPOs, Internet network failures present a challenge but only to a limited degree: data (images) that could not be received or sent in any given day can generally be received or sent the following day. By contrast, other ITES-BPOs that operate in segments that need real-time and continuous business process support are highly impeded by the poor quality of Internet services (see the value chain sections for more details). Internet services in Bangladesh have limited bandwidth, which effectively caps throughput to 7,000–8,000 images per month that can be uploaded to client-dedicated servers. As can be seen in table 7.13, the maximum available bandwidth is 5 megabits per second. For invoice processing and other BPOs, limited bandwidth reduces their ability to offer complementary voice and other help desk services to their clients. The current network infrastructure, therefore, is not conducive to ITES-BPO growth.

In this context, the industry's growth depends heavily on government's effective implementation of its long-standing plans for improvement of domestic and international connectivity. According to the Digital Bangladesh strategic plan, the government plans to expedite laying a second and even third submarine cable connection to ensure a minimal amount of redundancy and reliability in nationwide Internet connectivity. The plan contains initiatives to reduce the price of bandwidth (GOB 2010). It is anticipated that a rapid and robust implementation of these policy initiatives is needed to bring the country's Internet connectivity infrastructure at par with other countries competing in the international BPO market. Sri Lanka, for example, has four international submarine cables and fairly well-developed broadband, leased-line, satellite, and 3G and 4G cellular connectivity. India has an even more advanced connectivity network. By comparison, Bangladesh has the least capable network among countries with developed ITES-BPO service industries (see table 7.14).

Office space rents outside the few office facilities are increasing. The particular image-processing BPO highlighted in the value chain analysis has been able to access office space at the Janata Tower. At US$80 per square meter per year, the rental price is at least 50 percent below the estimated market price of US$120 per square meter per year. Moreover, the supply of electricity is backed up by central generators and the company does not have to spend additional resources on captive generation. At these prices, Bangladeshi office space rental costs are competitive compared with other countries (table 7.15). However, only a few among the more than 800 Bangladeshi ITES-BPO companies have access to such office facilities. According to interviewed companies, rents are increasing at 20–30 percent per year. Moreover, because of the poor electricity infrastructure (table 7.16), ITES-BPO companies have additional costs of captive

Table 7.14 Benchmarking the ICT Network and Overall Infrastructure in Bangladesh and Comparator Countries, 2012

Country	*Network readiness*	*Overall infrastructure*
Ireland	5.0	5.3
Malaysia	4.8	5.1
China	4.1	4.5
India	4.0	3.6
Sri Lanka	3.9	4.1
Egypt, Arab Rep.	3.8	3.6
Philippines	3.6	3.2
Bangladesh	**3.2**	**2.2**

Source: Compiled by Global Development Solutions, LLC, from World Economic Forum Global Competitiveness/Information Technology Reports, 2011–2012, http://www.weforum.org/issues/global-competitiveness.

Note: Network readiness is defined in World Economic Forum reports as "the degree to which economies across the world leverage ICT for enhanced competitiveness." Scale: 1 = underdeveloped, 7 = efficient by international standards. ICT = information and communications technology.

Table 7.15 Benchmarking Office Space Rental Prices, Bangladesh and Comparator Countries, 2012

Country	*Rent per square meter per year (US$)*	*Change from previous year (%)*	*Typical lease terms (years)*	*Typical rent free (months)*
Bangladesh				
Janata Tower 2012	80			
Dhaka, nominal market rates	120–250	+20; 30	1–3	0
Dhaka, including power generation	150–280			
Sri Lanka	227	—	—	—
Philippines	247	+3.5	3–5	2
India	360	0 to −11	3+3+3	1–4
Malaysia	484	−1.20	3	1–3
Canada	503	−2.5; +3.3	5–10	0–3
Vietnam	516	−7	3	1
Ireland	577	−17.40	10	18
China	677	−8	3	2

Sources: Bangladesh: Global Development Solutions, LLC. Other countries: CBRE, Q2 2012 market data, http://www.cbre.com/EN/Pages/Home.aspx.
Note: Data reflect the following cities and regions. China: Guangzhou. India: average for New Delhi (Gurgaon) and Bangalore. Vietnam: average for Hanoi and Ho Chi Minh City. Canada: average for Montreal and Toronto, suburban and downtown locations. Other countries: capital cities. — = not available.

Table 7.16 Benchmarking the Quality of Electricity, Bangladesh and Comparator Countries, 2011

Country	*Electricity quality*
United Kingdom	6.7
United Arab Emirates	6.4
Malaysia	5.9
China	5.5
Mauritius	5.1
Sri Lanka	5.0
Philippines	3.4
Vietnam	3.3
India	3.1
Pakistan	2.2
Bangladesh	**1.6**

Source: A.T. Kearney, http://www.atkearney.com/paper/-/asset_publisher/dVxv4Hz2h8bS/content/competitive-benchmarking-sri-lanka-knowledge-services/10192.
Note: Quality refers to electricity supply, specifically in perceived number of interruptions and voltage fluctuations. Scale: 1 = underdeveloped, 7 = efficient by international standards.

electricity generation that drive up rental costs significantly. When captive power generation costs are included, rental prices, which are nominally the lowest compared with other countries, increase to levels above those prevailing in the Philippines and Sri Lanka and approach those in Indian cities with significant ITES-BPO presence.

Value Chain Analysis for Invoice-Processing BPO Services

Invoice processing is a typical back-office BPO service. In the BPO value pyramid, invoice processing is a rule-based processing BPO that may also have some features of a problem-solving BPO in cases when help desk and similar features are provided. As such, invoice processing is a higher value-added service than data (image) processing services. Interviews suggest that the highest cost associated with providing invoice-processing BPO services is for data (image) processing (54 percent), administration and overhead (22 percent), and delivery and quality control of processed images (11 percent)—see figure 7.6.[18]

Most of the challenges and bottlenecks that pertain to the image-processing value chain also apply to the invoice-processing value chain. This section focuses on the finer details of issues already discussed or additional challenges in relation to invoice-processing BPOs.

Companies have major problems with Internet connection latency.[19] Connection latency is critically important to BPO firms because it enables them to provide services to their clients over shared network architectures in near real time. For the invoice-processing BPO firms, having access to a network with good latency would enable it to provide higher value-added services: invoices that were already entered and processed could be directly integrated into the clients' business process flow and databases via dedicated shared servers. The potential for increased profitability is substantial (table 7.17). According to industry professionals, with all certification standards in place, firms would earn

Figure 7.6 Invoice-Processing BPO Service Exporter, Value Chain Analysis, Bangladesh

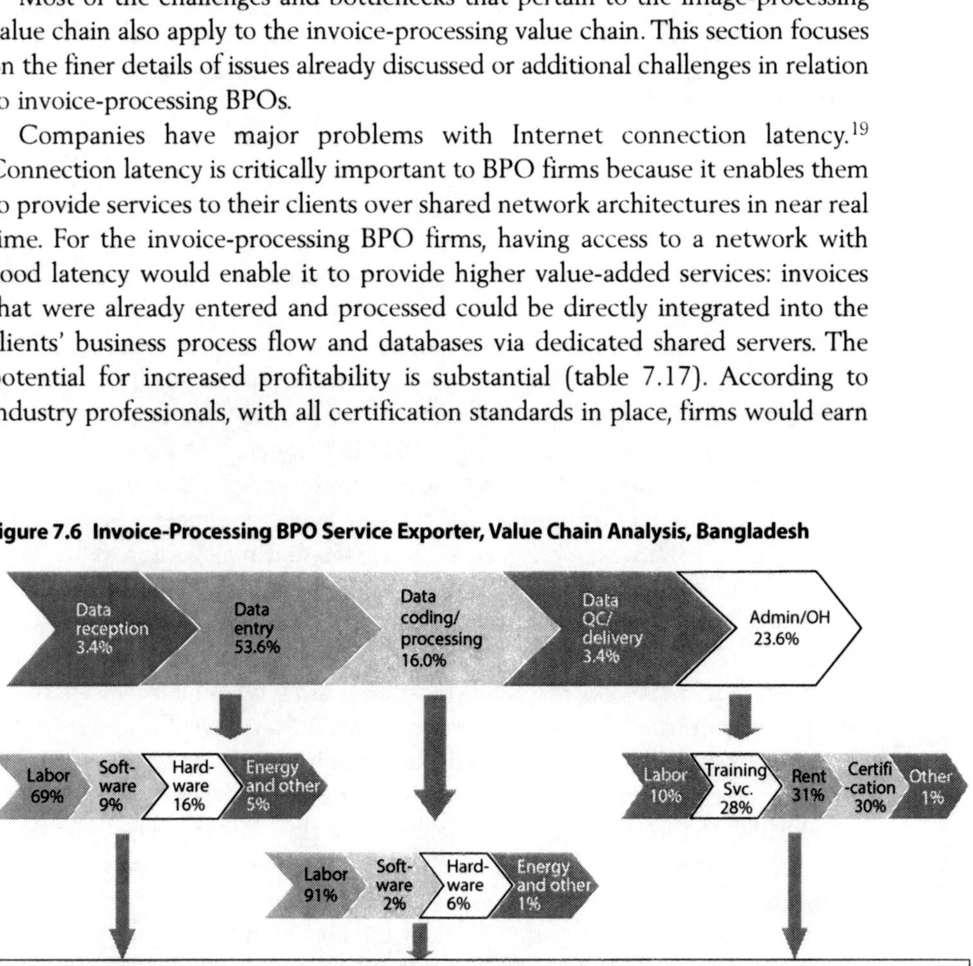

- Average monthly wage: US$100–US$200. For supervisor and managers, US$600–US$1,000.
- Turnover: 20–30 percent.
- Typical worker profile: 10–12 years of education, 18–25 years of age.
- Incoming workers' soft skills are poor.
- Internet unreliable: 29 blackouts in a year, causing major quality reputation problems with clients.
- Internet latency poor: unable to add voice and other continuous support services to client.
- Rental prices increased by 30 percent compared with last year.
- Certified to ISO 27001 standards. Other standards desirable but generally not affordable by SMEs.

Source: Global Development Solutions, LLC. QC = quality control; OH = overhead.

Table 7.17 Invoice-Processing Full-Service Value Chain Earning Potential, Bangladesh

	Sample invoice-processing BPO, full-service value chain			
Category	*Data entry*	*Data coding/ processing*	*Data integration into client business process flow/database*	*Business process workflow management*
Sales price per page index[a]	100	175	275	n.a.
Latency dependency	None	Limited	High	High
Characteristic	High competition, low margins (15%–20%)	Medium to high competition, reasonable margins (25%)	Medium competition, high margins (50%+)	Typically not outsourced by client

Source: Interviews, Global Development Solutions, LLC.
a. Index: 100 = price per page for data entry only. The value of each subsequent stage is compounded by adding the value of services performed at the previous stage(s). Areas where Bangladeshi BPOs currently operate are shaded gray. n.a. = not applicable.

three times more just by reducing the redundancy that is caused by poor Internet infrastructure.

With the current network latency levels, most shared networking applications cannot be used. Interviews suggest that roundtrip latency in Bangladesh is typically at or around 300 milliseconds.[20] Microsoft SharePoint requires a network latency of no greater than 250 milliseconds.[21] Moreover, network latency increases substantially each time a major international submarine cable breaks, as was the case on June 6, 2012, when Internet services were crippled (see figure 7.7). This example further illustrates that major improvements in the ICT network quality are a prerequisite for the ability of Bangladeshi ITES-BPO firms to grow and establish a reputation of quality and reliability with clients.

Moreover, small BPO firms, unlike most large firms, do not have international certification in place. The primary reason is the fact that certification is costly, as auditors must be hired from abroad—local auditors are not available for most standards certification (see table 7.18). In the case of the invoice-processing BPO highlighted in the value chain analysis, the firm reports having lost three potential contracts with U.S. commercial clients because of not having SAS70 certification. The firm is in the process of obtaining ISO27001 certification because it has a memorandum of understanding with a foreign client for a potentially very lucrative three-year contract if it complies with ISO27001. But, like other interviewed firms, the invoice-processing BPO reports financial difficulties with obtaining other certificates. In this context, providing support to firms for international certification could improve their competitiveness internationally.

In intellectual property protection, Bangladesh has one of the worst records in the world. Of the 144 countries surveyed by the World Economic Forum in 2011–12, Bangladesh's rank was 131.

Figure 7.7 Network Latencies, Bangladesh Telecommunications Company Ltd., 2012

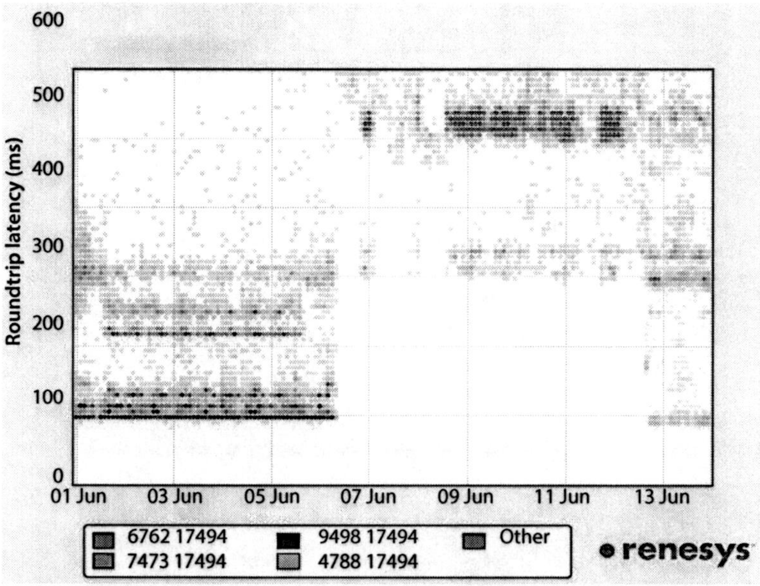

Source: http://www.renesys.com/2012/06/smw4-break-on-south-asia/.
Note: BTCL = Bangladesh Telecommunications Company Ltd.

Table 7.18 Reported Certification Costs, Invoice-Processing BPO, Bangladesh, 2012

Standard	*Estimated certification cost; one-time fee/annual fee (US$)*	*Certification required by*	*Local auditors available*
HIPPA	20,000/n.a.	U.S. government	No
SAS70	20,000/3,000	U.S. firms	No
ISO 27001	5,000/1,500	European Union	Yes

Sources: Interviews, Global Development Solutions, LLC.
Note: BPO = business process outsourcing; n.a. = not applicable.

Value Chain Analysis for Structural Engineering BPO Services

International competitiveness reports suggest that one area where Bangladesh has relatively good performance is in availability of scientists and engineers (table 7.19). There is potential for harnessing this competitive strength in the area of engineering services. At the national level, however, university-industry collaboration in R&D is weak. At the private sector level, some entrepreneurs have taken the initiative to hire highly qualified structural engineers to provide BPO services but, as the value chain analysis illustrates, critical challenges remain.

Labor costs dominate most stages of the structural engineering BPO value chain (figure 7.8). In the BPO value pyramid, structural engineering services are significantly more demanding in terms of labor skills and cost, as well as in task

Table 7.19 Benchmarking the Availability of Engineers and University-Industry Collaboration in R&D, Bangladesh and Comparator Countries, 2012

Country	*Availability of scientists and engineers Rank (scale)*	*University-industry collaboration in R&D Rank (scale)*
India	5.0 (16)	3.8 (51)
Malaysia	4.9 (20)	5.0 (17)
Sri Lanka	4.6 (32)	3.0 (118)
China	4.4 (46)	4.4 (35)
Bangladesh	3.8 (81)	2.6 (131)
Philippines	3.7 (91)	3.5 (79)

Source: Compiled by Global Development Solutions, LLC, from World Economic Forum Global Competitiveness Report 2012–2013, http://www.weforum.org/issues/global-competitiveness.
Note: Scale: 1 = poor, 7 = excellent, among the best in the world. Rank: 1 = highest ranked country, 144 = lowest ranked country.

Figure 7.8 Structural Engineering BPO Service Exporter, Value Chain Analysis, Bangladesh

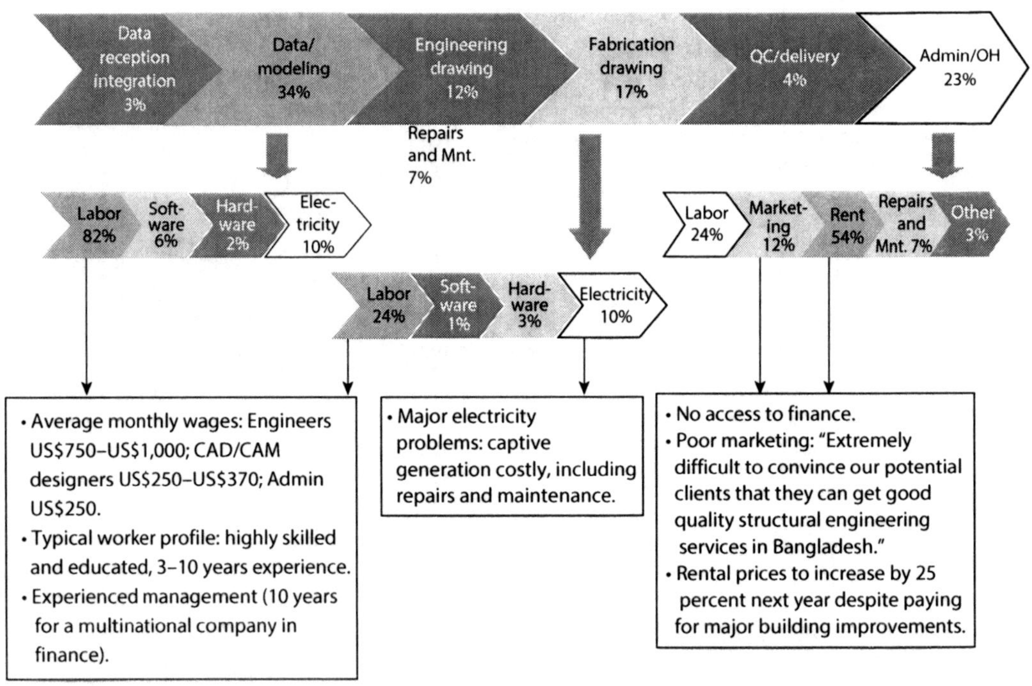

Source: Global Development Solutions, LLC.
Note: CAD = computer-aided design; CAM = computer-aided manufacturing; QC = quality control; OH = overhead.

complexity, compared with invoice- and image-processing BPO services. This particular firm employs highly skilled and experienced structural engineers and computer-aided design (CAD) and computer-aided manufacturing (CAM) designers that, compared with other BPO service providers, are much more expensive to retain. The firm's labor costs per employee are three to four times higher compared with other BPO service providers highlighted in this chapter. Moreover, the nature of the work is such that cash flow is more difficult to manage compared with other BPOs. Projects take longer to complete and operating expenses tied up in work in progress take many months to recover. As a result, structural engineering BPOs are highly dependent on good access to credit to finance their operations. As can be seen from the value chain analysis, however, financing costs are conspicuously missing; this is because the firm has no access to external financing.

Improving access to existing entrepreneurship and SME funds is anticipated to provide a significant boost to small and medium ITES-BPO firms. Interviews suggested that it took this particular firm six months to "make some inroads with a local bank for a US$120,000 loan." The firm was seeking better terms than the offered 15 percent annual interest rate, but negotiations with the bank were ultimately unsuccessful. In this regard, the firm is no different from most other firms interviewed: it is a self-financed operation. However, the major difference with most other firms interviewed is that this company is a sole proprietorship. Many other firms interviewed, including the image- and invoice-processing firms discussed in previous sections, are business units of IT, marketing, and other companies that are financially strong.

The marketing skills of small and medium BPO firms are extremely poor. In this particular example, interviews suggested that the BPO firm has an impressive list of clients. It has successfully completed structural engineering in the petrochemical industry for renowned firms like Exxon and Bechtel. Yet, according to the CEO, it was extremely difficult to convince potential clients that they can get good-quality structural engineering services in Bangladesh. This suggests that in addition to needing marketing skills improvements, SMEs would also benefit from a better image of the country as a whole. Like many other firms, the ITES-BPO highlighted in the value chain analysis can afford little funding for marketing. The company spends US$600–US$1,000 for search optimization services that increase the online visibility of the company on online search engines, such as Google and similar services.

Conclusions and Recommendations

Bangladesh's ICT industry is viewed by the public and private sectors as having high growth potential. Currently, its development is relatively low compared with other countries in the region. However, exports are on the rise and multinational corporations are investing in research and development centers in the country. In light of these advances, the sector needs to make many significant adjustments to address the issues raised in the value chain analysis.

The key impediments to success have already been acknowledged by the government as evidenced by ICT Policy 2009. Although the policy addresses all the major issues plaguing the sector, the government needs to prioritize and follow up.

One priority area for the government would be to provide quality Internet services at affordable rates. Uninterrupted connectivity with low latency and high bandwidth are necessities to compete in the global market, particularly for higher value-added ITES-BPO services. As stated in the Digital Bangladesh strategic plan, two additional international submarine cables should be installed to ensure a minimal amount of redundant capacity in case of failure of one of the three cables (GOB 2010).

Access to finance for SMEs is very important, but this issue is not unique to Bangladesh. Policy support can help improve access to existing funds (particularly the EEF and the JICA-funded SME loan facility). Analysis should be made to determine how to improve the EEF program's valuation tools, fund repayment policies, proposal evaluation, fund disbursement, supervision, and monitoring and evaluation.

Addressing the skills gap is another priority for the sector. Actions should include reducing the high school dropout rate and increasing the number and quality of graduate students. BITM could develop a combination of training programs, coaching, workshops, and certification for individuals as well as organizations. International experts can be instrumental in developing curricula and leading courses that will be relevant for multinationals requiring ITES-BPO services. The donor community can help in sourcing appropriate international experts. And, with donor support, curricula in the traditional school system should be adapted to international trends. Building on students' basic computer skills acquired from primary school, vocational secondary schools could offer courses appropriate to ICT and focus on the soft skills lacking in the market. Training would cover management practices, marketing techniques, and English language courses.

Finally, a focused and sustained promotional campaign—country branding and sector branding—and high-profile networking events that proactively address the main concerns of industry players in target markets would help better position Bangladesh. This strategy should be carefully thought out, in partnership with the private sector and international consultants. Among the goals could be to bring in an anchor investor in the captive BPO segment, which could have major positive spillovers for the sector as a whole.

Demonstrable and long-run commitment by the government is essential to boost investor confidence. For example, an IT/ITES business portal for the country could help develop a positive reputation for Bangladesh's ITES sector. Presenting the sector as a whole has advantages beyond individual companies attempting to place their URL at the top of the search list. Sector branding can also be done in partnership with private industry.

Notes

1. Data on the market value of manufacturing outsourcing are not available.
2. Since most business processes require IT support and rely on IT infrastructure, many complementarities between ITO and BPO exist. Nevertheless, ITO and ITES-BPO are two distinct services.

3. The industry nomenclature in India and other major ITES-BPO exporting countries commonly refers to BPO as business process offshoring, because most business process outsourcing in these countries is for clients in distant markets (the United States and the European Union). In Bangladesh, the industry uses the terminology ITES and/or ITES-BPO.
4. Data from http://www.xmg-global.com.
5. Data from Bangladesh Association of Software and Information Services, http://www.basis.org.bd/index.php/resource.
6. http://www.basis.org.bd/resource/About_BASIS_&_Bangladesh_Software_and_ITS%20_Industry.pdf.
7. PriceWaterhouseCoopers, 2005, "The Evolution of BPO in India," http://www.pwc.in/en_IN/ in/assets/pdfs/evolution-of-bpo-in-india.pdf.
8. Three other ICT sector associations exist in the country: Bangladesh Computer Samity is a group of computer and hardware vendors; the Internet Service Providers Association of Bangladesh is a group of Internet service providers; and the Bangladesh Association of Call Center and Outsourcing is a small group of voice-based BPO service providers that generated US$2 million in revenues in 2010.
9. The science and technology (including information technology) policy framework in Bangladesh was established in 1986 by the National Science and Technology Policy. In 1997, the government officially recognized ICT as a sector with high potential for affecting the development of the country. In 2002, the first ICT policy was formulated under the then Ministry of Science and Information and Communication Technology (MSICT). MSCIT was divided into two ministries, the Ministry of Science and Technology and the Ministry of Information and Communication Technology.
10. The ICT 2009 Policy guidelines stipulate that 5 percent of the annual development budget and 2 percent of the revenue budget are to be allocated to the IT sector. These guidelines generally are not followed either in budget allocations or in fund distribution and utilization. See, for example, the president of BASIS, quoted in *The Financial Express* (2010), and Uddin (2012) on the lack of specifics as to how the FY2013 budget for ICT sector and infrastructure development was to be spent.
11. As reported on the BASIS website, http://www.basis.org.bd/resource/BB-BASIS.pdf.
12. According to current foreign exchange guidelines (chapter 10, volume 1), http://www.bangladesh-bank.org/openpdf.php.
13. According to BASIS, strong monitoring of EEF fund utilization for the ICT industry has been a long-standing promise from Bangladesh Bank since 2009, but there has been no follow-up.
14. Information on how much was exported from the US$2 million voice-based BPO revenues is not available.
15. Image processing/vectorization falls within the graphic design segment of BPO services. Graphic design service providers in general provide a range of services, starting from the least complex clipping path (extracting objects or people from still imagery) to the most complex catalog designs and template conversions.
16. Images have varying complexities and some images require more time to be processed than others. The data refer to the average cost of processing images for this particular ITES-BPO service provider based on annual throughput of all images processed.
17. http://www.itu.int/ITU-D/ict/publications/idi/.
18. Costing per processed invoice page is confidential and can be requested separately.

19. In a computer network, latency is an expression of the time it takes (typically measured in milliseconds) for a packet of data to get from one designated point to another. It is most commonly measured as the time required for a packet to be returned to its sender (roundtrip latency).
20. Few interviewed firms reported lower roundtrip latencies of 150 milliseconds.
21. http://www.microsoft.com.

References

Abacus Data Systems. Company Website. http://www.abacusdatasys.com/data-services/data-entry.html.

BPAP (Business Processing Association of the Philippines) and Hewitt. 2010. "Gaining Momentum: State of Captives in the Philippines 2010." A BPAP-Hewitt Survey. http://www.trestlegroup.com/wp-content/uploads/2010/09/State-of-the-Captives-2010-FINAL.pdf.

GOB(Government of Bangladesh). 2010. *Strategic Priorities of Digital Bangladesh*, Draft, October 2010. Prime Minister's Office, Government of Bangladesh.

ITC (International Trade Centre) and KPMG. 2012. "Bangladesh Beckons: An Emerging Destination for IT/ITES Outsourcing." http://www.intracen.org/bangladesh-beckons-an-emerging-destination-it/.

Kathuria, Sanjay, andMariem Malouche, eds. 2016. *Strategies to Strengthen Bangladeshi Competitiveness: Thematic Assessments*. Washington, DC: World Bank.

PriceWaterhouseCoopers. 2005. "The Evolution of BPO in India." http://www.pwc.in/en_IN/in/assets/pdfs/evolution-of-bpo-in-india.pdf.

The Financial Express. 2010. "IT Leaders for Income Tax Exemption until 2021." http://www.thefinancialexpress-bd.com/more.php?news_id=103082&date=2010-06-14.

Uddin, Jamal. 2012. "Budget Lacks Specific Reflection of Govt's Policy for Dev of ICT." *The Financial Express*, June 09. http://www.thefinancialexpress-bd.com/more.php?news_id=132346&date=2012-06-09.

CHAPTER 8

Services Waiver for Least-Developed Countries and Market Access for Services Exports from Bangladesh: Opportunities and Challenges

Rupa Chanda and Selim Raihan

Introduction

The Eighth World Trade Organization (WTO) Ministerial, which was held in December 2011, yielded an important outcome for least-developed countries (LDCs). A decision was taken to grant preferential access in services to all LDC members on an unconditional basis to facilitate their services exports. This LDC waiver invokes an "enabling cause" and for the first time permits legal positive discrimination in favor of LDCs in the service sector under the General Agreement on Trade in Services (GATS), which until now has only permitted very narrow exceptions to the Most Favored Nation (MFN) clause. The waiver provides direct market access preferences to LDCs in the form of preferential quotas and exemptions from requirements. It also allows for other nonmarket access preferences, subject to authorization by the Council for Trade in Services (CTS).[1] An important potential outcome of this waiver is the facilitation of LDC services exports in modes and sectors of interest to them, particularly in labor-based services through the temporary movement of their nationals, or mode 4,[2] which has been a long-standing area of demand for low-income and least-developed countries under GATS.

Bangladesh can potentially gain from the LDC services waiver, especially from the possible facilitation of mode 4 exports. The country's advantages are its population of 150 million, its high population density, and its dependence on remittances and labor services exports. However, the true realization of benefits under this waiver remains unclear, as the granting of preferential access is voluntary on the part of all countries. The waiver may not be granted for the sectors and modes of greatest interest to the LDC members. Moreover, the operational aspects of this waiver remain unclear. Given these uncertainties, it is important for LDCs such as Bangladesh to determine which are the services and modes of export interest, and then to formulate a proactive strategy to benefit from this preferential access decision.

This chapter provides such an assessment of the market access opportunities as well as constraints to Bangladesh's exports of services. The aim is to identify particular services where Bangladesh is currently or potentially competitive, some of the current and potential markets to which it could export these services, and the external and domestic constraints to its services exports. This assessment is based in part on a review of existing secondary literature on Bangladesh's service sector and trade policy. The chapter also draws on insights obtained from meetings, focus group discussions, and interviews held with a variety of stakeholders in Bangladesh, including the government (the Commerce Ministry, line ministries, and regulatory authorities working in the service sector), academics, private industry, and nongovernmental organizations (NGOs).

LDC Services Waiver: Brief Overview

After years of negotiation, the LDC services waiver emerged as a major outcome of the Eighth WTO Ministerial in December 2011. The waiver was an important development-oriented result of the negotiations. Under this waiver, WTO members are authorized to grant preferences to services and service providers of LDCs. Benefits will extend not only to WTO LDC members, but to all LDCs as defined by the United Nations. The waiver refers to a new "Enabling Clause" for trade in services, limited only to LDCs.

As highlighted in Schloemann (2012), the waiver allows for classical market access preferences and opens up the possibility for allowing others, subject to an application and approval procedure. The waiver, as agreed, offers a two-tiered solution: (direct) market access preferences for LDCs are automatically allowed; other, nonmarket access preferences are not automatically covered. They can, however, be authorized by the CTS. WTO members may now, without further ado, grant LDC services and suppliers exclusive market access in otherwise closed sectors and modes of supply or provide them with incrementally relaxed market access to other members. Other measures discriminating in favor of LDC services and suppliers can be approved by the CTS, including preferences granted through selective (LDCs only) national treatment, preferential treatment with respect to domestic regulations, or even subsidies. Such preferences could make a significant difference to LDC service providers. As in goods, where technical barriers to trade and sanitary and phytosanitary measures reign supreme, it is regulatory issues that often pose the greatest obstacles to LDC services exports.

The report by the Chairman of the Special Session of the CTS of the WTO outlines the features of the LDCs services waiver (WTO 2011). Despite Article II:1 of GATS, services and service suppliers of LDCs may now receive preferential treatment in members' markets. The report calls for immediate and unconditional granting of such treatment. The objective of the LDCs services waiver is to promote the exports of those sectors and modes of supply originating from LDCs that are of particular export interest to LDCs. The report highlights that such waiver will last for 15 years from the date of its adoption (WTO 2011, 1–4).

Schloemann (2012) argues that lack of technical clarity about what preferences would be desirable and achievable and lack of political will to implement them might discourage use of the waiver. LDCs, individually and collectively, should proactively and systematically identify preferences that would benefit their services exports and translate these into concrete demands to WTO members. Schloemann (2012) calls for LDCs and their supporters to seek firm commitments wherever possible to enhance the predictability and reliability of their service providers, thus allowing them to make solid investment decisions for the future.

South Centre (2011) argues that to be effective, the types of preferences covered by the waiver would need to go beyond market access measures. The draft waiver decision limits its scope to the application of measures described in GATS Article XVI (market access). Other measures are subject to approval by the CTS, including the actions of high-income countries that discriminate against services and services suppliers of LDCs. South Centre emphasized that under this waiver, in practice, high-income countries could keep "economic needs" rules and nationality or residency requirements, even in sectors suitable for preferential access to LDC services and services suppliers.

There is a need to clarify rules of origin in the waiver. Restrictive rules of origin could be disadvantageous for potential access to foreign markets by LDCs. South Centre (2011) highlights that defining rules of origin in services trade is different and more complex than for goods. Services being intangible, it is difficult or nearly impossible to measure domestic value added. In addition, transformation of services is not as clear as the processing of goods.

Thus, it is evident that there are practical difficulties and many uncertainties about how this waiver can be operationalized. For Bangladesh to benefit from the waiver, it must first clearly identify opportunity segments, target markets, and market access barriers. It must assess whether it can carve out a preferential access niche whose value cannot be diluted by similar waivers to other LDCs. LDCs like Bangladesh should assess whether any domestic challenges prevent them from taking advantage of waivers granted. In light of these complexities, the following discussion examines Bangladesh's prospects in selected services. The aim is to assess in detail the significance of the services waiver for Bangladesh and to determine how the country may leverage the opportunities created.

Prospects in IT-BPO and Labor Services: Secondary Sources

Several services potentially could be targeted to enhance Bangladesh's export prospects. This section uses existing research to assess the export potential of two sectors: information technology–business process outsourcing (IT-BPO) services and labor services (specifically in areas such as nursing services). The section then examines the measures required to overcome existing constraints to these exports.

The selection of IT-BPO and labor services requires some explanation. In recent years, Bangladesh has made major strides in laying the groundwork for a diverse and successful outsourcing market. In particular, the information technology (IT) services industry in Bangladesh has been growing, serving international clients and domestic clients in the banking and telecom sectors. Bangladesh's emerging IT outsourcing players already have strong credentials and the Bangladeshi freelancer community has supplemented IT exports. Bangladesh is consistently ranked among the top freelance work locations on employment websites such as oDesk, eLance, and the like (ITC and KPMG 2012). The country offers a vast pool of young, trained, and English-speaking labor, which is available at costs almost 40 percent lower than in established destinations like India and the Philippines. Government authorities have demonstrated a determination to promote IT services industry in the country, including by providing cheaper bandwidth and alternate international cables, setting up technology parks, and providing tax holidays for export-oriented industries. The government's "Digital Bangladesh" initiative is helping set up information and communications technology (ICT) infrastructure for enhanced connectivity, ICT-based citizen service delivery, and an ICT-based education system. There is evidence that many global players, like Samsung, AMD, VizRT, and WorldBridge Global, are setting up operations in Bangladesh (ITC and KPMG 2012). The country has positioned itself as a key outsourcing destination by enhancing delivery capability and skill availability, lowering costs of operations, making focused investments in telecom and IT infrastructure, and highlighting success stories.

Bangladesh's economy is increasingly dependent on the export of human resources and the concomitant earnings in foreign exchange. Changes in the global labor market have meant an increase in the demand for skilled and educated people, in Arabian Gulf and Southeast Asian countries and in high-income countries. An overwhelming proportion of Bangladesh's international workforce consists of semiskilled and unskilled workers in the Gulf region and Southeast Asia. This traditional Bangladeshi market is now facing stiff competition from new entrants such as Cambodia, Nepal, and Vietnam.

Therefore, the government is trying to diversify its international labor force and develop strategies to send skilled workers and professionals abroad. Nurses from Bangladesh have migrated to the Gulf region and to Southeast Asia, including Bahrain, Brunei Darussalam, the Islamic Republic of Iran, Iraq, Kuwait, Libya, Malaysia, Oman, and Saudi Arabia. The government claims that promoting nurse migration underscores its commitment to the safe migration of women. There is a huge potential market for nursing services if Bangladesh can develop effective strategies.

This section provides more detailed discussion of IT-BPO and labor services. This is followed by a brief subsection that highlights factors affecting growth and competitiveness in some key input services, namely, transport and telecommunications services. These sectors have wider implications for export competitiveness in other parts of the economy, in goods and services. This subsection highlights the need to focus on a broad range of services and issues and to keep sector-specific export interests and economywide competitiveness objectives in mind.

IT-BPO Services

The global IT services market was valued at US$1.1 trillion in 2010, with a compound annual growth rate of 5 percent over the 2006–10 period.[3] IT services have been identified as a promising target sector for promoting services exports from low- and middle-income countries (LMICs) and LDCs, for promoting skilled employment, and for wider economic development. The sector has witnessed rapid growth in many LMICs and LDCs, including Bangladesh.

Bangladesh's IT-BPO subsector has grown from a negligible size to an industry worth US$350 million in annual revenues in 2009. Related software exports nearly tripled from a little less than US$13 million in 2005 to US$35 million in 2009 and further to $47.3 million in 2011.[4] IT and nonvoice IT-enabled services constitute the bulk of these exports. Table 8.1 shows the increase in IT exports between fiscal year 2005 (FY2005) and FY2010.

IT-BPO constitutes a small part of overall gross domestic product (GDP) and exports. However, the growth of IT-BPO has been significant, at an average annual rate of 40 percent over the 2004–09 period, driven by export trends as well as growing IT demand in the domestic market. According to the International Trade Centre (ITC) and KPMG (2012), in 2012 there were more than 800 IT and nonvoice ITES companies in Bangladesh, of which around 200 work on a global basis for outsourcing and project-based delivery models.[5] Many companies have been set up through joint ventures with overseas companies or as offshore development centers with 100 percent foreign capital. Voice-based business process outsourcing (BPO) services, although a small share of the total industry at present, have been growing rapidly. In 2012, Bangladesh had more than 60 call centers. According to the Bangladesh Call Centre and Outsourcing Association, in 2012 there were more than 15,000 agents working in this segment. BPO services revenues stood at US$2 million in 2010. Mamun (2012) stated that Bangladesh's software services exports would reach US$100 million in 2012.

Table 8.1 Exports of Software and ITES in Bangladesh, FY2005–FY2011
US$, millions

Fiscal year	*Value of exports*
2005	12.68
2006	27.01
2007	26.08
2008	24.09
2009	32.91
2010	35.36
2011	47.31

Sources: http://www.basis.org.bd/index.php/resource; ITC and KPMG 2012.

As of 2012, Bangladesh was exporting IT products to more than 60 countries. The main export markets are North America (accounting for 61 percent), followed by the European Union countries (13 percent), and East Asia, especially Japan (5 percent) (ITC and KPMG 2012). The United States still dominates as an export destination for Bangladeshi software companies. The other two important destinations are the United Kingdom and Canada. In recent years, other countries, for example, Australia and Denmark, have emerged as important export destinations. Several companies have achieved considerable success in Asian and African markets, including Japan, Malaysia, Saudi Arabia, Singapore, and South Africa. One of the most remarkable successes in recent times is the penetration by Bangladeshi software companies (although on a limited scale and for some niche product markets) into the highly competitive Indian market (BASIS 2011).

Growth in this industry is expected to continue with expansion of operations by Bangladeshi IT entrepreneurs and increased entry of foreign companies, many of which are setting up captive units in the country. Some international companies are interested in setting up BPO operations with a large number of seats (around 10,000) in the country. Bangladesh has been ranked high in competency for software services. Gartner, in its 2010 report, listed Bangladesh as one of the top 30 outsourcing destinations. Although most of the work done at present is low value added, such as website development and graphics design, Bangladeshi companies are gradually moving to middle-value software and application development as well as higher-end engineering and product development services.[6]

This growth in IT-BPO exports has been accompanied by considerable employment growth in this industry. An estimated 20,000 or more skilled and semiskilled professionals are employed in the IT-ITES sector. Another 35,000 IT-BPO professionals are employed in business enterprises, the government sector, and nongovernmental organizations. More than 10,000 individuals are estimated to be engaged in freelance outsourcing jobs such as editing, proofreading, data entry, and web research. Freelance billings were worth more than US$7 million in 2010, which placed Bangladesh seventh in freelance outsourcing earnings and Dhaka among the top five cities for such work (ITC and KPMG 2012).

A variety of factors have contributed to the rapid growth of IT-BPO. The labor force includes many English speakers and university graduates with well-established delivery capabilities. Bangladesh has more than 80 universities that produce around 185,000 graduates each year, including more than 14,500 graduates and postgraduates in IT and related areas (as of 2012). An estimated 5,500 graduates specialize in software engineering, thus providing a ready source of cost-competitive and competent labor for this industry.[7] There are specialized training institutes producing IT graduates and growing education-industry links help maintain a ready pool of professionals. Bangladesh scores favorably on labor costs (figure 8.1). Entry-level wages in the IT industry are over 50 percent cheaper than in other Asian countries and wage inflation is considerably lower (ITC and KPMG 2012).

Figure 8.1 Average Salary at Entry Level and Five Years of Experience, Bangladesh and Comparators, 2011
US$, thousands

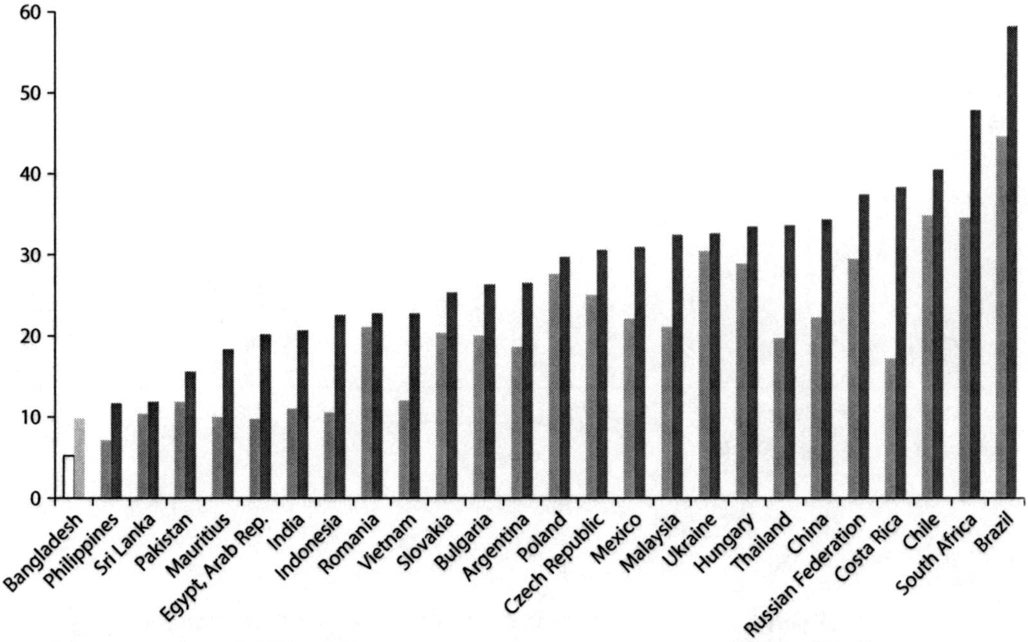

Source: Reproduced from ITC and KPMG 2012, 22, figure 8.

Bangladesh compares well on infrastructure costs. Real estate costs are significantly lower than in other competing destinations—for instance, 20 percent lower than in Delhi (figures 8.2 and 8.3). The sector has also benefited from growing teledensity, rising Internet penetration, falling bandwidth costs, and a growing and maturing market for telecom services. The rapid growth in freelance outsourcing has been driven by the ease of setting up operations, growing Internet penetration, and limited infrastructure requirements. Other contributors to sector growth include quality improvements in skill levels and delivery capabilities; quality and information security certifications obtained by Bangladeshi outsourcing vendors; and the ability of Bangladeshi companies to offer domain-specific services, owing to the country's large and growing domestic market in areas such as banking and financial services and telecom.

Government measures have also facilitated IT-BPO. The measures include technology parks established in Dhaka and surrounding areas to provide ready infrastructure, including network, connectivity and telecom, and power backups; ICT capacity-building initiatives; tax incentives; and passage of an IT Act to protect intellectual property rights and regulate e-transactions. Several government policies address the development of public ICT projects, specifically e-governance and office automation. The Sixth Five-Year Plan presents a vision of e-governance and promotion of the ICT sector (PC 2011).

Figure 8.2 Average Office Rent in the Central Business District, Bangladesh and Comparators, 2011
US dollars

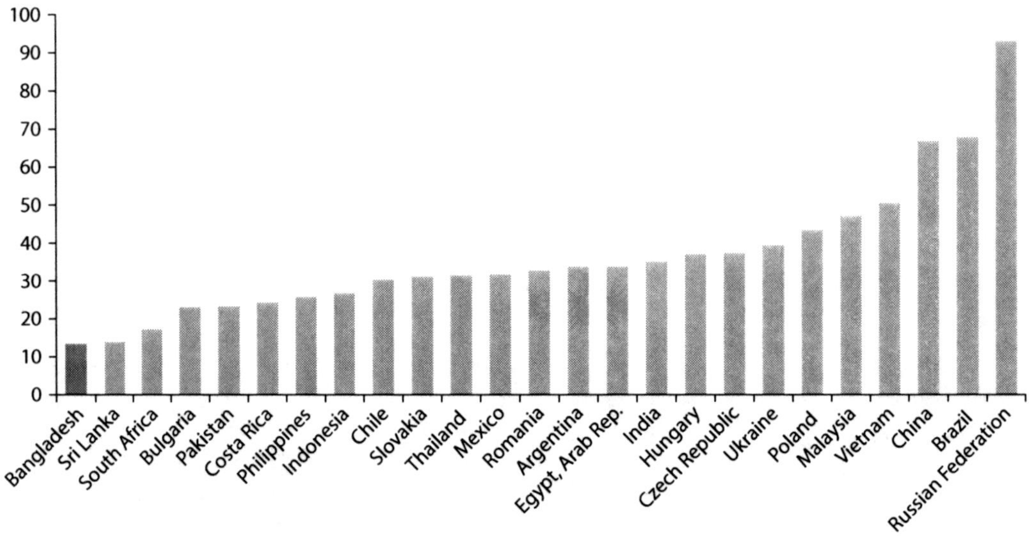

Source: Reproduced from ITC and KPMG 2012, 23, figure 9.

Figure 8.3 Potential Savings on a 25-Seat Development Center, Bangladesh and Comparators, 2011
percent

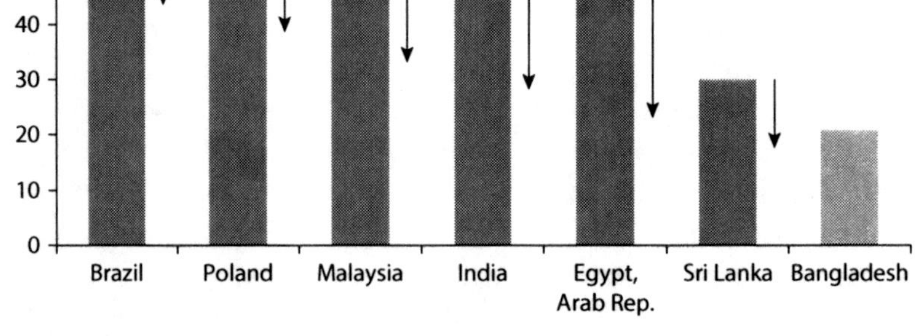

Source: Reproduced from ITC and KPMG 2012, 32, figure 10.

However, there are challenges to realizing the country's export potential in IT-ITES. This is reflected by the earlier evidence on the low value and share of computer and information services exports in Bangladesh. Other LMICs do better by comparison, including the Philippines, which has experienced rapid growth in IT services exports over the past decade.[8] By contrast, the share of software services exports in Bangladesh is less than 1 percent of total export earnings. Although the government has taken steps to address information security, the country still suffers from a negative image on protection of intellectual property rights. Fragmentation in the sector and lack of scale economies make it difficult for Bangladeshi companies to take up large contracts. There are problems of infrastructure, especially in power and bandwidth reliability and backup costs, and problems with access to finance and venture capital funds. High telecommunications costs are a major limitation. Lack of marketing skills and middle management knowledge are additional domestic constraints. Firms face problems of employee turnover (38 percent switching), absenteeism (19 percent), and lack of required skill sets. Low wage rates and intense competition are the main reasons for high mobility within the sector. Local workers lack expertise in higher value-added IT-enabled services owing to the small domestic market. Reports point to the need for more IT clusters and parks, more investment in skill building and infrastructure, and increased foreign direct investment (FDI) to facilitate growth. Finally, there is lack of overseas awareness about Bangladesh as a potential software services provider. Table 8.2 lists the main impediments to development of the sector.

For Bangladesh's labor exports, the key external constraints relate to mobility restrictions, including the movement of professionals because of immigration-related uncertainties, delays, and costs. Conditions would be improved by

Table 8.2 Domestic Constraints to the Development of Bangladesh's IT Industry
percent

Constraint	*1st Obstacle*	*2nd Obstacle*	*3rd Obstacle*	*4th Obstacle*
Access to finance (availability and cost)	23.8	7.7	8.1	5.7
Access to land	4.5	6.7	3.2	4.6
Business licensing and permits	5.4	5.7	1.6	2.9
Corruption	9.9	10.8	7.0	6.9
Crime, theft, and disorder	3.0	4.1	3.8	4.0
Customs and trade regulations	5.4	7.7	2.7	2.9
Electricity	26.7	20.6	14.5	8.6
Inadequate skilled labor	5.9	8.2	12.9	4.6
Labor regulations	2.0	1.5	3.2	1.1
Political stability	3.5	11.3	10.8	9.7
Tax administration	2.0	4.1	4.3	4.6
Tax rate	2.5	—	3.8	5.1
Transportation	—	1.0	10.8	10.3
Access to market	3.5	7.2	6.5	14.3
Access to technology	1.0	1.0	2.7	11.4
Copyright	1.0	—	2.7	2.9

Source: Shinkai and Hossain 2011, 11, table 8.
Note: Surveyed firms were asked to list their first four main impediments. The percentages give the share of firms that listed that particular issue as a first ranking impediment, second ranking, and so on. The numbers would thus suggest that electricity and access to finance are the main impediments.

speedier processing of visas, increased transparency in immigration rules and procedures, and separation of temporary from permanent entry.

Overall, as noted in a recent report for the U.S. Agency for International Development (USAID) Bangladesh IT-enabled services project, Bangladesh meets only the minimal requirements for software services exports, such as good telecommunications infrastructure, competitive labor costs, and good government policies (Carana Corporation 2011). The country's only clear market advantage at present is low-cost labor. But this is offset by high communications costs and is not sufficient for Bangladesh to enter new markets, especially given the country's lack of reputation as a quality provider and strong competition from other countries. To be more competitive internationally, Bangladesh needs much more focus on creating a supportive domestic business environment in this sector. Thus, a long-term growth strategy is required for building capacity, identifying target segments within the sector, and marketing—all of which will require considerable support from the government and development agencies.

Labor Services

Bangladesh's economy is very dependent on the export of human resources. Remittances have played a major role in the country's macroeconomic stability and alleviation of poverty (Raihan et al. 2009). The country is primarily engaged in exporting labor services for infrastructure development projects and for domestic work in the Middle East and some countries in Southeast Asia. Around three-fourths of Bangladesh's labor exports are for semiskilled and low-skilled services. Remittances and the number of workers employed are growing, but research indicates that, at present, Bangladesh cannot meet the growing demand in several occupational categories. Studies of skill requirements in destination markets highlight the scope for Bangladesh to diversify its labor services exports in the areas of target countries, occupations, and skill sets. Moreover, with growing competition from other LMICs in its traditional markets and segments, there is a need for Bangladesh to diversify its overseas employment pattern.

A recent study highlights that Bangladeshi recruiting agents are faced with high demand for low-skilled and semiskilled workers. Countries in the Middle East and Southeast Asia require masons, rod binders, carpenters, brick layers, and welders. The projected demand for various types of Bangladeshi migrant workers for FY2014 was more than 20,000 masons; around 31,000 carpenters; about 24,000 electricians; and around 7,600 mechanics, technicians, and foremen. The total estimated demand for Bangladeshi workers across various low-skilled and semiskilled occupations was 136,720 for FY2014 (Stamp 2010). Research indicates that Bangladesh is at present unable to meet this demand, as is evident from the fact that heavy premiums are being charged by the agents and ad hoc training centers and crash training programs have emerged for such jobs. The country is unable to satisfy demand in areas of global skill shortage, such as trained chefs and domestics who have proficiency in the language of the destination country.

The country faces several challenges, internal and external, to tapping this unmet demand. Many experts have pointed out that Bangladesh's migration policy and skill development programs have not strategically addressed shortages and demands in various labor markets. Lack of a targeted strategy has in turn resulted in problems such as inadequate training and orientation of migrant workers and growing competition from other labor-exporting countries. There are also regulatory challenges in tackling exploitation of migrant workers by overseas employers and recruiting agents, visa trading, and involvement of intermediaries at various stages of the recruitment and migration process. These issues raise the overall costs of migration for low-skilled and semiskilled workers and raise concerns about workers' rights and welfare. Addressing migration issues requires greater internal coordination of workers' agencies and institutions in destination countries, as well as intergovernmental coordination to manage the recruitment and migration process.

Legislative issues also constrain low-skilled and semiskilled labor exports. Although Bangladesh's regime for labor exports is becoming more liberal, policy is restrictive with respect to female migration. Since the early 1980s, successive governments have either banned migration of all categories of female workers except professionals or imposed restrictions on the migration of low-skilled and semiskilled women. At present, such women can migrate only with written permission from their husband, father, or brother. Such restrictions, which may be made on the grounds of safety and protection from abuse and exploitation, constrain the country's ability to export in segments that require female migrant workers. And there are external challenges arising from uncertainties and frequent changes in the immigration policies of destination countries like Kuwait and Malaysia. There have been instances of bans on recruitment of female Bangladeshi workers imposed by these countries.[9]

In addition to low-skilled and semiskilled labor exports, all the studies note that Bangladesh has the potential to increase exports of skilled and professional services. In 2010, only 387 professionals migrated for overseas jobs (Stamp 2010). For instance, there is scope to export English teachers and ICT professionals to Japan and nurses and caregivers to the United States and Canada. Bangladesh lacks a policy to regulate skilled labor outflows. Furthermore, such exports have been viewed from the perspective of "brain drain" rather than attracting returnees, brain circulation, and promotion of investments.

Bangladesh's ability to leverage the potential for labor exports effectively will depend on several factors. The factors include the state of the economy of the receiving countries and their immigration policies; the extent to which Bangladesh is able to diversify into new markets, occupations, and skill sets; Bangladesh's migration policies; and Bangladesh's ability to remain competitive with other exporting countries. Given its large population, Bangladesh will need a planned labor migration policy, embedded in a longer-term human resource development strategy, so that it can meet the skill requirements in international and domestic markets.

Nursing

A key skilled service export highlighted in many studies is nursing. Led by the United States and the United Kingdom, there is a huge global demand for nurses arising from demographic changes, aging populations, a surge in chronic diseases, physician shortages in primary care, and the need for nurses as case managers and for staffing new retail and worksite clinics (Siddiqui and Appiah 2008). However, studies indicate a decline in the numbers enrolled in nursing programs and nursing graduates in high-income countries (Aiken 2007). The United States had a shortage of 110,000 nurses (or 6 percent) in 2000 and is expected to face a shortage of 29 percent by 2020. Hence, the recruitment of foreign nurses from major nurse-producing countries, such as Australia, India, the Philippines, and South Africa, has become an attractive option for several high-income countries in recent years to meet their growing national nursing shortages (although such active recruitment has raised ethical issues). It is estimated that since 1997, the United Kingdom has admitted more than 90,000 international nurses from many countries and that one in ten of all working nurses in the United Kingdom is trained in other countries. Over the past decade, the number of foreign-trained nurse entrants into the U.S. nursing workforce has risen faster than the number of U.S. educated nurse entrants (Matsuno 2009). In the wake of these trends, nurse-sending countries, such as the Philippines and to a lesser extent India and China, have taken proactive steps to prepare their nurses to work in overseas markets and to meet the future demand for professional nurses and caregivers in Europe and North America.

Countries such as Bangladesh have the potential to supply this need for nurses, given their large labor force. However, nurse migration from Bangladesh remains small. In 1991–2004, around 21,000 female workers migrated from the country, mostly as housemaids and cleaners and others as semiskilled (mostly garment and factory) workers. A small share, around 5.7 percent, of these female workers consisted of nurses. Most of them went to the Middle East and the rest to Southeast Asia, mainly Malaysia (Aminuzamman 2007). Aminuzamman (2007) finds that since 2004 there has been a steady decline in the number of Bangladeshi nurses, notwithstanding growing demand overseas. These trends were in contrast to the experience of leading supplier countries such as the Philippines, which sent close to 90,000 nurses overseas over a period of 10 years during the late 1990s and early 2000s and supplied around 25 percent of all overseas nurses and 83 percent of foreign nurses in the United States. Clearly, Bangladesh has not been able to leverage the growing global demand for nurses, unlike other LMICs. This is because of a variety of constraints on the migration of nurses from Bangladesh.

One constraining factor is domestic demand. Bangladesh's current nurse-to-doctor ratio of 0.4 falls short of international standards of three nurses per doctor. There is an estimated shortage of more than 280,000 nurses (and 60,000 doctors and 483,000 health technicians) in the country. In the face of such shortages, a proactive export policy for nurses may not be immediately feasible or appropriate. However, a long-term strategy to meet domestic and global demand will require Bangladesh to build capacity, with the involvement of government, the private sector, private universities, and labor-exporting agencies. At present, government guidelines for nurse education prevent the private sector from offering nursing courses, which constrains growth. Several studies point to the need for massive investment in nursing education by government and private institutions to expand capacity.

Other constraints to nursing services exports include internal and external factors. Internal constraints include the lack of proper training, lack of appropriate skill sets, and the need to update training curricula and the quality of teaching. Current training facilities, standards, and curricula are not adequate. External barriers include nonrecognition of qualifications, language barriers, and prohibitive licensing requirements. Hence, as in the case of labor services exports more generally, Bangladesh's nursing services exports will require a strategic and planned approach, where there is focus on capacity creation in the domestic economy with spin-offs in exports.

Key Producer Services: Implications for Competitiveness

Services such as transport, logistics, telecommunications, and energy play a vital role in driving growth and competitiveness in any economy. In Bangladesh, examination of interindustry links shows that there is strong interdependence between industry and services. Input-output analysis for Bangladesh reveals that the service sector is the largest user of services inputs. Hence, lack of growth and capacity creation and lack of competitiveness in key producer services can impede the growth of industry and services. Telecommunications and transport and logistics services are two important producer services that can have ramifications for Bangladesh's export prospects in other important sectors.

This chapter does not discuss these two sectors in any depth. Trade facilitation and logistics services are discussed in Kathuria and Malouche (2016, chapter 6). Adequate transport and logistics facilities and connectivity are essential for economywide competitiveness and growth. For instance, shipping and distribution services are almost entirely imported from abroad and serve the exporting and importing sectors in Bangladesh. In addition, air freight services are used to carry cargo and clearing and forwarding agent services are used to clear inputs from the port or customs and for loading finished goods onto ships for export. Within the country, the garment industry makes use of road and rail transport services to bring the imported inputs to the production plant or to carry the finished goods to the ports. Such links highlight how the growth of transport and logistics services is essential for realizing export potential in other important sectors of Bangladesh's economy.

However, the sector is confronted by regulatory, political, and infrastructural challenges. Transport and logistics are not fully liberalized and vested interests prevent competition and entry of foreign providers. Political instability has caused projects to be stalled or delayed and has caused problems of cross-border communications stemming from disagreements with neighboring countries.

There can be many benefits from increased investment in and development of this sector. Transport (including shipping) services constitute a large part of Bangladesh's services imports and transport underdevelopment is the largest contributor to the country's trade deficit in services (see annex 8A). Shipping services account for a major part of the total use of services in key industries, including garments. In turn, exports of key products such as garments can augment exports of transport services, particularly shipping services, once the latter become more competitive. Likewise, there is need for FDI and capacity creation in segments such as port facilities and ship repair services in the short and medium run, laying the basis for possible exports of such services in the long run. There is also the potential to export port and transport services to the northeastern part of India by reexporting goods imported through Bangladeshi ports. Thus, there is a need to view the development of the transport and logistics sector within the larger context of strengthening overall competitiveness and facilitating exports in key industries, while reaping spin-off benefits through exports of these services in the long run.

The telecommunications sector is significant for various reasons: communications services are a critical input for other sectors, services and goods, and affect exports and imports. They have a key role in improving overall efficiency, productivity, and competitiveness and in export segments such as IT-BPO services, which are of growing interest for Bangladesh (see chapter 7, on information technology–enabled services).

Bangladesh has experienced considerable increase in teledensity, mobile phone subscriptions, and Internet penetration over the past decade, largely reflecting the entry of private providers and deregulation of this sector. There has been tremendous growth in the mobile telephony segment, including the business of several private sector operators. These are mostly joint ventures with foreign investment coming from India, Malaysia, Norway, and the United States. What is evident is that although there has been rapid growth, Bangladesh still has weak telecom infrastructure. Capacity and reach are still limited, especially in the fixed-line segment, highlighting the need for further investment in some segments.

FDI in the mobile segment of the telecom sector has been critical for improving service quality, increasing cell phone penetration, and providing Bangladeshi consumers with some of the most competitive cell phone call rates in the world. However, there are many concerns in the telecom sector that reduce its impact in segments other than mobile and even in mobile. Internet penetration, which has a positive impact on business productivity, is low (total of 3.3 million subscribers as of April 2013, of which 3.1 million were through mobile). The quality of Internet services is inadequate, falling well short of the goal of uninterrupted connectivity with latency and high bandwidth. The fixed-line segment is monopolized by Bangladesh Telecommunications Company Ltd., a state-run company, and this has reduced service quality and expansion in this segment. In addition, the decisions of the regulatory agency, the Bangladesh Telecommunications Regulatory Commission, have often been controversial, such as in the case of renewal of 2G licenses, and this has led to private sector perceptions of its politicization.

Primary Evidence on Prospects in Selected Services and Modes of Supply

Discussions were carried out with stakeholders in each of the aforementioned labor services exports, namely, ICT, nursing, and mode 4. Views were solicited on the opportunities as well as constraints in these sectors and modes from representatives in the private sector, government, and academic community. It appeared that the operationalization of the LDC service waiver was unclear to most of the stakeholders and the general view was that the waiver would probably not be of much benefit to Bangladesh. There was no awareness among stakeholders regarding any initiatives taken by other LDCs to obtain this waiver and thus no benchmark against which the government could pursue its interests. The discussions mainly emphasized the importance of undertaking domestic policy reforms and alleviating supply-side constraints if Bangladesh was to become competitive in services exports and benefit from a possible LDC service waiver. The interviews were held during May to July 2012. The findings from these discussions as well as the insights obtained from earlier primary work conducted for Bangladesh's service sector are presented here.

Most stakeholders held the view that after India, Bangladesh can become the most attractive ICT outsourcing destination in South Asia. Their claims are supported by some recent studies.[10] Bangladesh was ranked third among all offshoring countries of South Asia and best in competitiveness (BASIS 2010). It was evident from the interviews with stakeholders that Bangladesh's ICT sector has a significant advantage in labor and infrastructure cost. A recent report by Bangladesh Board of Investment supports this claim. The report mentions that a programmer's salary in Bangladesh is 40 percent of that in India, 50 percent of the Philippines, and 70 percent of Vietnam. Internet bandwidth charges are much lower than in many other countries. For example, compared with India, the cost is 50 percent lower (BASIS 2010). The stakeholders also emphasized the availability of ICT education facilities in Bangladesh.

Although the ICT sector in Bangladesh has almost all the necessary ingredients for success, according to industry stakeholders, there remain some perceived threats to the industry. Despite the cost advantages and availability of ICT education, the skills of the labor force in Bangladesh's ICT sector are not up to the required level. This reflects an outdated curriculum, inadequately trained teachers, and lack of adequate facilities in relevant institutions. The teachers in colleges under the National University as well as the new universities of science and technology are not sufficiently trained to adopt current trends in science and technology. The in-house and overseas training facilities are not adequate for the scientists who are working on cutting-edge technologies. Many staff members do not return home after the expiry of their training period and thus contribute to the poor performance or failure of projects. It was strongly argued by the stakeholders that without improvements in the skill sets of the ICT labor force, the country would not be able to exploit its potential, especially considering the stiff competition from countries such as China, India, the Philippines, and Vietnam.

The stakeholders highlighted another problem that was related to the lack of a methodical approach: companies in Bangladesh in general suffer from lack of documentation and work process skills. Companies also face difficulties in quality control.

The stakeholders perceived lack of finance as one of the major obstacles for Bangladeshi entrepreneurs in the ICT sector. Finance enables firms to undertake productive investment to initiate or expand a business. Availability of investment funds facilitates acquiring better technology to promote competitiveness. Most of the stakeholders complained that in Bangladesh investors faced credit constraints and had to pay high interest rates on loans unrelated to their performance. The problem is even worse for small and medium enterprises (SMEs), including the export-oriented ones. Banks are shy to lend to SME activities, as the banks do not consider SME activities to be attractive and profitable undertakings. In most cases, banks and nonbank financial institutions require collateral in the form of land and buildings. The value of real estate security is usually set much higher than the amount of the loan and many enterprises cannot raise such collateral. Furthermore, loan application forms for investment financing from banks are long, tedious, and redundant. Exporters outside Dhaka faced more problems with export finance than those in Dhaka. According to the stakeholders, there are emerging human resource constraints in this sector.

Although the country's ICT policy is favorable, Bangladesh may face a large "resource crunch" in the near future, because of brain drain and the growing attractiveness of other business sectors, which is pulling professionals away from an ICT career. There are also physical infrastructural constraints, chiefly the lack of continuous electrical power supply. Power generation capacity in Bangladesh is among the lowest in the world and power failures and load shedding are rampant. Frequent power failures and low voltage are large hurdles for software companies in Bangladesh. Domestic and international companies are working to find solutions, such as the use of low-power ICT equipment.

Stakeholders emphasized that the quality of Internet service in Bangladesh is worse than in countries like China, Sri Lanka, and Vietnam. The cost of Internet usage is high and the speed is limited. However, the stakeholders held the view that once 3G licenses were permitted, the situation would improve.

The stakeholders were emphatic that there is little coordination between policy making and implementation of ICT-related activities, which are carried out by several government entities. The lack of coordination acts as a barrier in carrying out the master plan of building a "Digital Bangladesh." Two ministries—the Ministry of Post and Telecommunications and the Ministry of Information—are primarily involved in dealing with ICT-related infrastructure, with input from the Bangladesh Telecommunications Regulatory Commission. The Ministry of Science and ICT promotes the ICT business sector through its wing, the Bangladesh Computer Council. The Ministry of Commerce is trying to promote ICT business through the ICT Business Promotion Council. E-governance activities are managed by two distinct government entities. The first is the e-government cell in the Prime Minister's Office, which is implementing the "Access to Information" program. The second entity is the Support to ICT Task Force under the Ministry of Planning. The lack of coordination among implementing authorities has caused setbacks in the progress of ICT development.

Stakeholder Recommendations

The stakeholders highlighted the need for formulation of a universal access and broadband policy for ensuring equity in ICT-based growth and development. To implement this policy, details of the relevant rules, such as the Patent Law, Secrecy Act, Consumer Protection Act, Trade Mark Act, Foreign Exchange Regulation Act, and Income Tax Act, should be taken into consideration so that there is no infringement of rights or violation of existing rules when implementing the ICT policy.

Stakeholders note that, in general, the Bangladeshi workforce lacks English language proficiency and there is room for improvement. There is a critical need to train the existing labor force in language and other skills. Training courses should be upgraded to reflect advanced technology.

There is vast scope for expansion of the ICT sector in Bangladesh, as is evident from the country's international ranking in teledensity and outreach. The stakeholders stressed the importance of advertising more vigorously the existing incentives, including fiscal and financial incentives, for attracting local investment and FDI in ICT through the public-private partnership initiative. There is much hope among most stakeholders that Bangladesh can be a successful supplier of ICT and software exports. Its main advantage is perceived to be opportunities for investors to reduce project costs significantly. However, as highlighted in the previous sections, Bangladesh's ICT sector suffers from some constraints and is not yet well known internationally. To improve the situation, the major focus of the country needs to be on export promotion. ICT firms should focus more on marketing activities such as commercial representation, networking, and advertising. If these issues are addressed, then there is scope for Bangladeshi ICT companies to generate much more revenue from the global market.

Stakeholder recommendations highlighted the need for domestic initiatives on multiple fronts to improve the supporting infrastructure and human resource capabilities and to create and promote the country's brand. The markets of interest were primarily the United States and the United Kingdom, although suggestions were not made specific to particular markets and were more generalized in nature. There were no proposals relating to the LDC services waiver; the discussions indicated a lack of awareness about the waiver as well as doubts over its significance. Stakeholders attached greater significance to addressing domestic capacity and quality-related issues to promote IT and BPO services exports.

Stakeholder Views on Nursing Services

Most of the stakeholders held the view that there is a huge potential market for exporting nursing services, but that Bangladesh has not been able to capitalize on this opportunity. The country has not been able to send a large number of nurses abroad.

Discussions with the stakeholders indicated that although there is demand for skilled nurses from Bangladesh in Middle Eastern countries, Bangladesh has not been able to supply these markets for several reasons.

The stakeholders perceived a huge demand for nurses in Saudi Arabia. An opportunity was created in 2003 when there was an outbreak of severe acute respiratory syndrome in the East Asian countries and Saudi Arabia imposed a temporary restriction on Filipino nurses. However, not many Bangladeshi nurses could meet the minimum requirements set by Saudi employers. Likewise, stakeholders felt that there was good potential for sending nurses to Kuwait. However, the basic requirement in Kuwait is a Bachelor of Science (BSc) degree in nursing for working nurses, and the number of BSc nurses is very low in Bangladesh.[11] In the United Arab Emirates, immigrant nurses are required to pass a difficult professional examination, which discourages foreign nurses from seeking a job in that market. There are also problems of language and standards that have to be met through professional training for the other Middle Eastern countries. In most cases, Bangladeshi nurses fail to meet these requirements.

Similarly, the stakeholders pointed out that although there is huge potential to export nurses to high-income countries in North America and Europe and to the Far East, several factors constrain the realization of this potential. The discussions indicated that Bangladeshi nurses fail to meet the high standards of the nursing profession in those countries and lack the required technical qualifications to apply for these positions. Language proficiency, especially in English, in general is low and the academic preparation of the Bangladeshi nurses is far below the requirements and standards set by Western nursing schools. Most Bangladeshi nurses lack various skills or requirements to pass the North American, European, and Australian examinations. Candidates generally have poor International English Language Testing System scores and high failure rates in the qualifying examination. Hence, Bangladeshi nurses do not feel confident to apply to these countries. Further, the entire application and examination system is costly for applicants. And there is a gross lack of information on the openings for nursing positions. Even today, Bangladesh does not have any recognized test center for such a recruitment process. And there is a lack of adequate coaching for the Commission on Graduates of Foreign Nursing Schools examination.

Aminuzzaman (2007) highlights several other constraints faced by Bangladesh in the context of nursing exports. The stakeholders were of the view that the situation had not improved since 2007. Bangladeshi nurses continue to lack behavioral and communication skills. They fail to understand instructions and follow-up procedures and are found lacking in interpersonal skills and a professional attitude. They tend to be reluctant to adapt to the new and changing environment. And Bangladeshi nurses fail to prove professional competence and respond to the challenges and the level of technical and professional demands placed on them under modern health management systems. They are unable to handle some of the sophisticated medical equipment. They are viewed as being "too conservative" toward their male counterparts and professional colleagues.

The stakeholders highlighted that although the nursing curriculum was revised nearly 13 years ago, its full and appropriate implementation had never taken place. The problem appears to be a mismatch between the curriculum and actual nursing practice, which is further hampered by ineffective and outmoded teaching methods, lack of appropriate tools for assessing students, and an ineffective mode of instruction.

Overall, the stakeholder discussions did not create an optimistic scenario about Bangladesh's prospects for nursing services exports. It was felt that Bangladesh would not be able to respond to the projected overseas demand. The current training facilities, standards, and curricula are simply not enough for the competitive employment market. In all respects, Bangladesh falls far behind the required professional standards.

Stakeholder Recommendations

The stakeholders felt that Bangladesh must follow a strategic and planned approach toward the export of nurses. The plan should address the country's immediate domestic requirements, but also help it gear up for export opportunities in the medium and long run.

The stakeholders suggested that Bangladesh could emulate nurse exporting countries like the Philippines, where nursing schools have teamed up with northern partners to create, develop, promote, and seek U.S.-based hospital and nursing home partners who wish to alleviate their nursing shortages. These partnerships have created strategic alliances with nursing schools, hospital systems, and other health care providers and helped create domestic as well as export capacity.[12]

Bangladeshi nurses must be better qualified to meet the growing demand from locally established private hospitals of international standard as well as the potential demand from the international labor market. The government of Bangladesh could come up with a special project to establish at least one international standard nursing college. This college could address the language barriers and nonrecognition of qualifications that are the two main obstacles to nurse migration. This could be done with technical assistance from development partners, with the standard of intake set at par with Western nursing institutes. The government of Bangladesh may also consider some of the following approaches to encourage quality intake of nursing students:

- Initiate a special program, with the assistance of international development partners, to introduce international nursing education in selected private universities.
- Help nursing institutes of selected private universities establish links with some elite nursing institutions. And help institutes obtain the necessary accreditations so as to improve nurses' technical competence. The ungraded institutes can train nurses to be sensitive to the cultural needs and considerations of various health care systems worldwide and thus create a truly globally competent nursing workforce.
- Encourage private institutes to introduce scholarship programs to fund the brightest students and place them in a quality nursing program.

Furthermore, the stakeholders suggested that the government could provide opportunities to private universities to use public medical colleges, hospitals, and other specialized health facilities for on-the-job training of student nurses. As an immediate initiative, the Ministry of Manpower, with the assistance of the Ministry of Health and Education, could form a task force to review and examine the potential for exporting human resources in the health sector without affecting domestic demand. All Bangladeshi embassies could participate in initiatives in collaboration with the Ministry of Manpower to prepare an inventory of projected demand for nurses in the global context, especially for Europe, North America, the Far East, and Australia.

As is evident from the nature of the recommendations, there were no proposals put forward by the stakeholders regarding the operationalization of the LDC services waiver. This was in part because of their lack of general awareness about the waiver and how it would be negotiated or implemented. The overwhelming view was that the need of the hour was domestic initiatives to upgrade quality, improve standards, build capacity, and work incrementally through intercountry dialogue at the level of the private sector and the government, specifically targeting markets such as Kuwait, Malaysia, Singapore, the United Arab Emirates, the United Kingdom, and the United States.

Stakeholder Views on Labor Services Exports

Stakeholders stressed the importance of labor services exports and associated international remittances as a source of foreign exchange for Bangladesh. However, they pointed to the many challenges in managing migration flows, not specifically mode 4 exports, although several of these challenges are pertinent to the country's mode 4 exports as well (as mode 4 is a subset of migration flows). The main concern of the stakeholders was the lack of a rights-based approach to migration, the lack of legal support, inadequate policies, and protracted implementation processes for safe migration (Siddiqui and Farah 2011). They also highlighted many problems that are faced by Bangladeshi workers overseas in their countries of employment, largely corroborating available secondary evidence in this regard. These problems may be summarized as follows:

- Procedural problems in some legal institutions in importing countries cause delays in the disposal of labor problem–related cases and in getting the proper payment for the laborers.
- Lack of awareness about labor rights in the importing country is a serious problem. As a result, foreign employers often treat Bangladeshi labor poorly.
- Bangladeshi migrant workers face nonadherence to the terms and conditions of employment by the sponsors. This has resulted in several other problems, such as nonpayment, underpayment, delayed payment, poor living conditions, refusal to provide air tickets at the time of exit, and so forth.
- Sometimes, as soon as the worker reaches the host country, the agreement is substituted by a new agreement that provides lower wages, substandard accommodations, and lower fringe benefits, and does not provide free food.

- Complex legal procedures in the host countries cause various difficulties for migrants. For instance, in case of accidents, it may take years to get compensation. Sometimes workers are repatriated after becoming handicapped temporarily or permanently by an accident, without receiving proper treatment or compensation.
- Female migrants face several problems in the country of destination. In many cases, females are confined to the residence of the employers and cannot communicate with others. They remain unreachable in case of an emergency or threat. In this context, it is important to mention that the Philippines has put a temporary ban on female migration. Indonesia has stopped sending females to Saudi Arabia. Sri Lanka is trying to expand its male labor market and reduce female migration. Under such circumstances, Bangladesh needs to be extra conscious regarding the security of its female migrant workers (Siddiqui and Farah 2011).
- A significant proportion of Bangladeshi workers become irregular for reasons operational in Bangladesh and in the countries of destination. Recently, Bangladesh has been facing stiff competition from newly emerging labor-sending countries of South Asia and Southeast Asia. The global financial crisis and political upheavals in the Gulf and North African countries have negatively affected labor migration from Bangladesh. Although in 2008, 800,000 Bangladeshis went abroad for work, in 2009 and 2010, the number was reduced by half. It is expected that in the coming years, workers from some African countries will participate in the Gulf labor market along with the newly entering Southeast Asian countries. This indicates that the competition for entry into the labor market is going to be tougher (Siddiqui and Farah 2011).

There are several problems related to domestic policies and institutional frameworks. They are as follows:

- Although the overseas employment policy has been in place for the past few years, successive governments have not developed any comprehensive action plan to implement it. The government is pursuing individual sections of the policy in a piecemeal manner. There is no monitoring and evaluation process built into the policy. Given the current competition in global labor markets as well as the need for better protection of the rights of workers, it is essential to develop a target-oriented action plan. The plan should ensure implementation of the overseas employment policy with built-in monitoring and evaluation systems to achieve goals and suggest incremental changes (Siddiqui and Farah 2011).

- Despite that the government of Bangladesh is committed to promoting short-term international migration, there is a lack of any planned program for accessing the rapidly changing international labor market. As a result, systemic methods for collecting information on labor needs in the receiving countries and on training requirements are not in place.

- The Ministry of Expatriates' Welfare and Overseas Employment (EWOE) is the most important apparatus in the government for managing migration. However, the ministry and its line agencies suffer from severe resource shortages. These include a shortage of skilled and competent human resources as well as inadequate infrastructure. Because of these shortages, many of the functions for protecting and promoting the rights and welfare of migrant workers cannot be delivered by the ministry (Siddiqui and Farah 2011).

- Bangladeshi workers are mainly employed in semiskilled and low-skilled occupations, where increasing competition from newly emerging labor-sending countries has resulted in a decline in wages and other conditions of work. As a result, there has been a decrease in the level of per capita remittances.

- Another problem is the mismatch between skill requirements and the available skill sets of the Bangladeshi migrants. Although there are several institutions that train Bangladeshi migrants, the curricula of these institutions are not frequently updated and have little vocational content, which is a major obstacle in promoting skilled migration. Moreover, the educational background of workers in the semiskilled and low-skilled job market is relatively poor. All these issues result in poor quality and lack of professionalism, which in turn make employers reluctant to stick to the terms and conditions of employment (Islam 2008).

- Bangladeshi trade unions have practical difficulties in working as an institution to collectively bargain with the country of destination. Although migrant workers' associations have emerged in Bangladesh and in the countries of destination, they lack the institutional capacity needed to advocate for the establishment of voting rights and a voice in the Bangladeshi parliament. Moreover, they have no representation in the management of the Wage Earners' Welfare Fund, which has been created through their subscriptions (Siddiqui 2004).

- The high cost of migration is the result of several causes that persist in the countries of origin and destination. Visa trading and involvement of intermediaries at various stages cause migration costs to spiral and the whole cost has to be borne by the migrants. For example, a work permit issued by the destination country's government is immediately sold in the local market. A work permit changes hands two or three times and when a Bangladeshi recruiter buys the work permit, the recruiter has to pay as much as US$2,000 upfront. Meanwhile, Bangladeshi recruiting agencies, local intermediaries, and dishonest public sector functionaries retain their margins from the same amount. Under these circumstances, when a migrant secures a visa she or he has to pay the entire amount, which is much higher than the actual cost. It takes more than a year for a migrant worker to recover the money spent to acquire the work permit (Siddiqui and Farah 2011).

- Migration is one of the least considered elements in the national development plan. Neither the five-year development plan nor the ten-year perspective plan has identified migration as a way to enhance development. Civil society has persuaded the Ministry of EWOE to incorporate migration as a thrust sector in the development plan. However, the Sixth Five-Year Development Plan does not have a separate section on migration. The ministry has been able to incorporate the issue of migration in various chapters (Siddiqui and Farah 2011).

- At present, the Bureau of Manpower, Employment, and Training (BMET), the line agency of the Ministry of EWOE, manages 38 technical training centers in Bangladesh. These training centers target local as well as international employment. There is a persistent tension in administering these training centers as two separate ministries. The Ministry of Labor and the Ministry of EWOE run these training centers under the supervision of BMET. About 2,000 trainers from these centers need urgent capacity building and training to conduct modern courses. Again, most of these technical training centers face major budget deficits. Moreover, the Bangladesh Technical Education Board of the Education Ministry, responsible for coordinating training and approving the training curricula within these centers, lacks adequate human resources to improve quality (Siddiqui and Farah 2011).

Stakeholder Recommendations

According to the stakeholders and in line with existing studies on the subject, several steps should be undertaken to resolve the problems related to labor migration from Bangladesh.[13] These steps can be grouped into four broad sets of measures pertaining to the following: (a) preparing the workforce to take up overseas employment through skill building and training; (b) facilitating the migration process; (c) ensuring safe migration and protection of workers through institutional arrangements and coordination with other governments; and (d) introducing institutional arrangements and policies to give strategic focus to labor exports. Most of these recommendations fall under the category of migration policies rather than mode 4 per se, but many are pertinent to the facilitation of services exports based on mode 4.

Preparing the Workforce

- Many labor-receiving countries have projections and plans for future development projects and concomitant labor needs. These projections need to be analyzed systematically, so that Bangladeshi workers can be trained to meet future overseas demand and can be marketed.
- The existing training institutes of BMET should be upgraded to help increase skilled migration. BMET needs to extend its training outreach through joint ventures with NGOs and private training institutes. BMET should disseminate information on the labor market to organizations that provide training and to NGOs. To ensure that the poor, men and women, have access to such training,

special scholarship programs should be established. These measures will require a major allocation of resources.

- Vocational training should be incorporated into mainstream primary and secondary school curricula and textbooks should include chapters on migration. To help improve communication skills, English should be introduced as a second language from first grade.

Facilitating the Migration and Remittance Process

- To ensure equal access for men and women to overseas employment, government restrictions on the migration of unskilled and semiskilled women workers younger than age 35 years should be rescinded. This should be coupled with better information and pre-departure orientation, and better support from Bangladeshi missions in destination countries.

- To increase access to employment through migration, the costs of migration should be reduced and access to low-interest credit should be created. A bank could be established by allocating resources from the Wage Earners' Welfare Fund. This bank could give loans to the poor at reasonable rates of interest by keeping mortgages on land or other properties. Since the Wage Earners' Welfare Fund is a contributory fund of the migrant workers, their views should be taken into account by the government.

- Before embarking on short-term contract migration, migrant workers should receive pre-departure orientation training. This should include the dissemination of information about the destination country, general job conditions, and the rights and duties of migrant workers under the legal regime of the country concerned and under international law. Instead of providing this training itself, the government may decide to encourage selected specialized agencies, NGOs, and migrant support groups to provide residential, pre-departure orientation training in migrant-prone areas on a decentralized basis.

- Bank officials should receive regular training, be aware of the importance of migrant remittances, and be motivated to make their services customer friendly.

- In an effort to ensure continuous employment and earnings on their return to Bangladesh, migrants should be informed about the need to save. To encourage small savers, proper incentive programs should be established. This may involve offering bonds, shares, and mutual funds at attractive rates. Migrant workers should be informed about the various forms of saving instruments offered by governmental, nongovernmental, and private agencies. Existing legal requirements may be relaxed so that selected microfinance institutions can mobilize the migrants' savings without providing credit.

- BMET should encourage NGOs and the private sector to offer special programs for the economic reintegration of the returnees. This may include helping them gain access to the formal banking sector, credit agencies for soft loans, land allotment on moderate terms, insurance schemes, and schemes organized under the Wage Earners' Welfare Fund.

Ensuring Safe Migration and Protection of Workers

- The Bangladesh missions in Kuwait, Malaysia, Saudi Arabia, and the United Arab Emirates should seek to draw the attention of concerned authorities in the respective countries to the negative consequences of work visa manipulation for both parties and urge them to take the necessary steps to halt this practice. The Ministry of EWOE should take the necessary legal and administrative actions against identified Bangladeshi procurers and middlemen engaged in the visa trade.

- The 1982 Immigration Ordinance in Bangladesh should be replaced by rights-based legislation reflecting the 1990 United Nations Convention on the Protection of the Rights of All Migrant Workers and Members of Their Families and other relevant International Labour Organization conventions. The government of Bangladesh has signed the 1990 Convention and, as a labor-sending country, it is in Bangladesh's interest to accede to this and other International Labour Organization instruments forthwith and to frame the necessary enabling national legislation.

- In an effort to reduce fraudulent practices experienced by migrants before departure, there is a need to create an employment exchange bureau or to regulate the *dalal* system.[14] Information on how to ensure safe migration should be disseminated through the mass media as well as through interventions at the grassroots level.

- BMET should concentrate on the regulation and monitoring of the international labor migration sector, rather than on implementing specific programs. The role of foreign missions in the labor-receiving countries should be redefined. Protection of the rights of migrant workers should be considered a priority concern. The government should consider establishing a migrant workers' resource center in each of the major receiving countries within the premises of and under the administrative jurisdiction of the Bangladeshi missions.

- Social protection measures relating to health, security, and accidents should be specified in the job contracts of semiskilled and unskilled workers. The predeparture orientation training should explain in detail to the migrants all such entitlements.

- The Bangladeshi missions should inform the authorities of the receiving countries about the difficulties faced by claimants in view of the stringent conditions in place in certain countries with respect to claims for compensation. This issue needs to be pursued in liaison with other labor-sending countries.

- The government of Bangladesh should negotiate with the receiving countries ways of simplifying the procedure for receiving benefits that fall due at the end of the contract period, so that the migrant can begin to process the claim well in advance and collect the amount before his or her departure.

- Information handouts on the health services available in the receiving countries should be prepared in Bangladesh and disseminated through the missions and various associations of migrant workers in those countries. Information should also be disseminated on HIV/AIDS. The current practice of forced repatriation of migrant workers who contract a disease such as HIV/AIDS should be discontinued. The sending countries should jointly seek to convince the receiving countries that the cost of medical care should be borne by employers when such diseases are contracted in the destination country.

- Expert bodies and civil society organizations should organize consultation meetings with local trade unions to familiarize them with migrant worker issues. In particular, organizations should be aware of the exploitation of workers in Bangladesh during the migration processing phase and the violations of the human and labor rights of migrant workers in the receiving countries. Links should be established between trade unions and migrant workers' associations so that they can complement each other.

- Trade unions should adopt innovative approaches to increase the union membership of migrants and make concerted efforts to develop links with the trade unions of the receiving countries. Trade unions should use international forums to campaign for the membership of migrants in the trade unions of the receiving countries.

- The issue of high visa costs should be placed in international forums such as the Global Forum on Migration and Development. A multilateral approach would help to stop visa trading in the destination countries. The governments of Bahrain, Kuwait, and Saudi Arabia are taking steps to stop this trade. Bangladesh should be involved with these sending countries to find effective solutions. In the Bangladeshi context, adequate legal steps should be taken to reduce the number of intermediaries to lower the high cost of labor migration.

Considering Institutional and Planning Issues

- To ensure effective streamlining of labor migration from Bangladesh, the government should declare migration as a "thrust sector" for the economy and should allocate the equivalent of at least 0.5 percent of remittances earned per fiscal year to the sector. Migration should be incorporated in the national development plans for effective management of the migration sector.

- The government should commit adequate resources to the migration sector. The Ministry of EWOE should propose the allocation of resources equivalent to 5 percent of annual remittances to organize services for migrant workers.
- The Ministry of EWOE should be redesigned with at least five separate departments, such as Facilitation and Regulation of Recruitment, Rights and Welfare, Labor Attaché Management, Long-Term Bangladeshi Affairs, and Policy and Research. Resource allocation for institutional reorganization must be ensured from the revenue budget and necessary infrastructure and human resource development should be funded from the development budget.
- Lack of coordination among the training-providing institutions and concerned ministries must be addressed through interministerial and interagency coordination. All the technical training centers should be equipped with updated training equipment. The capacity of the trainers should be regularly updated with continuous training of trainers. The Bangladesh Technical Education Board should set a minimum standard of training considering demand in the international market. Resources should be allocated for promoting skilled human resources at the grassroots level, under the revenue and development budgets.

The long list of suggestions made by the stakeholders to facilitate and manage migration flows clearly highlights that much remains to be done on the institutional, intergovernmental, and policy fronts if Bangladesh is to realize its potential in labor exports. It is worth noting that although these suggestions fall under migration policies, many of these are relevant to services exports through mode 4, such as for enhancing capacity, ensuring temporariness, identifying target markets and segments for exports, and ensuring the smooth flow of export earnings and their benefits to the local economy.

Roadmap for Promoting Services Exports from Bangladesh in the Context of the LDC Services Waiver

The secondary and primary evidence on Bangladesh's prospects for services exports indicates that there are four broad areas where the government needs to focus if it is to promote services exports in the context of an LDC services waiver. In order of importance, as emerged from the discussions, these areas are as follows:

1. Investment in infrastructure to remove physical capacity limitations and supply-side bottlenecks that currently affect exports of services where there is potential (as in ITC)
2. Investment in human capital to provide the required skill sets and competencies to leverage the country's potential in labor-intensive services exports via mode 4

3. Development of an integrated and strategic approach to build capacity and promote exports in selected services where the country has or is perceived to have potential
4. Negotiations at the multilateral, regional, and bilateral levels and initiation of dialogue with relevant institutions and stakeholders in selected countries to address market access interests and help domestic efforts to alleviate various internal constraints.

The discussion in this section highlights sector-specific policies for the selected services and modes. It presents a prioritized list of measures that need to be undertaken in these services with the specific objective of removing the main constraints affecting them and promoting these exports in the short and medium term.

Strategies for the IT-BPO Sector

Domestic supply side, capacity, and infrastructure-related factors are seen as predominant in shaping Bangladesh's competitiveness in IT-BPO services exports. Therefore, priority must be given to addressing these constraints.

A priority area is to bring down communications costs and improve the transmission infrastructure, issues that are currently hurting the IT-BPO sector. This will in turn require addressing the regulatory framework in the telecom sector. In particular, competition should be introduced in the fixed-line segment, which is currently dominated by the state provider, and a policy environment should be created that is conducive to FDI and technology flows in this sector. The associated benefits of lower connection costs, more reliable connectivity, increased investment in capacity, and ability to provide value-added services would generate spin-off benefits for the IT-BPO sector in the medium term.

Given the intense competition from other LMICs, it will be important to identify niche segments within the IT-BPO sector where Bangladesh can compete on low costs combined with quality. Some possibilities are in animation, transcription, legal process outsourcing, and engineering design outsourcing, as well as software solutions for specific segments, such as banking, insurance, and travel. The government and the industry will need to examine the emerging trends in this business worldwide, gauge demand and existing competition, and accordingly decide on where Bangladesh could position itself. There is a need to diversify into higher-value services and untapped markets in the Asia-Pacific region. Such a targeted strategy will need to be supported by government and industry initiatives for skill development and training and possible collaboration with trade associations in successful countries, such as India and the Philippines. Another target could be to capitalize on the segments where Indian companies are losing their competitive advantage because of rising labor costs in the tier-I Indian cities. Bangladesh could either directly try to attract this business onshore or encourage the setting up of near-shore services in the country as the backend for Indian IT and BPO firms, which are looking to lower costs and outsource (as Sri Lanka has done to some extent). Bangladesh could benefit from its geographic proximity to India and the fact that several Indian companies and IT training institutes are already present in the country.

The government needs to learn from the experience of other countries, such as the Philippines and India. It should provide special zones and corridors for the IT-BPO industry in the country where tax and subsidy incentives are granted to promote new IT-BPO establishments and facilitate exports. Such incentives and the provision of better infrastructure (including telecom bandwidth, real estate, and power) can help lower costs and enable scale economies for Bangladeshi firms.

The government, in collaboration with the industry association and leading firms, will need to invest in brand building and marketing Bangladesh as a quality provider of IT and BPO services. This will require delegations to other countries to showcase capabilities, engagement with overseas industry bodies in this sector, discussions with chambers of commerce of other countries through embassies and consulates, and leveraging the Bangladeshi diaspora in the United Kingdom and the United States.

In addition to initiatives on the domestic front, the discussions and an examination of the secondary evidence suggest the need for a strategic approach on the external front to promote Bangladesh's market access interests and improve its domestic capacity and build its brand. This can be achieved through bilateral discussions between the government of Bangladesh and the governments of target countries and through dialogue between industry associations and representatives in Bangladesh and their counterparts in other countries. Such incremental, confidence-building steps probably can pave the way for future discussions on the LDC services waiver, given the many uncertainties and complexities involved in implementing this waiver. Bangladesh's main interest in the IT-BPO sector would be with respect to mode 4 and visa facilitation, as they are most relevant for exports of IT-BPO services. There is, however, little that Bangladesh can specifically achieve on mode 4 issues, at least in the short run, through the services waiver. For example, a carve-out for Bangladeshi service providers under the waiver would not be practical and would not be accepted by partner countries like the United States. Hence, instead of the services waiver route, Bangladesh must follow a more realistic step-by-step approach that does not focus on preferences.

In particular, Bangladesh should negotiate for greater transparency in application of visa qualifying provisions such as economic needs tests, wage parity requirements, and prior work experience. These often affect the entry of LMIC and LDC IT service providers in other markets. In addition, it could try to negotiate for fast tracking of visas for business visitors and intra-corporate transferees going from Bangladesh to provide services—subject, for instance, to the company's meeting certain mutually agreed conditions (such as turnover, track record, contract value, and so forth). Such an approach has been argued in earlier papers on mode 4 strategies. It would not require granting any preferential access, but only streamlining administrative rules and procedures to facilitate entry, and would focus on select categories of service providers that host countries would be more willing to permit entry.

Intergovernmental and industry dialogue would be needed to highlight the benefits of facilitating mobility in the sector. The government of Bangladesh should interact with local industry to identify the specific entry conditions that are imposing a burden on the country's IT-BPO service providers. At the same time, Bangladesh should complement these efforts with improvements in its institutional capacity to govern labor flows, including ensuring temporariness and cooperating with other governments in case of violations and misuse of more liberal or facilitative provisions on labor mobility. By demonstrating its regulatory capacity in mode 4, Bangladesh will build confidence among its partner countries and then as a next step move toward special and differential treatment through the services waiver.

In the context of mode 1 exports like BPO, the government could seek, under the LDC services waiver, relaxation of conditions such as commercial presence requirements that are often tied to mode 1 commitments. Realistically, however, it is unlikely that there would be much benefit from such a relaxation of conditions if this waiver is extended to many other LDCs. An interesting possibility to consider in seeking a preferential waiver might be for the government to strategize on its own commitments, in services or in other areas of the WTO. For example, the waiver of commercial presence requirements for mode 1 exports of IT-BPO services could be linked to commitments by Bangladesh in areas such as telecommunications, technology imports, and technical assistance–related services. These commitments could be structured primarily to benefit Bangladesh's main partner countries for IT-BPO services exports (as its own commitments would need to be granted on an MFN basis).

Mode 4 access for IT services providers could be pursued outside the WTO through bilateral labor agreements and under comprehensive trade or partnership agreements, which would cover labor mobility at least for selected sectors or occupations or skill categories. But again, these initiatives must be seen as incremental, confidence-building steps toward realizing a longer-term objective of a preferential services waiver under GATS. Bangladesh could strategically target certain countries under these bilateral agreements, for instance Southeast Asian countries such as Japan, Malaysia, the Republic of Korea, and Singapore. Some of these countries have signed comprehensive agreements with India and could be open to similar agreements or addressing a subset of services-related issues with other LMICs in the region, including Bangladesh. Bangladesh has existing bilateral labor agreements with some of these nations. Finally, Southeast Asian countries may see a need to diversify to new export markets to beat competition and the growth prospects in the Asia-Pacific region.

Overall, even if the services waiver cannot be operationalized right away, Bangladesh should pursue a step-by-step approach. It should discuss relevant market access barriers with its main trading partners for IT-BPO services and, in parallel, pursue bilateral initiatives for facilitating labor mobility, technology transfer, and capacity building. At the same time, Bangladesh should improve its institutional capacity to govern labor flows, ideally in cooperation with its main trading partners, to show commitment and instill confidence in its efforts. Bangladesh should try to commit in areas where its partners would see benefits and would thus be willing to consider granting more favorable terms to Bangladeshi service providers. But realistically, no immediate benefits are likely from the services waiver and this can only be a slow process.

Strategies for Mode 4 and Nursing Services

The chapter has identified several challenges affecting Bangladesh's labor exports in skilled and less-skilled occupations. Therefore, there is a need for a coherent and more strategic approach to promoting labor services exports, along with a focus on target markets and occupations.[15] There is a need to integrate migration and labor export policy into Bangladesh's national development plans and employment policies. The strategy in the context of mode 4, including for nursing services, has to be twofold. First, the focus should be on skill building and capacity building for meeting domestic as well as overseas demand, given the predominant view that the prospects for exports in this sector are primarily affected by domestic capacity and quality-related constraints. Second, there should be a focus on negotiating with other governments, multilaterally and bilaterally. These negotiations should aim to remove market access barriers, to develop institutional arrangements and coordination mechanisms with other governments to protect the interests of Bangladeshi service providers, and to manage the movement of service providers. Some of the elements that would need to comprise these two focus areas are described in the following sections.

Steps to Promote Mode 4 Exports

Capacity building will be essential for promoting mode 4 exports. This will require preparing the workforce for the overseas employment process, providing skill development and training to meet the demands of overseas employers, and accrediting training institutions to improve training standards.

Another important element is to strengthen institutional and regulatory capacity so as to improve the management of the migration process internally; to coordinate with destination country governments to address issues of worker welfare and rights, repatriation, and recruitment; and to effectively monitor the demand for labor in overseas markets so that targeted strategies can be devised for specific markets. These steps will require institutional reorganization and coordination among concerned institutions and ministries in the country. Building institutional capacity to ensure the temporariness of labor flows to other countries would be essential to provide confidence to partner countries.

As for its negotiating strategy, Bangladesh could aim at sector- or occupation-specific agreements in a few select areas where there is a shortage overseas and where Bangladesh can supply capacity. At the least, issues such as necessity tests, transparency in the application of entry norms and conditions, and relaxation of burdensome requirements could be pursued. In some occupations, a more ambitious approach would be to seek quota-based access to specific sectors or occupations under bilateral labor agreements, subject to the capacity-building and institutional issues being addressed to manage labor flows.

It will be important for Bangladesh unilaterally to facilitate the inward movement of business visitors and incorporate transferees. This should not only reflect the interests of its own businesses, but should strategically demonstrate the country's willingness to liberalize to strengthen its position in market access–related discussions.

Bangladesh could seek the privilege of discussing a mutual recognition agreement using the services waiver. It could seek this privilege on the basis of the recognition provision under GATS, wherein countries are encouraged to extend their mutual recognition agreements to third countries and to provide third countries with an opportunity to enter into negotiations.

Steps to Promote Nursing Services Exports

For nursing services, domestic and international strategies need to be given priority.

Capacity building will be needed to promote skilled nurse migration from the country as the domestic shortage of nurses is a major constraint. For this purpose, the government should ease conditions that reduce the scope for private sector participation in nursing education. Updated training curricula and quality of teaching should be given emphasis. Nurses should be allowed from all educational disciplines instead of being limited to a science background for enrollment in the BSc nursing program. To ensure knowledge in necessary science courses, students with a nonscience background could be required to undertake a pre-course in those subjects to bridge the gap.

The government could focus on high-value, skilled nurses for export by encouraging the establishment of international standard nursing colleges in partnership with Western nursing institutes and by encouraging private universities to set up international standard nursing institutes. This would not only augment the supply of nurses for the export market, but also would raise overall quality and standards in the domestic market. The government could learn from other countries, such as the Philippines, which has had proactive policies to send nurses abroad and has built a reputation in the global market as a supplier of nurses.

Given the high demand for nurses in many of the target markets (including Japan, Korea, the United Kingdom, and West Asia), Bangladesh could explore the scope for negotiating preferential market access in the form of a limited quota for its nurses in selected countries. The quota given by Japan to Filipino nurses under the Philippines-Japan Economic Partnership Agreement could serve as a reference, although it may not be realistic to expect Bangladesh to enter into a comprehensive agreement with Japan along the lines of the Philippines agreement. A sector-specific agreement that caters to select skill sets in the health care profession, in particular nursing, could be considered.

As a future step, Bangladesh could then seek to obtain similar commitments multilaterally under the services waiver.

There is a need to discuss bilaterally with other countries issues such as the equivalence of qualifications and to sign mutual recognition agreements. Bangladesh (along with six other countries) has already signed an agreement with Malaysia that allows its nurses to practice there, subject to obtaining a Temporary Practicing Certificate from the Nursing Board of Malaysia and meeting certain minimum requirements.

The government could also facilitate access to its own health sector in areas such as the entry of researchers, educators, and institutions to improve standards of training and transfer of knowledge and to build domestic capacity in nursing. Unilateral measures to grant access to its own market can help it to pursue its own market access interests in future discussions.

Concluding Thoughts

As the outlined elements of the strategies across the selected services and modes suggest, the government needs to adopt a multipronged approach to promoting services exports. It must first and foremost address capacity constraints, skill and human resource inadequacies, and regulatory issues in the domestic market. On the external front, Bangladesh should take a step-by-step approach by first initiating dialogue with other governments. It should enter into greater exchange of views with industry associations and representatives to facilitate an appreciation of the external barriers faced by Bangladeshi providers in selected sectors and modes of interest. Once such discussions create trust, then the more difficult issues can be addressed and the LDC services waiver route could be considered. Without a gradual buy-in from key partner countries through bilateral dialogue and confidence-building measures, operationalization of a services waiver does not seem feasible.

Central to this process will be the identification of relevant services, markets, and issues. As is evident from the discussion of Bangladesh's service sector competitiveness, there are only a few areas or occupations that Bangladesh can target. These are mostly labor-intensive services, some professional such as IT-BPO and engineering, some semiskilled such as nursing, and some low-skilled such as construction. The target markets could include existing markets such as the United States, the United Kingdom, and some of the West Asian countries, but a more strategic approach would aim to diversify target markets and thus include emerging ones where opportunities are yet to be realized and where competition may be less intense. The latter could include markets in Southeast Asia and the Asia-Pacific region. To identify these services and markets, discussions with domestic industry and stakeholders will be essential. The difficulty, however, will be to identify issues that are specific to Bangladesh and that cannot be easily extended to other LDCs or, even if extended, would not really undermine any preferences gained by Bangladesh. An examination of the primary and secondary evidence does not indicate any such special areas or issues.

This is evident from the predominant view that domestic reforms and supply-side issues hold the key to improving prospects for services exports and the failure of the stakeholders to provide any concrete areas where the services waiver could be leveraged. In this regard, it may be useful to continue with many of the earlier proposals that were included in the LDC communication on mode 4. One such proposal is for a more transparent and streamlined regulatory setup for mode 4, with reduced scope for application of potentially discriminatory measures such as economic needs tests and burdensome licensing procedures. This would bring benefits to Bangladesh. Although these benefits may not accrue exclusively to Bangladesh, the same will likely be the case with any LDC services waiver. These existing proposals on mode 4 could provide the momentum and direction for further discussions pertaining to a services waiver, where many issues still remain to be clarified and the approach is not yet certain.

Overall, the analysis in this chapter suggests that the LDC services waiver, while attractive in theory, may not yield much in practice to an LDC such as Bangladesh. This is because Bangladesh cannot necessarily differentiate itself, as its sources of comparative advantage and the challenges it faces in the service sector are common to many other LDCs. Moreover, a major institutional challenge in effecting this waiver will be the lack of institutional and negotiating capacity. As the discussion has highlighted, much will depend on strategic negotiations with selected countries. However, this latter process itself will require capacity building, something that is lacking in LDCs like Bangladesh. Hence, if a beginning is to be made, then the Bangladeshi government must first understand the services waiver better, as there is little awareness or understanding of this proposal at present. The overseas missions should discuss with the selected governments and industry bodies to gauge the latter's views on the potential opportunities created by the services waiver, how this waiver could be implemented, and whether Bangladesh can obtain any meaningful preferences through the waiver.

Another important point emerges from the analysis. There are inherent challenges in the existing multilateral framework in the granting of preferential treatment by a high-income country to an LDC. This is especially true of services, where there are many behind-the-border barriers and regulatory issues are paramount, making preferences more difficult to maintain compared with the case of goods trade. Hence, the systemic implication of this waiver is that although it is apparently voluntary in nature, it is unlikely to work as a one-way concession that would be granted by high-income countries to LDCs. There is bound to be some implicit quid pro quo in this process and LMICs will need to negotiate to exercise this option. Therefore, beyond identifying sectors and markets where the waiver could be pursued, it will be equally important for Bangladesh to identify what it could unilaterally commit that is also in line with its own long-term interests. The discussions with other governments must thus also be used to gauge what kinds of unilateral and other initiatives Bangladesh may be expected to undertake to instill confidence in its trading partners and be able to obtain better terms and conditions for its service providers.

Annex 8A: Services in Bangladesh's Economy: Trends and Key Features

Services Output and Employment

The service sector has grown in importance in Bangladesh's economy over the past three decades. From a value of US$9.5 billion in 1980 (including construction services), the service economy in Bangladesh more than tripled in size in real terms (2005 constant prices) to US$33.6 billion in 2005 and stood at US$46.1 billion in 2010. It was three times the size of the agricultural sector and 1.5 times the size of the secondary sector in 2010.[16] Table 8A.1 highlights the relative sizes of the three sectors over the 1980–2010 period and the growing role of the service economy in Bangladesh.

Although the secondary sector has in general posted the highest growth rates, over the past two decades, services have exhibited the most steady and consistent upward growth trend relative to the other sectors. As shown in figure 8A.1, services have grown consistently in the range of 4–6 percent year-on-year in this period, in contrast to industry and agriculture, which have shown much more volatility. Table 8A.2 further highlights the steady increase in the average growth

Table 8A.1 Trends in Bangladesh's GDP and Sector Composition, 1980–2010
US$, millions

Total GDP	**20,712.16**	**30,201.62**	**38,007.27**	**49,054.23**	**64,418.63**	**88,924.11**
Agriculture	5,705.7	7,250.0	7,760.6	9,843.9	11,134.3	13,815.0
Industry	5,509.2	7,444.9	10,760.8	14,079.9	19,671.3	29,025.7
Services	9,497.3	15,506.7	19,485.9	25,130.4	33,613.1	46,083.4

Source: UN Least-Developed Countries Services Waiver and Market Access for Services Exports from Bangladesh: Opportunities and Challenges, org/unsd/snaama/dnlList.asp.
Note: GDP = gross domestic product.

Figure 8A.1 Annual Growth Rate, by Sector, Bangladesh, 1991–2010
constant 2005 prices, percent

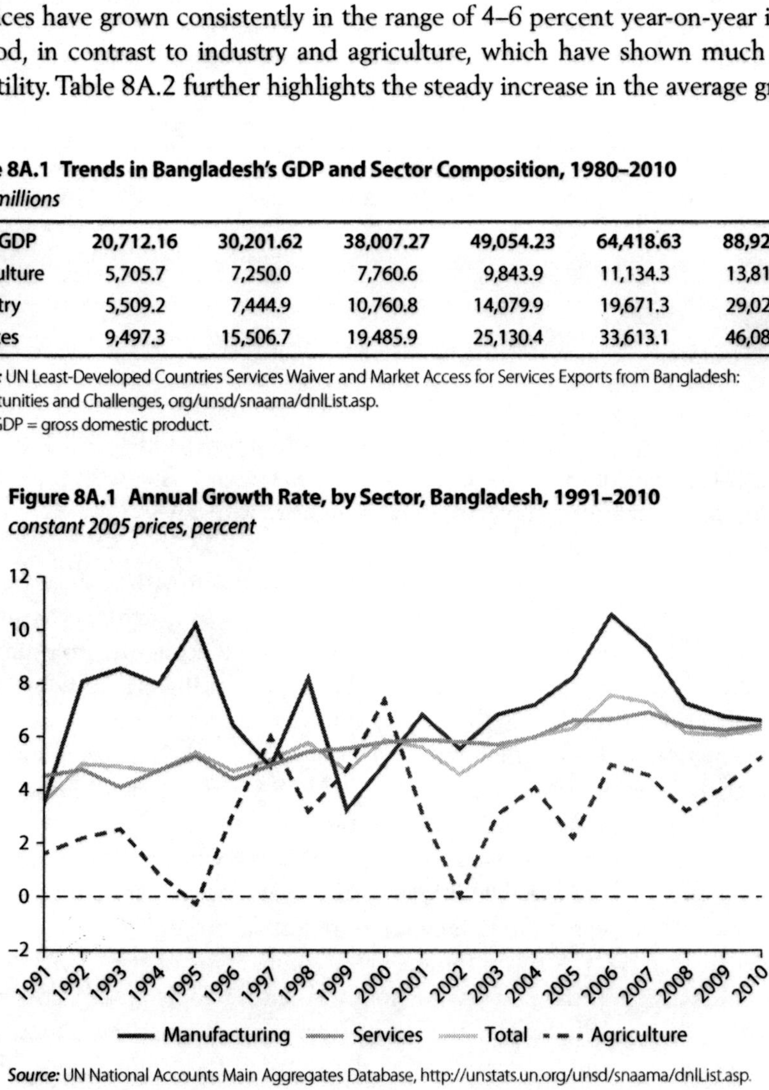

Source: UN National Accounts Main Aggregates Database, http://unstats.un.org/unsd/snaama/dnlList.asp.

Table 8A.2 Average Annual Growth Rate, by Sector, Bangladesh, Selected Years
percent

Years	*Total*	*Agriculture*	*Manufacturing*	*Services*
Average annual growth rate				
1995–2000	5.3	4.0	6.3	5.2
2001–05	5.6	2.5	6.9	6.0
2006–10	6.7	4.4	8.1	6.5
CAGR				
1981–90	4.1	2.2	3.8	5.2
1991–2000	5.1	3.3	6.9	5.0
2001–10	6.2	3.5	7.6	6.3

Source: UN National Accounts Main Aggregates Database, http://unstats.un.org/unsd/snaama/dnlList.asp.
Note: CAGR = compound annual growth rate.

Table 8A.3 Sector Share in GDP, Bangladesh, Selected Years
percent

Sector	*1980*	*1990*	*1995*	*2000*	*2005*	*2010*
Total GDP	100	100	100	100	100	100
Agriculture	27.5	24.0	20.4	20.1	17.3	15.5
Manufacturing	26.6	24.7	28.3	28.7	30.5	32.6
Services	45.9	51.3	51.3	51.2	52.2	51.8

Source: UN National Accounts Main Aggregates Database, http://unstats.un.org/unsd/snaama/dnlList.asp.
Note: GDP = gross domestic product.

rate of services from 5.2 percent in 1995–2000 to 6.0 percent in 2001–05 and further to 6.5 percent in 2006–10. The sector has grown in line with the overall economy, as indicated by the compound annual growth rates (CAGRs) during these years.

Hence, the service sector has broadly mirrored overall growth in the economy and has helped promote economic stability, given its consistent performance. The share of the service sector has also grown in the economy, from around 46 percent of GDP in 1980 to a little over 50 percent of the economy by 2010, along with a similar increase in the share of the secondary sector in the economy. Higher growth rates for industry and services have led to their growing shares in the Bangladeshi economy, as illustrated in table 8A.3. Services, including construction, accounted for over 50 percent of the economy in the past two decades and had a share of almost 60 percent of GDP in 2010 (while the share of industry has also grown from less than 30 percent to nearly 40 percent in this period, with manufacturing constituting the bulk of industrial output).

Table 8A.4 shows the subsector shares of components of the service sector and their CAGRs over the past few decades. The most significant service subsectors in output are distribution; transport, storage, and communications; construction; and community, social, and personal services within other activities.

Table 8A.4 Trends in Subsector Services Output, Bangladesh, 1980–2010
percent

Year	*Construction (ISIC F) as % of GDP*	*Wholesale, retail trade, restaurants, and hotels (ISIC G–H) as % of GDP*	*Transport, storage, and communications (ISIC I) as % of GDP*	*Other activities (ISIC J–P) as % of GDP*
1980	3.236	12.495	7.981	22.142
1990	4.735	11.660	8.800	26.149
1995	5.212	11.749	8.442	25.866
2000	6.158	12.170	8.615	24.287
2005	7.013	12.739	9.240	23.187
2010	6.972	12.807	9.859	22.184
CAGR				
1981–90	6.62	3.78	5.16	5.61
1991–2000	8.13	5.58	4.93	4.08
2001–10	7.32	6.69	7.53	5.29

Source: UN National Accounts Main Aggregates Database, http://unstats.un.org/unsd/snaama/dnlList.asp.
Note: CAGR = compound annual growth rate; GDP = gross domestic product; ISIC = International Standard Industrial Classification.

Table 8A.5 Share of Employment and Labor Force by Occupation and Sector, 1999–2009
percent

Item	*Agriculture*	*Industry*	*Services*
Employment share			
1999	59.5	15.4	25.1
2007	53.5	18.9	27.6
2008	53.5	18.9	27.6
2009	53.5	18.9	27.6
Labor force by occupation			
2000	62.1	10.3	27.6
2005	48.1	14.5	37.4
2008	45.0	30.0	25.0

Sources: ILO 2008. For 2000 and 2005, figures for labor force by occupation: United Nations, A World of Information, http://data.un.org/CountryProfile.aspx?crName=Bangladesh. For 2008, figures for labor force by occupation: Central Intelligence Agency, World Factbook, https://www.cia.gov/library/publications/the-world-factbook.

These subsector trends in services output reflect the importance of a variety of factors in shaping service sector performance in Bangladesh. These factors include deregulation and policy reforms in areas such as telecommunications, the role of rising incomes, and domestic demand in driving growth in segments such as trade and distribution services or community personal and social services.

However, although services have grown in importance in domestic output, their contribution to employment has not been as rapid in Bangladesh (as is also true for the South Asian region at large). The share of services in total employment stood at less than 30 percent in 2009 compared with over 50 percent in agriculture, notwithstanding the latter's declining share of output (table 8A.5).

Table 8A.6 Disaggregation of Service Employment, by Sector, Bangladesh
percent

Sector	*Percent*
Electricity, gas, and water	0.61
Construction	6.71
Wholesale and retail trade	(...)
Hotels and restaurants	47.56
Transport, storage, and communications	24.39
Financial intermediation	4.27
Real estate and associated activities	31.10
Public administration, defense, and compulsory social security	15.85
Education	(...)
Health and social work	(...)
Other community and personal services	15.85

Sources: Labor surveys and Census of Bangladesh, 2005–06 survey data.
Note: ... = negligible.

The employment trends reveal that services have exhibited low employment elasticity in Bangladesh (as is also true for the rest of South Asia).[17] According to Basu and Maertens (2009), the employment elasticity of services with respect to output has been lower than that in industry and agriculture and has declined over the past few decades. Hence, employment absorption in services has not kept pace with the rate of growth of output. Disaggregated information for employment elasticity in individual services as provided by Basu and Maertens (2009) also confirms this fact. The subsector distribution of services employment presented in table 8A.6 shows that segments such as hotels and restaurants trade and distribution; transport, storage, and communications; and real estate account for the bulk of service sector employment in Bangladesh. Given the proprietary and small-scale sector nature of many of the latter services, the employment data suggest that a large part of services employment may be informal.

Services Trade

Exports

Bangladesh's services exports trebled over the past decade, from a little more than US$800 million in 2000 to around US$2.4 billion in 2010.[18] As highlighted in table 8A.7, the contribution of traditional services, such as transport and travel, declined over the decade from around 50 percent to about 20 percent of total services exports, while that of other services, in particular, communications, other business services, and to some extent computer and information services, grew over this period. In value terms, other business services constitute the largest segment in other services and grew almost sixfold in value and increased their share in total services exports by around 33 percent between 2000 and 2010. Likewise, communications services grew more than tenfold in value terms over this period and significantly increased their contribution to total services exports.

Table 8A.7 Value and Share of Exports of Service Subsectors, Bangladesh, Selected Years
US$, millions, and percent

	2000		2005		2010		
Sector	*Value (US$, millions)*	*Share (%)*	*Value (US$, millions)*	*Share (%)*	*Value (US$, millions)*	*Share (%)*	*Rank*
Commercial services	283.192	100.00	474.21	100.00	1,209.41	100.00	107
Transport	91.368	32.26	113.009	23.83	173.591	14.35	118
Travel	50.421	17.80	70.009	14.76	81.221	6.72	158
Other commercial services	141.403	49.93	291.192	61.41	954.598	78.93	72
Communications	21.532	7.60	23.906	5.04	277.67	22.96	
Construction	0.194	0.07	14.156	2.99	6.909	0.57	
Insurance	3.513	1.24	5.027	1.06	6.841	0.57	
Financial services	13.083	4.62	17.972	3.79	40.841	3.38	
Computer and information	3.243	1.15	18.713	3.95	37.756	3.12	
Royalties and license fees	0.058	0.02	0.261	0.06	0.517	0.04	
Other business services	99.253	35.05	210.013	44.29	582.147	48.13	
Personal, cultural, and recreational services	0.527	0.19	1.144	0.24	1.925	0.16	

Source: UNCTADSTAT database, http://unctadstat.unctad.org/ReportFolders/reportFolders.aspx?sCS_referer= &sCS_ChosenLang=en.
Note: The shares in the table were calculated after excluding "Government services not included elsewhere."

Thus, the service export data for the past decade suggest that Bangladesh is increasingly moving toward new services and indicate the role of two main factors, liberalization (albeit partial) of subsectors such as information and communication services and business services over the past decade or so and the country's comparative advantage in labor-based services. The growth in communications services exports reflects the impact of liberalization and deregulation of services such as telecommunications, while the growth in other business services, comprising of segments such as engineering, consulting, and other professional services, reflects Bangladesh's large pool of labor and the growing opportunities in emerging services to export skill-intensive and professional services.

Two features are noteworthy about Bangladesh's exports of services. First is the low growth in tourism services exports and the country's poor ranking in this segment. This feature is suggestive of constraints related to infrastructure and connectivity, as well as possible lack of focus on developing this sector for exports. Second is the low value of computer and information services exports (although growth has been high because of the low base value), which is striking given the growing demand for software services in the global market and the emergence of other LDC exporters of computer services. This feature is suggestive of the fact that Bangladesh, notwithstanding its potential in labor-based and skill-intensive business services, may not have been able to leverage its potential fully in this segment and could be facing competition from other low-cost LDC exporters of IT and IT-enabled services.

Imports

Bangladesh's services imports registered a considerable increase over the past decade, from US$1.6 billion in 2000 to US$4.4 billion in 2010. In contrast to the case of its services exports, however, the share of traditional services, such as transport, actually increased, more than tripling from US$1 billion in 2000 to US$3.4 billion in 2010. The share of transport services in total services imports increased from 66 percent to over 80 percent over this period.[19] This growing dependence on imports of transport services in part reflects the demand from the ready-made garment sector and Bangladesh's reliance on foreign transport carriers, given its capacity constraints in transport and logistics (as highlighted by many experts and in many reports). There has been a more than trebling of imports of other business services in value terms, reflecting the growing importance of these supporting services to the economy. However, in value and share, transport services dwarf all other segments.

Overall Trade Orientation and Competitiveness

Combining the service export and import trends, it is evident that Bangladesh has had a persistent overall trade deficit in services, which has grown from around US$800 million to nearly US$2 billion in the past decade (tables 8A.7 and 8A.8). This deficit is concentrated in traditional services, such as transport and travel, whereas there has been a positive trade balance in other commercial services, on account of emerging segments such as communications and other business services. In global rankings, Bangladesh features below the top 100 countries as a service exporter, although its rank is slightly higher in the case of "other commercial services" exports, owing to the category of other business services. Bangladesh ranks among the top 100 service importing countries, reflecting its higher import as opposed to export orientation in services, but this is primarily on account of its import dependence in transport services. Figure 8A.2 illustrates the trends in the services trade balance at the aggregate and subsector levels.

These service trade figures highlight two important points. First, Bangladesh is potentially more competitive in nontraditional services that rely on information and communications technology and the availability of abundant and low-cost labor, and in services that have been liberalized (although the potential in computer and information services appears to be unrealized to date). Second, at present Bangladesh may not be competitive in traditional services such as transport and travel, where infrastructure availability and supply capacity are critical for delivery and where there is need for further liberalization and policy reforms or for greater policy thrust to promote exports (as has been argued in various studies of the country's infrastructure and logistics services sectors).

Table 8A.8 Value and Share of Imports for Service Subsectors in Bangladesh, Selected Years
US$, millions, and percent

	2000		*2005*		*2010*		
Sector	*Value (US$, millions)*	*Share (%)*	*Value (US$, millions)*	*Share (%)*	*Value (US$, millions)*	*Share (%)*	*Rank*
Commercial services	1,523.35	100.00	2,011.36	100.00	4,128.30	100.00	71
Transport	1,012.76	66.48	1,544.73	76.80	3,440.64	83.34	51
Travel	289.91	19.03	136.27	6.77	260.60	6.31	109
Other commercial services	220.68	14.49	330.36	16.42	427.06	10.34	109
Communications	7.39	0.48	20.62	1.03	20.23	0.49	
Construction	2.15	0.14	1.07	0.05	6.29	0.15	
Insurance	91.07	5.98	150.65	7.49	26.32	0.64	
Financial services	30.75	2.02	13.27	0.66	45.35	1.10	
Computer and information	1.52	0.10	4.26	0.21	5.42	0.13	
Royalties and license fees	4.42	0.29	2.75	0.14	17.64	0.43	
Other business services	83.29	5.47	137.72	6.85	305.70	7.40	
Personal, cultural, and recreational services	0.10	0.01	0.03	0.00	0.13	0.00	

Source: UNCTADSTAT database, http://unctadstat.unctad.org/ReportFolders/reportFolders.aspx?sCS_referer=&sCS_ChosenLang=en.
Note: The shares in the table were calculated after excluding "Government services not included elsewhere."

Figure 8A.2 Trade Balance in Services, Bangladesh, Selected Years
US$, millions

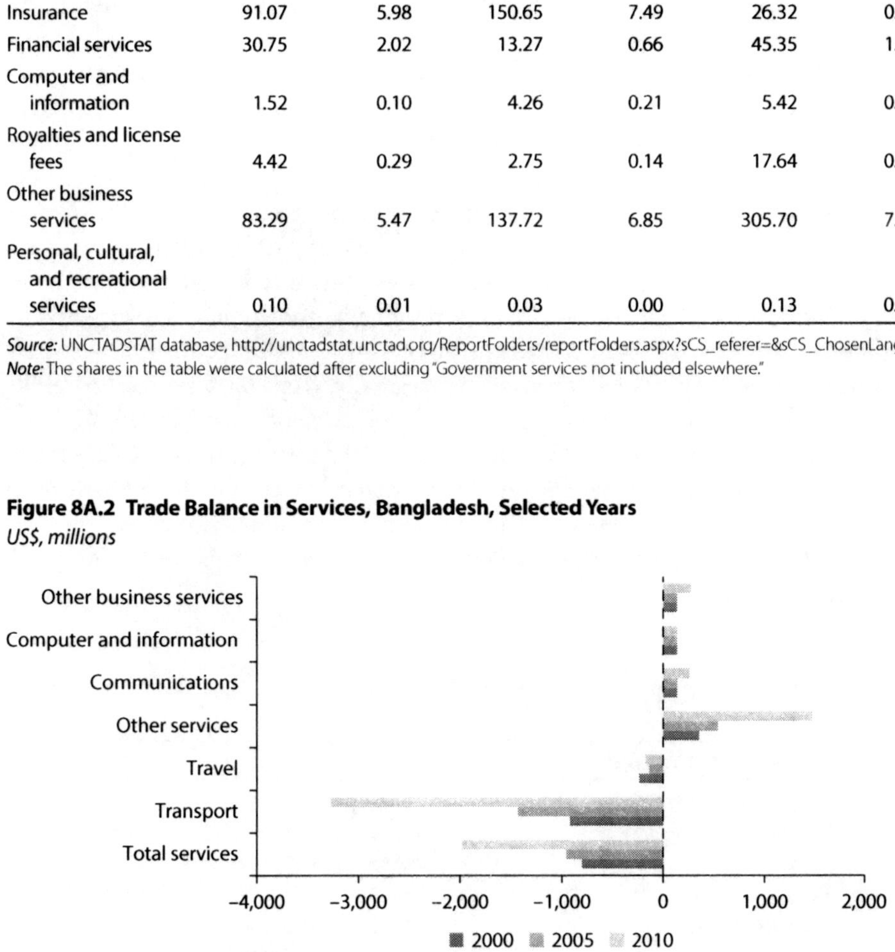

Source: Calculations based on UNCTADSTAT database, http://unctadstat.unctad.org/ReportFolders/reportFolders.aspx?sCS_referer=&sCS_ChosenLang=en.

The growth trends in the various segments of services similarly confirm the growing and likely potential of some emerging services in the future.

The revealed comparative advantage (RCA) indexes for Bangladesh's services exports similarly highlight that the country is relatively competitive in communications and other business services, with RCAs of 1 or more, while the RCAs for transport and travel services have consistently been less than 1 and have declined over the past few years. Placing the RCA values against the growth trends and shifts in composition of the services export basket, it appears that Bangladesh's traditional exports are affected by domestic constraints arising from inadequate infrastructure and lack of supportive policies. The decline in the RCA value for computer and information services, notwithstanding the skill-intensive nature of this segment, is noteworthy, especially against the much higher RCAs for other business services and communications services. The decline in computer and information services is indicative of the country's untapped potential in this segment.

Bangladesh's overall RCA for services exports has been less than 1 and stagnant over the past decade, in contrast to its RCA for goods, which has consistently been greater than 1 and has risen slightly over the past decade (table 8A.9). The country has registered higher growth in goods as opposed to services exports over the past two decades. This is reflected at the regional level, where Bangladesh's export performance in goods has been superior to that in services, as highlighted in figure 8A.3. The country's share in world services exports has risen only marginally, from 0.05 percent in 1990 to 0.06 percent in 2010, compared with an increase in its world share of goods exports from 0.05 percent in 1990 to 0.12 percent in 2010. The share of services exports in total exports has remained at around 11 percent over the past decade, lower than that for the other large countries in South Asia, while the share of services imports in total imports has been in the range of 15–18 percent.

Table 8A.9 RCAs in Services, Bangladesh, Selected Years
percent

Total commercial services	*2000*	*2005*	*2010*
Other business services	1.9169	2.3415	1.9037
Communications services	4.1406	4.9121	10.1303
Transportation	0.6545	0.5509	0.6728
Travel	0.5007	0.3342	0.2634
Financial services	0.5516	0.4356	0.4672
Computer and information services	1.1188	0.6385	0.5342
Construction services	1.5859	0.3002	0.2229
Insurance services	0.6064	0.5641	0.2475
Personal, cultural, and recreational services	0.3334	0.1110	0.1111
Royalties and license fees	0.0092	0.0002	0.0066

Source: Calculations based on UNCTADSTAT database, http://unctadstat.unctad.org/ReportFolders/reportFolders.aspx?sCS_referer=&sCS_ChosenLang=en.

Figure 8A.3 RCAs for Goods and Services Exports in Bangladesh and South Asia, Selected Years
percent

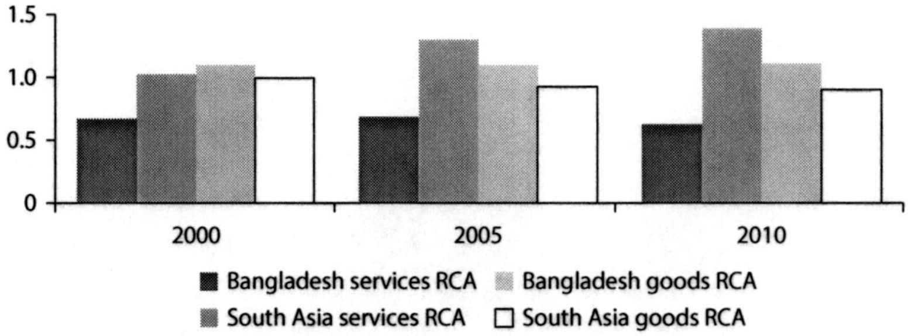

Source: Calculations based on UNCTADSTAT database, http://unctadstat.unctad.org/ReportFolders/reportFolders.aspx?sCS_referer=&sCS_ChosenLang=en.
Note: RCA = revealed comparative advantage.

Exports of Labor Services

Bangladesh, like the rest of South Asia, is an important source of migrant workers and professionals to the rest of the world given its large pool of low-skilled and skilled labor. Data on overseas employment, provided by the Bureau of Manpower, Employment, and Training of Bangladesh, highlight the rising trend in overseas employment of Bangladeshi workers over the past three decades. It increased from around 200,000 workers in 2000 to 800,000 workers in 2008, with female workers constituting about one-sixth of all migrant workers in 2011 (figure 8A.4).[20]

Corresponding to the rise in overseas employment, there has been a huge increase in remittance inflows, from less than US$1 billion in the 1990s to nearly US$2 billion in 2000 and to US$11 billion in 2010 (figure 8A.5). The significance of labor services exports is evident from the high share of remittances in Bangladesh's GDP, rising from a little over 4 percent in 2000 to nearly 14 percent in 2009.[21] Bangladesh ranks among the top 10 remittance recipients in Asia.

These large inflows of remittances have macroeconomic and development implications for Bangladesh's economy. Studies indicate a strong multiplier effect of these remittances on the rural areas of Bangladesh, such as through increased consumption spending and increased investment in health and education relative to nonmigrant families. Another channel is through the establishment of enterprises and small businesses by returnee migrants or their family members, which are generating employment and creating markets for locally produced goods and services.[22] Thus, the management of migration and associated remittances is an important issue for Bangladesh.

The main destination markets are Saudi Arabia; the United Arab Emirates; selected countries in Southeast Asia, such as Malaysia and Singapore; and the United Kingdom and the United States (figures 8A.6 and 8A.7). These constitute the main source countries for remittances. Other markets include Australia,

Figure 8A.4 Number of Bangladeshi Workers in Overseas Employment, 1976–2000

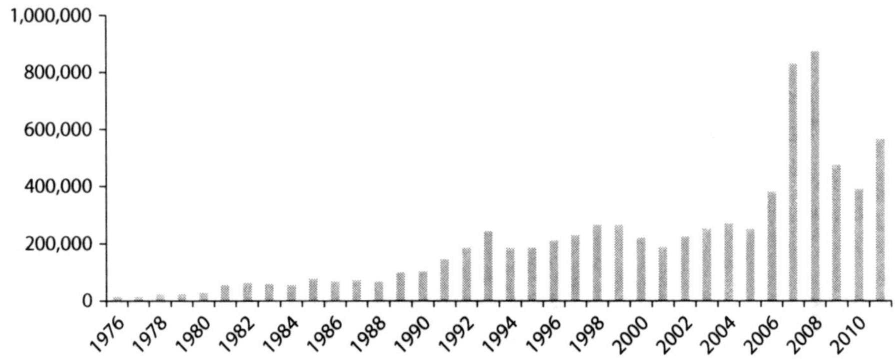

Source: Bureau of Manpower, Employment, and Training, http://www.bmet.org.bd/BMET/statisticalDataAction.

Figure 8A.5 Remittances from Bangladeshi Workers Overseas, 1976–2010
US$, millions

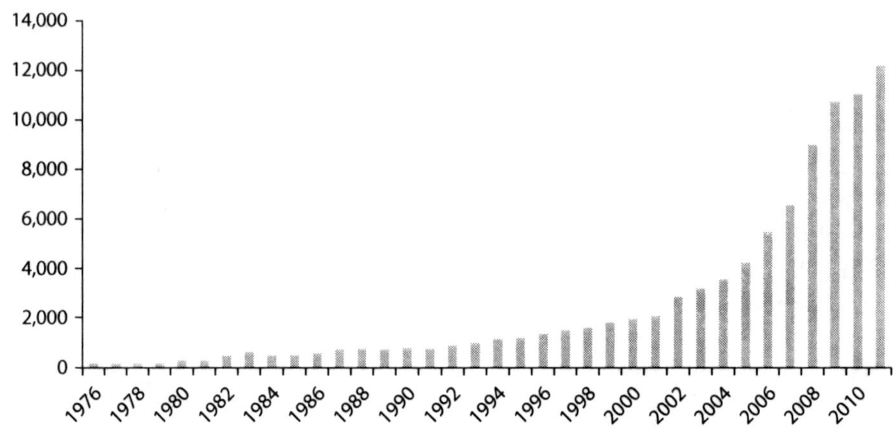

Source: Bureau of Manpower, Employment, and Training, http://www.bmet.org.bd/BMET/statisticalDataAction.

Belgium, Canada, France, Germany, Italy, Japan, the Netherlands, New Zealand, South Africa, Spain, and Switzerland. Saudi Arabia alone accounts for nearly half the total number of Bangladeshi migrant workers.

Bangladesh's mode 4 exports are dominated by low-skilled workers, followed by skilled and semiskilled workers, according to government sources. This movement is mostly in the form of contract labor. Table 8A.10 highlights the skill-wise categorization of Bangladesh's labor exports. The table highlights the declining trend in professional labor exports and the significant rise in low-skilled labor exports, which are mainly in occupations such as domestic work; construction (masonry); transport operations; and manual trades such as carpentry, fabrication, welding, and cleaning.

Figure 8A.6 Overseas Employment in Major Countries, 1976–2010
percent

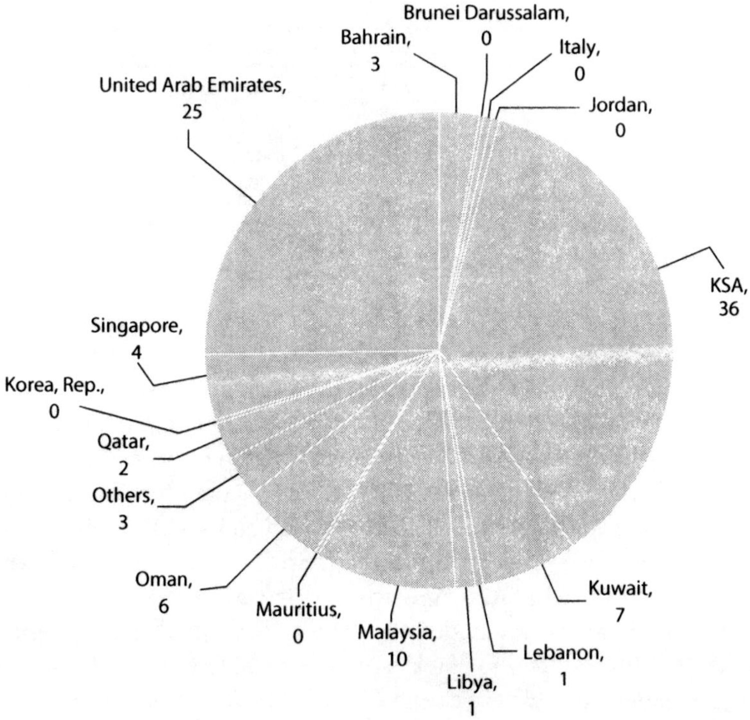

Source: Bureau of Manpower, Employment, and Training, http://www.bmet.org.bd/BMET/statisticalDataAction.

Figure 8A.7 Remittances from Major Countries, 2010
US$, millions

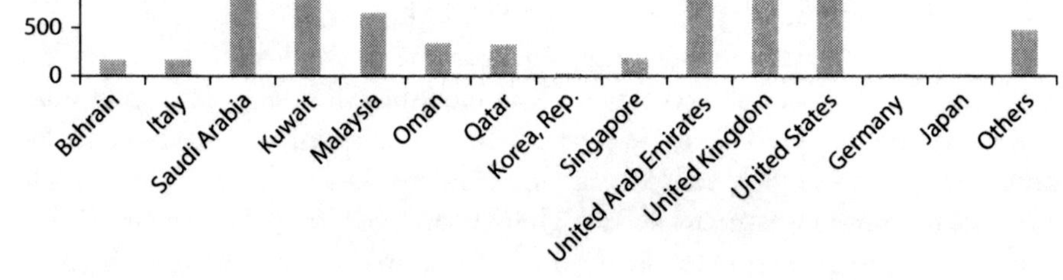

Source: Bureau of Manpower, Employment, and Training, http://www.bmet.org.bd/BMET/statisticalDataAction.

Table 8A.10 Skill-Wise Breakdown of Bangladeshi Overseas Workers, 1990–2011
number of workers

	Category				
Year	*Professional*	*Skilled*	*Semiskilled*	*Low skilled*	*Total*
1990	6,004	35,613	20,792	41,405	103,814
2000	5,940	42,742	30,702	109,581	188,965
2005	1,945	113,655	24,546	112,556	252,702
2011 (up to December)	1,129	229,149	28,729	308,992	568,062

Source: Bureau of Manpower, Employment, and Training, http://www.bmet.org.bd/BMET/statisticalDataAction.

There is also movement of skilled workers from Bangladesh to English-speaking high-income countries, such as Australia, the United Kingdom, and the United States. However, these numbers are small in comparison with the large number of low-skilled workers working worldwide and particularly in the Middle East, and relative to the other larger countries in South Asia. As per the U.S. Department of Homeland Security data for 2009, there were a mere 389 persons engaged on H1 B visas and 46 on L1 visas from Bangladesh, which were even fewer than the number of Sri Lankans working under these categories in the United States. Similarly, in the case of the United Kingdom, the number of applications under the Highly Skilled Migrant Program has been small, at 200 or fewer for most years. Overall, the overseas employment data for Bangladesh suggest the country's comparative advantage in less-skilled labor services exports, the concentration of market access interests in the Middle East at present, possible domestic and external constraints to increasing professional services exports, and the potential to diversify in markets and skill categories.

FDI in Services

The bulk of inward FDI to Bangladesh has been in services. According to the International Trade Centre, FDI in services accounted for over 60 percent of total FDI over the past decade and increased in value from US$370 million in 2000 to around US$900 million in 2008.[23] Figure 8A.8 highlights the significance of the tertiary sector as a destination for FDI inflows, particularly since 2003.

In the service sector, there has been a noticeable increase in FDI inflows to communications and financial services over the past decade, reflecting the FDI liberalization undertaken in these areas. Together, these two segments alone accounted for around 80 percent of total FDI inflows in services (table 8A.11).

Putting the various trends in output, employment, trade, and FDI together, it is evident that Bangladesh is competitive in labor-based services. Its export interests are in mode 4, while its import interests are mainly in capital-intensive producer services such as transport, finance, and insurance, through mode 3. The data on trade and investment flows highlight the scope to grow services exports in new and emerging services; the need to address likely infrastructural, financial, and regulatory constraints in various traditional services whose exports and

Figure 8A.8 Trends in FDI Inflows, by Sector, 2000–09
US$, millions

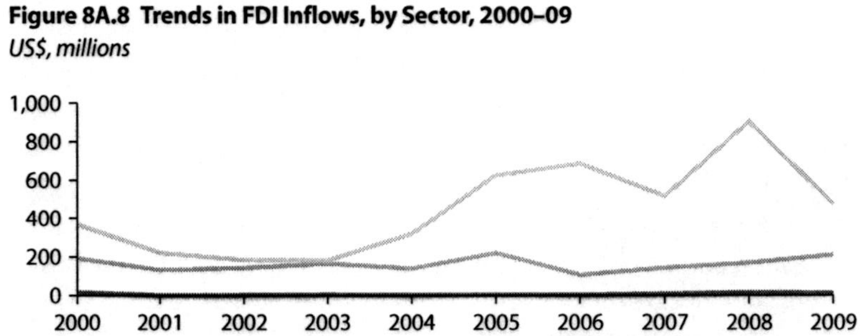

Source: International Trade Centre, Investment Map, http://www.investmentmap.org/prioritySector.aspx.
Note: FDI = foreign direct investment.

Table 8A.11 Value and Share of FDI Inflows in Selected Sectors, Selected Years
US$, millions, and percent

	2000		*2005*		*2009*	
FDI inflows	*Value*	*%*	*Value*	*%*	*Value*	*%*
Total FDI inflows	**578.6**	**100.00**	**845.3**	**100.00**	**700.2**	**100.00**
FDI in nontertiary sector	208.7	36.07	221.7	26.23	223	31.85
FDI in tertiary sector	370	63.95	623.8	73.80	477.1	68.14
Transport, storage, and communications	5.4	0.93	282	33.36	250.1	35.72
Finance	51.5	8.90	130.5	15.44	161.5	23.06
Electricity, gas, and water	301.1	52.04	208.3	24.64	51.2	7.31
Unspecified tertiary	8.9	1.54	3	0.35	11.6	1.66
Business activities	0.2	0.03	0	0.00	1.8	0.26
Construction	—	0.00	—	0.00	0.7	0.10
Wholesale and retail trade	1.7	0.29	—	0.00	0.1	0.01
Health and social services	0.4	0.07	—	0.00	0.1	0.01
Hotels and restaurants	0.8	0.14	—	—	—	—

Source: International Trade Centre, Investment Map, http://www.investmentmap.org/prioritySector.aspx.
Note: FDI = foreign direct investment; — = not available.

competitiveness indicators have declined over the years; and the potential role that FDI in such services could play in enhancing the competitiveness of key producer services with positive spillovers for the rest of the economy.

Based on this discussion of Bangladesh's export interests and strengths in services, the LDC services waiver could potentially yield benefits to Bangladesh in services that are labor intensive and where labor mobility is an important mode of delivery. Hence, services such as IT, construction, health care, and various professional services are potential areas where the services waiver could bring benefits, specifically in the context of modes 1 and 4. At the same time, the discussion suggests that to leverage opportunities in these areas, Bangladesh would need to address various domestic constraints and may need to use the WTO services negotiations and bilateral discussions strategically to address these constraints.

Notes

1. Information on the waiver is provided at http://www.wto.org/english/news_e/sppl_e/sppl223_e.htm; http://ictsd.org/competitiveness/140321/; Klep (2012).
2. Mode 4 is the "presence of natural persons." See http://www.wto.org/english/tratop_e/serv_e/gatsqa_e.htm.
3. http://www.researchandmarkets.com/reports/71491/global_it_services.
4. Bangladesh Association of Software and Information Services (BASIS), http://www.basis.org.bd/ index.php/resource.
5. According to BASIS (http://www.basis.org.bd/index.php/resource), there are more than 500 IT and information technology–enabled services companies registered in Bangladesh, employing more than 12,000 IT professionals. Of these, over 20 percent export their products and services to more than 30 countries and around 6 percent have been set up with foreign capital. Numbers from other sources vary to some extent but are broadly in this range.
6. A Bangladeshi company, Eyeball Technologies, has developed the Blackberry Playbook's Video Chat for Blackberry Messenger for a Canadian company. The company SSD Tech has developed mobile platforms for VAS (value-added system) for international companies. The company Graphic People has been creating promotional material in various languages for Dell. R&D centers have been set up by multinational companies such as Samsung.
7. Bangladesh Association of Software and Information Services, http://www.basis.org.bd/index.php/resource.
8. Software services exports by the Philippines grew from US$423 million in 2007 to nearly US$1 billion in 2011, registering average annual increases of around 30 to 40 percent. See http://www.industryweek.com/global-economy/philippine-software-exports-hit-nearly-1-billion.
9. Much of this discussion is based on IID (2011), Karim (2011), and Stamp (2010).
10. See, for example, a study by the Japan International Cooperation Agency mentioned in BASIS (2010).
11. There are four kinds of nursing education in Bangladesh (Aminuzzaman 2007): (a) bachelor's and master's degrees in nursing; (b) diploma in nursing, (c) diploma in midwifery, and (d) diploma in orthopedic nursing. In 2012, government (38 institutions) and nongovernmental institutions (five institutions) offered nursing education that was affiliated with the Dhaka Medical University (Soomal 2012). The Nursing College, under the University of Dhaka, offers a master's degree in clinical nursing.
12. There was a mass migration of Philippine nurses to the United States in the latter half of the twentieth century. Before the Philippines became independent in 1946, the United States sponsored nurse training there, including the study of English, that was comparable to the work culture and training of nurses in America. The first big wave of nurses from the Philippines came after 1948, as part of the Exchange Visitor Program. This program allowed people from other countries to come to the United States to work and study for two years to learn about American culture. With the cycle of nursing shortages after World War II, the exchange program became a recruiting vehicle for hospitals in the United States and many Filipino nurses were hired through the program. Another big upsurge in migration from the Philippines occurred after 1965, when the U.S. immigration laws—which had favored northern European countries—were changed, allowing more people from the Philippines and Asia

to immigrate. The new law allowed nurses to come to the United States on tourist visas, even without prearranged employment. Entrepreneurs in the Philippines set up more nursing schools to meet the demand and the number of nursing graduates soared. In the 1940s, there were only 17 nursing schools in the Philippines, compared with 170 in 1990 and more than 300 in recent years. (Source: http://www.minoritynurse.com/article/philippine-nurses-us%E2%80%94yesterday-and-today.) There are examples of support from the USAID's Office of American Schools and Hospitals Abroad (ASHA) to the Philippine nursing schools. (Source: http://www.unitedboard.org/Portals/0/Content/ASHA%20grants%20announcement.pdf.)

13. This section is based on Siddiqui (2004) and Siddiqui and Farah (2011).
14. *Dalals* are brokers who act as the middlemen in recruiting and placing migrant workers with overseas employers.
15. Studies have identified several categories of short- and medium-term export interest for Bangladesh. Occupations of short-term interest include nursing and midwifery, secretaries, personal service workers, guards, sales persons, farmers, miners, building finishers, painters, machinery mechanics, metal workers, handicraft workers, printers, food-processing workers, machine operators, domestic helpers, cleaners and launderers, drivers, caretakers, agricultural laborers, and construction workers. Occupations of medium-term interest include managers, physicists, chemists and related professionals, health professionals (other than nursing), teachers and professors, computer professionals, finance and sales associate professionals, metal molders, welders, structural preparers, textile and other product machine operators, and porters.
16. http://unstats.un.org/unsd/snaama/dnlList.asp.
17. Employment elasticity measures the ratio of employment growth to growth in output, where an elasticity of 1 implies that every percentage point of GDP growth is associated with a percentage point of employment growth.
18. http://unctadstat.unctad.org/ReportFolders/reportFolders.aspx?sCS_referer=&sCS_ChosenLang=en.
19. http://unctadstat.unctad.org/ReportFolders/reportFolders.aspx?sCS_referer=&sCS_ChosenLang=en.
20. http://www.bmet.org.bd/BMET/statisticalDataAction.
21. http://www.bmet.org.bd/BMET/statisticalDataAction.
22. Raihan et al. (2009).
23. http://www.investmentmap.org/prioritySector.aspx.

References

Aiken, L. 2007. "U.S. Nurse Labor Market Dynamics Are Key to Global Nursing Sufficiency." *Health Services Research* 42 (3): 1299–1320.

Aminuzamman, S. 2007. "Migration of Skilled Nurses from Bangladesh: An Exploratory Study." Development Research Centre on Migration, Globalisation and Poverty, University of Sussex, Brighton.

BASIS (Bangladesh Association of Software and Information Services). 2010. *Bangladesh Association of Software and Information Service, Annual Report 2010.* Dhaka: BASIS. http://www.basis.org.bd/index.php/resource.

———. 2011. *Software & Service Product Catalog.* Dhaka: BASIS. http://www.basis.org.bd/index.php/resource.

Basu, Kaushik, and Annemie Maertens. 2009. "The Growth of Industry and Services in South Asia and Its Impact on Employment: Analysis and Policy." In *Accelerating Growth and Job Creation in South Asia*, edited by Ejaz Ghani and Sadiq Ahmed, 81–140. New Delhi: World Bank and Oxford University Press.

Carana Corporation. 2011. "Information Technology Enabled Services—Bangladesh." USAID Bangladesh IT Enabled Services Project, Dhaka.

IID (Institute of Informatics and Development). 2011. "Facing the Challenges of Labor Migration from Bangladesh." Policy Brief 4, Dhaka.

ILO (International Labour Organization). 2008. *Global Employment Trends Report*. Geneva. http://www.ilo.org/wcmsp5/groups/public/@dgreports/@dcomm/@publ/documents/publication/wcms_150440.pdf.

Islam, N. 2008. "Migration Scenario: Nature, Patterns and Trends." Bureau of Manpower, Employment, and Training, Dhaka.

ITC (International Trade Centre) and KPMG. 2012. "Bangladesh Beckons: An Emerging Destination for IT-ITeS Outsourcing." ITC and KPMG, Geneva.

Karim, Z. 2011. "Temporary Movement of Natural Persons (TMNP): Prospects and Constraints of Bangladesh." *Canadian International Journal of Business Management* 6 (2).

Kathuria, Sanjay, and Mariem Malouche, eds. 2016. *Strategies to Strengthen Bangladeshi Competitiveness: Thematic Assessment*. Washington, DC: World Bank.

Klep, Maroussia. 2012. "WTO Gives Special Treatment for Service Providers from LDCs." MediaGlobal News, March 16. http://www.mediaglobal.org/2012/03/16/wto-gives-special-treatment-for-service-providers-from-ldcs/.

Mamun, Abdullah. 2012. "Software Exports on a Roll." *The Daily Star*, February 23. http://archive.thedailystar.net/newDesign/news-details.php?nid=223559.

Matsuno, A. 2009. "Nurse Migration: The Asian Perspective." ILO/EU Asian Programme on the Governance of Labour Migration Technical Note, International Labour Organization, Geneva.

PC (Planning Commission of Bangladesh). 2011. "The Sixth Five Year Plan." PC, Dhaka.

Raihan, S., B. H. Khondker, G. Sugiyarto, and S. Jha. 2009. "Remittances and Household Welfare: A Case Study of Bangladesh." ADB Economics Working Paper Series 189, Asian Development Bank, Manila.

Schloemann, H. 2012. "The LDC Services Waiver: Making It Work." *Bridges Africa Review* 1 (4).

Shinkai, N., and M. Hossain. 2011. "Productivity and Performance of IT Sector in Bangladesh: Evidence from Firm Level Data." *Bangladesh Development Studies* 34 (2): 1–22.

Siddiqui, T. 2004. "Decent Work and International Labour Migration from Bangladesh." Presented at National Policy Dialogue: "Globalisation, Decent Work and Poverty Reduction: Policy Alternatives" under the Decent Work Pilot Programme of Bangladesh. Dhaka, Bangladesh.

Siddiqui, T., and M. Appiah. 2008. "Institutional and Regulatory Reforms for Producing Nurses for Overseas Employment." Policy Brief, Refugee and Migratory Movements Research Unit, University of Dhaka, Dhaka.

Siddiqui, T., and M. Farah. 2011. "Facing the Challenges of Labor Migration from Bangladesh." Policy Brief, Refugee and Migratory Movements Research Unit, University of Dhaka, Dhaka.

Soomal, P. K. 2012. "Nursing Education in Bangladesh: Analysis through an Ethnonursing Lens and Critical Social Theory." A project submitted in partial fulfillment of the requirements for the degree of Masters in Nursing in the School of Nursing, Faculty of Human and Social Development, University of Victoria.

South Centre. 2011. "Analysis of Draft Waiver Decision on Services and Services Suppliers of LDCs." Analytical Note, South Centre, Geneva.

Stamp, Maxwell. 2010. "Study on the International Demand for Semi–skilled and Skilled Bangladeshi Workers." Prepared for the TVET Reform Program, Bangladesh.

WTO (World Trade Organization). 2011. *Preferential Treatment to Services and Service Suppliers of Least-Developed Countries*. Report by the Chairman, Ambassador Fernando de Mateo, Geneva. Geneva: WTO.

APPENDIX

Diagnostic Trade Integration Study: Comments by the Ministry of Commerce, Government of Bangladesh

The task of the Diagnostic Trade Integration Study (DTIS) of Bangladesh was assigned to the World Bank by the Government of Bangladesh under the Enhanced Integrated Framework for Trade Related Technical Assistance to Least Developed Countries. This study aims to analyze internal and external constraints and identify future work for further integration of the economy of Bangladesh with the world economy, keeping in view the end goals of job creation and poverty reduction, as well as the enhancement of citizens' welfare. The report seeks to identify gaps in physical and institutional infrastructure as well as future policies in these areas, with a view to consolidating Bangladesh's strengths in existing markets as well as diversifying export products and export markets.

The final version of the DTIS report was submitted by the World Bank in December 2013, a draft of which was presented in a validation workshop with the active participation of relevant stakeholders in Dhaka. The stakeholders from the government and private sectors made valuable comments and suggestions on various issues of the report for further amendment. It was also viewed that in some cases the information and analysis provided in the report did not properly reflect the real scenario of the country. The Ministry of Commerce of the Government of Bangladesh prepared a list of comments and requested the World Bank study team to revise the report, accommodating the concerns of the Ministry. The World Bank team attempted to address some of the concerns of the Ministry and the stakeholders. But many areas of the report remained unchanged and the World Bank expressed its inability to conduct further modification.

The concerns raised by the Ministry of Commerce and the stakeholders in the validation workshop are the following:

1. Market diversification (Pillar 1: Breaking into New Markets, volume 1, chapter 3) is rightly identified as a necessity of the economy of Bangladesh. To this end, the DTIS report suggests only two options to address the issue of market diversification. These are trade facilitation and promotion of economic integration with Asia. There is no doubt that further integration with Bangladesh's two neighbors and leaders of the world economy, China and India, will be beneficial for Bangladesh. However, there is a need to explore other markets, such as markets in Africa, South America, and Western Europe. Moreover, the possibility of using existing trade policy tools, such as regional trade agreements, should be explored. The Closer Economic Partnership Arrangement with major trading partners, including involvement in the Association of Southeast Asian Nations (ASEAN), Regional Civil Society Organization Engagement Mechanism (RCEM), and Trans-Pacific Partnership (TPP), is not addressed in the report. Further, it is not clear why in addressing market diversification issues, such as transit, trade facilitation with India is addressed. Seemingly, these issues are not connected with market diversification.
2. Volume 1, chapter 3, of the report mentions that "[t]ariff escalation appears to be the outcome of pre-budget consultations with producer groups only, without consultation with other stakeholders." But this is not the case. Thorough discussions with the representatives of all the sectors are undertaken in preparing the budget.
3. The study ignores the issue of establishing a deep sea port, which is essential to reduce the transaction/transportation costs of trade.
4. Breaking into New Products (Pillar 2, volume 1, chapter 3) is another important area of the study. The study states that "a large number of quality-related laws and regulations in Bangladesh influences trade and unduly disturbs the free flow of imports." However, the report does not identify those specific laws and regulations. Moreover, it is not clear how those laws and rules impair product diversification. It was viewed that the report requires more analysis of the new products in terms of diversification, market penetration, promotional drives, etc. to guide policy makers to adopt appropriate policies.
5. The Ministry of Commerce earlier suggested to merge Pillar 3 with Pillar 4, and call it "Building a Supportive Environment," and separate "Building Institutions for Trade Policy Coherence and Implementation" as a pillar, which is crucial for achieving overall trade competitiveness as well as economic growth and good economic governance in Bangladesh. The Ministry of Commerce, Export Promotion Bureau, Bangladesh Tariff Commission, Bangladesh Foreign Trade Institute (BFTI), National Board of Revenue, Bangladesh Accreditation Board, Bangladesh Standards and Testing Institution, and other related public sector institutions need to be

strengthened for better service and quality. The development of private sector institutions might also be taken into consideration. Strengthening BFTI to fulfill its mandated role to work as a forum/platform for increased interaction between the government and the private sector is essential for ensuring coherence in formulating and implementing trade related policies. Emphasis may be given to institutional strengthening for attracting more private and foreign investment.

6. In volume 1, chapter 1, the statement "[b]ecause of protection, production is not necessarily competitive: many sectors have high effective rates of protection" appears to be an overstatement and very generalized in nature. The study was required to be more specific.
7. In volume 1, chapter 1, the statement about monetary policy is contradictory.
   (a) The current account surplus and excess foreign reserves means that local money supply should increase, and that should force the interest rate to go down. But in Bangladesh that is not reflected in the interest rate. The reasons for this should be examined.
   (b) The current account surplus also implies less demand for foreign exchange and, as a result, the taka should appreciate and currency appreciation has a clear anti-export bias. In such a scenario, what the government and the monetary authority should do needs to be explained.
   (c) Lower inflation in Bangladesh cannot be attributed to a single monetary phenomenon, because inflation has gone down while local money supply has increased. Thus, under the present scenario, lower inflation could be a supply-side phenomenon.
   (d) The report notes prudent monetary and fiscal policy, but also financial weakness. This seems contradictory.

   There was a need for critical examination of the monetary policy of Bangladesh, which has not been done. Rather, the study has made a contradictory statement.
8. A proper focus could be given to the capacity building of associated departments/organizations of the Ministry of Commerce. For example, BFTI could play a favorable role in ensuring a constant stream of training for Ministry officials on trade and commerce. The Action Matrix should identify the required interventions for the capacity building of BFTI and other relevant organizations (as per their roles).
9. The World Trade Organization (WTO) cell within the Ministry of Commerce is fully responsible for dealing with the activities and various works of the rules-based WTO system. The cell serves as the focal point for formulating Bangladesh's position under the ongoing multilateral negotiations, following up the activities under the WTO Agreements, and taking the necessary actions. Unfortunately, the report provides little attention to the ongoing activities of this cell. The Action Matrix could outline the appropriate interventions required for improving the negotiation skills of the officers of the cell. A similar approach may be considered for other cells/wings of the Ministry of Commerce.

10. As per the terms of reference and concept note of the DTIS, there should be a separate chapter and specific focus on service sector development. However, the portion of the DTIS relating to the development strategy for the service sector is far below the expectations, although the volume on sector studies includes two chapters, namely the least developed countries (LDCs) service waiver (volume 3, chapter 8) and ITES (volume 3, chapter 7). Proper action or strategies for the overall development of the service sector are not mentioned in the main report or in the Action Matrix. The operationalization issues of the LDC services waiver are not analyzed in the study. The DTIS should outline at least the major policy interventions and institutional reforms required for development of the service sector. The report may also consider the development of a detailed "service sector export and import policy." The report may propose to establish a separate "service cell/wing" in the Ministry of Commerce and Export Promotion Bureau to promote development of the service sector. Other possibilities could also be explored, such as the creation of a "Services Business Promotion Council," ways and means to negotiate preferential access in trade in services under the LDC waiver decision, and use of the Aid for Trade fund for developing and undertaking the projects for implementing the recommendations in the areas of trade in services.
11. The content of the section "Trade Policy Reforms to Reduce Anti-Export Bias and Balance Consumer Interests" (volume 1, chapter 3) does not match the title of the section. Almost every analysis and suggestion is concentrated on imports. No policy shortcomings related to exports have been discussed under that topic.
12. The report mentions that "[i]n Bangladesh, lack of export diversification arises in large measure from distortions related to variations in export facilities across sectors, including special bonded warehouses (SBWs) and cash incentives" (volume 1, chapter 4). However, no alternative policy option is suggested in the report. This should be addressed by thoroughly examining various export facilities.
13. Trade facilitation in the report is very narrowly focused, concentrating mainly on trade facilitation measures affecting trade with India. The text on this topic should be rewritten, with broader coverage. The role of a deep sea port is not taken into consideration, which may play an important role in trade facilitation and facilitating Bangladesh as a trading hub.
14. Volume 2, chapter 8, titled "Attracting Foreign Direct Investment in Bangladesh," mentions that the role of the Board of Investment as a one-stop service center is crucial for attracting foreign direct investment (FDI) in Bangladesh, because other developing countries and LDCs are competing in this field. The main constraints as identified in the report are: bureaucracy, corruption, electricity shortages, inadequate access to land and finance, skill shortages, ineffective implementation of measures to attract FDI inflows, and lack of confidence in sustained sociopolitical stability. In addition, the report identifies several constraints in attracting FDI to metropolitan areas

(electricity, political instability, governance, access to land, and access to finance) and non-metropolitan areas (low demand for goods and services, rising inflationary pressure, seasonal inaccessibility of roads, and cost of finance). Identification of these constraints is an important finding of this study. However, the study fails to provide any recommendations for addressing these constraints.

In addition, the study lacks sector-wise analysis of FDI inflows, comparison of FDI inflows with other countries at a similar level of development, and identification of sectors that have potential for attracting FDI.

15. In volume 3, chapter 2, the sector study "Light Engineering: Bicycles" mainly assesses the performance of bicycle industries in the value chain in the context of global competition. The objectives of the value chain analysis are set to examine the entire process in terms of costs, productivity, constraints, solutions, and competitiveness (compared with China and Vietnam). However, the Action Matrix does not reflect any suggestions for enhancing the industry's cost competitiveness or participation in the global value chain.
16. In volume 3, chapter 6, "The Pharmaceutical Sector in Bangladesh," provides a good analysis of the present scenario of the pharmaceutical sector in Bangladesh based on secondary information. It is plausible from the chapter that stakeholders' consultations have taken place, but no clear reference is made in this respect. The study team should perhaps consult the Directorate General of Drug Administration, Ministry of Health and Family Welfare, and concerned private sector representatives.

    The study is based on outdated data, for example data for imports of active pharmaceutical ingredients for 2007, although we have updated information. One of the objectives of the study is to identify the causes of failure in taking advantage of the post-Trade Related Aspects of Intellectual Property Rights (TRIPS) environment, which is properly reflected in the study. However, the study does not provide any recommendations on measures to be taken after the expiry of the TRIPS transition period on pharmaceuticals for LDCs.

Environmental Benefits Statement

The World Bank Group is committed to reducing its environmental footprint. In support of this commitment, we leverage electronic publishing options and print-on-demand technology, which is located in regional hubs worldwide. Together, these initiatives enable print runs to be lowered and shipping distances decreased, resulting in reduced paper consumption, chemical use, greenhouse gas emissions, and waste.

We follow the recommended standards for paper use set by the Green Press Initiative. The majority of our books are printed on Forest Stewardship Council (FSC)–certified paper, with nearly all containing 50–100 percent recycled content. The recycled fiber in our book paper is either unbleached or bleached using totally chlorine-free (TCF), processed chlorine–free (PCF), or enhanced elemental chlorine–free (EECF) processes.

More information about the Bank's environmental philosophy can be found at http://www.worldbank.org/corporateresponsibility.

green press INITIATIVE

CPSIA information can be obtained at www.ICGtesting.com
Printed in the USA
LVOW09s0312181016

509124LV00013B/44/P

9 781464 809248